Pigeon Cove

*from a lithograph
produced in 1886
by
George H. Walker
& Co.*

Lynne –
Best wishes to you
for a great opening of
school!
George
August '96

Loading Granite at Knowlton's Wharf, an oil painting on wood by Alfred J. Wiggin dated 1852, which hangs in the Sandy Bay Historical Society. The large house at the right was built about 1825 by William Torrey, who came from Quincy to operate the Flat Ledge quarry. It was later the home of artist Aldro T. Hibbard and his studio replaced the shed and barn. The Sanborn house at far left remains a home to this day.

Town on
Sandy Bay

Town on Sandy Bay

a history of Rockport, Massachusetts

by

Marshall W. S. Swan

Published for the

TOWN HISTORY COMMITTEE

by

PHOENIX PUBLISHING

Canaan, New Hampshire

The drawing of a Chebacco boat from Sandy Bay used decoratively
throughout the volume was based on a watercolor sketch in Jonathan
Parsons' hand arithmetic book dated 1836.

Swan, Marshall Wilbur Stephen
  Town on Sandy Bay.
  Bibliography.
  Includes index.
  1. Rockport, Mass.—History. I. Title
F74.R68S92   974.4'5   80-15578
ISBN 0-914016-72-5

Printed in the United States of America
by Courier Printing Company.
Binding by New Hampshire Bindery
Design by A. L. Morris

CONTENTS

FOREWORD

How It Came About

T HIS BOOK has been a long time in the making, at least a hundred and fifty years. For it was more than a century and a half ago that Ebenezer Pool, Jr., then a young man of about thirty, began jotting down bits of local history about which he had heard or read. Frequently, he included notes about events in which he personally had participated. By the time of his death in 1878, those memoranda had come to fill six closely written, bulging notebooks. As early as 1854, when Rockporters were celebrating the hundredth anniversary of Sandy Bay's independence as the Fifth Parish of Gloucester, orator-physician Lemuel Gott drew extensively upon the Pool papers. From them and other informative materials he prepared a "Centennial Address," which gave a history of Rockport from its early explorers to his own time. Because it took two and a half hours to deliver, Dr. Gott's narrative was related in two parts that snowy day, half in the afternoon, the rest during the evening exercises. Next, in 1860, came John J. Babson's monumental *History of the Town of Gloucester, Cape Ann, Including the Town of Rockport.* That 610 page volume had two shorter sequels, the *Notes and Additions* of 1876 and 1891. All three accounts abound with nuggets of Rockport's story, especially its earlier years.

By 1884 Rockporters had begun to sense a need for a town history all their own. So, at their annual town meeting they chose a committee to secure from Dr. Gott, by then living in retirement at Berlin, Massachusetts, a copy of his manuscript from 1854. For his generosity the town meeting voted the sum of $50.00 "as a token of regard for the lecturer." Simultaneously, the Committee made arrangements with the heirs of Ebenezer Pool to draw upon his memoranda, so that they might also be "wrought into a history of the town." Both sets of documents were extensively rewritten for publication. At their annual meeting on March 2, 1885, Rockporters next voted that one thousand copies of Dr. Gott's address together with "other items of special interest" should be published in book form and "sold to citizens and others at cost price."

In due course there emerged from the printing office of the local newspaper, the *Rockport Review*, a 295 page *History of the Town of Rockport*. Although it carried the date 1888, even advance copies were not off the presses until November 1889, a few days before the death of the principal compiler, John White Marshall, who the year before had published a long survey of Rockport's past and present in Hurd's *History of Essex County*. In reviewing the long-awaited book, the *Cape Ann Advertiser* wrote that it would cost $1.50 or $1.65 "by mail; post paid," but that it would be "an almost indispensible book for every native of Rockport." And so it was and still is. By now it is a rarity. Those occasional copies which turn up in antiquarian book shops usually bring a high price.

Forty years passed. Then, in 1930, when Massachusetts observed its Tercentenary, a number of members of the newly established Sandy Bay Historical Museum discussed the possibility of preparing a fresh, expanded history of Rockport. Although many commemorative labors were undertaken at the time, a town history was not one of them. Another forty-odd years slipped by, during which another generation of Rockporters had made and passed into history.

With the national Bicentennial era came a revival of interest in the past and a renewed awareness that a people without a past can have no future. Lest the town lose any more visual reminders of its corporate heritage, Rockporters established a town history committee and charged it with the task of assembling and producing a pictorial record of the community. This task was strikingly brought to fruition with the publication in 1975 of *Rockport as it Was . . . A Book of Pictures,* edited by Dr. William D. Hoyt and printed by the late Richard Tarr. By now, the stock of that popular volume is being exhausted rapidly.

Out of the enthusiasm engendered by the "picture history" came a resurgence of interest in preparing a new narrative account of "our pleasant town by the sea," as the men of 1888 characterized Rockport. A committee was gathered, various plans of operation were considered, and a method of procedure was agreed upon. Some of the earlier enthusiasts fell by the wayside, others withdrew for lack of time and for changing personal priorities. Most members stayed the course. To those hardy colleagues, the author is truly grateful.

How It Was Planned

From the outset the Committee recognized that it had to have a clearly defined plan for operations. Charting such a course called for several major decisions, some of them made with difficulty, many with reluctance, all only after hours of deliberation. There was prompt unanimity that the book should be physically attractive and make enjoyable reading. Though meticulously researched, and thereby relieved from some errors of previous publications, the new history was to have a broad, enduring appeal. Its style should avoid both garrulous informality and academic formalism. It was with some regret that the Committee agreed to abandon the genealogical approach so dear to many nineteenth century local historians. The medley of more recent Rockporters, it was realized, would have little interest in old-family trees, while old-family seekers had ready access to Babson's genealogical excavations. Because Peter Smith's 1975 reprint of Babson's *History* once again made available the earlier story of Cape Ann, the Committee decided to devote primary attention to the Rockport which had secured its municipal independence in 1840. Wisely, though, it acknowledged that just as United States history did not begin on July 4, 1776, so Rockport's must cover its century and a half while still a part of Gloucester. Similarly, the Committee concurred that its picture of Rockport should be set in the wider context of developments beyond parochial borders. Towns, like people, do not evolve in isolation.

Thanks to contacts made by Eleanor Parsons, there was the great good fortune of early selecting Phoenix as the prospective publisher of this volume. The Committee met repeatedly with Adrian Paradis and A. L. Morris of Phoenix and aided by their counsel blocked out the overall format of the book. A shared desire to include an almost lavish array of illustrations inevitably meant reducing the narrative substantially. Tables, prefatory material, and a comprehensive index necessitated still further trimming of the basic text. Accordingly, the Committee was faced with the uncompromising reality of compressing 350 years of Rockport history into about 400 pages. In shaving parlance, that meant "once over lightly."

The following pages have been deliberately titled "*A History of Rockport.*" They represent only one-third of the material gathered for the first draft of the book. Chapter by chapter the texts were scrutinized by the dauntless members of the Committee, each with his or her special competence. From their considered observations were extracted revised, scaled-down versions. From those in turn emerged the final text. All who labored to produce this book hope, thereby, that errors of commission will be minimal. No one is more rueful than the Committee, and the author in particular, that more events, more people, more anecdotes, could not be squeezed into this present volume.

As for the omissions, inevitably they are legion. Thus, it is the truly pious hope of this "doorman to the past," of his colleagues on the Town History Committee, and the entire company of research assistants and other helpers named in the Afterwords following the story, that this volume will be but a prologue. Rockporters, young and old, present and yet to come, are urged to supply the gaps, to offer other interpretations by talks, articles, brochures, photographs, reels upon reels of oral history tapes, studies of specialized topics and themes. Rockport has many other "histories" waiting to be told. That doughty captain-admiral, John Smith, who cruised along our coast in 1614, making our first map and giving us our first real place names, summarized history as "the memory of time, the life of the dead, and the happiness of the living."

Marshall W. S. Swan

February 27, 1980

Town on
Sandy Bay

Part 1

In the Time
of Small Things

 OCKPORT, *all six and a quarter*
square miles of it, embraces the outer
limits of Cape Ann, that promontory
which juts out into the Atlantic Ocean some dozen miles from the mean coastline
of Massachusetts Bay. Beyond roll the vasty deeps, a silver mine of fish which
lured the firstcomers. Beneath lies limitless granite, the living rock which drew
hundreds of immigrants to the island-cape, and for a century provided a
livelihood for them and their dependents. Around are scattered the coves and
headlands, the beaches, the woods, and the peace which attracted artists and
visitors to the town when fishing and quarrying were no more. Rockport's
destiny was determined in geologic time and by glaciers, thousands of years ago.

Hardscrabble and dense woodland discouraged even the Indians from
settling there. A handful of excavated artifacts, though, suggest that a few
native Americans were the area's first summer boarders. Moving down from

upcountry, they fished and gathered clams during warmer weather. Most of those transients, however, summered at Gloucester, as piquant French reports related. It was French, not English explorers who were the first white men known to have landed in today's Rockport. The location was Whale Cove, the date July 16, 1605, and the attraction was an Indian invitation. But for the ambivalent behavior of other Indians in 1606, when Champlain returned to Le Cap aux Isles, as he called Cape Ann, Rockport might have begun as a French colony.

Ten years were to pass before the indefatigable Capt. John Smith published the first of his enthusiastic books promoting what he christened "New England." Methodical mapmaker and careful recorder of all he saw, he noted back in 1614 the three staples which would provide initial revenues for a town on Sandy Bay: timber, fish, and stone. It was those successive publications of John Smith which moved the ancestors of many a Rockporter to migrate hither. One eager reader was Pastor Francis Higginson, who brought his entire family in 1629 and in turn produced his own avidly read account of Essex County in 1630.

Some two hundred years were to pass between the time Cape Ann acquired its first permanent residents (1639-40) and the year Rockport—two sevenths of the area—was incorporated as a town in its own right, independent of Gloucester (1840). Still earlier there had been the disheartening attempts by the men of England's Dorchester Company to establish a support group for their annual fishing projects (1623-26). Those, too, are a part of Rockport's story; for a tenacious remnant of those "land men" refused to return to England, preferring to cast their lot with the New World—at Salem, then later all along the North Shore. Cape Ann would be resettled; in 1642 its church was "gathered," and the town was named Gloucester.

Future Rockport remained uninhabited for a half century more. During that time Cape Ann as a whole grew hesitantly, precariously hugging its peninsula so inaccessible over land. Yet there were advantages in that isolation. The vexations of boomtown Boston and Salem were avoided. Newcomers were assimilated more gradually. The needs of survival rather than of salvation tempered the blasts of Puritan theocracy. Cape Ann was happily spared the menace of resident or peripheral Indians. Thus, in its way, the community could focus on the business of living. Even the deviltries of local witches were airy, though several Cape Ann gammers were committed to prison for a time.

Except for sheltering occasional fishermen at Folly, Pigeon, Long, and Straitsmouth coves, future Rockport initially provided only safe and unrestricted feeding grounds for swine and nonproductive cattle and horses. It was its virgin timber stands which brought the first exploiters to the area (1667), yet 1688 came before the town began making land grants in what is now Rockport.

Only by the early 1690s did Sandy Bay get its first family, the Richard Tarrs from Saco, Maine. The second, John Pool's, moved in from Beverly in 1700. Both breadwinners were lumbermen; both were drawn to "ye Cape" by its trees.

Once families had built homes by the brook at the Front Beach, others tried their luck. First to arrive were the families at Folly and Pigeon coves. Soon lots at the Southern Woods and shore were occupied. Further expansion occurred at the bay. Roads were laid out to connect central Gloucester with the clusters of cottages along the shore and those growing families with each other. By 1724 the residents described themselves as a "neighborhood" and petitioned for land for a schoolhouse. By the time the community lost its founding fathers in 1727 and 1732, their sons and some other men were taking up the burdens of government so critical to the well-being of all towns.

Unlike most communities which tried to establish an independent parish church first off, future Rockport waited until 1738 before petitioning for tax money to provide for a home-based preacher during the winter months. Complaints of excessive hardship in getting to church five or six miles away, especially in winter and for those people without horses, produced the desired results. Future Rockport was on its way to becoming a parish by itself and, eventually, an independent town.

It would take another sixteen years, however, for Sandy Bay to achieve parochial independent status. During that period what would become Rockport would welcome its first wharves for fishing and coastal traders. It would acquire its first burial grounds and would suffer the loss of some thirty-one of its children by diphtheria. Smallpox, too, would visit the area and take its toll. On the other hand, the Great Awakening would rouse citizens to a fresh awareness of their relationships to man and God. In anticipation of its independence as a new, fifth parish of Gloucester, the townspeople of future Rockport would build their first meetinghouse and call their first resident minister, Ebenezer Cleaveland. On January 1, 1754, Sandy Bay received the privileges enjoyed by other parishes of the province of Massachusetts Bay.

1

"BACKWARD,
TURN BACKWARD, O TIME"

"Our New Paradise"

I T WAS JUNE 29, 1629, a Friday. The morning was foggy, the wind calm. As the sun climbed higher, however, the mists burned off. Before long, on all sides of the rolling ship, alert passengers began spotting infinite multitudes of mackerel. Hugging the shoreline, the *Talbot* slid through waves festooned with buttercups and sea anemones. Landward, every hill and hollow were "full of gay woods and high trees." By noon, wrote Francis Higginson in his diary that early summer day, the ship had borne down to within a league of Cape Ann.

Two months and two days had passed since the *Talbot* had cast off downstream from London. The weather had held reasonably clement, except for May 27 when "the winds blew mightily, the rain fell vehemently, the sea roared and the waves tossed us horribly." Most of the landlubbers had suffered the agonies of seasickness, including Parson Higginson's wife, who "was something ill by vomiting" but she "is now much better for the seasickness." He rejoiced that on ship "I have been strangely healthful." Only three of the 130 voyagers had been committed to the depths: two sickly children and one "notorious wicked fellow that was given to swearing." Unhappily, Mr. Goff's great dog had been washed into the vasty deeps, and "five beastly Sodomitical boys" had been caught at a wickedness "not to be named."

At eight o'clock and midnight the crew had sung a psalm and offered a prayer "that was not read out of a book," while the

4

passengers—outward bound to plant a new Eden in a New World— held morning and evening services daily. For secular diversion, the voyagers had been treated to porpoises, a vast sunfish, jellyfish as big as a man's fist, a turtle, huge whales "huffing up water as they go" and, on June 11, "a mountain of ice shining as white as snow like to a great rock or cliff." Yet after two cramped months at sea they rejoiced on the twenty-fourth when "we all had a clear and comfortable sight of America."

After rounding Halibut Point and cautiously negotiating the Salvages, Straitsmouth, Thacher's and Milk islands, the helmsman found it too dark to venture into Cape Ann Harbor. Cranky winds drove them all seaward again until four o'clock Saturday afternoon, when the skipper ran for port and finally dropped anchor. "It was a fair and sweet evening." Four of the men lowered the tender, rowed over to Ten Pound Island, and brought back ripe strawberries and gooseberries and "single sweet roses." On the eve of their first Sabbath in America, Francis Higginson wrote with gratitude: "God was merciful to us in giving us a taste and smell of the sweet fruit as an earnest of his bountiful goodness to welcome us on our first arrival." As for his band of stalwart Puritans, "all are desirous to see our new paradise of New-England." Spied by Governor Endecott's mariners, "who rested the Sabbath with us at Cape Ann," they were piloted on Monday to their new home at Salem.

An energetic promotor of colonization, Pastor Higginson hurried descriptions to friends in Leicestershire of what he had found "at Cape Anne and at Masathulets Bay." These were eagerly circulated in old England by the autumn of 1629, and three editions of his *New-England's Plantation* were issued at London during 1630. The second and third included a shopping list for prospective emigrants: meat, malt, oatmeal, peas, cloth, leather, tools, iron and steel, glass, and so on. "When you are once parted with England," he reminded them, "you shall meet neither with taverns, nor alehouses, nor butchers', nor grocers', nor apothecaries' shops to help what things you need." Yet his enthusiasm would do credit to a board of trade promotional folder: "A sup of New England's air," he insisted, "is better than a whole draught of Old England's ale." More to the point was Higginson's advice to procure a copy of Capt. John Smith's "booke of the description of New England" and study it from page 203 to the end.

"Backward, Turn Backward, O Time"

"Few of her founders gave so much and got so little as Captain John Smith," decided Samuel Eliot Morison. For a century and a half that feisty soldier has been remembered almost exclusively because of a twelve-year-old Virginian named Pocahontas. Yet John Smith devoted nearly two decades to the development of New England. He it was who actually put New England on the maps. Without setting foot on Rockport soil, in 1614 he identified the three staples which would become the mainstay of its people: timber, fish, and stone.

Sharpened by youthful escapades in Europe, then further honed by his grinding ordeal in Virginia, the keen captain sailed for New England on March 3, 1614. With his two ships and their seasoned crews went a single passenger—an Indian named Squanto, destined for immortality through the Pilgrims. Impervious to the seduction of precious metals, Smith focused on fish and furs. Once arrived off Maine, "while the sailors fished, myself with eight others of them [who] might best be spared" beat down the coast, assaying the potentials of the region. When his half a dozen maps proved so much waste paper, he himself drew a map "from point to point, isle to isle, and harbor to harbor, with the soundings, sands, rocks, and landmarks." Profoundly impressed by his daily discoveries, John Smith determined to publicize the area.

On returning to England, he set about coordinating a program for colonization. His descriptive tract of sixty pages was hurried through the press in June 1616. To secure additional attention he dedicated it to the king's Privy Council. Then he had a brilliant, though belated idea. Why not involve the royal family?

Through connections he presented to the adolescent crown prince a copy of his *Description of New England* together with his meticulously drafted map. The future king was then entreated to change the "barbarous" names on the latter for proper English ones, so that posterity might boast that "Prince Charles was their Godfather." The ruse worked. Some of His Highness' alterations stuck—for instance, the river he named for himself. Others did not. Cape Cod remains as fishy as ever, despite the royal attempt to rebaptize it Cape James for the reigning monarch. Another sacrifice fell on future Rockport, on an echo of Smith's own hazardous past in Eastern Europe.

Cruising down the coast of Massachusetts in 1614, he had come upon "a great bay, where we found some habitations and cornfields,"

homesteads of the Agawam Indians. To the southeastward "doth
stretch into the sea the fair headland . . . fronted with three isles."
Recalling his captivity more than a decade before, he named the cape
for a Greek girl from Trebizond to whom he had been given by her
braggart suitor. "The beauteous Lady Tragabigzanda, when I was a
slave to the Turks, did all she could to succor me," he called to mind,
adding that in the moments of his deepest thralldom the one hope he
had clung to was the love of Tragabigzanda. So with nostalgic
gratitude he bestowed her name upon that fair headland, only to have
Prince Charles rechristen the promontory Cape Ann, in honor of his
mother. Today, the beauteous Tragabigzanda is memorialized only in
chronicles and by a short street near Gloucester's Bass Rocks. "Alas for
American mythology," sighed one historian.

Prior to his enslavement, however, Captain Smith had been the
victor in three successive jousts with Turkish soldiers during a prolonged siege in Transylvania. In the initial encounter the Englishman
drove his spear through the eyepiece of a Turk's helmet, "face, head,
and all." The second challenge, involving lances and then pistols, also
resulted in the infidel's losing his head. The third exchange was with
spiked battle-axes and curved broadswords. Again the young Christian unhorsed and decapitated his opponent. As a reward, Prince
Sigismond Bathory granted Smith a patent for a coat of arms bearing
three Turks' heads on a shield. More than a decade later, on reaching
the Cape in Massachusetts with its three isles "seen far to seaward in
regard the headland," John Smith dubbed the islands the three Turks'
Heads. In later Rockport, the name was to be relegated to a hotel. The
islands acquired individual designations: Straitsmouth, Thacher's,
and Milk.

To the ancestors of many a Rockporter John Smith's successively
revised, updated maps and the promises of his promotional books
were enticing. Reports of the "greatness of timber" for houses, buildings, and ships, descriptions of wide ledges of stone, "strangely divided
with tinctured veins of divers colors" for buildings, slates, furnaces—
these stimulated emigration. Even more energizing was New England's "chiefest mine," the "silver stream" of cod, mullet, turbot, haddock, hake, cusk, mackerel, cunners, herring ("if any desired them"),
bass, perch, salmon, and sturgeon ("whose roes do make caviare"), not
to forget the eels, crabs, lobsters, mussels, oysters, clams, and periwin-
kles with which the captain baited his hooks for colonists.

"Backward, Turn Backward, O Time"

John Smith's massive *Generall Historie of Virginia, New England, and the Summer Isles* was published in 1624 and was the folio recommended by Francis Higginson. Reprinted in 1626, 1627, and 1632, it became a combination Baedeker and bible for emigrants. In it, the well-informed author wrote: "By Cape Ann there is a plantation" where they have "set up a fishing work," and he prayed "the eternal God protect and preserve" it. Unlike the eloquent Higginson and those who preceded and followed him, John Smith never settled on his Massachusetts shores. Yet that far-traveled captain, to whom was finally awarded the title "Admirall of New England," claimed in print: "Of all the four parts of the world I have yet seen . . . I would rather live here than anywhere."

Champlain and His "Lords of Themselves"

If John Smith did not go ashore at future Rockport, neither did several other English voyagers who preceded him in these waters and with whose narratives he was familiar: Bartholomew Gosnold, Brereton, and Archer, who overshot the Cape in 1602; Martin Pring, whose mention of it is said to be the first record in the annals of Cape Ann; or George Weymouth, who journeyed in 1605, reportedly to promulgate "God's holy church," but who kidnapped five Indians and took them to England. Although records of the Iberian explorers are skimpy, what could be the promontory of Rockport was labeled "Cabo de Santiago" on the Gomez-Ribero map of 1529. In the interest of historical veracity, it should be added that, wishful thinking and ethnic jingoism to the contrary, there is not any evidence on which to base the tales of Thorwald and the alleged Viking love affair with the headlands and harbors of the town. "Here I should like to fix my dwelling" is a nineteenth-century fantasy of Professor Eben N. Horsford of baking powder fame, as is the "fair city of the Norsemen, founded on the banks of the classic Charles."

To the French falls the distinction of being the first recorded white men to walk on Rockport's shores. Late on July 15, 1605, sailing south from Cape Porpoise, Samuel de Champlain sighted Cape Ann. The next day he reached the peninsula and made notes of three islands off the mainland, "full of woods of different kinds," as well as of another low, treeless, flat ledge, "where there are breakers and which extends a little farther out to sea than the others." This was the Salvages later memorialized in T. S. Eliot's *Four Quartets.* Champlain, who was also charting his journey, called the area "Cap aux Isles."

He and his companions caught sight of a canoe manned by five or six Indians. After sidling up to the French barque, they paddled to what was probably Whale Cove and danced upon the beach. The pursuing French gave each Indian some biscuits and a knife, "which caused them to dance better than before." By means of sign language the landing party persuaded the natives to draw a map on the sand. Smoke signals and other signs lured the French farther around the Cape, where they anchored near "a small island," variously identified as Thacher's, Milk, or Salt. More biscuits and knives were dispensed during that two-hour sojourn. The onset of a brisk breeze summoned the French back to their ship and thence away from the island-cape. That July 16, 1605, Rockport had received its first summer visitors, day trippers at that!

Summer boarders were another matter. From time to time undiplomatic questions are raised about Rockport's savages, the indigenous ones, that is. The usual reply is that the area had few if any resident Indians, presumably because it was too heavily wooded to sustain an agricultural population. Only a few Indian relics have been unearthed in Rockport proper, mainly on Pigeon Hill and at Folly Cove, though Gloucester has produced a more varied array.

Champlain's narratives of 1605 and 1606 provide the chief firsthand description of those native summer boarders, who migrated to the coast, where they fished, went clamming, and lived in huts. They cleared land by burning, then planted corn, pumpkins, squash, beans, and artichokes. Wearing garments of grass and hemp rather than fur, they were described by the French as painting their faces red, black, and yellow. The men cut the hair on the crowns of their heads and, through plucking, avoided beards. They played pipes, "though with less harmony than our French shepherds," and "whistled through their noses and gamboled." For defense they relied on clubs, spears, and bows and arrows. To their overseas observers they lacked both government and religion being, rather, "lords of themselves."

Champlain and his associate, de Poutrincourt, related a few anecdotes of their brushes with Cape Ann's natives. On the former's detailed map of Gloucester Harbor, "Le Beau Port," as he called it, is depicted the near ambush perpetrated by the Indians against the unsuspecting ship's crew as they washed their dirty linen off Rocky Neck. The sheltered harbor notwithstanding, the Gallic visitors decided against a permanent settlement at the Cap aux Isles, because the

"Backward, Turn Backward, O Time"

attitude of the large native population was ambiguous. Thanks, then, at least in part to the local Indians, Rockport was never part of a French colony.

"Before We Were the Land's"

This prologue to the drama of Rockport has moved backward. Before the end of the beginning, a few paragraphs should be devoted to the land itself. The special relationships between Rockporters and the living rock, myriad boulders, and stingy soil with which for centuries they struggled will repeatedly appear as this history unfolds. When viewed from above, the most salient characteristic of the town is that it rests at the tip of a promontory. Although today Cape Ann is an island, as it was at the end of glacial period, it became one only after colonists cut through its narrow neck to facilitate ship transport.

Rockport's foundation, granitic bedrock, composes about nine tenths of the area, much of it rich in hornblende, making it easily workable yet highly durable. Up into the cracks of granite were forced molten rock ranging from black basalt to white quartz. More than 360 of these "dikes" can be seen inland in the exposed quarries and out along the shoreline. The day-to-day cutting in Rockport's quarries was regulated by what happened millions of years ago. On top of the bedrock is a thin layer of smaller rocks and soil varying in thickness from a few inches to 150 feet. This "drift deposit" came as the glacial ice sheets pushed down from the north like huge bulldozers which moved countless boulders in addition to the smaller stones. These "erratics," some weighing in the tons, are so profuse that settlers had a shortage of tillable land. Smaller boulders piled one on another make the characteristic fencing of the town.

A scarcity of soil for filtering groundwater resulted in impurities penetrating wells and springs. By 1888 a U.S. Geological Survey made the alarming statement that "at least three-fourths of the sources of the domestic water supply . . . are liable to contamination," a challenge with which the townspeople had to grapple along with the trials of sewage disposal. The town's most striking geological feature is a two-hundred-foot-high drumlin. Surviving from the first ice age, reshaped by the second one, cleared for farming by the town's early settlers, Pigeon Hill was quickly recognized as an invaluable landmark for mariners. At a town meeting in March 1713 the voters decided that "for a publick good" the crown should "lie common, still, perpetually,

Landmark Lane in 1914. The grassy road to the top of Pigeon Hill was not yet lined with houses and the big elm halfway up the slope was a distinguishing feature of the countryside. (Hoyt)

to be for a sea mark." A beacon it remains, as it has since the first fishermen came to these shores.

ADDITIONAL READING

The story of Francis Higginson and his family has been told in Thomas W. Higginson, *Life of Francis Higginson* (New York, 1891). Higginson's journals and *New-England's Plantation* were issued by Alexander Young, *Chronicles of the First Planters of the Colony of Massachusetts Bay* (Boston, 1846) and in a number of later reprints—at least three since 1970.

The standard edition of John Smith's works is Edward Arber and A. G. Bradley, eds. *Travels and Works of Captain John Smith,* 2 vols. (Edinburgh, 1910).

The definitive treatment of the earlier explorations is Samuel Eliot Morison, *The European Discovery of America: The Northern Voyages A.D. 500-1600* (New York, 1971). A popular survey of later explorations is Henry F. Howe, *Prologue to New England* (New York, 1943).

Highly readable is Samuel Eliot Morison, *Samuel de Champlain* (Boston, 1972). The six-volume edition of Champlain's writing is Henry P. Biggar, ed., *The Works of Samuel de Champlain* (Toronto, 1922-36).

For those inclined to learn more about the rocks of Rockport, two works provide a thorough grounding: Nathaniel S. Shaler, *The Geology of Cape Ann, Massachusetts* (Washington, 1890), and John H. Sears, *The Physical Geography, Geology, Mineralogy and Paleontology of Essex County, Massachusetts* (Salem, 1905). A good popular survey was written by Diana D. Fisher, "Cape Ann's Rocks of Ages," *Rockport Horizon,* May 12-25, 1978, pp. 5-6.

"Backward, Turn Backward, O Time"

2

IN THE BEGINNING

The Stage Is Set

IT ALL BEGAN with fish,—Massachusetts, that is,—and on Cape Ann. From the days of the Cabots, European sailors had been braving the North Atlantic in pursuit of them. It has been estimated that as many as five hundred fishermen were working the New England deeps by the time of the Pilgrims. Even those elect, when asked by King James how they proposed to live, replied: "By fishing." To which the monarch dryly observed: "So God have my soul, 'twas the Apostles' own calling."

The Council for New England, a group of imaginative businessmen and clergymen from the west coast of England, secured a patent on February 18, 1623, to establish "a particular plantation." That year saw the beginnings of Cape Ann and, following successive jugglings of patents, charters, and companies, of the Commonwealth of Massachusetts. Late that the spring the Dorchester Company of investors secured a fifty-ton vessel named the *Fellowship,* loaded it with men and provisions, and sent it forth. Their experienced master hit things right; laden with a full cargo he scudded back to Europe only to reach the Spanish market after prices had plummeted—a lost of some £600.

Left behind to winter-over in the country at Cape Ann were fourteen "extra men." Even their names are unknown today, those pioneer Gloucestermen; yet they were the first white settlers to make a home in this area. Their presence was quite possibly discovered either by the Plymouth planters themselves or by the fringe at Wessagusset. In September, Edward Winslow was hurried back to England to obtain more supplies, people, and a patent. Although he was successful in his mission, even to wangling a patent for "a known place there commonly called Cape Ann . . . and the islands within said bay," his return was delayed because all the able seamen had been hired by the "Western men."

Those activists were tackling a new plan proposed by Rector John White of Dorchester. His idea was to induce some settlers to remain in New England as a support group for the fishing fleet: to build shelters; plant crops; catch venison, fowl, and fish; make salt; and have all in readiness for the seasonal arrival of the company's fishing boats. White envisaged an expansion into a colony, which would cut timber for ships, make pitch and tar, grow hemp for sails and cordage, and graze sheep. Vital to his scheme were resident ministers to tend to the cure of souls and rescue the perishing American heathen. In all, an association of 119 sponsors was duly formed with a capital of over £ 3,000. "Compassion towards the fishermen and partly some expectation of gain prevailed."

Those expectations were never realized, alas. When two ships landed from England, the spring of 1624 must have brought relief and joy to the fourteen extra men on Cape Ann. Yet autumn carried back grim news to the underwriters. Their ships' catches had been small, mishandled and chalked up a £ 1,700 loss. Behind at Cape Ann the *Fellowship* and the *Friendship* had put ashore thirty-two more landmen, whose wages and provisions would cost the company a minimum of £ 500 more. Although the Plymouth colonists had also hurried men to Cape Ann to build a house and fish-drying stages, they declined to challenge the western squatters, because their own title was flawed.

Among the newcomers to Cape Ann were Thomas Gardner, to oversee the plantation; John Tilly, to manage the fisheries; and John Woodbury from Somerset, who "brought cattle and other things to Cape Ann for plantation work, and built a house and kept their cattle and set up fishing." Many Rockporters today trace their family lines to some of those stouthearted reinforcements. The next year the optimistic English merchants raised an additional £ 2,000 and dispatched three ships to Cape Ann waters. These malfunctioned but then landed so bulky a catch it could not all be transported promptly. By the time it did get to Europe, it too fell victim to an English-Spanish war and glutted French markets. Concurrently, the landmen at future Gloucester were growing fractious despite the efforts of Roger Conant, hired from Nantasket to govern and manage the whole settlement. A near fatal exchange of gunfire was incited between Miles Standish and a fire-eater named Hewes, who was openly exploiting the Pilgrims' fish stage at Gloucester Harbor. That same vexing summer John Tilly appropriated salt left for others on Ten Pound Island by the ship *Phoenix*.

By 1626 the ill-starred Dorchester Company went bankrupt. Fishing losses, the "ill chosen and ill commanded" support group, and the sale of the company's three ships at disastrous prices had run up cumulative liabilities of over £ 3,000. So "the plantation was dissolved and deserted by the said joint adventurers," grieved Pastor White. Three centuries later Professor Morison pithily commented: "The Dorchester Adventurers appear to have been a group of public-spirited men who wished to do something for their country, a little for the Indians, somewhat for the fishermen, and a good deal for themselves." They failed on all counts. Or did they? John White's own assessment, written in 1630, was this:

As in building houses the first stones of the foundation are buried underground and are not seen, so in planting colonies the first stocks employed that way are consumed, although they serve for a foundation of the work.

Most of the landmen returned to England, but a saving remnant elected to remain. On deciding that today's Salem might prove more promising, in the autumn of 1626 Conant, Balch, the Grays, Woodbury, Palfrey, Knight, Tilly, Gardner, Norman, Allen, and three or four other families "transported themselves" to Naumkeag. By spring they were established in their new quarters. In England a proper patent was assured, and a ship brought them additional cattle. Their summer crops flourished; winter was kind; and June 1628 provided a cargo of needed clothes, salt, grain, cattle, food, and settlers. About September 8 the *Abigail* dropped anchor with still more families and a new governor, John Endecott, charged by his board to "be of good courage, go on, and do worthily." By the spring of 1629 the Massachusetts Bay Company dispatched the fleet of ships carrying the Francis Higginson household and some three hundred fresh settlers. From them would begin the return northward.

Thus it was that from the fourteen extra men at Cape Ann in 1623, through the Dorchester Company's landmen of 1624-26, and the New England Company's plantation at Salem in 1627-28 emerged the Massachusetts Bay Colony in 1629. In 1691 it absorbed the fragile

Plymouth plantation and so created a united Commonwealth. At just that time on the shores of Sandy Bay, Rockport acquired its first family.

"A Plantation Called Gloucester"

For more than a decade after the exodus to Salem, Cape Ann was devoid of homesteaders. Despite tradition and a lost "ancient manuscript," there is no surviving evidence to sustain assertions to the contrary. A number of transients passed through, however, and a few remained in Rockport waters, beginning with the calamitous shipwreck of August 1635, which drowned all Pastor Avery's family and the brood of his cousin, tailor Anthony Thacher. From that tragedy future Rockport would receive two place names (Avery's Rock and Thacher's Island) and American literature some thumping verses by Whittier, "The Swan Song of Parson Avery." The twin lighthouses later built on the island named for Thacher grace the official seal of the town.

In March 1639 the General Court at Boston sent three men to see if the narrow neck at Cape Ann might be "cut thorow" to facilitate shipping. Then in late May colonial bigwigs decided to revive the plantation at Gloucester by offering most favorable terms to those who intend to promote the fishing trade. A committee was designated to lay out a settlement, and all stocks employed in fishing were to be free from taxes for seven years, "to encourage our own people to set upon it." Set upon it they did, notably Osmond Dutch and Thomas Milward. The former wrote to his family in Dorset cautioning them to bring "some refreshments besides the ship's provision" on their voyage to Cape Ann. He particularly recommended

some suger and fine ruske or bisket, a little barrell of ale to make warme meate, and oatmeale, and currants and a little spice, and some fine flower and eggs, and a few chikens with a henne or two, and a little butter and honey.

Before long arrived spiritual direction. Thomas Lechford noted that "at Cape Ann, where fishing is set forward and some stages builded, there one Master Rashley is Chaplain, for it is far off from any Church." By 1642 a number of chronicles mentioned the church which had been "gathered" at Gloucester.

In the Beginning

In his journal on May 18, 1642, John Winthrop wrote: "At this Court was established a Plantation called Gloucester." Boundaries were surveyed, and the "first ordering, settling, and disposing of lots" was completed. Perhaps as early as the autumn of 1641 Pastor Richard Blynman had moved to Cape Ann from Marshfield, accompanied by his satellites, several of whom had voyaged with him from Wales. At incorporation the parish was "but a small number, about fifty persons." Like many clergymen, Blynman found it impossible to satisfy all his flock. So once again he upped anchor and, in late 1649 or 1650, at the invitation of John Winthrop, Jr., moved southward to Pequot (New London, Connecticut), siphoning away from Gloucester some fifteen families.

During the Blynman tenure, however, the town had been organized, land grants made, clerks chosen for the market, for the civil defense band, and for keeping the town records. Gloucester paid its first tax bill to the Bay Colony in 1642 and got its first license "to draw wine." The Cut was dug making Cape Ann an island, and occasional citizens were found guilty of being scofflaws, profane, "living from their wives," laboring on the Sabbath, and even being adulterous. Some shipwrights created such a ruckus as to bring down investigators from the governor's council to deal with "the Gloucester business."

More constructively, brand marks were agreed upon to identify Cape Ann horses, and steps were taken to conserve desirable timber. In 1644 a half acre was set off "for a common burial place." Saw mill privileges were voted in February 1653. One Gloucester resident proposed to manufacture salt in what is now Rockport, where "is wood and fitting water for that work without inconvenience to the town." Slowly, the town spread out. In 1654 Edward Johnson of Woburn concluded that the principal reason it was no more extensively populated was its isolation, "lying out towards the point of the Cape" and that "access thereunto by Land" was "uneasie." Yet, the potentials of the fishing trade and good timber for shipping were "very beneficial," if only Gloucester had "men of estates to manage it."

The early 1660s brought to town a remarkably able manager in the person of the Parson John Emerson. He was paid £60 per year, one quarter of it in cash, the remainder in marketable Indian corn, peas, barley, fish, beef, and pork, plus cordwood to heat his parsonage. Before long he made astute investments in three grist and log mills. It was during his pastorate that the Richard Tarr family became Rockport's pioneer residents.

Town on Sandy Bay

In the 1660s the town commenced paying attention to the areas which in 1840 would be set off as Rockport. Cape Ann was heavily wooded well into the eighteenth century. Over the horizon, especially at Salem and Boston, lucrative markets loomed temptingly for that cordwood and lumber. On January 20, 1667, voters succumbed by permitting logging to a distance of 660 feet up from the sea from Brace's Cove around the entire coast to Plum Cove. To head off any threats from unauthorized squatters, the town meeting of April 25, 1668, forbade "planting ground upon the Cape." Placed off limits for settlement was the whole of future Rockport—in fact, the land from Annisquam to the place "where the fence doth stand in Starknaught Harbor."

During the succeeding twenty-year embargo the town felt seriously menaced on three occasions. The first was King Philip's War (1675-76). Open hostilities did not occur at Cape Ann, but drafts were levied and sixteen Gloucestermen eventually received bounty lands for their services against the Indians when "pressed by our Committy of malisha." Fortunately, only one draftee died. In March 1676, as a response to the stepped-up defense effort Cape Ann reported the construction of "two garrisons, besides several particular fortifications." Their locations are no longer known. It has been suggested that one may have formed a portion of the old house still surviving at 188 Granite Street, Rockport. All evidence points to its antedating the land grant (1688) on which it was built and the arrival of Rockport's first permanent family in the early 1690s.

The second threat came in 1680 when the heirs of John Mason filed claims to annex much of Essex County. Gloucester bore its share of the common defense. From Cape Ann by "our messengers for England" petitions were sped to "our Most gracious and dread Soveraigne." In London the Mason claims were disallowed, and Essex County settlers breathed more easily—until Indian claims to the area arose in 1700.

With the revocation of the Massachusetts Bay Charter in 1684 came an almost despotic new governor, Sir Edmond Andros. His arbitrary restrictions and high-handed measures lit fires of rebellion throughout his jurisdiction. In 1688, the same year in which today's Rockport was finally opened for development, seven dauntless Cape Anners dug in and refused to collect Andros's imposed assessments. Hailed into Salem court, they were hit with fines of more than £ 42. Understandably, there was open rejoicing on the Cape when irate Bostonians rose and imprisoned the governor and his sycophants. With a "full and

In the Beginning

18   clear vote in the affirmative," Rockport's mother town supported the
Glorious Revolution in England and the resumption of government in
Massachusetts which reflected the original charter of the pioneer
settlers on Cape Ann.

ADDITIONAL READING

The origins of Massachusetts were related by John Winthrop, William Bradford, Edward Johnson, and William Hubbard. Thomas Hutchinson's *History of the Colony and Province of Massachusetts Bay,* ed., L. S. Mayo, (Cambridge, 1936), is the enduring eighteenth century treatment. In our own era, James T. Adams, *The Founding of New England* (Boston, 1927); Samuel E. Morison, *Builders of the Bay Colony* (Boston, 1930); and Charles M. Andrews, *The Colonial Period of American History, the Settlements, Vol. I* (New Haven, 1964), make illuminating and pleasurable reading.

The two basic accounts of the Cape Ann story, on which all others are based, are John White, *The Planters Plea,* first published anonymously in 1630 but reprinted several times, including a Tercentennial facsimile edition by Rockport's Sandy Bay Historical Society; and William Hubbard, *General History of New England to 1680,* currently available in at least three reprint editions.

A later trailblazer was John W. Thornton, *The Landing at Cape Anne* (Boston, 1854). The various studies by Frances Rose-Troup on John White, Roger Conant, and the North Shore settlements, and especially her *Massachusetts Bay Company and Its Predecessors* (New York, 1930), are indispensable.

For the early history of Cape Ann, John J. Babson, *History of the Town of Gloucester* (Gloucester, 1860; reprinted, 1975), is still the monumental work, along with its *Notes and Additions* (1876 and 1891), neither of which has been reissued. The former contains a wealth of genealogical items; the latter has additions and corrections to the basic history. None of the three works was adequately indexed.

Earlier records of Gloucester were microfilmed by the Early Massachusetts Records Inventory in 1972 and are available at the Carnegie Library in Rockport and the Sawyer Free Library in Gloucester.

3

TARRS, POOLS, AND PIONEERS

J UST WHEN was Rockport founded? It was officially incorporated on February 27, 1840, on being set off from Gloucester by the Massachusetts legislature. Rockport's earliest surviving building is quite possibly part of the house at 188 Granite Street and may date from 1675-76. Some land lying in today's Rockport, however, may have been granted as early as 1658. The first extensive land grants, though, were made on February 27, 1688, when the qualified voters decided to distribute their common lands "at ye Cape."

Every householder and every man, "upward of one and twenty years of age" who had been born in the town and was still living and paying taxes there, was to receive a six-acre parcel, chosen in a lot drawing. Eighty-two units were laid out from Lane's Cove, around "holybut point," past "piggion cove," to today's Millbrook in Sandy Bay. Thus ended the embargo of 1668 against settlement at the Cape. Restrictions there were: against selling, against hunting or hounding cattle or swine, and against insufficient fencing. These restraints stemmed from the town's longtime practice of using future Rockport as an open summer feeding ground for all dry cattle, nonworking oxen, and all horses except those "for the saddle or collar." Scarcely had the lots been laid out, however, than they began to change hands, thus inaugurating Rockport's still thriving real estate business.

None of the 1688 land grants was immediately taken up by homesteaders. To the Richard Tarrs of Saco, Maine, belongs the honor being Rockport's first family. The town dates its settlement from their arrival at Sandy Bay sometime in the opening years of the 1690s. Who were they, those first comers? Richard was forty-five or forty-six when they arrived, and Rockport's first lady, Elizabeth Dicer Tarr, was twenty-four or twenty-five. The couple had probably been married in Saco or nearby, where her father owned land abutting Tarr's. The older groom was seemingly a widower with two youngish sons, William and John, who came along with their father; stepmother; and possibly their half sister, Elizabeth, born January 10, 1690, or more likely 1690/91. At the age of eighty-four Richard Tarr deposed that he and his family lived on their farm in Maine "till the Indian Wars began in Sixteen Hundred Ninety Two." There he had earned his livelihood as a lumberman, having hired a sawmill to which he hauled logs from the surrounding Maine forests. The founder father came to Sandy Bay, according to his great-grandson Jabez in 1840, to "be near to help load the wood coasters, which belonged to Gloucester and freighted wood from here . . . and also to go as a hand for them when wanted." To begin with, the Richard Tarrs had only a small shelter indeed, possibly acquired from transient woodcutters. On the slope behind what is now 113 Main Street, they settled down and biblically multiplied upon the land. In 1930 a marker was erected there to commemorate Rockport's first home.

What was it like, that community to which the Tarrs had made their way? From Parson Emerson in July 1690 one learns that Gloucester had sent fifteen volunteers for service against the French in Canada. Another seven had been drafted "to the Indian Wares." When forty-seven more were called up, Cape Anners were distressed at being left unprotected militarily and deprived of stout hands to get in hay and harvest, "so that wee must of necessity be forced to kill our cattell and [are] in great danger of being famished." The town's oldest extant tax list (1693) consists of eighty-five names. Richard Tarr's 12 shillings, 8 pence put him well into the lower half of the payers. That only six sloops, one boat, and one shallop were taxed is evidence that fishing was not yet the major source of income. The shipbuilding being carried on at Gloucester may later have lured Rockport's second family to town. The only church was four to five miles from Sandy Bay off

joined only in November 1709 at the age of forty-two when her children, ranging in age from eighteen to six, were also baptized and taken into membership. Despite long-standing regulations, the Tarrs' new hometown paid no schoolmaster until 1698. There was one midwife but no doctor other than the minister. Sick but still mobile citizens went as far as Lynn for treatment.

Houses at Cape Ann were not log cabins but of the seventeenth-century English construction still to be seen throughout Essex County. Gloucester records of 1668 speak of Hugh Rowe's house with its "daub" sides and ends and thatched roof. The interiors were scantily furnished by modern standards. Surviving inventories, including the one from Richard and Elizabeth Tarr's own cottage, remind readers of the heap of living it took to make a pioneer house a home. As late as 1713 the town was still paying bounties of 30 shillings for grown wolves killed within Gloucester. As for bears, antiquarian Ebenezer Pool, writing in the mid-nineteenth century, spoke of a bear talked about by Henry Witham "some 120 years" ago. It had been driven into the water and killed by the latter's "Uncle Babson." Presumably, someone spotting its skin drying on a peninsula beside the cove at Sandy Bay dubbed the place "Bearskin Neck."

Rockport's first family faced other hardships as well. Down on the Tarrs swooped the scourge of witchcraft, for Cape Ann did not escape "the prodigious war made by the spirits of the invisible world." Before the battles were over, eleven women were dragged to the bar of justice for assorted "diabolical acts." In July 1692 the twenty-four-year-old Ebenezer Babson, his aging mother, and bachelor household were beset "almost every night" by skulkers, as the jittery John Emerson wrote to the Mathers in Boston. The "devil and his agents" required some sixty militiamen from Ipswich before they mysteriously evaporated—an episode which later inspired Whittier's jingly narrative, "The Garrison of Cape Ann." Subsequently, Babson denounced two of his female neighbors. Others charged included Richard Tarr's mother-in-law, Elizabeth Austin Dicer, committed to prison at Ipswich. On December 15 he personally signed a bond for yet another local victim. It is the earliest surviving document fixing him as a resident of Gloucester and speaks well for his courage during a time of public hysteria. If mother Dicer did return to live with her daughter's family after her release, such tales she must have had to tell.

Less menacing were the hampering ordinances on cattle, fencing, registration of horses, ringing swine, restricting geese, and dividing rams from ewes to prevent ill-timed conception. There were decrees governing catching, "pickling," and drying fish to offset the lamentable "ill-reputation on this Province and the fishery of it." Above all were strict controls on thatch banks, timbering, and sawmills. As incentive pay informers received half the fines levied against violators.

Despite all this, the Richard Tarr family stuck it out at their house on the slope above "Davissons Run." To the joy of grandmother's release from prison was added another daughter, Honor, on May 20, 1693, quite possibly the first white child born in Rockport. She was followed by Richard in 1695, Joseph in 1698, Benjamin in 1700, and others in the new century: Caleb (1703); Samuel (1706); Abigail (1709); and Sarah, who arrived on September 11, 1716, when her father was seventy and her mother forty-nine. All were baptized in Gloucester's first parish church. In March 1697 Richard Tarr was permitted to fence in three or four acres "against the house he lives in at Sandy Bay." Although this was not an outright grant, he was never called on to surrender it. In 1701 he was allowed an additional ten acres, provided he looked after the aged and impoverished Arthur Churchill, a former associate in Maine. Subsequently other acreage was acquired and developed by Rockport's proliferating first family.

Next the Pools

The end of the decade signaled change. The town purchased from belated Indian claimants a clear title to the whole area—some ten thousand acres—for £ 7. Even before 1700 the isolation had begun to ease. Transient fishermen stopped over at Pigeon Cove, Long Cove, and the Straitsmouth district, and there were lumbermen and loaders with whom Richard Tarr was associated. A rash of land transfers had broken out following the grants of 1688, harbingers of settlers to come. In 1695 John Babson received two or three acres at "the strait mouth point to set up fishing upon"; in 1696 Joseph Eveleth got six acres "at the Cape," his grant referring to "the house that was his father's." The General Court in 1699 awarded Straitsmouth Island to Capt. James Davis, because he had been "at much charge and expense in the late wars." That March, John Day bought land in the Loblolly Cove-Emmons Point area, only to sell it in 1704 to William Cogswell, who may have put up one or two lean-tos for Chebacco fishermen. The younger John Emerson secured acreage "at Sandy Bay upon the point commonly called Davisson's Neck." Those properties would be purchased by Rockport's second permanent family and include their initial housing.

John Pool, a twenty-year-old native of Taunton, England, arrived in Beverly about 1690. In August 1693 he married the thirty-three-year-old widow of his employer. Sarah Pool proceeded to augment her Woodbury brood of seven children with seven Pools, six of them sons. Her vigorous groom was a carpenter and shipwright, who in April 1700 closed a deal for Emerson, Jr.'s property at Sandy Bay. The price was £ 160 and the mortgage was paid off by 1709. In the autumn of 1700, presumably, Pool transported his family to Rockport, thereby doubling its resident population to fourteen—still more if some of the Woodburys came along.

Up-and-coming John Pool soon branched out. His first venture was to secure a privilege to erect, jointly with Thomas Witham, "a grist or corn mill on the brook that runs down into the sea." Power was to be provided by the dammed-up stream which still blesses Rockport. How much corn was ground there is questionable, for Pool was a lumberman and made his success with timber. By rationalizing operations he controlled the whole production: cutting, hauling, sawing, transporting by ships of his own construction, and provisioning from his expanding fields and family. He is credited with supplying "hemlock timber also the limbs of the trees" for Boston's new Long Wharf, begun in 1710. As a descendant once wrote: "these means gave him the advantage of accumulating property quite fast for those days."

Even for those days also, John Pool accumulated wives quite fast. Sarah birthed Jonathan, Miriam, Robert, Ebenezer, and Joshua in Beverly. In November 1701 Caleb became the first Pool to be born in Rockport. John, Jr., in 1703 ended her progeny. That year the father's fellow townsmen tapped him for jury duty at Salem. In 1707 John Pool and three other worshipers at the first parish church were given permission to build stables there for their horses on Sabbath days. Although pressure for schooling mounted to the point that the town was obliged to hire a schoolmaster, the Pools solved their own problem by sending son Jonathan to Beverly to learn the fundamentals. In his old age Jonathan enjoyed relating his youthful experiences on returning to Sandy Bay to teach his brothers and—one hopes—his sisters. How the young Tarrs were taught is not known, perhaps at home or

The Francis Tarr homestead in 1893, with Mrs. Sally Lane Tarr (1803-1894) in the doorway and her daughter, Mrs. John Noble, on the step. (SBHS)

possibly at Gloucester's dame school, set up "to learn children to read, knit, and sew."

More public offices and more land came to John Pool, but in November 1716 his wife left him for greener pastures. She was succeeded in 1717 by Sarah Dodge, who died in February 1718, and in June 1719 by Elizabeth Holmes of Salem, who survived a year and a half. Last came widow Abigail Ballard of Lynn, Pool's fourth wife in five years. She rejected his initial proposal but changed her mind. In recognition of her reversal, they named their son (1722) Return. In later years "Turn's orchard" was a familiar spot for Sandy Bay youngsters. At least one daughter, Abigail, was also born to the couple.

Left, Right, and Center: Other Pioneers

To the Tarrs and Pools at Sandy Bay were soon added neighbors to the north and, a bit later, to the south and in the bay itself. To Folly Cove moved the Samuel Lanes, Thomas Wise, Benjamin Hoppin, and William Woodbury, a wheelwright from Beverly. In 1702 the Samuel Gotts purchased land and built what is said to be the oldest gambrel-roofed house remaining on Cape Ann. A Wenham weaver, he brought

The unusual half-gambrel house built by Samuel Gott in 1702 near Halibut Point, Pigeon Cove. (Hoyt)

with him a wife and two or three children. One more wife and twelve children followed. By 1707 he was a juryman and had increased his property; later he joined the town church and became a militia lieutenant—a mark of his popularity.

To his wife's brother, William Andrews of Chebacco, Gott sold three lots by "a Cove usually called Hoop Pole Cove." As that farm grew to fifty-five acres, the two Mrs. Andrewses produced six children at what became Andrews' Point. William's sister Elizabeth married Joshua Norwood of Annisquam in September 1704. They, too, moved to Pigeon Cove. While residing at the Garrison House they had a bumper crop of fourteen children. After purchasing land at Gap Cove near Straitsmouth, they sold their first house on March 15, 1732. Down in Pigeon Cove itself, at the building known since 1853 as the "Old Castle," lived the Jethro Wheelers, who bought the land from Norwood in December 1712. The date of their house is uncertain, guesses ranging from a very dubious 1678 to 1717, when it is first mentioned in a mortgage deed. For nearly two centuries it sheltered Pigeon Cove families until it became a museum and community center. To the Pigeon Hill drumlin came the Thomas Harrises, Edward

Tarrs, Pools, and Pioneers

The "Old Castle," a Wheeler home in Pigeon Cove, was built about 1715. Before its restoration, this ancient dwelling housed four families at the same time. (Hoyt)

Braggs, Richard Langsford, and Joseph Thurston. By 1713 nearly all the common lands on the hill had passed into private hands.

To the south of Sandy Bay moved Peter Bennett, another wood-loader, who lived near Pebble Beach. On Milk Island (a bird sanctuary since 1927) he and the Peter Emmons family of Loblolly are supposed to have pastured their cows. Although Grovers from Beverly had been "warned out" of Gloucester—a procedure widely used to protect towns against potential tax burdens—Josiah; Edmund, a weaver; and their respective families were ensconced there by 1720, if not before. Into Sandy Bay proper moved the John Davises from Ipswich via Casco, Maine, with their son Samuel. From Beverly by 1719 came weaver Jabez Baker, John Wonson, Samuel Clark, and Joshua Kendall; all formed links to the Tarrs. In 1730 smallpox invaded, carrying off a number of residents.

People called for roads. Within five months in 1707 two highways were laid out. The earlier ran from the Meeting House Green "to the now dwelling of Mr. John Pool." Its Main Street portions over "the great hill" are still in daily use. In October a road was laid out from Annisquam to "the southwest corner bound of Samuel Gott's land." The next year brought a second massive land grant allocation between

Town on Sandy Bay

Samuel Gott's deed of August 18, 1711 to William Woodbury covering the land which became the Babson Farm (now the Old Farm Inn) near Halibut Point. (SBHS)

Long Cove at Sandy Bay, the head of Starknaught Harbor, and the "great fresh pond." Today's Mt. Pleasant and South streets had specific provisions for seven access ways to the several loading places on the shore "where wood useth to be loaded." Curiously, the land grants of 1688 had failed to provide for a road. It was not until 1716 that today's Granite Street was approved from Halibut Point across the Back Beach to the Millbrook.

By 1725 the last of the town's common acreage had been assigned. Slowly the community waxed and became cohesive. Already a year before, in response to an appeal from John Tarr, John Pool, Jabez Baker, "and the rest of the neighborhood at the head of the Cape," the commoners had granted nearly an acre on today's Main Street by "the head of Sandy Bay . . . for the use of a school forever . . . for the Godly instruction of children and teaching them to read and write good English." By the time Sandy Bay had become a "neighborhood" its second generation were already taking up varied civic functions held by their fathers: jurymen, highway surveyors, hog reeves, tythingmen, constables. At the first annual town meeting following the death of

Tarrs, Pools, and Pioneers

Reproduction of rubbing from the gravestone of John Pool, the second settler of Sandy Bay. (Phillips)

Rockport's first settler, scions of the first three pioneers were appointed to posts of public trust: Benjamin Tarr and John Pool, Jr., as constables and the younger Samuel Gott as tythingman. Caleb Pool, the first male of his line to be born at Sandy Bay, was designated surveyor. The neighborhood was well and truly functioning.

The year 1727 was long remembered throughout the province for a violent earthquake. On May 20 Sandy Bay had been shaken by a tremor of another kind, the death of John Pool at the age of fifty-seven, leaving behind a mulatto servant valued at £ 30 and an estate of over £ 2,800, to be divided between his widow and many children. He was buried on his own land "in the little meadow" beside his first three wives. Three years later Richard Tarr, octogenarian, also found time running out. Unlike Pool, he drafted a detailed will. In the spring of 1732 he, too, was laid to rest in his own hard-won acres, some of which were soon to be bequeathed to his fellow townsmen for their first burial ground on the knoll which gently dips to the ever changing ocean. In far away Virginia, another founding father—that one of an entire nation—was born. His name was George Washington.

ADDITIONAL READING

Babson's *History of Gloucester,* together with his *Notes and Additions,* relate the beginnings of Rockport. Also important are the *History of the Town of Rockport* (Rockport, 1888), and Allen Chamberlain, *Pigeon Cove and Its Early Settlers and Their Farms* (Boston, 1940). The Rockport volume contains the comprehensive "Centennial Address" of Dr. Lemuel Gott (1854) and Anthony Thacher's chilling narrative of his shipwreck in 1635. The Mathers' reports are readily procurable in successive editions of the *Magnalia* and *Remarkable Providences.* Samuel Eliot Morison published an informative account of Thacher, Avery, and Salvages as well as of T.S. Eliot's interest in the disaster: "The Dry Salvages and the Thacher Shipwreck," *The American Neptune,* 25, no. 4 (October 1965): 36-50.

Readers interested in the early architectural history of the area should consult *The Monograph Series Records of Early American Architecture,* especially the following: Frank C. Brown, "Cape Ann: Some Earlier Colonial Dwellings"; Daniel O. Brewster, "The Cottages of Cape Ann"; M. S. Franklin, "The Cottage Interiors of Cape Ann"; Thomas Williams, "Some Old Houses of Pigeon Cove, Massachusetts"; and Stuart Bartlett, "Garrison Houses Along the New England Frontier," (reprinted, 1979).

For the scholarly reader there is, regrettably, no substitute for a patient culling of the manuscript town records, the two volumes of the commoners' records at the city clerk's office in Gloucester, and above all the volumes of Ebenezer Pool's papers at the Sandy Bay Historical Society. These were transcribed (errors and all) and typewritten by valiant WPA workers. There are no detailed indexes to the memorabilia, and Pool himself on many occasions repeated his material in differing versions.

For more about the commoners and their activities see Roy H. Akagi, *The Town Proprietors of the New England Colonies* (Philadelphia, 1924; reprinted, Gloucester, 1963), and Herbert B. Adams, *Village Communities of Cape Ann and Salem,* John Hopkins University Studies in Historical and Political Science, vols. 9-10 (1883), pp. 323-401.

For documentation on the Indian payoffs see Sidney Perley, *The Indian Land Titles of Essex County* (Salem, 1912). Also of interest is Horace P. Beck, *The American Indian as a Sea Fighter in Colonial Times* (Mystic, Conn., 1959).

Tarrs, Pools, and Pioneers

The story of King Philip's War is grippingly presented in Douglas E. Leach, *Flintlock and Tomahawk* (New York, 1958). Two works which provide helpful background material are Harry M. Ward, *The United Colonies of New England–1643-1690* (New York, 1960), and Charles M. Andrews, *Colonial Self Government 1652-1689* (New York, 1968).

Two studies of shipbuilding are Joseph A. Goldenberg, *Shipbuilding in Colonial America* (Mariners Museum, Newport News, Va., 1975), and Bernard and Lotte Bailyn, *Massachusetts Shipping 1697-1714* (Cambridge, 1959).

For two penetrating views of life as lived by prominent men of the period probably nothing is more revealing than the *Diary of Cotton Mather 1681-1724* and *The Diary of Samuel Sewall, 1674-1729.* Both works are available in modern reprint editions of two volumes each.

In his *History of Gloucester* Babson included a large folding map showing the location of the homes of the earlier settlers. This was beautifully reproduced for the bicentennial by the Bearskin Press of Rockport.

4

GROWING PAINS

FOLLOWING the death of Richard Tarr, more than two decades would pass before the Cape achieved the status of an independent parish. There would be a time for a generation to be born, raised, and married—time, too, for others to die and join the great majority. For the town as a whole there would be growing pains. As Cape Ann acquired new residents, its population centers developed self-consciousness. The one parish, one church, one marketplace of Richard Tarr and John Pool became five disparate ones during the lifetimes of their children.

First came the west parish of 1716. Annisquam "after much debate" was set apart on June 11, 1728, as the third parish encompassing everything to today's Pigeon Cove and "the southerly side of Pigeon Hill pasture." Among the signers of the new church's covenant were Samuel Gott, Jethro Wheeler, and Joseph Thurston. Though an attempt failed in 1738 to gather in Sandy Bay, the road which had been cleared across Dogtown from Squam to John Pool's place greatly facilitated contacts between both settlements.

With churches and ministers of their own, residents next called for grammar schools for their children, called so shrilly that they even brought suit against the town. To resolve their complaints and those rising from the Cape a committee of eight was appointed to study the matter. Jonathan Pool, himself a "schoolmaster, scribe, and farmer," was Sandy Bay's representative. Finally, at a town meeting on November 4, 1735, voters accepted a rotational system.

Of the town's seven "squadrons," Sandy Bay was number six. Its bounds stretched from the Squam parish line "by the easterly end of the wood lots to Mr. William Tarr's house, from thence to the Cape Hedge, so-called." Each district was to have the grammar school master in proportion to the amount it contributed to the town tax. Each "squadron" was also obligated to provide a convenient schoolhouse "free for all the inhabitants of ye town." The school cycle ran for three years. "The Cape's proporsion is for three months"; but the third parish rated five and a half. Thus, future Rockport had acquired its own elementary school in 1725 and, for a few months every three years, its own grammar school. With one exception it is not clear which teachers taught at Sandy Bay. He was Jonathan Pierpont (1695-1785), a graduate of Harvard in 1714. On March 11, 1747, he received £ 38 "for keeping school at the Cape eleven weeks and for his board during that term."

The year of the educational compromise brought Gloucester its first selectman from "ye Cape." Edmund Grover was elected on March 1, 1735. "For time spent in the Town service the year past" he was paid £ 6 10s. on February 17, 1736. Some two weeks later he was reelected, as he was for a third term on March 8, 1737. The next year Grover carried out a significant trust: on September 18, 1738, he was voted £ 36 12s. 6d. as reimbursement for 160 pounds of powder which he had provided for the town's stock. As the decade drew to a close, defense became a growing concern. Yet Cape Ann voters were always reluctant to spend their own funds for protection so long as provincial ones might be squeezed out. That year Gloucester's stock of ammunition was "now six half barrels of powder and one thousand pounds of bullets."

Other Sandy Bay men were also coming to the fore. In 1737 Samuel Davis was one "drawn by lot (according to ye directions of ye law of this Province) to serve in ye Jury of Trials at the next sitting in Salem." In 1738 Gloucester voters chose Edmund Grover's son Nehemiah to serve as constable, only to "unchoose" him on discovering that he "doth not appear to be a freeholder." Edmund's namesake, though, was named a tax collector. Two years later another luminary of the fifth parish-to-be, Jabez Baker, was elected selectman. For swearing in its officers the town's treasurer paid £ 3 18s. 2d., the "expense for the Selectmen and Licker at the house of Mr. James Stevens." Into the neighborhood of Sandy Bay had moved such other newcomers as the Henry Withams; Elias Cook and his wife Sarah; the Thomas Dressers; Edward Jumpers; and the elder John Rowe, who married Mary Baker in 1736 and was to have a shoeshop on what is now 85 Main Street. Rowe is said to have opened a tavern on the hill opposite a road "leading to the Burying-ground." In 1775 the only Sandy Bay man listed as an "Inholder" was a John Rowe. In 1788, "John Row, Jr.," was licensed to retail spirits from his house.

As the Cape acquired new residents, however, it also lost some. Smallpox was to invade Cape Ann periodically for generations. In the late autumn of 1730 the town set up a barricade at the Cut and paid watchmen to watch the barricade. On February 3, 1731, John Babson was awarded £ 2 "for his trouble in moving out of his house to accommodate Joseph Tarr, who we was doubtful was going to have the smallpox." In Tarr's sloop "Jacob Rowe was sick with the smallpox." On his death, four of his townsmen were paid for burying him and for "damage" to their clothing. The danger subsided gradually.

Then, between February 5 and 20, 1737, the town was startled by "a Blazing Star" which had a "small head at ye west and a dim sharp stream at ye eastern end." On the sixth, a Sabbath, "just before night, we heard a pretty loud earthquake." Were these thought to be omens? The comet of 1769 certainly was. In any event, Death rode into Sandy Bay in the late winter of 1738 when Essex County as a whole was ravaged by an epidemic of diphtheria. Various Tarrs paid their tolls, the John Gotts gave all their brood, and it seems that perhaps twenty-two grandchildren of John Pool were carried away by the "throat distemper." "By the late sickness we have had thirty-one of our pleasant children taken from us by death," lamented members of the twenty-seven families then living in the neighborhood. This was the time when the town augmented the cemetery, then measuring four by nine rods, which had been given to the Cape people by the Richard Tarr family. The body of little Daniel Barber, a grandson of Jabez Baker, may have been the first interment. A few slate stones still remain as chilling reminders of that grim episode in Rockport's history.

"Yet we have reason to bless God for sparing so many," bravely reflected the survivors; "there is still living in our neighborhood more than 140 persons." Among them were several aging pioneers, paid boarders living with relatives or with members of the community. Widow Elizabeth Tarr, seventy years old in 1736, was running out of

Growing Pains

So the honourable the Committee from the Generall
Court 532

The Memoreall of the Subscribers humbly
Sheweth — That they live nearer the old
than the New Meeting House in the first Parish
in Glouster. That they have put in a Peti:
tion to the honourable Generall Court that they
might not be set off with Such as have Petitioned
for a New Parish. That they persist in their
former Sentiments and most Earnestly pray that
they may not be set off with them that desire
another Parish may be set off but continue to
belong to the first Parish in said Town if it Shall
be thought convenient that there be another
Parish set off And Your Petitionrs as in Duty bound
Shall ever pray &c
Dated at Glocester May y 17th 1739.

James Wallis
Nathanael Sawyer
Nymphus Stacy
Caleb Pool
Caleb Town
Boniamin Tarr
John Pool

James Parsons
William Tarr

Samuel Daues
James Haraay
Samuel Clark
Joshua Kindel
Thomas Dresser
Samuel Tarr

Petition of Sandy Bay inhabitants to remain in Gloucester's First Parish, May 17, 1739. (Mass. Archives)

Town on Sandy Bay

funds. To avoid having her become a public charge, the town agreed to give her children the ten acres she and Richard had used since 1701, provided that their sons would post £ 500 against any future calls for town assistance. Other townspeople were paid in cash; for instance, Thomas Oakes in 1738 and 1739, "for taking care of his mother-in-law Jane Somes . . . and for her funeral charges and expenses"; Samuel Clark for his father-in-law, John Davis; Capt. Samuel Davis "for keeping his Father Davis."

When necessary, children were also provided for by the town. Little Ebenezer Davis, "being about two years old," was taken in by the Harrises, Samuel and Thomas, Jr. In February 1744 public funds supplied 50 shillings for shirting for the wee one. At the end of the month the selectmen paid out £ 15 "half of the sum we agreed to pay" for raising him "Till he is twenty-one years old." Then, too, there was the customary system of indenturing and apprenticing young people. On December 14, 1741, Ebenezer Pool paid £ 40 for John Wonson's time, asserting that the youth "has bound himself to me as a Term Boy." Thus, among themselves the people of future Rockport were becoming an increasingly cohesive community. Before long they, too, manifested a desire for autonomy as a parish.

The Campaign Begins

Once it began, the process took over fifteen years—from March 1738 until December 31, 1753. In the end, people's persistence triumphed. The first step was taken in the late winter of 1738 (not 1737, as is frequently said). Churchgoers from Sandy Bay asked their own first parish in Gloucester to permit them to hire a minister for three winter months and to return to them one quarter of their compulsory church taxes to pay for such winter preaching. At the March 14 meeting the vote was a tie, 19 to 19; a second vote elicited 28 nays but only 20 yeas. Undaunted, in early June the Sandy Bay contingent appealed to the General Court at Boston emphasizing that most of them lived between five and six miles' distance from the meeting-house and had great difficulties in getting to church, "especially in the winter time when tis almost impracticable for such of us as have horses to do it and utterly so with respect to those who have none." Stressing that they were "poor and low in the world" yet wanted to be "blest with opportunity to hear God's word preached," they beseeched the governor and legislature to intervene. Their petition, signed by thirty-two men, provides the earliest-known list of Sandy Bay residents.

The entire matter was quickly blanketed into a bitter controversy festering at the center of Gloucester, where a new church building had been erected. Step by step the Sandy Bay people marched with the forward-looking, commercially oriented members of the harbor area, including old Pastor White. The result was that proddings from the General Court and repeated nudgings from Tarrs, Grovers, Bakers, Clarks, Davises, Pools, Harrises, and others did secure winter preaching at Sandy Bay and funds to pay for it, "so far as forty shillings per sabbath will go." In a test case, Eleazer Grover applied for and got his church tax rebate. So commenced the formal parting of the ways, "so long as all they of the Cape, viz. those who live on the north side of a line from Beaver Dam to the Cape Hedge so called continue with us and pay their rates to the First Parish." Even more surprising was the concession made in August 1740 that the Cape might be set off as a separate parish whenever the residents "are able to maintain a Gospel Minister among them."

Who was found to preach there during the dozen years that the arrangement held is not known, though Moses Parsons (Harvard, 1736) may have been one. First parish financial records mention only sums disbursed not the preachers. The initial years of the 1740s brought to Cape Ann a whirlwind revival, the Great Awakening. Accounts from Pastors White and Bradstreet indicate that the effects were dramatic, though not tempestuous. Young people began "to read, sing, and pray." Soon more children "would pray to admiration." A "desirable child about seven years old" had died at Sandy Bay in 1738, lamenting "on her death bed that she never heard a sermon in her lifetime." Quarreling, swearing, drinking, etc. were laid aside. People were "anointed afresh," even "crying out in time of divine service under a sense of their sins."

Sins had to be acknowledged before the whole congregation. Failure to give satisfaction meant being barred from communion. Among the recorded peccadillos were Samuel Gott's and Thomas Ayers' suspensions "for ye sin of drunkenness," James Parsons, Jr.'s, "profane speaking" and the "evil and uncharitablness" of the fight between Ens. John Rowe and Col. Epes Sargent. John Pool II was embroiled in a series of incidents including an uncontested "breach of the Seventh Commandment" (in 1753 when he was fifty), and later still for his neglect in not attending the ordinances because of "a private difference between him and one of the brethren." Regrettably, no account survives of the only appearance in town of George Whitefield, the greatest of all awakeners. Of a service in Boston, though, Thomas Prince wrote he had "never seen anything like it before, except at the time of the general earthquake."

To the residents of Sandy Bay earthquakes would come soon enough; storms they had with them always. The winter blizzard of 1740-41 had been particularly bitter, carrying off four men but washing ashore limes and lemons from their cargo. Mariners clearly needed a safer haven in the area. So in 1743 Benjamin Tarr and John and Ebenezer Pool secured a grant at what was called the "Whirlpool" in today's old harbor for a wharf. Said to have been 72 by 20 feet and built of timber and stone, it was the first Sandy Bay pier. Each of the owners was also allotted space for storage purposes.

The economic outlook of the 1740s was bleak, as Parson White wrote to Boston, because of the war with Spain and the fears of war with France. The price of fish was low, that of salt very dear. The price of corn had doubled in part, as White growled, because the French "can sally out and take over corn-vessels." In June 1747 Mark Parsons and his crew escaped safely when a fully manned armed boat from the *Don Pedro* captured their sloop just off the Cape, as they were homeward bound from Maryland. Only about ten of the town's seventy vessels were employed in fishing. "Our people are scattered abroad in the world to get their bread . . . many serving as volunteers in his majesty's service."

Yet the leaders at Sandy Bay foresaw that their future lay in commerce. Accordingly, future Rockport erected its second wharf not long after the crusade to capture the French fortress of Louisbourg. That project enlisted strong support throughout Cape Ann, including a vessel of Jethro Wheeler's. As the future governor, Thomas Hutchinson, boasted: "Five or six well-fed Marblehead or Cape Ann men catch as much fish as ten or twelve meagre French men in the same time." The two wharves furnished a modest shelter into which neighborhood coasters and a banker or two could be docked to discharge cargo or be refurbished between fishing trips. Yet only two years later Benjamin Tarr himself lost a sloop.

Growing Pains

By the Treaty of Aix-la-Chapelle (1748), Sandy Bay had grown to some thirty-five homes with about forty families, plus the hamlet at Pigeon Cove, which had lost pioneer Samuel Gott in November 1748. Antiquarian Pool estimated the total population at about 260 by 1750. On January 28, 1751, the first parish reluctantly agreed to relieve their Cape members from paying any taxes to the parish for two years, to commence "from the twenty-fifth of March next, provided they maintain a gospel minister among them all that term and relinquish any demands they have or may have upon the Parish."

The delighted residents let no grass grow under their feet. Acting like an already independent parish, they voted "to Beuld a Meeting house." Rockport's first book of records commences with the minutes of a so-called Parish meeting on March 18, 1752, though an earlier notation dated "1752 February the 1 day," reads starkly thus: "Voted to have the Enocolation in Mr. Bakers and Mr. Withams houses." This is the only surviving evidence at Sandy Bay of the smallpox which invaded Cape Ann in early 1752.

Capt. Samuel Davis, Ebenezer Pool, and John Rowe were put in charge of the future parish. A month later Henry Witham and Jonathan and Ebenezer Pool were elected assessors and Ebenezer Grover collector. On April 14 it was stipulated that the money should be turned over to "Mr. Cleaue Land," the earliest-known mention of him at Sandy Bay. By autumn plans for a joint meetinghouse with Annisquam had been jettisoned and a frame erected at "Mr. Smith's Pasture" (about 59 Mt. Pleasant Street today). Friction, however, resulted in transporting the structure down to a site east of the present Baptist church.

A fresh "petistion" for independence was submitted to the group at Gloucester Harbor on March 12, 1753, where it finally passed. On May 11 the bay reassembled, elected a parish committee, chose a threesome to negotiate with Pastor Ebenezer Cleaveland for another year, appointed Jonathan Pool—the former schoolteacher—to be their clerk, and yet another trio to number and price the pews, of which Capt. Samuel Davis was to be treasurer and caretaker. With some trepidation the neighbors tackled the matter of a "petistion in be half of the inhabetence of the Cape" to be dispatched to "the Genneral Corte" requesting separation. Edmund Grover, Henry Witham, John Rowe, and Caleb and Ebenezer Pool composed the drafting committee.

Town on Sandy Bay

At Boston their gallant efforts were accepted. When the first parish raised no objections, on December 31, 1753, the Provincial Council ordered, and on January 1, 1754, the lower house of the legislature and Governor Shirley concurred, that the petition from the Cape be granted. The boundary line of the petition was extended "on a North Course from Beaver Dam to Squam-Line," and the people and property lying "Notherly [sic] and Northeasterly thereof to Squam Parish were to be made a seperate [sic] parish, and do Duty and Receive Privilege as other Parishes within this Province do or by Law ought to enjoy." The Sandy Bay parish, Gloucester's fifth and last, was thereby chartered.

ADDITIONAL READING

In addition to Babson's accounts are the manuscript records of Gloucester town, commoners' and selectmen's sessions, and the various documents of the first and third parishes on deposit at the Cape Ann Historical Association.

At the Massachusetts Archives are the relevant civil, ecclesiastical, and military papers. The published *Journals of the House of Representatives of Massachusetts* are invaluable. Edwin Gaustad, *The Great Awakening in New England* (New York, 1957), relates the whole story; John White's description of the first parish is in Babson's *Notes and Additions*, vol. 2, pp. 124-27. Parson Bradstreet's letter appeared in *The Christian History*, 14 (August 13, 1743): 187-89.

For the smallpox and "throat distemper" see Claude M. Fuess, ed., *The Story of Essex County* (New York, 1935), especially Robert K. Vietor, "Medicine and Public Hygiene," vol. 2, pp. 829-77. A good military overview is Howard Peckham's *The Colonial Wars, 1689-1762* (Chicago, 1964). But to get the flavor of the campaigners, one should at least sample the pungent *Louisbourg Journals, 1745* ed. Louis de Forest (New York, 1932).

Part 2

From Parish to Town

ROM THE DAY *the first white men strolled along Rockport's shores until the area became part of the fifth parish of Gloucester 150 years elapsed. Only 86 years would pass between the establishment of Sandy Bay parish (1754) and the incorporation of the town of Rockport (1840). But such years they would be. Think what a native-born octogenarian would have seen by the time he voted in Rockport's first town meeting. There would have been periods of quiet desperation, exhilarating change, grinding conflict and dynamic peace – in about equal proportions.*

At the time of his birth, his village would have been dogmatically church centered; by the time of his town's birth, both its villages would have become commerce oriented. Caesar's dues would be being rendered first. During the patriarch's first decade his community would have grappled with its meeting-house and minister and with multiple civic challenges: tax assessments, rate collections, the keeping of public records, primary schools for youngsters, and a rotational grammar school for higher levels. There would have been vexatious relations with the third parish at Annisquam, periodic incursions of smallpox, devastating winter storms, the melancholy parching of summer droughts, even disconcerting earthquakes.

Beyond his sheltering coves would have rumbled the drums of discord. It is easy to assume that an age which lacked telecommunications also lacked an awareness of events over the horizon. Not so at Cape Ann—with its far-ranging coastal traders, fishing vessels, college-trained clergymen, and dispossessed Acadian refugees. Indian raids in Maine, French invasions from Canada, privateering on the high seas—all would have cried out for militant response. Stalwarts from Sandy Bay, including the "fighting parson," would have replied swiftly.

In his second decade Rockport's graybeard of 1840 would have become acutely aware of the mounting tensions between his parish-town-province on the one hand and his mother country across the seas. In his early teens he would have heard of the new, high-handed taxes being imposed from England and of the havoc they would raise with his neighborhood's way of life. He would have seen his father riding off to town meetings at Gloucester with increasing frequency, meetings no longer concerned with routine matters such as roads, rebates, roaming hogs, licenses, and regulations but with rights, liberties, even defense. By his mid-teens there would have been grisly tales about the massacre at Boston and the violence in Gloucester against Customs Collector Fellows and "Saville the Informer."

In Sandy Bay itself, however, life would have gone on at his church and in the community. At the former a pew would have been found for a choir and a new hymnbook adopted by the congregation. In 1768 Parson Cleaveland would have gone off for a spell, on Indian matters. In the harbor a stout long wharf would have been constructed and a pound fenced in for stray animals. Everyone would have found inflation troublesome, even more so the boycott of English goods, especially tea. On Thacher's Island the erection of two lighthouses would have fascinated him and his friends, and a string of coastal shipwrecks would have sobered them noticeably. And what of those increasingly anti-British sermons preached by the minister in the 1770s? How would the neighbors react to the blockade of Boston and the series of countermoves, first throughout Massachusetts, then down the entire American coast? War would have broken out by the time the old man had turned twenty-one.

Many a Sandy Bay man born in the 1750s responded to the call for independence. A few were alive in 1840. Some of them had fought at Bunker Hill and remained through the siege of Boston; fewer signed up for the

Continental army, while John Rowe, Jr., even became a professional soldier. Once hostilities turned southward, most Sandy Bay striplings preferred to ship out on privateers. But from 1775 on Cape Ann as a whole suffered increasingly from loss of men, economic crises, shortages of food, disease, and natural disasters. By the time of the signing of the peace treaty at Paris in 1783, the village was pitifully poor and bereft even of its minister. Residents might have echoed the words of another clergyman who wrote: "We are poor, and cold, and have little meal, little wood, and little meat; but thank God, courage enough."

From the war's end, however, things took a turn for the better in future Rockport. Because its fishing ventures were mainly confined to offshore areas, smaller boats could be put into service rather expeditiously. By the early 1790s Sandy Bay had a fleet of over sixty vessels at sea. The stability which followed in the wakes of the new Constitution and a stronger federal government added a buoyancy to the townspeople, although a few did leave the community to take up land grants in Maine, given as a bounty to war veterans. New arrivals soon took up homesites in both the fifth parish and the Pigeon Cove area. The community secured its first medical doctor in 1792, its second in 1798, and a secondary school of its own in 1797. The doctrine of universal salvation had swept into Gloucester during the Revolution. By its appeal to so many Sandy Bay church-goers, it provided a means of helping to finance repairs to the decaying meetinghouse. Thus, the century came to a close on a wave of unexampled prosperity throughout the fifth parish.

Between 1800 and the outbreak of the only war in which Rockport was ever invaded, the octogenarian of 1840 would have been in his prime, the mid-forties to mid-fifties. By then he would have had well-grown children and perhaps a grandchild or two. If he had been a fisherman, he would have benefited greatly from the rising prices of cod, pollock, and haddock; he might also have joined in the trend to catch and market more mackerel. Federal bounties for fishing vessels would assuredly have pleased him, though not the crippling Embargo, Enforc-ing, and Non-Intercourse Acts imposed by the government. Fresh improvements to the piers at the Whirlpool and Long Cove would have seemed notable steps forward for the commerce of Sandy Bay. So, too, would have been the new roads, the daily stagecoach service to Gloucester Harbor, and the establishment of a fire company for Sandy Bay, although a bucket brigade. In 1804 would have risen the imposing new meetinghouse, to be followed by the expansion of other religious bodies, at first the Universalists and Baptists. By 1810 the town of which Sandy Bay was so vigorous a parish would have grown to nearly six thousand residents.

The War of 1812, so unpopular with most New Englanders, created few serious hardships on Sandy Bay and Pigeon Cove. Even contemporaries admitted that fishing and privateering proved a profitable wartime business. It did, however, bring enemy troops and vessels into future Rockport and scatter a few cannonballs throughout the village. The fort on Bearskin Neck and the doughty volunteers, dubbed "Sea Fencibles," proved far from impregnable, but both have enriched local color in the generations since and the volunteers themselves were benefited by the pensions they were finally granted.

The quarter century which followed set every wheel of business in motion. Sandy Bay and its neighboring Cove became almost a boomtown, having doubled its population in two decades. Fishing became big business, on a modest scale, and a mighty sea serpent boggled the minds of many who pursued it in 1817 and later. Larger wharves were erected, and between 1836 and 1840 a breakwater was constructed (with federal money) at Long Cove. Pigeon Cove had already pioneered its own harbor facilities in a laudable fashion. In 1835 Straitsmouth acquired a lighthouse to complement the twins at Thacher's. A Marine Insurance Company was floated. Anthracite coal came to Rockport in 1832 but failed to kindle an enthusiastic response.

Far more important for generations to come were the invention and production of isinglass, on which Rockport would long hold a monopoly, and the beginnings of the granite business in 1823, an industry which would in time sustain the chief burden of Rockport's economy. In 1825 the parish won a post office for itself; in 1827 the town initiated its first newspaper (the Gloucester Telegraph); and in 1830 both the harbor and Sandy Bay inaugurated a lyceum series to further enlighten the people. To accommodate their members, churches were built by the Baptists (1822) and Universalists (1829). From 1839, the Methodists shed their beams from their chapel on Jewett Street. To dampen other lights came two fire engines–tubs, not buckets–to Sandy Bay in 1829 and 1830. The age also brought the first of the temperance societies which labored so persistently to keep Rockport sober. Also contributing to Rockport's gravity those years were drownings, a murder, further expansions of the cemetery, and the purchase of a parish hearse.

So self-reliant did the fifth parish become that attempts were initiated in 1817 and again in late 1827 to set the area free. Gloucester's other parishes raised few objections, and the Telegraph supported independence for Sandy Bay. Caution, however, especially on matters of financial liability, prevailed for the time being. But, on the train of further expansion by the time Rockport's hypothetical voter of 1840 had reached the venerable age of eighty-five he would have been assured of living in an independent town.

5

"AN ASSTABLESSHED PARISH BY OUR SELVES"

T HINKING BACK over his childhood, James Russell Lowell remarked, "New England was all meeting-house when I was growing up." It was even more so in the previous century. The earlier records of Sandy Bay parish place the local church at the center of community life. To the rhythms of daily existence it set the beat and tolled the bell. As early as November 1753 the fifth parish began putting its house in order. Ebenezer Grover, Thomas Dresser, and Caleb Pool were designated "to adjust accompts with the Committee that was Chosen to Beuld the Meeting house." No contemporary descriptions of the structure remain as it stood on its irregular lot of some 68 by 120 feet at the head of Long Cove, unprotected by breakwater or seawall. At its eastern corner was the block from which worshipers mounted their curveting "gay nags" to return home.

Historian Pool described the building as thirty-six feet square, two stories high, without a belfry or steeple. On the south side was a porch through which the congregation entered and from which a staircase rose to a narrow gallery, which may have flanked three sides of the interior. The main floor had a central aisle, on either side of which were pews. Near the pulpit were three long seats, and the pulpit itself is claimed to have boasted an overhead sounding board. There is supposed to have been "one seat for colored people." A Massachusetts Bay assessors' list for 1754 credits Gloucester with 61 of the 439 blacks "sixteen years old and upwards" in Essex County. Numerous references to them survive in the journals of Pastor Samuel Chandler who, like his elder colleague, ministered to their needs. On November 22, 1753, he was at the Cape marrying a white couple and also "Caesar and Flora." A decade later Ebenezer Cleaveland joined two others: Negro Dick, a servant of Capt. William Norwood's, and "Philis," a slave to widow Baker, "relict of Captain Jabez." Philis met death in a poisoning scandal, but under the Massachusetts constitution Dick was liberated, became Richard Freeman, and lived on at Sandy Bay to reach his eightieth year.

The new little meetinghouse had few amenities to counteract its bareness. In March 1756 its parent first church voted "at the request of the 5th Church in Gloucester, newly embodied" to donate one flagon. Five years later, Cape parishioners received a legacy of £ 3 from their deceased elder, Jabez Baker. From the bequest and other sums a silver chalice was purchased. Deacon Witham was requested to find "a stone jugg" or something suitable "to git and hold wine." To store all these, in 1761 Deacon Ebenezer Grover was asked to build "under ye deacons' seat a conveniency to keep ye church vessels."

Though the building may have been unimpressive even in a time of small things, from its inception it nurtured a group of dedicated men and women. It "blowed exceedingly hard and exceedingly cold at the Bay" in early 1754. Bad weather persisted until late spring. It was May 16 before the first legal meeting of the fifth parish was held. Several officers were then elected; Mr. Cleaveland was engaged for another year; and Benjamin Tarr, parish constable, was singled out to collect the taxes of the new precinct. Thanks to his extant list, dated October 21, it is known almost precisely who resided in the area.

There were in all thirty-seven taxpayers plus two "estates." Roughly half of the residents lived mainly by agriculture, the other half from the sea. Two men paid no taxes and four others paid no poll taxes. The three Clark men seem to have been overlooked somehow. Only two vessels were deemed large enough to be assessed. One was owned by the estate of Capt. Jabez Baker, Jr., drowned in September 1753; the other by Ebenezer Pool. In all, Benjamin Tarr was to gather £ 26 6s., of which £ 12 3s. 6d. was the town tax. Babson calculated that in its inaugural year the fifth parish contained about one twenty-fourth part of the total valuation of Gloucester.

These were the neighbors who turned to the civic and ecclesiastical tasks before them in 1755. On February 9 the first parish dismissed ten men "in order to their incorporation into a distinct church by them selves called the fifth church in Gloucester": Edmund Grover, Jabez Baker, Nehemiah Grover, Henry Witham, Johnathan Pool, Samuel Davis, John Rowe, James Parsons, Jr., Samuel Clark, Jr., and Eleazar Lurvey. On the thirteenth, a Thursday, Pastor John White incorporated the church with the assistance of Annisquam's Bradstreet, his colleague Chandler, and the fourth church's Mr. Rogers.

Next the newly established church had to call a minister. For the better part of two years worshipers at the Cape had been ministered to by Ebenezer Cleaveland, a native of Canterbury, Connecticut, and a lineal descendant of the *Mayflower* Hopkinses and other Pilgrims. With his brother he had been expelled from Yale by its conservative faculty for repeated attendance at revival meetings with their family and other prominent members of their home church. So deeply had the Cleaveland boys imbibed "erronius Doctrines," they were "filled with such a strong and lively Impression of divine Things, as made them come home Singing along the Streets." On being suspended from Yale, Ebenezer, then not quite twenty, married a local girl, Abigail Stevens, also from a born-again, New Light family and a descendant of Massachusetts' historian-soldier, Edward Johnson. The youthful groom took up his religious studies with Eleazar Wheelock; schoolteaching seems to have covered the financial needs of the newlyweds.

The installation of John Cleaveland at Essex, Massachusetts, was the magnet which drew his younger brother to Cape Ann. Seemingly, the latter's sermons, prayers, and conduct satisfied the fisher-farmer people at Sandy Bay, anxious for a minister of their own; probably he refrained from singing along the streets of the village. John Rowe, Ebenezer Grover, and Caleb Pool were named the committee to "treet" with Mr. Cleaveland "about his Principels." On Friday, February 28, 1755, the parish concurred with the church vote "in Chusing Mr. Ebenezer Cleaveland for their Pasture." On Monday, May 12, the parish swore in its elected officers and voted to pay Cleaveland "Sixty Pounds Sallerry yearly."

A month later Cape parishioners tackled the problem of housing for him and his family. As his "Settlement" fee, the minister was to have £ 53 6s. 8d. and "to Gitt the house frame ready to rais by the first of

October next," close to the junction of today's Main and School streets. By the last day of October plans were launched for his installation. Francis Pool was chosen to procure "a quesen" (a cushion) for the ordination. Samuel Davis, Jr., was elected to "intertain the ministers and mesengers" coming from other parishes for the inaugural event for which he was to receive 10 shillings for each man, presumably from the "Provision . . . to be maid for them by the whole Parish." Interestingly enough, no known account of the great occasion itself—even the actual date—has survived.

On Sunday, November 9, Cleaveland was admitted to membership in his own church. On November 26 he is said to have performed his first marriage there. United were Ralph Haycock and Martha Burnel. Edmund Grover and Jabez Baker were named ruling elders, and Samuel Davis and Henry Witham were appointed to the deacons' bench. Communion was to be observed once very six weeks "through all the seasons of the year." As wives of the deacons, Elizabeth Davis and Rachel Witham were exempted from paying the 2-shilling contribution to stock the communion table. Two days before his thirtieth birthday Ebenezer Cleaveland signed the records of the fifth parish meeting as pastor, adding the initials "V.D.M.," a Latin abbreviation for "by the word of God, minister." Reluctant Yale had not yet granted him a college degree.

Rumblings

The mid-1750s was a period of seismic disturbances. November 18, 1755, was long remembered through out the Western world for "the great earth quake." According to some local jottings found by Babson, at "half-past four in the morning was the most shocking earthquake as ever I knew in this land. It shattered a great many chimneys in this town and in other towns." Then, on December 19, came another "loud rumbling of an earthquake—no shaking but a jarring like thunder." Never loathe to shake up their backsliders, the clergy of Cape Ann capitalized on those tremors. Despite the bitter cold, on December 24 "a full congregation" turned out at the harbor "to humble ourselves under the tokens of God's Displeasure in the Earthquake." The fourth parish kept its fast on January 1, to which Ebenezer Cleaveland came from Sandy Bay to do the praying. Then the new Cape parish held its own fast on January 29, although its disappointed pastor was in bed, "sick of a fever." The Reverend Mr. Chandler supped at Ebenezer

Pool's. A sudden whirlwind on April 24 frightened jittery worshipers out of church, and on May 8 the whole province—keenly aware of the market for Massachusetts fish in Catholic Iberia—set apart the day for a fast "on account of the Earthquake which was desolating Lisbon, Portugal." Only three days afterward, about 8:00 P.M., Cape Ann heard yet another low rumbling of an earthquake. People everywhere were on edge.

Much louder and more lasting rumblings began troubling them soon, though the mother country didn't declare war on France until May 18, 1756, and it took until August 4 for the war to be proclaimed at Boston. Far from being blinkered from developments beyond their horizon, Cape Anners were quite alert to events and trends. At a town meeting in 1754 they had instructed their representative to the General Court to vote in favor of the Albany plan for the federation of colonies. As for the persistent French-Indian turmoils Babson tersely commented: "Not many towns had a larger interest at stake in the war than Gloucester."

When training days for the militia were increased, women and children were warned of the threats their men might be asked to combat. A fast on August 26, 1755, specified intercessions for "our armies and expeditions" and singled out "General Bradstreet's [sic] defeat near Ohio." (It was Braddock's defeat which so drastically changed the fortunes of George Washington.) Next came prayers for "general Shirley's marching to Niagara." Lastly, the town made special mention of the forces of "general Johnson at Crown Point."

On September 20, "the companies met to enlist soldiers to go to Crown Point." Muster rolls signed out there in October included many Gloucester names, among them the two John Rowes from the fifth parish and the third parish's former constable, Capt. Jonathan Fellows. Chaplain Chandler ministered there until December. Other local soldiers took off to upper New York and Canada, some to be captured and held prisoner, a few never to return. Reinforcements of quite another kind were welcomed by the church at Sandy Bay, which formally received fifteen women dismissed to its care in 1756 from the harbor parish: the two Anna Bakers; Mary Grover; Deborah Davis; Rachel Witham; the two Elizabeth Clarks; Elizabeth and Mary Harris; Abigails Rowe and Parsons; Rebecca Tarr; and Elizabeth, Hannah, and Martha Pool. As was the custom, they would sit, segregated, across the meetinghouse aisle from their men.

"An Asstablesshed Parish By Our Selves"

Until after the fall of Canada, town fishing vessels would be fired upon by privateers. So was a Gloucester schooner, overtaken by Spaniards while returning from Martinique. The town, however, fitted out a few privateers of its own, including William Ellery's. In an appeal for defense assistance Gloucester deplored "the small number of their men commonly at home, the greatest part of them being generally employed in the fishery or otherwise absent at sea." Then, too, in the autumn of 1756, Cape Ann had its first encounter with refugees, when the Acadian French were uprooted from their farms and scattered throughout American colonial communities. Longfellow later immortalized these wretched victims in his poem *Evangeline*. Cape Ann was paid £ 6 for quartering twenty-four of them in "the Neuter-French house," prior to their relocation at Wenham and Methuen. The Doucett family—Joseph, Ann, their ten children—and the infirm "Widow Eliza Janvire" of Manchester were thirteen whom Gloucester took in.

Yet despite war threats daily routines continued at home and at the Bay meetinghouse. Widow Mary Gamage, a daughter of Joshua Norwood, was hired to be sexton at 9s. 4d. a year, a job she held for nearly a decade along with serving as a neighborhood midwife. The new parish voted in 1757 to buy two volumes for their minutes, and two years later the church also purchased "a book to keep ye church records." Costs came from two Spanish dollars given "to the 5th Church of Christ in Gloucester by Elder Jabez Baker and Deacon Samuel Davis." But the scribes moved slowly, for in April 1762 voters reiterated that the "Old Records" should be put into one volume. To expedite matters, in the spring of 1765 Elder Pool and Deacon Whitham were chosen "to assest the Clark in setteling the old Records" in a single book. Today those precious volumes are cornerstones of Rockport's history.

Comings and Goings

Storms and droughts complicated the community's struggle for survival in 1757. Disheartening news of the capture of Fort Henry arrived at Cape Ann on August 13. On the fifteenth, "we had alarm guns firing and drums beating to send one quarter part of the militia to the frontier, invaded by French." Parson Cleaveland outdid himself with a series of monthly fasts, and Henry Comerford got permission to sell spirits "to enable him more advantageously to carry on his business of supplying the fishery" at the harbor. On Thanksgiving, after about

plentiful table, in good order, in peace and quietness." One hopes his
Sandy Bay friends experienced similar bounty and joy. On March 16,
1758, the humdrum of the Cape parish was quickened when Chandler
married widow "Madam" Stevens to the recently bereaved Elder Edmund Grover, both of them octogenarians. A week later he visited with
the newlyweds and their "children together" at a party in the harbor.

In April, following another earthquake and fresh militia maneuvers, the town was agog over the departure of its troops to Ticonderoga
and transports to Halifax and Louisbourg. Pigeon Cove's William
Andrews, Jr., is said to have died while returning from the latter
campaign. Unable to lag behind, Parson Cleaveland extracted from his
church people (but not from the Parish as a whole) permission to go as
chaplain to the regiment of Col. Jedediah Preble. He was on duty from
June 12 through November 15. There is no indication that his
parishioners hired a substitute. From the diaries of both his clerical
brother John and medical officer Dr. Caleb Rea of Danvers, one gets
vivid pictures of life at the front and on the frontier. The electrifying
news of the fall of Louisbourg in 1758 to the Anglo-American invaders
reached Sandy Bay at a time when the bemused parish treasurer was
troubled "Concerning the behindments" of unpaid taxes. To celebrate
the victory the returned Parson Cleaveland mounted another of his
fast-and-prayer days. When the excitement of the fall of Quebec hit
the town on October 12, 1759, there was "great rejoicing; illumination;
firing of cannon here." At the annual provincial Thanksgiving on
November 29 everyone had cause for gratitude on the Cape where, as
the minister put it, "is the habitation of cod fish, an unimpaired source
of Treasure, a rich revenue, a wholesome repast, delicate diet, the
reward of dripping toils of the fisherman, who live in the spray, and
labor on the verge of the ocean."

The second half of 1760 again took Parson Cleaveland away—for
twenty-four weeks as chaplain to the troops of Col. John Whitcomb.
Great was his rejoicing at "our victorious and final Reduction of
Canidy." But on his return there was another smallpox alarm. Samuel
Pool's family was quickly evacuated to the Boston Pest House in
Ebenezer Collins's boat. Also that January, memorial services were
conducted on receipt of the news of the death of King George II, a
reminder that the town, however remote, was still part of the far-flung
British Empire. In 1761 death took three of the industrious Grovers:
Nehemiah on January 13, Elder Edmund (the old bridegroom) on

"An Asstablesshed Parish By Our Selves"

February 5, and Deacon Ebenezer on October 25. Another earthquake in March so shook the Cape that "all got up." Also that March voters decided that "the fish yard shall be fenced in for three year." From mid-May until "a plentiful rain" arrived on September 4, Sandy Bay was again parched by drought.

The next year was even grimmer in some ways. Bitter cold and deep snow, in places five feet deep on the level, was followed by a "melancholy dry time," when prices for corn and hay fairly rocketed. That summer Sandy Bay had its infrequent turn hosting "free Scool" and thereby eased the drain on flattened pocketbooks. Finally, on October 9, 1762, the whole town joined in the province's Thanksgiving for success in war, and a peace treaty was formally signed on February 10, 1763, at Paris.

January 1764 marked the tenth anniversary of the creation of Sandy Bay as "an Asstablesshed Parish by our Selves." There is no record of any special celebrations, though the town as a whole was in the throes of another religious revival. One convert was Alice Meserve, "brought into light last night as she was seeking Christ in the cellar; very full and flaming." Snow, cold, and another outbreak of smallpox curtailed travel and canceled church services and midweek lectures. Only on March 15 could a day be dedicated to "humiliation, prayer, and thanksgiving relative to the infectious disorder."

At the Cape parish there was indeed much for which to give thanks after ten years of independence. The community had been legally chartered; its citizens had met the challenges of local self-government; its neighborhood school program was functioning; and the neighborhood had built a church, called a minister, provided a communion service, and begun a choir. The resting place for its beloved dead had been enlarged and modest economic facilities prepared for its living. Finally, it had learned to equate liberty with vigilant interdependence. On March 7, 1764, a local diarist recorded: "Last Monday evening remarkable Aurora Borealis; pillars of smoke and flashes of light; the northern part of the hemisphere seemed almost of a blaze." For future Rockport the decade ahead would become an epoch of smoke, flashes, and blaze.

Minutes of the Sandy Bay parish meetings were carefully transcribed by Calvin Pool for the *Essex Institute Historical Collections,* vols. 21 and 22 (1884-85). For accounts of the Cleaveland brothers' collision with Yale, see John Cleaveland's journal in the *Essex Institute Historical Collections,* vol. 107 (1971), pp. 143-72, and Thomas Clap, *The Judgement of the Rector and Tutors of Yale College* (New London, 1745). Intimate views of the Ticonderoga campaign are given in "Journal of the Rev. John Cleaveland," *Essex Institute Historical Collections,* vol. 12 (1874), pp. 85-103, 179-96; and vol. 13 (1875), pp. 53-63.

For the French and Indian War service see Nancy S. Voye, *Massachusetts Officers in the French and Indian Wars, 1748-1763* (Boston, 1975), and Robert E. MacKay, *Massachusetts Soldiers in the French and Indian Wars, 1744-1755* (Boston, 1978).

For the sad tale of the dispossessed French Canadians see George F. Dow, "The French Acadians in Essex County," *Essex Institute Historical Collections,* vol. 45 (1909), pp. 293-307.

"An Asstablesshed Parish By Our Selves"

6

COLLISION COURSE

IN HIS OLD AGE John Adams sagely concluded that the radical change "in the principles, opinions, sentiments, and affections of the people"—not the military action—was "the real American Revolution." And so it was with Cape Anners. As early as the year the Cape parish was set off, Gloucester joined its neighbors in vociferously attacking a London tax proposal as being "inconsistent with the natural rights of mankind." But it was the Molasses Act of 1764 and subsequent taxing restrictions which finally propelled Cape Ann, the province, and all the American colonies into rebellion. The General Court forecast that a strictly enforced customs act would mean the collapse of a fishing business worth £ 164,000 annually and unemployment for five thousand seamen from vessels valued at £ 100,000. To that blow was added the Stamp Act of 1765, by which Parliament stretched its hand into the pockets of every American colonist. While delegates from six colonies were preparing a joint "Declaration of Rights and Grievances," Cape Anners turned out "at a very full meeting" on October 7, 1765, and unanimously warned their representatives to the General Court to make no concessions whatever. When on November 1 the act took effect, bells tolled, flags were lowered to half-mast, and business ground to a halt.

Yet life went on. At the Sandy Bay meetinghouse, once again "Mrs. Gammidge [was] chosen saxton for this year"—at long last with a pay hike to 10 shillings; Parson Cleaveland's salary remained pegged at

£ 66. 13s. 4d. Out on the streets, voters were annoyed by roaming animals, so they allotted £ 35 to John Pool and John Rowe, Jr., to construct a pound for strays. When news of the tax repeal reached the town in May, however, the selectmen did the unusual; they released a whole cask of gunpowder, "to be used towards expressing our Joy." Surely many fifth parish families joined their fellow townsmen in quite literally "having a blast." Still, 1766 was a hard year. A fire destroyed a harbor warehouse, sail loft, and their contents. Locally, mountainous springtime waves swept seven fishing boats to destruction and catastrophically damaged several others. Cape Ann lost some forty seamen that year. To the selectmen's appeal, on March 3, 1767, the General Court granted the town a reduction of £ 50 in their province taxes, "in consideration of their sufferings and losses."

Since fishing and coastal trade supplied the main revenue of the fifth parish, increased docking areas were needed for the expanding fleet. To a petition from Ebenezer and John Pool and Benjamin Tarr the commoners offered to the parish "Bair Skin Neck So Called with all the Common Land that may be spared near Long Cove," together with "the Land the fish Houses stands on Belonging to the Little Boats." As a price, they insisted that within three years the fifth parish build a wharf of two hundred by thirty feet, "back of the Old Wharff" which would rise sixteen feet at "ye Head of ye Wharff from Low water Mark." Two days later Sandy Bay concurred in having a wharf on "Bear Scin Neck flatts," stipulating, however, that costs should not come from a tax levy on the parish but rather from such entrepreneurs as would build the "Peer" to specifications.

That same spring singing at the meetinghouse should have improved, for the fifth parish voted "to Provide a Place for the queristers [choristers] to Set in" and to have it ready "by the first Sabeth in March next." The solution found was "to bye Lurvey's Pue." Just where Eleazer Lurvey himself planned to move is not recorded. Perhaps he was one of the singers. Nor is it known what songs those sirens rendered. The Cape parish may have followed the mother church's lead and lined out hymns from the modified *Bay Psalm Book.* On March 5, 1767, however, the bay congregation voted "individually" that "we will for the future sing in our public assembly Doctor Watts' *Psalms and Hymns.*" According to Lemuel Gott, Captain Young and Thomas Dresser were "head singers."

From 1766 on the Cape also took a more progressive line on education. At the end of March the parish voted to take over "the

Schoolhouse." Costs for refurbishing it on its new site on the grounds of the present Congregational church were covered equally from parish funds and from its proprietors. A private school building was erected in the early 1760s on John Pool's land at "Groat" Hill overlooking the Front Beach. One version has him constructing it to rent out; the other says that it was built by proprietors. Both stories agree that it was in use until about 1800, when it was sold to James Parsons, in 1797, who was still living in it in 1859 at the age of eighty-four. In 1767 Thomas Dresser and Joshua Tarr were asked to "look out for a Scool Dame." In 1768 residents voted for "a scool master this winter." At the March 19 parish meeting, however, John Rowe, Jr., was designated to "carry a paper about to see if they will sign for a school master or mistress." The verdict was for a "Scool Master if they Gitt one the summer insuing." By 1769 parents again were asked to sign petitions "one for a man Scool and one for a woman Scool." In 1770 the Cape decided not to send "more than two Scolers to the Scool a Peice." Seemingly, teachers were paid so much per pupil, and tax funds for education were scarce—a shortage which lasted until long after the Revolution.

Outside the town storm clouds began piling up. Two regiments and a British flotilla reached Boston in September 1767. Although Lord Townshend had stiffly withdrawn internal taxes, he substituted levies on glass, lead, paint, paper, and tea. As a response, on December 21, 1767, Cape Anners steered for rebellion by joining a one-year boycott against some fifty-five imported products and "the use of Superfluities." Instead, they supported domestic manufactures of all types and elected colleagues to obtain written support for both schemes from all inhabitants and households.

At Sandy Bay the period was rife with uncertainties. With the death of Pastor Bradstreet, the Annisquam church asked Cleaveland for help. By April 1763 he was being shared between the two congregations at an augmented salary of £ 80. A number of considerations led to negotiations for some kind of merger between Annisquam and the bay. The fifth parish did appoint a committee of five (four of them Pools) to discuss with Squam counterparts "upon what tearms thay Shall Joyn with us." Agreement was reached to accept all whom the General Court "shall see fit to Set of to us."

Other links with Annisquam grew stronger, especially for those of the bay who found it easier to cross Dogtown Common than to travel around the Cape to the harbor. As Sandy Bay developed economically, the matter of an improved road from Squam to "the Wood Lots" and from the Wood Lots to Sandy Bay was raised at a town meeting in 1765. After an initial defeat, the proponents achieved conditional success. On March 17, 1766, the town agreed to the layout, on the explicit understanding, however, that no public funds would be paid to console anyone whose land was taken over for the roadway. To spruce up the meetinghouse at Sandy Bay, the parish voted in March 1768 to have Lt. John Rowe get a christening basin, an hour glass, "and frame to stand in." A more sober addition was the new "burying cloth" for the parish. Pending resolution of an Annisquam alliance, the Cape congregation decided "not to Seat the Meeting House," that is, to make a reseating to accommodate the anticipated influx. In an attempt to brighten all outlooks, on May 11 the town instructed their delegate to the General Court "to use his interest and Endeavors to prevent any Exize upon spirituous Liquors."

On July 14, 1767, the fifth parish lost its second John Pool. His surviving will, bequests, and inventory reveal much about how someone of his station lived. His real estate holdings included a house, barn, gristmill, 220 acres of land, plus a "Pigeon Hill Pasture," a lot of five acres at Andrews farm, a "quarter part of a blacksmith shop," "one old fish house," "1 pue in the meeting house," and his interest in "the Wharffe in the Whurlepool Cove." Lemuel Gott's "Centennial Address" to the contrary, there is no known extant evidence that John Pool, Jr., had even one let alone "several" slaves, although in 1771 one of the Cape's two "life servants 14 to 45 years of age" lived at Isaac Pool's, John's executor.

The fighting parson of Sandy Bay was also in sporadic turmoil during those years. In 1765 he is said to have been at Fort Edward, New York, as a military chaplain once again. In October 1767 his mentor, Eleazar Wheelock, urged him to go to "the Ohio" as a missionary to the Indians "with a view to continue Years, if not for life among them." Requesting a prompt reply, he finally got a most muddled one dated March 17, 1768. Cleaveland assuredly did not wish to devote his life to saving Indian souls, perhaps losing his own scalp in the process. By using his household and Sandy Bay as excuses, he wiggled his way out: "I have an expensive family that commands my care and attention and have taken charge of a poor people who are resolutely engaged not to dismiss me: I have no body in these parts who encourage but all use their intrist to discourage and hinder me." Yet only two months later the community agreed that its minister might be dismissed for six months "to go to the Mohawks"—without pay, of course. His financial receipts show "I was absent 14 Sabaths." To insure preaching in Mr. Cleaveland's absence, Eleazar Lurvey was asked "to lookout after a Minister," and an agreement was concluded with one "Mr. Adams to prech four Days if he will come for four [Spanish] Dollers per Day."

Following the venture to the Mohawks, Wheelock requested Cleaveland and his own son Ralph to survey New Hampshire, today's Vermont, and eastern New York to find an ideal location for an Indian charity school. The Parson's letters and final report of December 17, 1768, make arresting reading, above all his views of the crucial Indian congress held late in October at Fort Stanwix. Such tales Cleaveland must have brought back to Sandy Bay, that forty-three-year-old minister whose survey was largely responsible for the site of today's Dartmouth College. And such drudgery he must have found on his return to the Cape.

During the parson's absence his own town had been the scene of violence. In September 1768 a mob of seventy-odd Cape Ann vigilantes stormed the house of Samuel Fellows, the newly designated collector of customs, but failed to find him. The next July, Fellows surely savored a sweet revenge when he helped sweep "a Prisoner out of the Hand of Justice" and into a Loyalist armed schooner in Cape Ann Harbor. Yet already in October 1768 Gloucester had observed a day of fasting and prayer because of the critical state of affairs in the British nation—"the precarious situation of our rights and liberties in these colonies on account of the oppression and the impositions laid upon us." In 1769 poverty began to grind down seaport communities in particular. At Sandy Bay even the minister was so hard pressed that he cried: "I dare not at all time appear out of my house, as the sheriff has special orders to take nothing but my body." Cleaveland's salary had been raised to £ 70, yet in September the parish offered surety for its pastor's debt of £ 2.

Violence

The new decade brought the first serious violence. Three weeks after the Boston Massacre of March 5, Cape Ann had its own outburst. Jesse Saville of Annisquam, employed by the royal customs controllers, was dragged from his bed by a group of Cape Anners disguised as blacks and Indians. Beaten and yanked by his hair and heels four miles to the harbor, he was tarred and carried in a cart "almost naked and exposed to Cold, Scorn and Derision." With a lighted lantern in his hand, he was forced to declare that he was "Savil the Informer." Yet the town's high-minded patriots could track down none of the mobsters except "George, a Molatto Man-Slave, the property of Samuel Plummer." He was tried, lashed, fined, and imprisoned.

Later that spring the town elected monitors for their boycott, "especially respecting the importation of goods and the selling or using of tea." Francis Pool was the watchdog who patrolled fifth parish households. Perhaps out of a genuine concern for their hard-squeezed pastor, the parish raised his salary to £ 80 in 1770. Despite the hard times, by 1773 they found money "to Put on the Clabords on to the meeting house that is wanting." In 1774 came construction of "a singing seat" in the front of the gallery pews and, in November 1775, yet another call "to Mend the Meeting House." Also requiring public funds was that troublesome old "Buryingyard fence" and "a Good Pare of Bars" for the gate. A need for additional graves had brought expansion in 1760 and 1767. Recurring reminders of mortality were the shipwrecks along the reefs of the Cape.

In the spring of 1771 the General Court purchased Thacher's Island for £ 500 and arranged to build "a lighthouse or houses and a convenient house for the keeper," an overdue protective measure. Another was a mutual covenant signed in 1774 by fifteen town businessmen to cover their vessels "from hence to the fishing banks and back." Smaller fishing boats, such as those of the Cape parish with crews of two or at most three, were not included, nor were the four bankers claimed by Ebenezer Pool and tradition as belonging to Sandy Bay at the outbreak of the Revolution: *Morning Star, Rising Sun, Friendship,* and *Little John.*

As more inflammatory beacons were lighted, Cape Anners decided that the Watch House Fort, or Battery House, should be refurbished to protect their gunpowder and ammunition. Then the selectmen warned Richard Silvester, the king's customs inspector and a supporter of Tory Governor Hutchinson, to quit the town. By Christmas, voters were blatantly joining other colonists to oppose tyranny in all its forms in the defense of "our Rights and Liberties, which are dearer to us than our Lives." A local Committee of Correspondence was named as a link with the expanding continental system. At Sandy Bay a scribe from the past died at eighty-two—Jonathan Pool, Rockport's original schoolmaster.

In 1773 a darker pall was cast over Cape Ann fishermen and their merchant colleagues, first by smallpox, then by taxed tea. The events of Boston's Griffin's Wharf on December 16, 1773, could never have taken place but for the support of people throughout the colonies, Gloucester included. In a history-making session on December 15, at 3:00 P.M., Cape Anners voted five declarations against tyranny and dutiable tea ("that detestable herb"). Their texts were dispatched to the *Essex Gazette* for all to see just where their town stood. By the time of publication, however, 342 chests of precious Indian tea had already been floated in Boston Harbor, that "nest of locusts."

Pastor Cleaveland, like his fellow ministers throughout the area, had long been exhorting his congregation into disaffection. His two published sermons show him subtly then openly denouncing tax gatherers and other royal despots. The first excoriations were delivered on October 10, 1773, and bore the title *Sinners Persisting in Sin.* The second blast, on July 31, 1774, was entitled *The Abounding Grace of God Towards Notorious Sinners.* Lambasting "the most abject temper of tools and vassals," the parson lauded "the benevolent temper of heroic Sons of Liberty." "No nation," he bellowed, "has a right by the laws of equity to tyrannize over their brethren." In the Sandy Bay meeting-house he accused "our rightful Sovereign" of violating his coronation oath "by establishing popery in one of his colonies," of putting his royal hand to bills against "our charter rights," and of sending ships of war and armed troops "to force on us those arrogant and unrighteous measures." Was it libertarian sentiments like these or a lack of felons or just plain budget cutting which led his parishioners to vote "not to build a pair of stocks" in March 1774?

When General Gage dissolved the General Court, Cape Ann's five delegates to the Essex County meeting in September passed resolves to support "our rights" and if need be to "encounter even death." Thus, when their popularly elected representatives rose one by one, declaring their assent, the householders of future Rockport took their stand for freedom. Next, the town responded to the October call of the new Provincial Congress for a revitalization of the militia. At training maneuvers the company based largely in the fifth parish chose John Rowe as its captain, with Mark Pool and Benjamin Tarr as lieutenants, and Isaac Pool as ensign. Rowe's commission, dated December 22, 1774, was signed by Ebenezer Cleaveland, "President," and Joseph Thurston, "Scribe." It deftly combined references to "loyal Subjects," "our Patriots," and "Provincial Charters." Rowe's specific task was "leading, ordering and exercising us the said Sixth Company in arms."

In early January 1775 Cape Ann moved forward again and paid its taxes, not to the British representatives, but to the rebel Provincial Congress. It also took steps to recover from Tory-minded Epes Sargent the gunpowder in his possession. Lt. Mark Pool of Sandy Bay was named one of the committee to recoup it. The crisis heightened on April 2. A vessel brought news that the king had proclaimed "a rebellion at this time exists," that the government was sending reinforcements, and that as of July 20 the five recalcitrant New England colonies would be denied access to all North Atlantic fisheries. Violators would forfeit their vessels, cargoes, and all supplies. Since by 1775 about one quarter of the people in seaport communities lived on fresh fish, Lord North's bill spelled ruin. Reaction was instantaneous. Cape Anners voted to "sort the Town's Musket Balls," purchase fifty small arms for the town's use, have "a number of Cartridges" made, and raise fifty minutemen to train twice weekly. With their fishing rigs knocked from their hands, they reached for their muskets. When the church steeple tolled midnight on April 18, 1775, Cape Ann began the most fateful day in its history.

ADDITIONAL READING

The plethora of recent accounts of life in the American colonies between the Treaty of Paris in 1763 and the Battle of Lexington and Concord in 1775 portray bright backgrounds against which to view future Rockport during that decade of anxiety.

For the critical period of the Massachusetts Provincial Congress, and countless references to Gloucester's delegates and their toil, consult *The Journals of Each Provincial Congress . . . 1774 and 1775* (Boston, 1838). To see how Gloucester was part of the world beyond the Cut a helpful study is Richard Brown, *Revolutionary Politics in Massachusetts . . . 1772-1774* (Cambridge, 1970). An uncommonly attractive portrait of another town at this era but one which shows how Gloucester's development was typical of the Massachusetts experience is Robert Gross, *The Minute Men and Their World* (New York, 1976).

On the local scene there are again the parish and fifth church records, the various volumes of official documents kept by Gloucester officials of the time, the diaries of Samuel Chandler in Babson's *Notes and Additions*, vol. 2, and Ebenezer Cleaveland's two published provocative sermons and some of his letters.

Bettye Pruitt, the *Massachusetts Tax Valuation List of 1771* (Boston, 1978), offers an unsurpassed statistical picture of the town and its inhabitants on the eve of the Revolution.

7

"TO ENGAGE WITH
THEIR LIVES AND FORTUNES"

T HEY WERE OUT on the fishing grounds when the news
came—twenty boats of them,
according to tradition. Where else should fishermen be on a midweek
working day if not plying their trade? It is further related that a mes-
senger quickly pulled out to warn them, that they all returned and were
soon up in Gloucester Harbor, armed with whatever they could lay their
hands on. By then, however, reports had come in of the British turnback
from Lexington and Concord. By night grim calm had settled down on
the homes and inns of Cape Ann.

Friday, April 21, brought together "the qualified Inhabitants of the
Town of Gloucester" for the first of eight years of wartime town meetings.
On Monday they got down to business. First, they chose a committee of
safety, of whom the Sandy Bay members were Isaac Pool, Deacon Jabez
Rowe, and Joseph Thurston. Barnabas Dodge, who owned much of
Pigeon Hill, was also included. Next, an intensive security patrol was set
up. Pursuant to the call for a full-scale Massachusetts army, the company
of minutemen under Capt. Nathaniel Warner and Ebenezer Cleaveland, Jr., was dissolved, and every militia captain was ordered to "inlist
proper men out of his Ward and that the Inlistment begin tomorrow at
ten o'clock."

Voters agreed that any person not able to pay for mending his gun
might have it repaired at the town's charge. Dependent families would be
looked after, a gun and a blanket furnished to each volunteer, and

IE CONGRESS OF THE COLONY OF THE
MASSACHUSETTS-BAY.

John Row Esquire

GREETING.

E, repofing efpecial Truſt and Confidence in your Courage and good Conduct, Do, by thefe Prefents, conſtitute and appoint you the faid *John Row* to be *Captain of the First Company in the* Regiment of Foot *Whereof Ebenezer Bridge Esq is Colo* raiſed by the Congrefs aforeſaid, for the Defence of faid Colony.

You are, therefore, carefully and diligently to diſcharge the Duty of a *Captain* by leading, ordering, and exerciſing the faid *Company* in Arms, both inferior Officers and Soldiers, and to keep them in good Order and Diſcipline ; and they are hereby commanded to obey you as their *Captain*, and you are yourfelf to obferve and follow ſuch Orders and Inſtructions as you ſhall, from Time to Time, receive from the General and Commander in Chief of the Forces raiſed in the Colony aforeſaid, for the Defence of the fame, or any other your fuperior Officers, according to military Rules and Diſcipline in War, in Purſuance of the Truſt repoſed in you.

By Order of the Congreſs,

Jos Warren Preſident P. T.

Dated , the 19 day of *May* A. D. 1775.

Secretary P. T.

Capt. John Rowe's commission in the Foot Company of Col. Ebenezer Bridge's regiment, May 19, 1775. (SBHS)

recruits rewarded with 20 shillings' wages in advance. Later, promised as a bounty, was a coat "in the common plain way, without lapels, short, and with small folds," pewter buttons to be affixed. Given such bait, the initial response of unemployed fishermen to drumbeating recruiters was lively. Cape Ann alone raised four full companies and generously provided soldiers for two others. Spring burst with all its radiance. On May 16, wrote Parson Fuller, "trees full in their blossom. Prospect of a Fruitful year. Planting and sowing in my garden."

The majority of the soldiers from Sandy Bay enrolled in Capt. John Rowe's company, but the men of future Rockport saw Revolutionary War service in many units and many places, on both land and sea. Although their commissions dated only from June 16, the thirty-seven-year-old Captain Rowe, who had seen service in the French and Indian War, signed on as of May 19, as did his lieutenant, Mark Pool, and Ens. (or 2d Lt.) Ebenezer Cleaveland, Jr. Captain Rowe then lived at "the third house

"To Engage With Their Lives and Fortunes"

built between Pool's Bridge and Squam Hill," today's 5 Holbrook Court. On May 29 Sgts. Daniel Barber Tarr, William Haskins, and William Foster joined the ranks, along with five corporals and twenty-nine privates. Others were recruited up to June 13, by which date the core of the unit had set off for headquarters at Cambridge. Along the line they picked up another sergeant, William Davisson. They reached "Mystic"—probably Medford, not the Mystic River—by midday on June 16.

The next day at Bunker Hill, John Rowe had fifty-nine men in his company, not the mythical sixty-six who answered a "sudden alarm." Six of his later recruits did not sign up until July 14 and 19, a month after the "very smart engagement." There is no evidence that Daniel Barber Tarr and not John Rowe himself gathered those troops. Enlisted they were: thirty-eight from Sandy Bay, ten from the "Farms" neighborhood, seventeen from intown Gloucester, and Davisson from close to headquarters. None was over forty; only three were over thirty; twenty-two were in their twenties; and seventeen were in their teens, including the fourteen-year-old William Rowe and sixteen-year-old John Rowe, Jr., sons of the captain. Of the forty-four privates, all but six were fishermen or sailors. Most of their equipment came from public funds charged to subsequent wages. Such were the men who marched to Bunker Hill, helped dig the immortal dugout, construct the hay-stuffed railfence, and man them both so nobly. What they did there for independence should never be forgotten; their losses—Josiah Brooks, William Parsons, Francis Pool—should ever be gratefully remembered by Rockporters.

Yet that was only the beginning. The demands of the military dragged on until the end of 1775. A few reenlisted "by the request of Genl. Washington," as they fondly reiterated in their old age, and saw out the siege of Boston. Others stuck through the successive debacles of New York and on to the rout at the Battle of Trenton. A handful served in the Continental troops throughout the war or at least in various campaigns; the younger John Rowe was to make a career for himself as a soldier. Parson Ebenezer Cleaveland was a campaigner for nearly three years, though not with his parishioners, as is generally stated. Nor did he march off with them to Bunker Hill. Cleaveland was chaplain to Jonathan Ward's regiment, besieging Boston from positions in Roxbury and Dorchester Heights. When not at "home on furlow" in 1776 and 1777, he was at various engagements in New York under Col. Paul Dudley Sargent. By September 8, 1777, the parson was discouraged by the poverty of his

Cape parish and contemplating a new career as a land agent for Dartmouth College at Landaff, New Hampshire.

The latter half of 1775 and much of 1776 was a period of preoccupation with coastal defense. Out patrolling the shoreline was a contingent of Captain Whipple's company under Lt. Joseph Lane and 2d Lt. Benjamin Tarr, Jr., of Sandy Bay, instructed to make at least weekly visits to "the watch at the Cape" to see "if these men attend their duty." Then came a summons to the first parish meetinghouse on the afternoon of June 24, 1776, "to Act on a Matter of the greatest Consequence that was ever laid before this or any other town in America." Voters took their decisions by walking. The result?

125 walked from the East side of the House to the West side by which they Voted in the affirmative, that if the Hon.ble Congress for the Safety of these Colonies declare them Independent of the Kingdom of Great Britain, they do solemnly engage with their Lives and Fortunes to support them in the Measure. Those that were Contrary minded was desired to walk to the Eastward but there was none that did.

The next entry in the town's record book for 1776 is the text of the Declaration of Independence. It was read out in all the churches. Annisquam heard this blessing: "May God bless these free and independent states till time shall be no more, with liberty, peace and safety! May America be Emmanuel's land. Amen and Amen!"

Digging In

The story of Cape Ann during the war has been grippingly related, principally from the maritime point of view. Another narrative should be compiled covering the war on land and the hardships at home. It would be a dark one, beginning with the decision to "remove and secure, if practicable," the lamps and oil from the lighthouses on Thacher's Island. Also to be removed were "the keeper of said lights, with the several boats, cattle, etc." Many months later the province decided to erect a warning beacon at Gloucester (on Governor's Hill). Pigeon Hill may also have housed a watch and guard.

No one appears to have identified the British frigate *Milford* that June morning in 1776 as it cruised toward Sandy Bay. An overly exuberant Mark Pool convinced Captain Rowe to round up an armed crew in a pair of fishing boats and take over what appeared to be a clumsily worked merchant ship. At the critical moment from around Halibut Point sailed Newburyport's pride, the *Yankee Hero*. The "flotilla of fearless fools" hailed the *Hero*, boarded her, and set out in pursuit of the frigate. The *Hero* discovered its mistake too late. In the struggle before the eyes of their families and neighbors along the shores of Pigeon Cove and Sandy Bay four men were killed, including schoolmaster-soldier Hugh Parkhurst, who had survived the Battle of Bunker Hill. Twelve were wounded, including Ebenezer Rowe and Parson Cleaveland's son-in-law, Reuben Brooks, who later died in a Halifax prison. All were taken prisoner, some not to return for several years, others sooner—including John Rowe and Mark Pool—but only after enduring prison ships and smallpox in Canada and New York. On April 24, 1777, Capt. John Rowe was raised to the rank of first major in the militia regiment of Essex County under Col. James Collins.

More rewarding was the capture off Straitsmouth of a British cargo vessel loaded with cattle. But privateering was the glittering lure which carried off so many men from the fifth parish—just how many will never be known, owing to the lack of surviving crew manifests—but reasonable conjectures run to about forty. The privateer brig *Tempest,* for example, was struck by lightning in the Gulf Stream and went down, carrying among her crew eight young men from Sandy Bay: Nehemiah Boynton; Daniel Oakes; Joshua Pool, Jr.; Daniel Stillman; and four Tarr cousins; Henry, James, Moses, and William. Also lost to lightning, claimed Ebenezer Pool, was the man who had painted the lightning and thunderbolts on the stern of Capt. Isaac Somes's *Tempest.*

In the autumn of 1777 some good news came: "Gen'l Burgoyne and his army are all prisoners and to be sent home to England. Rejoicings at Boston, Salem, Marblehead, Portsmouth, Newbury, and at Gloucester." Several Cape parish men took a special interest in that operation, for they did guard duty at the prison camp on Winter Hill: among those from John Rowe's company were William Jumper, Samuel Low, Jacob Lurvey, Jonathan Parsons, Mark Pool, and John Youlin. But good news was scarce in comparison to the heartbreaks from poverty, inflation, disease, and hunger. Because of the blockade, unemployment began pinching early. Larger ships were drawn up on shore and decayed like the drying flakes. Despite attempts to control prices, the value of paper money plummeted. Word of Cape Ann's hardships brought four benevolent Quakers to town to survey relief measures. During December 20-22, 1775, they gave help to 159 Cape Ann individuals and to 224 of the dependent children. Among the Sandy Bay recipients were Samuel Clark, "an aged man"; Lois

in-law Betty, with her children; Joshua Norwood; Rachel Davis; Abigail
Jumper; Caleb Tarr's wife Hannah; Sarah Rowe; Elizabeth Rowe; and
Mary and Ruth Boynton. At Salem they had already given 10 shillings to
the wife of Thomas Giles and their five children—soon to become residents of future Rockport. In March 1776 they made a "Seccond Vissit to
Glocester on Cape Ann," during which they bestowed donations to 117
adults and their 194 children.

Locally, several inland towns shared their own meagre stocks with
Gloucester, yet as early as January 1776 the town had had to risk
dispatching two vessels to Virginia for grain. By the end of the decade
grains were so scarce a boy is said to have walked to Beverly to purchase
three bushels of barley. The town records abound with entries dealing
with funds for the poor, loans for charity, purchases for the needy, and
appeals for tax abatements. The raid and break-in at the storehouse of
Col. Joseph Foster at Beaver Dam Farm is one of Cape Ann's living
legends of the period.

In 1777 and 1778 smallpox again brought fear, misery, and death
to the whole community. The years 1779 and 1780 were particularly
virulent. At Sandy Bay people voted on January 4, 1779, to permit
inoculation but only in five houses: "Mr. Baker's, Captain Francis
Pool's, Henry Witham's, William Harskins', and Decon Grover's."
Furthermore, no one was to "EnockoLate" until having gone to "the
Pest Houses and there to Stay till Clensed." The disease carried away
several residents, including Caleb and Ebenezer Pool, Mrs. Abigail
Rowe, and widow Elizabeth Clark. As a public health measure, all were
buried near the seashore, west of Whale Cove in the South End. Ruth,
the widow of William Andrews, Jr., of Pigeon Cove, died of smallpox
on July 22.

Another loss was Parson Cleaveland, his wife, and some of his
family. They were victims, not of smallpox, but of poverty and inflation. Protracted negotiations on Cleaveland's return from the army
finally collapsed when his impoverished congregation could no longer
pay him a living. When a stipend of ninety quintals of fish would not
suffice, he finally secured his dismissal in mid-June 1780 and moved to
New Hampshire.

During the earlier 1780s Sandy Bay managed to secure occasional
preachers, some of whom also served the parish as teachers. In order
to use their schoolhouse, however, voters found it necessary to evict
the crippled William Clark from the building. Either he or his brother

Samuel was apparently the author of some grim religious warnings first published in 1769 but reworked into political propaganda in 1776 and issued as *The American Wonder: or, The Strange and Remarkable Cape-Ann Dream.* Far more frightening was the "Dark Day" of May 19, 1780, when all became so still and murky that candles and lamps had to be lighted at noon. Residents—both pious and sinful—wondered if Judgment Day had come. Subsequent views were that forest fires had produced a thick, high cloud cover overhead, not to mention prayers on bended knees below.

Added to unemployment, poverty, shortages of food, abysmally debased currency, smallpox, and loss of a minister were the heavy snows of 1780-81. Starting with a roaring northeast gale, drifts soon piled up over fences, even darkening the second-story windows of some Sandy Bay cottages. It snowed at least part of the time for twenty-seven consecutive days. Thanks to the cold and the icy crusts, however, people could move about once they dug themselves out. Yet for thirteen weeks sleds or sleighs were needed. Ebenezer Pool enjoyed recounting the miraculous survival of one of his grandfather's twenty sheep, which was buried in an enclosure next to the barn for twenty-nine days yet managed to live off the turf and its own wool.

As the war crept southward, New Englanders were freed from bleak constraints. After the surrender at Yorktown in October 1781—Eleazar Grover was there to see it—draft calls were halted. In April 1783 hostilities were formally suspended. How Cape Anners reacted to the news is not known. On the hill where Fitzhugh Lane's house now stands there was a solitary, venerable oak tree with a twenty-three-foot circumference. Despite its decaying condition, it had long been a popular resort for townspeople. As part of the celebration ceremonies, said Babson, its hollow trunk and leafless branches were brilliantly illuminated.

The ship *Robin Hood* brought the news of the peace treaty from London on October 22, 1783. It must have seemed bittersweet to those who lived in the Cape parish and who had lost so much to achieve it. The tale was concluded by Sandy Bay's John Rowe, Jr., who wrote that in June, 1784,

I was stationed with the garrison at West Point, at which place I commanded the last guard which was mounted by the troops which still remained of the revolutionary army. The keys of the Fort I delivered into the hands of Lieut. Bliss,

Town on Sandy Bay

Did Benjamin Tarr ever think of himself as an usher? Assuredly not. Yet, when he ushered in the new century in 1700, his was the only family living in what is now Rockport. With two Pools he built their community's first and third wharves. To him was given the task of gathering the first taxes of independent Sandy Bay parish. At his death in 1782 he ushered in a new, free nation. Ben Tarr was laid to rest in the plot of earth his family had given to his neighborhood. Perhaps his coffin was graced by the new burying cloth his parish had purchased that March. Despite its wartime losses, Tarr's community had seventy-five males and no slaves, the latter having been declared free by the courts. In his parish thirteen men owned vessels assessed at £ 1,404. Ebenezer Pool estimated that the harbor held twenty fishing boats and four larger ones able to resume trips to the various North Atlantic fishing banks. In all, Sandy Bay consisted of between sixty-five and eighty houses and some five-hundred people. Its total value was calculated at £ 9,538. As for the whole town of which the fifth parish was still the smallest unit, it had a population of 3,893 white men and women, of whom 355 were widows and 37 were blacks. Benjamin Tarr had helped Massachusetts emerge from the chrysalis of a province into a sovereign state. His thirteen disparate colonies had earned recognition as the United States of America. Could they now become a biblical "Emmanuel's Land"?

ADDITIONAL READING

It would be a work of supererogation here to suggest reading matter on the American Revolution as a whole. The choice is almost limitless, even those items confining themselves to Massachusetts. Of particular help are Allen French, *The First Year of the American Revolution* (New York, 1968), and his *Siege of Boston* (New York, 1911).

Thomas J. Fleming, *The Story of Bunker Hill* (New York, 1960), presents a gripping narrative of the one great struggle to which men of future Rockport gave so much.

Three helpful books are R. N. Tagney, *A County in Revolution* (Manchester, 1976); Benjamin W. Labaree, *Patriots and Partisans* (New York, 1975); and Joseph Garland's absorbing *Guns off Gloucester* (Gloucester, 1975). For the genealogically oriented, Babson's *History* and the unpublished Pool papers are well larded with names and data concerning privateers and the men who sailed them, while the privately published journals of the Reverend Mr. Daniel Fuller (1775-97) also show much of Gloucester during and after the Revolution. For the Friends, see Henry J. Cadbury, "Quaker Relief during the Siege of Boston," *Publications of the Colonial Society of Massachusetts*, vol. 34 (1943), pp. 39-179.

"To Engage With Their Lives and Fortunes"

For those interested in the military records of individuals, consult the seventeen-volume *Massachusetts Soldiers and Sailors of the Revolutionary War*. Pension and service records have been microfilmed by the National Archives and are readily available both in Washington and the regional depositories. For data on officers there are editions of Francis B. Heitman, *Historical Register of Officers of the Continental Army . . . 1775-1783*.

For a remarkable adaptation of a religious tract into revolutionary propaganda see Samuel Clarke, *The American Wonder; or, The Strange and Remarkable Cape-Ann Dream* (Salem, 1776).

Town on Sandy Bay

8

CHANGE AND DECAY

IF THE TRUTH WERE KNOWN, after the Declaration of Independence was read from the pulpit, probably none of the worshipers who remained in their pews at Cape Ann and heard their country prayed for in scriptural oratory paid much attention. Visions of America as a biblical commonwealth had vanished with the Puritans, long before. But that their new nation should become a "New Order of the Ages," as its great seal proclaimed, was another matter. By 1784 even the fisher families and farmers in future Rockport were buoyantly optimistic. Hadn't their own militia helped vanquish Europe's sharpest soldiers? Hadn't their cove-trained sailors outmaneuvered Britain's best? What might they not do in peacetime?

To be sure, their town as a whole had suffered severely during the Revolution. More blows came with peace. On July 2, 1783, Great Britain closed the British West Indies to American shipping, and on August 30, 1784, France shut off its American possessions to foreign traders. Soon it was calculated that about one third of America's fishermen were being squeezed: they were too poor to live where they were and were too poor to move away and begin anew.

Future Rockport, on the other hand, had early been outclassed in the building and manning of schooners for either bank fishing or extended coastal trade, although occasional individuals had shipped on such vessels. Daniel Barber's gravestone silently testifies to his death at far-off Antigua on November 8, 1735. Except for the four ships said to have been skippered by Henry Clark, Ebenezer Grover, Jr., William Haskins, and Joseph Thurston, Jr., the boats of Sandy Bay and Pigeon Cove were small, only partly decked over, and restricted to inshore catches. Thus, as the war turned southward they were able to resume fishing sooner than larger seaports with bulkier ships. For cod, haddock, and pollock their sturdy Chebacco boats were ideally suited. As the market grew, so did the fleet. Offsetting the wartime losses of young and middle-aged men, a stream of boatbuilders, sailors, and hand-liners moved to Sandy Bay from Chebacco itself, Gloucester's old town parish, Annisquam, and the Farms. By 1786 it proved advantageous to repair the old wharf to help accommodate the increased activity.

It seems pretty clear that soon after hostilities ended ship construction recommenced in Long Cove. Full of hopes, Daniel Thurston and his son are said to have fitted out a schooner for the banks, while Benjamin Hale and Daniel Young also ordered a new vessel, the *Lucy*. Built near the Whirlpool dock by Capt. John Rowe, "a ship and house carpenter," she weighed forty-nine tons and for two or three years had as her skipper Captain Young himself. For a time, William Haskins may also have been skipper of the *Lucy*. In 1793 statistically minded Lucretia Norwood reported sixty-two sailing vessels of five to ten tons at one time in what is now Rockport Harbor. Another scorekeeper saw forty boats there in 1797, each weighing between ten and fifteen tons. With but minor fluctuations, the sea proved to be the making of postwar Sandy Bay.

Even the inland portion of the fifth parish attempted to produce a bonanza in fish, but that catch got away. In 1784 the town meeting did vote to stock Cape Pond with alewives; Salem's observant Reverend Dr. William Bentley noted them with interest while visiting the area in 1799. Nothing further seems to have been done about developing the spawning ground or hatchery until 1816. Then, once the stream was reopened to the sea, ample stocks were dumped into the flowing waters, and on December 14 the state legislature passed an act regulating that fishery. As late as 1827 the town was selling fishing rights to anticipated annual runs. Alas, few alewives adopted Cape Pond as home port. Sandy Bay fishermen were obliged to follow the sea, not their brook.

At times the sea followed the men, bringing damage, disaster, and death. In September 1783 a Dutch ship was blasted by a line storm and sank off the Cape with a loss of 303 people. In October 1784 a local boat capsized on the north side of the peninsula, drowning seven. Strangely, the one man saved is said to have been the only one who could not swim. In 1792 Daniel Young and Isaac Jacobs were drowned on treacherous Milk Island Bar while bound from Sandy Bay to Salem. Milk Island was also the scene of the fatal wreck of the *Renown* on December 15, 1797. The year before, it was Little Good Harbor Beach and Salt Island which witnessed the loss of the *Industry* and all hands. Six bodies were recovered for burial. The coastline of today's Rockport has rarely been without tangible evidence of the perils of the deep.

Not all storms were mortal, fortunately; but the combined gale winds and record tides which converged on Sandy Bay about May Day, 1787, carried John Tarr's ten-ton fishing boat right out of Long Cove, over the road, and into the Roberts family's meadow adjacent to today's Baptist church. Bearskin Neck was flooded, and eight inches of water poured over the floors of the fishhouses there; flotsam and jetsam were picked up from village homes for weeks afterward. For most people, it was the storm of the generation.

The year 1787 will be forever memorable in American history for the momentous decisions taken during the Constitutional Convention. Not a trace of those highly charged debates survives in any known Sandy Bay document, although one hint of patriotic pride crept into the cape parish records that summer. On July 7 a warrant was issued "in the Name of the Goverment [sic] and People of the common Wealth of Massachusetts." Perhaps it served to remind voters of the need to buttress the authority of their new state.

The autumn before, a group of desperate western Massachusetts farmers led by Daniel Shays protested debased paper money, home foreclosures, and imprisonment for debt. When twelve hundred of them tried to seize the Springfield arsenal in December, reliable towns were called on to supply troops. Of the four thousand raised, Gloucester responded with a full company of sixty-six. Except for three deserters, they served a month and a half, for which they were paid £ 3. Among others Sandy Bay provided the captain, veteran John Rowe, Jr., whose wages were £ 12, though Congress had adopted a decimal system of coinage based on a hundred-cent dollar on August 8, 1786.

Change and Decay

On November 3 Cape Ann held its first general muster for many years; over 350 men—including those from the fifth parish—participated, as they also must have in the subsequent "convivial cheer." The "drinking [of] several patriotic sentiments" was accompanied by the "discharge of a field piece to each." It would also be amusing to know if any Cape parish girls were among the thirty young ladies, "inspired with the love of industry," who produced ninety-nine skeins of excellent yarn at a federal spinning match in October 1788. Whether Sandy Bay held services to bless "the Day of the Commencement of the Constitution and Inauguration of the government" is no longer known. But both John Rowes and their many former comrades in arms can be expected to have rallied to their local tavern and raised a bumper to the president-general, whom they used to see on Cambridge Common. Some of them might have stayed on and talked about neighbor John Blatchford's *Narrative of Remarkable Occurances Detailing his Sufferings in the Revolutionary War, while a Prisoner with the British*. "Taken from his own mouth," the book claimed, it had been printed by Thomas Green at New London, Connecticut.

That same autumn the town acquired its first U.S. customhouse, followed by a post office. For some years after the Revolution the town lost several residents to Maine, where bounty lands were granted. From Sandy Bay went some Clarks, Dressers, Gosses, Finsons, and Rowes. Still, in 1789 Sandy Bay's taxes were $560, and Jabez Tarr was to gather them from 133 men, according to Ebenezer Pool's reckonings. In 1790 the state's tax on Gloucester was £ 239. 10s. 3d. Of this the first parish was assessed over £ 40. Of the remaining four parishes, however, Sandy Bay parish emerged with the highest assessment (£ 24. 14s. 7d.). The energy of its inhabitants, at times a seeming "Operation Bootstrap," had proven their vitality. In 1790 the government conducted its first census, Gloucester's total being 5,317, of whom 41 were blacks. The separate parishes were not enumerated independently. The people of Sandy Bay and Pigeon Cove found themselves riding a billow of well-being. As the minister of the harbor parish wrote: "It was a time when unexampled prosperity ensued."

Freed from the dolors of war, residents turned to such civic concerns as their elected officials, their schools, and their church. With the exception of John Rowe in 1778, only Pools and Tarrs served as fifth parish members of the town's board of selectmen from 1768 to 1798.

Scions of the older families would continue to appear among parish and town officeholders, although increasingly they would bear fresh first names—an indication of the emergence of the third and even fourth generation. But after the Revolution the broadening power structure of the parish found places for, say, Jabez Richardson (purportedly the bay's first baker), William Haskins (an emigrant from Maryland who had fought with distinction at Bunker Hill), Daniel Young (an assessor by 1785), Aaron Sargent (collector in 1786), Benjamin Hale (school committeeman, 1787), William Swanson (monitor, 1787), and Asa Todd (monitor, 1794). A clubby exclusiveness did not characterize the community's body politic.

Schools began vexing the taxpayers by 1790. The two original buildings were sagging noticeably. In fact, vandalism had elicited a $5 reward on January 11 to "any person that shall find out who broke the lock of the door and the clapboard of the House and prove it." Parents living south and east of the brook entering Long Cove started agitating for a separate school. Funds from uptown were so limited, however, that no action was taken; on the contrary, in 1792 limitations of not more than two scholars per family at one time were imposed. Likewise, "no scholar that is more than Twenty-one Years of Age shall goe to school on accnt of Public Money the present Winter Unless by the Committee's consent."

That year newcomer Dr. James Goss, a twenty-five-year-old physician from Billerica, settled down in Sandy Bay, by then a parish of some seven hundred people with perhaps another two hundred over in the Pigeon-Folly Cove district of Squam parish living in about ninety houses. All would have been heated by wood. As an economic sidelight, Ebenezer Pool noted that his father, master of the coastal sloop *Ruby,* transported fuel purchased at Camden, Maine, for $0.75 a cord and sold it in Sandy Bay for $2.25 per cord. Dr. Goss's talents were quickly tested by an epidemic of diphtheria, the old "throat distemper," which is said to have carried off sixty-two children within a few weeks in 1793. Prior to his arrival the Cape parish had had no doctor of its own, though for generations Mary Norwood Gammage had "officiated in the medical line among her sex." Then, too, widow Dorcas Grover Dresser, whose husband, Thomas, Jr., had "died in the Revolution or soon after," turned to good works and "became a nurse woman and much of the time kept an infant school with Dorcas, Jr., assistant." Soon after arriving, Dr. Goss was also asked to teach school—"for this season." He accepted; the schoolhouse was cleared;

Change and Decay

76 and a committee was appointed to provide "a Lach, some glass and other necessary improvements." Was one of them, perhaps, Noah Webster's popular new *American Spelling Book?*

By 1796 repairs would no longer suffice, and so began a prolonged wrangle over a new school and funds to build it. In a burst of irritated energy the taxpayers gave complete "liberty" to anyone who wished to build "a Proprietory School House on Parish Land." This offer was seized on by parents as a solution. A group of fifty-eight men, at $27 per share, soon raised $1,566 for the new structure. It was erected on the site of the parish house of today's Congregational church, and on December 27, 1797, Ebenezer Parsons signed a receipt, still extant: "Received of Mager Pool" $1,014.50 "in full" for its construction. Into the classroom went, as successive schoolmasters, "collegiate" Joseph Cummings of Topsfield; William Saville of Gloucester (1798-1803); David Jewett from New Hampshire only to become beloved minister of the first church; and William Whipple, who taught at Sandy Bay for some twenty years. Among the first class of students was Rockport's future antiquarian, the ten-year-old Ebenezer Pool.

"Preching"

From the diminishing number of church members in good standing, the post-Revolutionary War residents were far more concerned with rendering their dues unto Caesar than unto God. Nonetheless, the parish did have its obligations before society, not to mention the state legislature. Accordingly, each year a perfunctory vote was passed "to have preching" and a committee was asked to "treet with a minester" or to "Settle the Gospele Among us as Soon as Canveniently may be Done." Year after year the job proved inconvenient, even when the Cape sought out a "young ortherdox" chap to "Supplie the Desk." Financing in 1786 was to be "by Way of Conterbushen for the Pressent." Few takers, even novices, could be found on those terms. To brighten their corner voters agreed to repair their deteriorated church edifice. Back in 1784 they had shaken their heads about preventing "the Boys Riteng or Cholkeng about the meeting house." In 1787 they allocated half of the revenue from leased parish lands "so that the porch of the meeting house might be rapaired, so far at least as funds permitted." With the prospect of a new pastor named Mansfield in the offing, in March 1793 parishioners agreed to "obtain glass Sufficient to fill all vacant places"—funds to come from "the burying place Tax."

At a 7:00 A.M. meeting on August 19 the neighbors went all-out and ordered six new psalmbooks and six singing books. To "take the lead of the Singing for the future," they selected schoolmaster-physician James Goss and John Cleaveland, a son of their former minister. Two weeks later John was saddled with another job: "Take care of the Boys and Girls to keep peace on service time." In 1796 Dr. Goss was entrusted with the prickly task of writing "to Mr. Cleaveland at Amesbury to return a gilt Psalm Book, which was supposed to be [i.e., believed to have been] carried there."

Behind that awkward assignment lay the fact that after some years of visits to their former parish, Ebenezer Cleaveland and his wife had returned to their family at Sandy Bay in 1786 or 1787. However, when another opening of sorts called him to Amesbury, they rumbled off to labor in that vineyard from late 1793 or 1794 to well into 1797. With the parson, perhaps, had migrated a fifth parish psalmbook with gilt lettering or even with a gilt fore edge. When the couple turned back to Sandy Bay the next time, they would remain there, surrounded by previous fellow worshipers, until the last trump.

To Pastor Cleaveland and his fellow Calvinists the arrival of the Reverend Mr. John Murray preaching the final salvation of the whole human race must have seemed truly scandalous. A blooming Independent Christian Society within the Cape parish must have boggled the venerable pastor's mind. Yet several of the signers of its charter of compact in 1785 were Sandy Bay parish residents: among them five Pools, five Norwoods, John and Ebenezer Gott, Joshua Gammage, and Benjamin Tarr, Jr. In 1788 still others, including Thomas Oakes, agreed to be taxed to pay the Reverend Mr. John Murray's salary. By 1792, at the time of incorporation, additional fifth parish people, including Benjamin Marshall, had joined.

The "gross errors and popish absurdities" of the Universalists were to be preached from Cleaveland's old pulpit every fourth Lord's Day from March 1788. The price demanded for preaching such heretical doctrine was "One fourth part of the Cost arising therefrom in the reparation" of the meetinghouse. Thanks to those unlikely compromises with theology and grudging support from public funds, Sandy Bay parish maintained preaching of a sort through more than twice the biblical seven lean years. At the last annual parish meeting of the century in 1799, Cape voters laid out their priorities in unmistakable terms: "After settling all Charges that the parish owe," the com-

Change and Decay

mittee might then "lay out what money remains in preaching, according to their judgment."

If the fifth parish congregation had ever sung the lines "change and decay in all I see," they would have found them appropriate to Sandy Bay. Happily, however, their emphasis would have been on change. Some of the postwar changes were transient—for instance, the fifty French men, women, and children who arrived at Long Cove in four shallops on October 10, 1794, from the island of St. Pierre, from which they had been driven by the English. Of these visitors making their way down the American coast to the French consulate at Boston, Babson wrote: "The homes at Sandy Bay being opened to them, they went on shore and had their wants liberally supplied." Four years later the neighbors had a great whale driven ashore into "steep bank cove." It was seventy-six feet long from the tip of its tail to the edge of its jaw. Before a high tide carried off the corpse, Solomon Norwood was enterprising enough to render some forty barrels of oil from its blubber. Despite rather poor sleighing, several visitors came down from Gloucester to ogle the curiosity, which left behind a permanent reminder of its sojourn—the name Whale Cove.

A more constructive addition to the parish came in 1794, a well dug at Dock Square, into which a white oak pump was placed through a platform of planks. Costs were covered from subscriptions raised from neighbors and fishermen by Ebenezers Cleaveland, Jr., and Pool. Six years later the commoners voted "to grant to the inhabitants of Sandy Bay a small piece of land near Long Cove whereon they have erected a pump, the said piece of land to be kept sacred for the use of said inhabitants forever, and if converted to any other use the same to revert to the Commoners again." In 1798 Nehemiah Knowlton purchased a barn frame at Essex and had it moved by boat to Sandy Bay via the increasingly busy Long Cove landing. Also in 1798 arrived Dr. John Manning and his family, who were to contribute so notably to the community down the decades. He had moved first to Gloucester Harbor but in November 1798 became Rockport's second resident physician. That year the town assessor's returns for "Eastward and Sandy Bay" listed 213 dwelling houses and 83 outhouses with a total evaluation of $103,258. The homes were grouped under three evaluations: $100-$500, $500-$1,000, $1,000-$3,000. Of these the fifth parish had, respectively, 155, 42, and 16; the whole of the third parish had none of the most expensive, 4 in the middle bracket, and 127 of the lowest evaluation—further evidence of prosperity at the Cape.

Since the original Tarr gift, the fifth parish's cemetery had already been enlarged twice. By 1792 voters had to decide whether to take more common land or buy footage from Stephen Pool, who also offered to sell them another pall, though it needed some "tossels" to complete it. They bought both "a good Decent burying Cloth" as well as Pool's, which would have served for the two pairs of biers, "1 Small and one large," which they also purchased. By 1796-97 they resolved the cemetery problem by discontinuing the old road, which traversed the then burial ground at an angle from the Millbrook to Main Street, and by moving the east (front) wall down the hill but "not infringing on the lower main Road." Unneeded land which had been roadway was sold to Thomas Robards and John Rawlings. Removed was the old house belonging to Thomas Robards, Jr., in which widow Mary Kendall lived. It blocked the new road by the burial ground. At the March 26, 1799, parish meeting, the people of Sandy Bay voted for a second time to build a gate for their burying place.

"Tradition" reports—and one would like to believe it—that old Parson Cleaveland led his community in a memorial tribute to his former commander in chief and their country's first president when George Washington died on December 14, 1799. Pastor Forbes's sermon on the occasion at Gloucester Harbor was later published. If such a tribute was held at Sandy Bay, among the scores of mourners would have been the surviving old guard from the war which had made America free. At their head would have marched Maj. John Rowe. What long thoughts would have run through the mind of that frail old soldier, soon to join his general, as he returned to the farm on Pigeon Hill he had purchased from Captain Dodge in 1784? What memories, what visions did he see from his parlor during those last months as he looked out over the quiet town stretched along the coves below?

ADDITIONAL READING

An invaluable source for material on Essex County's past, including Cape Ann, is William Bentley, *The Diary, 1784-1819,* 4 vols. (Salem, 1905-14), reprinted by Peter Smith (Gloucester, 1962).

Indispensable background material for anyone interested in shipping and fishing are Samuel Eliot Morison, *The Maritime History of Massachusetts 1783-1860* (Boston, 1941), and Raymond McFarland, *A History of the New England Fisheries* (New York, 1911).

The story of the first church of Rockport (fifth parish, Gloucester), was carefully outlined by Israel Ainsworth, *Two Anniversary Discourses* (Salem, 1907).

The keystone history of the Universalists in this area is Richard Eddy, *Universalism in Gloucester, Mass.* (Gloucester, 1892).

Change and Decay

The helpful, though not exhaustive compilation on doctors is Russell Leigh Jackson, *The Physicians of Essex County* (Salem, 1948). Sandy Bay and later Rockport get short shrift, however.

What purports to be a wartime report straight from the mouth of the young man who related it is *The Narrative of John Blachford.* Originally published in 1788, it was printed in full in the *Cape Ann Gazette* in July 1860. In 1865 at New York Charles I. Bushnell privately reprinted the work with notes and an introduction.

9

RING IN THE NEW

DID ANYONE IN SANDY BAY parish stay up late Tuesday night, December 31, 1799, to usher in the new century? Was there, perhaps, a watch night service in the old meetinghouse, conducted by the still older Parson Cleaveland? At the harbor, Pastor Forbes delivered a long centennial sermon. Were any of the livelier young people of the fifth parish daring enough to hold a quiet New Year's Eve-turn-of-the-century sociable? The law decreed "that no Guns, Pistols, Crackers, or Squibs shall hereafter be fired in any of the Streets or Alleys in this town." Who was the first person in Rockport-to-be to write the words Wednesday, January 1, 1800? Was it some old-timer proud to record that he or she had "made it"? Or was it some stripling at the new Proprietors' School?

If those questions must remain unanswered, a beguiling view of the area as it was the summer before survives. Pastor William Bentley of Salem drove to Cape Ann in his chaise and meticulously entered many observations about the town in his diary.

The Annisquam meetinghouse was "not in very good repair but better than at Sandy Bay," he decided. At Folly Cove and Halibut Point he was intrigued by all the mooring stones with their sunken trees. There were fishhouses and the town's three hundred boats, "half of which belong to the part called Sandy Bay." Of the small wherries, he noted that in good weather they could make two trips a day, hooking as many as five hundred cod and haddock. He himself caught several of

81

82

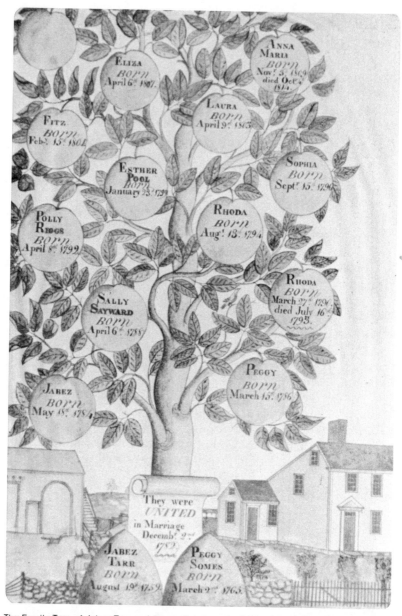

The Family Tree of Jabez Tarr and Peggy Somes, one of five similar watercolors by William Saville, dating from 1817 to 1826, in the archives of the Sandy Bay Historical Society. The house shown stands today at 153A Main Street. (SBHS)

Town on Sandy Bay

the latter, "but the wind breezing, I was too sick to persevere." Driving around the Cape, he stopped to see treacherous Salt Island, the Foster farm at Beaver Dam, and the view from Cape Pond heights before he descended into Sandy Bay. Although "Mr. Rollins, a Trader" (John Rawlings) was away on business, his wife entertained Bentley with "a most excellent fish dinner." At the Rawlingses', too, art collector Bentley was attracted to some drawings of funerary monuments "in memory of some deceased children, done by one Saville, a Schoolmaster." Refreshed, the minister resumed his visit through the settlement, "stretched along upon several coves." Of it he wrote that May day:

It had no houses which express the wealth of Cape Ann Town, but it had none of the marks of poverty which many houses in that place display. The Houses are small and of two stories and generally painted. The Doors are commonly on the side so as to afford a good front room and back kitchen, with a bed room back of the front entry. Some are double.

These were Bentley's notes about the school and church:

The School house was neat. The Door was at the Eastern end but there was a partition between the Doors in the same frame to keep the stairs leading above seperated [sic] from the room below. There are two windows on a side. The roof hipped with a Belfrey. The House painted green and roof red. The Meeting House is small and the body filled with seats, much neglected, roof rotten and open, standing near the shore below the School House.

He inspected Straitsmouth and "the Light Houses on Thacher's Island" and commented on "the very decent appearance of the women and children, which have good forms and most florid countenances united with an uncommon cleanliness in their dress." After dinner he bounced over "a miserable road," from which, however, he did enjoy "a pleasing view of Pidgeon Hill" with its few remaining trees and "the verdure everywhere on its sides." There was talk, he mentioned, of raising "a Monument" on the crest as a landmark to assist mariners. Beside the way he saw "several neat Houses and two neat School Houses of one Story well painted." Back at Halibut Point and Folly Cove he was fascinated by many flat stones, split into "all dimentions," but difficult to transport because of the ocean waves and the rough roads. The bachelor cleric wrote warmly of the expansive Gott farm, its eccentric owner, its sand, locust trees, sassafras, "the best oak timber on

Ring in the New

the Island," and Gott's "several nurseries of trees." At a farewell dinner Bentley raised this parting diplomatic toast: "The hospitality of Cape Ann, may it be preserved in our National Character." So appeared Sandy Bay parish in 1800 with its 673 males, 631 females, and 20 more people "entered since enumeration." For tax purposes, its evaluation was $192,000.

Following the war scare of 1798, fishing was speedily resumed, prices rose encouragingly, and Sandy Bay's fleet was substantially augmented with newer vessels running between fifteen and twenty tons. Then as now suitable moorings were at a premium. On January 11, 1803, Epes Woodbury, a mariner, sold for $40 "one half of a berth and Stump in Pigon Cove so colled unto William Norwood mariner . . . with the prevlages there belongon. this Stump formable belonged to Daniell marthant." In addition to cod, haddock, pollock, and hake, mackerel had risen in popularity and price. Early in the new century Stephen Pool is said to have devised a new method of catching them. By keeping them fresh in seawater, he marketed them at Salem, Boston, and even down to Hingham. The method caught on.

More important by far was the expanding system of government subsidies. Dating from July 4, 1789, the program would run till 1854. Three eighths of the bounties went to the owners and five eighths to the crew. For some sailors there was the added chance for employment on naval vessels being constructed "to protect ourselves," notably the *Constitution, Herald, Essex, Merrimac,* and *Congress.* "All of these had several Sandy Bay lads, young men, and more middle aged men, some 40 or more of them." In later years Ebenezer Pool raised his estimate to sixty.

Gains, however, were garnered from the sea this decade, as in every other of Rockport's history, only to the accompaniment of losses, sometimes cruel ones. But some benefit came to the neighborhood when a cargo of wood from Maine was lost at Sandy Bay in 1811 and was then "taken away by citizens of nearby towns," as Pool archly put it. Hints of dark traditions remain about Cape Anners' lack of respect for flotsam. On other occasions grief came from the cold. A whole generation of fifth parish families reminisced about Friday, January 19, 1810, when the temperature fell some 65 degrees in a few hours and brought the "coldest day and most violent gale ever recorded in our history." It also caused the tragedy of young Rachel Pool, housekeeper for her maternal grandfather. Venturing out for kindling wood, she got chilled to the bone. She hurried back to the stove to warm herself, was momentarily overcome with the heat, and fell forward into the fire. From searing burns, she lost her eyesight and, blinded, the young man she was planning to marry.

Other losses occurred early in the new century which reminded the community of its past. Among them were the deaths of Revolutionary War Col. Joseph Foster and Pastor Eli Forbes, whose care for Sandy Bay people had been deeply appreciated. At the bay itself, in 1805 was buried "Old John Blatchford," believed by many neighbors to have been well over one hundred years old. His tale of the freezing of London's Thames River was a popular neighborhood anecdote.

Faith

The very day that the storm of October 9, 1804, was wreaking its havoc, a new adventure in faith was dedicated: the "Old Sloop" (to-day's imposing Congregational church). By 1802 inhabitants could no longer cope with their decaying meetinghouse. A new one was voted to adjoin "the new school house land." Costs were to be levied "according to the town valuation of 1803," three fifths to the "Orthodox" and two to the Universalists. The cornerstone was laid with Masonic rites on July 4, 1803. Reportedly present were the aged Pastor Ebenezer

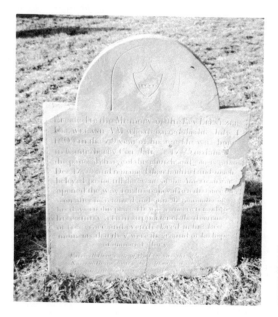

Gravestone of the Rev. Ebenezer Cleaveland (1725-1805), first pastor of the Congregational Church, in the Parish Burying Ground on Beach Street. (Photograph by William D. Hoyt)

Ring in the New

Cleaveland and his successor-to-be, David Jewett. On July 19 the sale of pews for the new church was initiated. Of the 121 places sold for $9,009, pew no. 57 was bought by Parson Cleaveland for $92. He preached in the new building on a few occasions and in November is said to have baptized nineteen children on that one day. The first boy was his great-grandson, Samuel H. Brooks. On July 4, 1805, however, the seventy-nine-year-old widower pastor slipped away, having murmured to a friend: "I trust in the same God that I did when the bullets flew about my head." Appropriately, he was buried from the church he had initiated. On October 30, 1805, Jewett, who had already endeared himself to the community as a schoolteacher, was ordained minister of the fifth parish church with its ten members. He served his growing flock and community with devotion for over thirty years.

The Congregational church was not unique in sharing Jeffersonian prosperity. Increased attention was paid to highway maintenance. For instance, what is now King Street was widened from the Millbrook (Pool's Bridge) all the way to the foot of Squam Hill. The eight gates which had long barred the road from Sandy Bay to Pigeon Cove were taken down, a gesture symbolic of the opening up of life in other respects. With expansion, however, came diversity of opinions.

The Orthodox were already sharing their meetinghouse with the Universalists of Sandy Bay, but by 1807 that arrangement was to lead to rancor, physical disruption, and twenty years of litigation which engendered an enduring bitterness. The Universalists undertook to build a new meetinghouse at Gloucester Harbor, the architect being Col. Jacob Smith. By then one fifth of the society's members lived in the fifth parish. Dr. John Manning was one of the four-member committee. The cornerstone of the edifice was laid with Masonic rites on September 5, 1805. Among the brethren of Tyrian Lodge was Benjamin Tarr IV. Of the fifty-two subscribers to the building fund, Sandy Bay's Joseph Baker had two shares; David P. Tarr and teacher William Saville, one share each. In 1808 Saville was chairman of the committee for the new hymnbook printed for the society at Boston. Pool stated that Saville wrote the last hymn in the volume.

In November 1804 Baptists commenced their spiritual activities in Sandy Bay homes—a response to initiatives taken by Capt. Benjamin Hale, converted from smuggling during the Anglo-French wars. Then in March or April 1805 James Woodbury, a descendant of Sarah Pool, was publicly baptized in the ocean. Intolerant demonstrations were staged by three separate groups on May 27, 1807, when Elisha Williams of Beverly baptized William and Martha Hale Smith at the Front Beach. Blank cartridges were fired from the cannon on Bearskin Neck, and a "company" of not so young men, characterized as "individuals of the baser sort, but claiming respectability," tramped back and forth along the cemetery wall, beating drums and tooting disruptive fifes. A dog was subjected to a mock baptism. Yet eighteen Baptists constituted their church on March 30, 1808. It was incorporated in June 1811 when a law was passed exempting Massachusetts residents from paying a parish tax provided they were members of a separate, incorporated religious body. Devotions were first held in the homes of Samuel Huston, Stephen Robards, and in the spacious new house of Deacon Ebenezer Pool in Dock Square, begun in the fall of 1805 and completed in 1813.

Health services in the fifth parish improved further with the arrival of Dr. William Ferson to share responsibilities with the physicians James Goss and John Manning. In 1805 the deaths of some fifteen children from diphtheria in about two days, "besides many others before and after," no doubt taxed all medical abilities, as had the typhoid epidemic of 1797. Local agriculture came under fresh scrutiny. Of the estimated 105 to 110 houses in Rockport-to-be in 1800, only ten to a dozen could have been described as farms. It is thought that all the neighbors owned only thirteen to fifteen yoke of oxen and had still fewer horses for plow and barnyard tasks. So little hay was raised in the area that most of the fodder required for winter use had to be imported by barge from the salt marshes of Essex, Rowley, and Ipswich. Early in the new century, however, the experiments of John Gott, Thomas Oakes, and Caleb Norwood, Jr., began to be emulated. Seaweed was used for fertilizer. Several acres of swampland were transformed into grasslands and cornfields, thereby curtailing imports.

In 1804, under a law of the state, Gloucester was divided into eleven school districts, each administered by a local "Prudential Committee." Sandy Bay had three of its own; the Pigeon Cove area had another, land having been given for a school there by James Norwood, perhaps as early as 1797. The elder Stephen Knutsford was probably the first schoolmaster in the North Village. In 1808, the middle or first district of Sandy Bay got its long-awaited new building at "School House Beach," about where Main and Beach streets join. Two of the fifth parish's young men became trailblazers during this decade by going off to Harvard College. Joseph and John Manning were graduated in 1808 and 1810, respectively; Charles followed in 1819.

Clouds

Unclouded Sandy Bay began to darken as the war worsened between Napoleon and the British. On December 22, 1807, the American Embargo Act prohibited all American or foreign vessels from leaving the United States for foreign ports. The value of fish plummeted, cod being bartered for "country produce," and the market for scale fish becoming nearly nonexistent. Political tensions shot up like rockets. On August 22, 1808, a Gloucester town meeting requested the president, in vain, to suspend the embargo.

Cape Ann itself was divided between its Jeffersonian Republicans and their hostile Federalist neighbors. Sandy Bay's Dr. Manning was a prominent Federalist supporter. Like his associates, he must have been grieved when Madison won the presidency. More disturbed were the local fishermen and mariners, who suffered keenly from the embargo and still more from the Enforcing Act of January 9, 1809, which permitted port collectors to seize goods which even "appeared" to be destined for foreign ports. Sandy Bay men, with many associates, quietly turned to smuggling well before the embargo was lifted. In November 1809 the state paid Gloucester $1,008.50 for pauper assistance.

For a brief respite prosperity returned: fish prices rose; trading resumed; and housing construction, which had flourished for half a dozen years before the embargo, also picked up. Most significant were two moves by the legislature on behalf of the harbors at Pigeon Cove and Sandy Bay. On January 22, 1808, the General Court granted to the town "one half a township of land in Maine, to be held out for sale within three years." The purpose was to raise money for "filling up a gap between a point of land, called The Pilions and the great ledge at the mouth of Pigeon Cove at the foot of Pigeon Hill, about twenty rods upon a rocky foundation." When sales stalled in 1812, a one-year prolongation was granted. Those acres were finally auctioned off in Boston for 20 cents each.

Far more successful was the incorporation by the General Court on February 25, 1811, of the Sandy Bay Pier Company by Josiah Haskell, Jr., Nehemiah Knowlton, David Story, and others. Once the weakened old wharves were taken down, the stone foundations of a sturdy new one were laid near the Whirlpool harbor. The dimensions were specified as 287 feet long and not less than 60 feet wide, "together with a projection twenty feet square" on the south side joining the head of the wharf. The Sandy Bay Pier Company established thereby was to outlive a half dozen generations.

Somehow, each decade of Rockport's history has generated gobbits of back-fence gossip or fireside chitchat for the residents. This era, for example, had another earthquake, "a Great Eclipse of the sun; stars visible in the daytime" (June 16, 1806); a hanging (Moses, the son of Stephen Pool, on May 11, 1810; was it suicide? an accident? a penalty?); and—of course—a fish story (a twenty-eight-foot shark, whose liver allegedly produced 103 gallons of oil for Cap. John Gott). The earthquake took place one evening soon after sunset the third week of November 1805. "It caused some rumbling noise," recalled Ebenezer Pool, "but not heavy." Its principal interest stemmed from the fact that it had been "predicted" by Caleb Pool some months previously in the meetinghouse—"he then deranged," remarked his antiquarian cousin. Caleb Pool was vouchsafed a series of revelations which catapulted him from a Deist to a New Light Christian. That experience convinced him (with ghostly assistance, no doubt) to write and privately publish at Salem his *News from Heaven by Visions, Communicated Miraculously.* The preface to this thirty-one-page rarity was dated June 17, 1805; the visions stemmed from the Apocalypse, though with scatterings of local touches.

It took no visionary to forecast the near future, however. Fifth parish people had learned that their lives were linked to vicissitudes beyond their control. In good times they basked under improvements. By 1805, for instance, the stagecoach to Gloucester, which had been initiated by Jonathan Lowe on April 25, 1788, with twice-weekly trips, was offering them daily, four-horse service to the harbor. Organized fire protection was inaugurated at Sandy Bay in January 1807 by twenty public-spirited men—each with his pair of staunch leather buckets and two tough three-bushel bags, subject to annual examination and periodic musters. The regulations were printed in 1808.

By 1808 Sandy Bay was richly provided with innholders and retailers of spirituous beverages, dispensing cheer, seven from their shops, three more "on the square," and two from their homes. All the sellers had been certified by the selectmen as having "maintained good Rule and Order in their respective Houses or Shops and have conformed to

Ring in the New

the Laws and Regulations respecting Licensed persons, and are firmly attached to the Constitution and Laws of this Commonwealth." In 1807 Samuel Huston was approved by the court at Salem to become an innholder at Sandy Bay.

But in times of strain the fifth parish and their neighbors at Pigeon Cove shared such restraints and burdens as the two embargoes, the Non-Intercourse Act, and the British impressment of American sailors. By the close of the decade a storm from the Northeast rolled in toward Cape Ann. Soon Rockport-to-be would shake at its turbulence.

ADDITIONAL READING

Marshall Smelser, *The Democratic Republic 1801-1815* (New York, 1968), is a short, readable account of the period and is available in a paperback edition. The ponderous six volumes by Henry Adams are formidably detailed but have been abridged.

Eli Forbes, "A Century Discourse, delivered on the 1st of January, 1800," *A Family Book* (Salem, 1801), pp. 268-97.

Caleb Pool, *News from Heaven by Visions Communicated Miraculously to and Explained by Caleb Pool, of Gloucester* (Salem, 1805).

A general sketch of the town as a whole was put together by Alfred M. Brooks, "A Picture of Gloucester about 1800," *Essex Institute Historical Collections,* vol. 87 (1951); pp. 333-38. On the churches and some houses James F. O'Gorman has written attractive reports in "The Search for Jacob Smith," *This Other Gloucester* (Boston, 1976), pp. 16-29.

A fine account of the early days of the Proprietor's School was printed in the *Cape Ann Advertiser* of Friday, September 21, 1866.

10

"MR. MADISON'S WAR"

THE WAR OF 1812 was also the War of 1813, 1814, and 1815. From the day it was declared until Congress ratified the Treaty of Ghent, a state of belligerency existed between the adolescent United States and its parent country for more than two years and eight months—a year longer than America's participation in World War I. Fought out on fresh water and salt, from Canada to the Caribbean, against British, Canadian, Indian, and Spanish enemies, it gave the United States some heroes (Andrew Jackson, "Tippecanoe" Harrison, Oliver Hazard Perry, Capt. James Lawrence); some slogans ("We have met the enemy and they are ours"; "Don't give up the ship"); some epithets ("War Hawks"; "Old Ironsides"); and a national anthem. As debits, it took the lives of some 2,260 American soldiers and sailors, burned the White House and parts of Washington, and brought into the coves and streets of Rockport-to-be the only enemy invaders in the town's history.

Like most conflicts, the War of 1812 had a number of causes. For the coastal towns, however, maritime issues predominated, notably the impressment of American sailors by British naval vessels. On June 18 Congress declared war on Britain, a move bitterly resented by the Federalists and commercial interests. Seacoast states from New Jersey northward voted 3 to 1 against the president's war message. As the conflict progressed, its unpopularity grew. In the hope of encouraging the secession of New England, where "Mr. Madison's War" was so resented, the British refrained from seriously enforcing a blockade north of Long Island Sound until 1814.

On Cape Ann political differences and party factionalism had become rampant by the elections of 1812. A coalition of Federalists and antiwar Republicans locally outvoted the war party by 494 to 401. Even after war had been declared officially, Gloucestermen went on record at a county convention held at Ipswich on July 21 with their bitter denunciations and their concern for the "awful and alarming situation of the country." They did, however, appoint a committee of safety and take measures to strengthen local defense through town militia and artillery companies. Back on January 26, 1807, the state legislature had approved a petition from John Burns and other fifth parish men asking permission to raise a Light Infantry Company. It was attached to the county's Second Militia Regiment.

For the first year and more the war failed to trouble the area. Even later, events were viewed and reviewed through a convenient haze. Ebenezer Pool, who lived through them and was at times an active participant, recorded them with more than his usual casualness. His versions, frequently differing from each other, also differed with those related by Lemuel Gott in 1854, and with those published by Babson in his *History of Gloucester*. One impression, however, shines brightly. As Pool put it: "From 1810 to 1815 or the end of the English War with the U.S. fishing in-shore was a profitable business. . . . Privateering was good in 1813 and 1814." Dr. Gott was more subtle: "Our fishing interests, with some little interruption, proved highly profitable and the mass of the people obtained a comfortable living in peaceful pursuits, but some for purposes of plunder and more rapid gains embark in privateering."

A few incidents should be recounted again, as accurately as the discrepancies of the sources will permit. Once the English began harassing the Massachusetts coast, likely targets for the privateers out of Nova Scotia were coastal vessels carrying cargoes to and from Maine. On occasion these anchored in Sandy Bay for protection. Their pursuers, claimed Pool, "were always driven off by our people." He cited only one illustration, however. That was of a privateer named the *Commodore Broke* (or *Buck* or *Brack*), which in August 1813 stood into Sandy Bay pursuing a coaster. In the process the enemy blasted a mixture of shot into the peaceful settlement. (Ebenezer Pool claimed that enemy privateers "often fired their shot into the buildings of the town.") Local men hastened to return the fire from the end of

Bearskin Neck, where even before the fort was built they had installed a six-pound cannon. The British ship veered off after being hit by a cannonball. It either "entered the schooner under her transom, and, passing under deck, came out near her stem, above the water" or "shot through her from stem to stern." Babson's colorful version of the skirmish added the unlikely feature that "the men at Pigeon Cove gave her several musket-shot as she passed their shore: but she got off without further damage."

Clearly, Cape Ann required better protection against the depredations of British naval vessels and Canadian privateers. The fort at the entrance to Gloucester's inner harbor was strengthened; the old fortification upon the Stage Fort underwent repairs and acquired some barracks; two companies of state militia were drafted; and a third one, also drafted, was pressed into service by the national government. Early militia laws had exempted mariners from compulsory military training. So, when the embargo was lifted, fisherman were particularly anxious to be included in the category of mariners. Hence, in 1810 all the field officers and captains in the Cape Ann regiment signed a petition to the General Court, claiming that

a large portion of the soldiers liable to do military duty in the 2nd Rgt., 1st brigade, and 2nd division of the militia . . . are fishermen, a class of citizens whose activity, honesty, usefulness and industry are well known to your Honors. We firmly believe the fishermen are not behind their fellow citizens in patriotism and courage and that they would cheerfully shoulder their muskets and strive to discipline themselves for the service of their county, if they could be excused from military duty during the fishing season.

The legislature cautiously acceded on February 28, 1811. Fishermen would forthwith be "deemed to be mariners, and as such exempted from military duty, while they are actually employed as aforesaid." Yet with the crunch of 1814, that welcomed exemption was repealed.

At Sandy Bay a company of "Sea Fencibles" was enlisted, with initial barracks at the entrance to Bearskin Neck; in 1814 plans to build a fort out on the point were put in motion. Subscriptions were taken locally, and a horseshoe-shaped fort was erected at a cost of $400, $500, or $600, depending on which chronicler is to be trusted. Surviving until 1837, it was modestly equipped with two (or three or four) cannon and furnished with nine (or ten) guards, housed in an adjacent watch-house, and paid $8 a month. To the British cruising off the coast it

"Mr. Madison's War"

looked more formidable than it was, and they planned a blitz operation.

Invasion

The "Battle of Sandy Bay" appears to have run pretty much as follows. Stationed off Cape Ann, in response to "the allarms and the damages that Rockport privateers and ships" were allegedly creating, were one or more English ships. The frigate *Nymph* captured a Sandy Bay boat skippered by Capt. David Elwell. Forcing him to serve as a pilot, the *Nymph* sent ashore two (Gott said three) barges with muffled oars. The time was soon after midnight (or 1:00 A.M. or 2:00 A.M.) on a densely foggy September 8, 1814. The armed barges bore some twenty men apiece. One of the boats pushed into Long Cove and landed its crew at a place known as the "Eastern Gutter," whence the men proceeded stealthily to the fort and at the end of the neck. There they quickly captured the sleeping sentry, and the nine (or ten or twelve or fourteen) guards in the watchhouse, which they set on fire. They spiked the fort's two (or three or four) cannon "which were borrowed," broke the wooden wheels on the gun carriages, threw the whole lot over the wall, and with their prisoners they left the useless fort.

Meanwhile, another barge had rowed to the other side of the neck and down into the Whirlpool dock area. There some of its crew may have "boarded some coasting vessels at anchor in the bay." In the process they seem to have fired at a mast of a sloop. By then the sky was lighter and the fog was lifting. As the somnolent residents awoke, startled, one of the more alert raced to the meetinghouse and began pealing the bell, creating a rumpus which alarmed both the invaders and the dormant Sandy Bayers. In an attempt to silence the clamor, the British on the barge leaving the Whirlpool dock fired their six-pounder at the steeple. They ripped one of the west supports with a ball still preserved among the Church's memorabilia. In so doing, however, the concussion sprang a bow plank; the barge quickly shipped water and sank before all its crew could land safely. The two officers and several of the men escaped over the neck to the Long Cove area, where at the "Gutter" they hijacked a whaleboat belonging to Ebenezer Davis and made it back to the *Nymph* in safety. Lemuel Gott's version has only the lieutenant in the whaleboat while the others pulled a fishing boat confiscated from James Parsons and William Lurvey.

Meanwhile, the English barge in Long Cove, also alarmed by the hullabaloo, rowed out toward the bay with the prisoners from the fort and watchhouse. In the retreat they were fired upon by three Cape stalwarts using small arms, "the writer being one of them," proudly noted antiquarian Pool, along with William Lurvey and John Davis. The British retaliated with their six-pounder, three "firings" being made by each side; "but no one was killed"—or even injured that foggy dawn.

As for the remnant from the sunken barge, twelve (or thirteen or fourteen) were soon taken prisoner. One man "secreted himself through the day for fear of being discovered by the inhabitants who he [thought] to be savages." On the contrary, the people of the fifth parish provided hospitably for their prisoners, keeping them at the large house of James Tarr at the foot of "the great hill" (today Poole's Hill), near the junction of King Street, Summit Avenue, and Railroad Avenue. Details of the subsequent exchange of prisoners are anything but clear, perhaps because the Sandy Bay people involved acted questionably, if not extralegally, and found it prudent to fuzz up and even conceal some of the evidence against them.

Babson, allegedly on reports derived from actors in it, related that the alarm at the fifth parish spread rapidly and brought down from Gloucester Harbor military reinforcements under Colonel Appleton. When an exchange of prisoners was proposed (by whom?), the colonel decided he lacked authority. While awaiting a decision from higher echelons, he detached a platoon under Lt. Charles Tarr to guard the prisoners. During the night, however, "a number of men in disguise rescued the prisoners from Tarr, and effected an exchange." This sounds as if some Cape parish men did indeed take matters into their own hands. Given the subsequent turn of events, they may well have done just that.

No such hints are to be found in the narratives of Pool, however. He stated merely that in the evening the British prisoners were marched to Pigeon Cove, were joined by their one fugitive brother who had been hiding out, and were ferried back to the *Nymph* in a boat owned by Capt. Daniel Wheeler. In exchange for their captured men, the British released Capt. David Elwell, the sleepy sentry, "our six men" (or nine), and "several others which belonged elsewhere" (or two Salem men). In his "Centennial Address" of 1854, Dr. Gott admitted that while the British were being held prisoner orders had come from Salem to Sandy Bay to move them to the internment camp at Salem. "But our people judged it best that they should be exchanged for Americans and they thought that this course would conciliate the Capt. and prevent further trouble." And in fact it did.

From that time whilst stationed of Cape Ann he gave the Boat Fisherman free liberty to fish unmolested, which they had been doing to a great profit . . . so that the war was a benefit to this business in our part of the town.

James Parsons got his fishing boat back. To compensate him for the loss of his whaleboat, Ebenezer Davis received the raised barge, "well built and copper fastened," which was in use for years afterward. The pistols, pikes, cartridges, small arms, and cutlasses of the British prisoners were divided up by the committee of safety. As a keepsake, Ebenezer Pool proudly showed a carving knife he owned made from a cutlass. The real trophy was the small cannon raised from the sunken barge, "retained as town property for firing by anyone on any public day, fourth of July, etc." It weighed 649 pounds; was about four feet long; had a five-inch bore; and, predicted Pool, "probably will be kept for a memorial for years to come." Today it rests with its bronze plaque on the lawn of the meetinghouse it assailed that misty dawn.

The Folly Alarms

Two other wartime incidents occurring at Rockport-to-be deserve brief attention. The first has been dubbed the "Folly Cove Alarm." Shortly after their misadventure with the *Nymph*, "some say it was September 19, 1814," Cape people who had once experienced a Yankee *Hero* tangled with a British *Leander*. A frigate of that name was cruising northwest of Folly Cove in the morning. Spotting a fishing boat owned by Nathaniel Parsons, the *Leander* fired a 32-pound shot at it. The ball was later picked up in the garden of the absent Walter Woodbury, whose wife "took about $1,500 silver and hid it in their orchard and was near when the shot fell." The fishing boat put for the shore in haste, pursued by one or more of *Leander*'s barges, which, under a flag of truce, demanded to inspect it.

The crew of one barge killed a nearby grazing cow and would have taken two more, according to Pool's narrative; but luckily an alarm was raised by neighbors, and Capt. David Elwell hurried over with "some 70 men and lads" from the Sea Fencibles of Sandy Bay and Capt. Charles Tarr with "about 80 men armed and equipped partly with musket balls that were taken from the sunken barge of September 8."

They are said to have carried with them a nine-pounder, two six-pounders, small arms, and "the old Revolutionary soldiers." Having heard the *Leander*'s cannon, the "Yankee Blues" from Annisquam under Capt. Isaac Dennison, Jr., also mustered quickly, as did Capt. Ebenezer Tarr's Squam militia. In all, Babson reported that some four hundred soldiers appeared; Pool's customary enthusiasm led him to say "about 600 men armed as estimated." Whatever the number, their firm stance warned off the potential British cattle rustlers.

Also at Folly Cove occurred the incident involving Epes Woodbury related in Gott's "Centennial Address." He boarded an American privateer which had (mistakenly, one assumes) captured a boat of his as well as its skipper. Woodbury had made the mistake of thinking the privateer was British. Hoping to bribe the "enemy" captain, he carried along a quarter of veal. The American privateersman then made another mistake; he mistook Woodbury for a Tory. To punish the supposed traitor, he laced the grog he offered him with a powerful shot of jalap. The purgative "operated powerfully" and prostrated poor Woodbury. This practical joke was neither the first nor the last experience which people from future Rockport had with privateers during the United States' second war with Britain. As with the Revolution, though, the names and service terms of local seamen are now pretty much unknown.

One of the earlier American vessels plying this area was the *Cadet* of Salem. "Manned in part from here," it was for a time commanded by Capt. David Elwell of the *Nymph* encounter. Gott credited him with clearing the impressive sum of $12,000, stating that he and his crew never had an open military engagement but did board some vessels and "took some prizes." This type of "protection" system was also operated by the British. Privateersmen would overtake an enemy vessel, capture it, but often release the boat and crew once a ransom had been paid. There was also the occasional connivance between ostensibly "neutral" vessels and commercial interests ashore. Babson related a flagrant example of this involving the neutral Swedish schooner *Adolph* and its barefaced smuggling. Babson also recounted a number of events involving the Gloucester privateers *Swordfish, Thrasher, Orlando, Madison,* and the merchant ship *Pickering.* Although these vessels presumably had local crews, the men's names are not to be found on available registers.

Several fifth parish and Pigeon Cove mariners are said to have been captured on privateers or merchant vessels and incarcerated in the prisons of Halifax, Chatham, on the Thames River (William T. Abbot), and Dartmoor (Benjamin Colby, Joseph Bailey, and "one from Folly Cove"). Abbot was away from home about nine months. Yet all the privateersmen are believed to have returned safely in due course, some having previously earned substantial shares of prize money. Daniel Stanwood Wheeler served on the U.S.S. *Wasp* but died in 1816, having had an extended career in the local infantry militia company, of which he became ensign in 1806, lieutenant in 1807, and captain in 1809. He also built and ran the tavern in Pigeon Cove (167 Granite Street) from 1805 onward. Actually, only a few local men may have been war victims, and even their fates are uncertain. Samuel Lane and Joseph Tucker, Jr., son of a Revolutionary War participant, were possible casualties in the fighting at Lake Champlain. According to the third parish records, John Morgan and James Robinson died in the army in 1814. the latter in Vermont.

Thus, as Babson graciously summed up the effects of the war on the town, it was trade that was the greatest sufferer from Mr. Madison's War. "Though many of the people were deprived of accustomed gratifications, there was none of that want of the necessaries of life, which, in the Revolutionary struggle, was so severe and distressing." One incident of distress occurred on November 8, 1813, when fifteen-year-old Mina Dowsett died convulsively from rabies said to have resulted from a dog bite the preceding March. One welcome gratification at Sandy Bay was the installation of two stoves in the ten-year-old meetinghouse, one the gift of Pastor Jewett's mother-in-law, the other bought by contributions from the church's growing congregation. Although the old enemy of weather made a savage attack on Folly Cove and the north side of town on October 1, 1814, the "violent cold Tuesday" of January 31, 1815, ushered in heartwarming news: *PEACE!*

When a rider on a foaming, sweaty horse brought the news to Cape Ann, the younger Thomas Knights of Sandy Bay happened to be at Gloucester Harbor. For a printed handbill reporting the ratification of the treaty "he had to pay twenty-five cents." As he in turn galloped home, he met Col. Isaac Dennison on "the Great Hill" and gave him the handbill. "The Colonel brought it here." Celebrations were quickly organized that February 22. At the harbor the large meetinghouse was brilliantly lighted. "For the first time its venerable walls resounded patriotic songs, mingled with shouts of merriment and joy." Soon afterward Cape Ann had a "grand ball." Ebenezer Pool recorded that the news "caused much joy" in Sandy Bay and that there was "a great celebration" during which "a great illumination took place in most of the dwelling houses in the village." Guns were fired, he recalled, and toasts were given with three cheers, "at Allen's Head, Fort Point, and on Hale's Point fired a cannon."

NOTES

In view of the significance, locally, of the escapade involving the *Nymph*, it is worth noting a contemporary account of the incursion written by one Samuel H. Russell on September 12, 1814, while stationed at Fort Sewall, Marblehead:

On Monday Evening of the 5th inst. the Enimie, consisting of 3 barges, landed at Sandy Bay & catcht them a Napping & took all in the Fort prisoners, but providentially allarmed the town which caused the ringing of the bell & firing of allarm Guns, at which they made the best of their way of, with their prisoners, after getting a certain distance of, they fired from one of the barges at the Meeting house, the second shot drove the bows of the boat out & set them all swimming, the Americans, with 12 of the Enimie, swam to the shore but have since been smuggled of by some of their friends.

N.B. You will observe I say in my letter that all the Americans swam ashore, which is a mistake: five of them happen'd to be in one of the other barges who was made prisoner of.

A second, widely divergent press report was included by Babson in his *History of Gloucester:*

Thursday, Sept. 9, 1814.–About daybreak, three barges full of men, from three frigates and a seventy-four, landed at Sandy Bay, and took possession of the fort, in which were four guns and fourteen men. The men were made prisoners. They then turned the guns upon the town, and fired upon the Meeting-house, where the alarm-bell was ringing. The artillery and militia companies, and soldiers from the fort, were immediately on the march (the artillery in thirty minutes from the alarm). A skirmish took place, in which several were killed and wounded on each side; the number not known. Our troops finally succeeded in driving off the enemy after they had spiked the guns at the fort and thrown them overboard, and succeeded in taking thirteen prisoners by one of their barges upsetting. Great credit is due to the militia and regulars of Gloucester for their activity. It is said they turned out to a man in a very few minutes. Great consternation prevailed at the first alarm at Gloucester; as it was represented the enemy had landed three thousand troops, and were marching directly into the harbor. Four of the fourteen prisoners escaped from one of the barges by swimming, and one was drowned.

A third, still different account appeared some sixty years after the skirmish. Signed only "Web Foot," it was published in the *Cape Ann Advertiser* of Friday, March 19, 1875, and added some local color, if few solid facts.

ADDITIONAL READING

Two publications which are helpful for those interested in tracking down soldiers from the War of 1812 are the *Records of the Massachusetts Volunteer Militia Called out . . . during the War of 1812-1814* (Boston, 1913) and "Prisoners of War from Massachusetts, 1812-15," *Essex Institute Historical Collections*, vol. 63 (1927), pp. 135-44, 217-32, 323-27.

"Mr. Madison's War"

11

ENTERPRISE

"**T**HE COMMENCEMENT of another peace," rejoiced one resident of Sandy Bay, "set every wheel of business in motion." And how they hummed between the Treaty of Ghent (1815) and the incorporation of Rockport (1840). Fishing and commerce boomed on shore and at sea; regeneration of the spirit reached for the sky.

Federal bounties for fishing resumed, and March 1819 brought welcome increases. Cod was eagerly sought for, fetching $5 per quintal locally and $6 at New York. Fish oils brought $1 a gallon. No fifth parish men parlayed their fish into fortunes, but Nehemiah Knowlton sailed the *Java* to New York and on his second trip cleared $600 at the very time Jabez R. Gott squeezed out $100 for teaching school in Sandy Bay.

Well before 1820 William Norwood and Charles Wheeler of Pigeon Cove ventured south, then turned to follow northbound mackerel schools. They were joined by schooner Capt. William Goss, Jr., and Ebenezer Davis. Mackerel became an all-season goal, especially after the invention of a baitmill about 1820 and Abraham Lurvey's better method of running lead around hooks and jigs. More profitable yet was Norwood's system of salting, curing, and sealing his catches. Lobstering was regulated as of February 20, 1824. The protected area included the "Harbor of Sandy Bay, from Gap-head on the east side to Pigeon Cove on the north side." With the completion of the Erie Canal, "western" markets became increasingly accessible. In 1825 Rockport-to-be was credited with 14,875 quintals of fish, 3,283 barrels of mackerel, 676 boxes of herring (from Maine), and 1,093 barrels of fish oil. In bounty payments it received $5,025. About 1837 a new trend in marketing set in, led by Caleb Tarr, Jr., and John W. Marshall, who bought fish fresh and split from the boats and in turn sold to markets. Prices were fixed at an "on board" rate by those rising middlemen. In all, Sandy Bay then had a fleet of some eighty-five sail with a tonnage estimated at 1,250 tons.

Raymond McFarland sketched this engaging picture of a boy of the time:

Long before a lad could nib a quill, or make a pot-hook, or read half the precepts his primer contained, he knew the name of every brace and stay, every sail and part of a Grand Banker and a Chebacco boat, all the nautical terms. . . . By the time he had seen his tenth birthday he was old enough not to be seasick, not to cry during a storm at sea, and to be of some use about a ship, and went on his first trip to the Banks.

That same lad and his family would also have learned to cope with the storms and the havoc along their coast, for scarcely a year passed without damage. Sandy Bay escaped the worst of the hurricane of September 1815, though the old piers were heavily hit. Four years later there were the freak tidal waves in early June which drowned young Benjamin Low when his "canoe," loaded with fresh fish, was upset near the harbor entrance. The gale of February 1820 moved a fifteen to twenty ton boulder at Bearskin Neck about twenty feet. Damage to the drying flakes was far more significant.

In mid-March 1828 Moses Pool was blown out to sea in his wherry, but after thirty-six hours, with only two cakes of ship's bread to eat, he managed to reach Baker's Island. At Whale Cove in 1830 a woman trapped in a wrecked Nantucket sloop was extracted from a hole cut in the deck. At the home of Joseph Smith she gradually recovered. Then, too, the very landscape was altered by the southeast gale of 1830, when Starknaught Harbor was inundated, the southwest creek blocked off, and a new channel opened down toward Cape Hedge. In mid-January 1831 a thirty-hour snowstorm halted stage traffic and there was no preaching in all Cape Ann, "tho' there were at least ten ministers in the town," noted Pool with some scorn.

Enterprise

Not all maritime ventures were aboveboard—even after the war. When American ships were denied the West Indies, the U.S. Navigation Act of August 1818 closed American ports to British vessels from there. Once again, enterprising smugglers violated the laws. The schooner *Washington* smuggled a cargo of rum into Sandy Bay where it was stowed away in barns, woodpiles, and fishhouses. An informer, living at Solomon Pool's, brought customs officers down from Gloucester Harbor. They confiscated the contraband and levied on Pool a fine of $500. "Mr. Joseph Smith barely escaped the loss of a like sum." The vessel itself was scuttled but later raised and sold.

Cape Ann was growing—Sandy Bay faster than any of the five parishes. Pigeon Cove, too, was expanding. A local reckoning in 1818 gave the fifth parish 1,506 inhabitants and about 160 houses—an explosion of nearly 100 percent in just over two decades. By 1830 the bay's population reached 1,783, in 336 families, and in 196 dwellings, according to the federal census. Ebenezer Pool mentioned with filial piety that there were 115 children and adults named Pool living there, plus 15 "married females" who were also descended from Rockport's second family.

The call of the running tide was being answered by more and more men and boys. Alert to their commercial interests, enterprising businessmen of Sandy Bay saw that there must be facilities to which to return. In 1811 the Sandy Bay Pier Company had been incorporated, demolished the eighteenth-century wharves, and at the cost of $9,000 laid down a new stone one some seventy feet to the north in the Whirlpool harbor area. Once the war was over the company promptly constructed the southwest wharf, primarily to accommodate lumber and wood shipments. Still not satisfied, in 1817 the firm added a third pier. Costs for these improvements ran to some $50,000, an impressive capital outlay.

By the spring of 1826 enterprising Pigeon Covers were also improving their commercial interests. On June 26 the state legislature chartered the Pigeon Cove Pier Company "for the purpose of erecting and maintaining a stone pier" to be 164 by 100 feet. The incorporators were Nehemiah Knowlton, Walter Knowlton, Abraham Lurvey, William Pool, Daniel Tuttle, and Daniel Wheeler. Incorporation of the Pigeon Cove Harbor Company was signed on February 5, 1831. It was capitalized at $100,000 by Charles Wheeler, John W. Wheeler, David and Gorham Babson, and their associates. In July 1830 they had petitioned to improve Pigeon Cove, which "lies open and exposed to the influx of the ocean," by constructing a breakwater "on the North East side of said cove, commencing at the Pillions (so-called) and extending in a South Easterly direction to the Great Ledge, which lies at the mouth of said Cove, and from said ledge in a south westerly direction to another ledge which is covered at low tide." The crux of their plan was "to ask and receive, for their benefit, from all vessels, rafts, or other articles coming within the said basin, such dockage or rents, and such wharfage on all goods and property as shall be landed or taken off within their limits." Before long, Daniel Wheeler and his colleagues sold out to the Harbor Company. Not to be outdone by the North Villagers, on March 5, 1832, the Sandy Bay Pier Company wrested legislative permission to acquire a large chunk of real estate on Long Cove in order to make "a safe and convenient harbor."

Although the coast was blessed with twin lights on Thacher's Island, there remained the constant menaces of Salvages and Straitsmouth. On April 8, 1835, the federal government took over Straitsmouth Island, "for the sole purpose of erecting and maintaining a lighthouse" there. Benjamin Andrews was given the task of maintaining the operation. He was not liable "to serve as a juror, or to perform military duty." The next year commenced the earlier of Sandy Bay's two federally nurtured breakwaters, the one running out from the tip of Bearskin Neck toward the Headlands, which made a genuine harbor out of the already bustling Long Cove. The stone was locally procured and, after being estimated by Samuel Giles, "weigh master," was paid for by Washington—at a cost of some $190,000, according to Ebenezer Pool. The old fort was taken down in 1837 and put into the lengthening breakwater. Wharves were built out on the north side of the harbor and from the south side of Long Cove Brook. Annually appropriated funds dried up before completion of the breakwater, though political influence was sought for years from Congress. Sandy Bay became so heavily engaged in commercial fishing that it launched its own Mutual Marine Insurance Company in January 1827. The capital was raised from thirty-six shares (expanded to forty in 1831), and the principal direction was provided by Isaac Dennison, Jr., and Ebenezer Pool, Jr. Some twenty years later the company dissolved and a new one was created.

One marine enterprise surfaced repeatedly in August 1817—a sea serpent! This was the first such visit since John Josselyn in 1639 told about "a sea-serpent, or snake, that lay coiled up like a cable upon a rock at Cape Ann." This new arrival was repeatedly seen and described by several sober citizens in sworn testimony before a committee of scientists sent to investigate it on behalf of the Linnaean Society of New England. Their published reports and drawings and those sent to the Royal Society of London still make entertaining reading. "The hardy and patient crews of two fishing smacks, armed at all points, commanded by two vigilant and brave captains, of the name of Pool, came from Sandy-Bay, and remained a whole week." Although the serpent came within a few rods of the Pools' nets on August 27, "he went off without entering." A month later, however, Gorham Norwood and Moses Colby and his son were mowing in a field near Loblolly Cove. Out wiggled a snakelike creature. Thinking it might be progeny of the talked-of sea serpent, they killed it and carried it to Sandy Bay village—"it was viewed by many people, it being a training day at that place." Later they sold the corpse to John Gott. On reaching Boston, the "baby" was exhibited for a fee. Off and on for a century, the "Gloucester Sea Serpent" provided an unusual inducement for tourist-eager hotelkeepers. Not until 1877, however, did the creature perform again for many respectable spectators at Rockport.

Ashore

By no means were all Sandy Bay-Pigeon Cove residents occupied with fishing enterprises. Agriculture got fresh deference, especially after the icy winter of 1816-17, remembered as "eighteen hundred-and-frozen-to-death." Reportedly the only corn to ripen that summer was at Pigeon Cove in a small, sheltered spot whose owner hoarded it all for seed. Whereas in 1800 only about ten Sandy Bay men supported their families by farming, by 1827 some twenty-seven to thirty did so; instead of the dozen pairs of oxen in the parish there were sixty. Comparable increases were to be noted in cattle and other livestock. Instead of relying on imported hay, by 1825 local farmers had a surplus for selling. The raising of potatoes and grain began in earnest. By 1824 the local farmers harvested about three thousand bushels of grain and milled it nearby.

Land became more desirable, for both agricultural and speculative purposes. In 1819, for example, the acute David Babson and William and John Fears purchased the five-acre sea mark on Pigeon Hill for $525. In September 1820 Babson gave $4,000 for the "Babson Farm" property at the junction of Granite Street and Gott Avenue. Shortly before Rockport became independent, enterprising Ezra Eames bought up ledges of granite along the highway in Pigeon Cove. In 1839 he picked up David Babson's interest in the "top field" of Pigeon Hill and later the Fear's rights, too. In 1840, the thirty-nine-year-old Eames built the modish Greek Revival house for himself at 96 Granite Street—by all odds the most impressive home in the area.

Diversification of commercial interests became increasingly noticeable following the War of 1812. Urbanization called for more amenities. For summer refrigeration, in 1830 the village got what may have been its first commercial icehouse. The improvement of stoves led Abraham Doyle in 1832 to bring to town some casks of anthracite coal. The eighty tons brought in about 1838 by Capt. John S. Giles sold for $8 a ton but moved slowly for a full year.

Two fresh commercial exploitations were begun within a year of each other: isinglass in 1822 and granite in 1823. Both would take hold promptly, and both would provide livelihoods for a century to come. Isinglass was a semitransparent, pure form of gelatin used for generations in glue; in jellies; in the settling of beer; in thin sheets for curtains on carriages, open trolley cars, and automobiles. It was made from the "sounds" (air bladders) of fish, especially hake. In 1822 a Bostonian named William Hale came to Sandy Bay and commenced buying sounds from fishermen on Bearskin Neck at 3 to 5 cents a pound. He cleaned them, dried them, and with wooden rollers shaped them into ribbons and sheets of isinglass. The process was patented in 1823; but heavier pressure was required, so double sets of metal rollers were constructed and turned by three or four people at 40 cents to 50 cents per day. Production was carried out in a two-story building on the northwest side of the neck. In due course the business was taken over by Jabez Rowe and William Norwood, who organized the Sandy Bay Isinglass Company. A newspaper advertisement of December 28, 1827, offered "American Isinglass for sale at factory price. A line addressed to the Subscriber for any quantity will meet with punctual attention." The agent was Jabez R. Gott. Sandy Bay held a monopoly on this commodity until the patent expired.

Another newspaper advertisement placed in a Boston paper on April 17, 1823, sparked the granite business, which in turn would sustain so much of Cape Ann's economy and permanently transform its character. Having cut some five hundred tons of cellar and foundation stone along the shore behind today's chapel at Pigeon Cove, Nehemiah Knowlton offered it for sale. From Quincy, Massachusetts, which had quarries of its own, came the enterprising "Major" Bates.

Enterprise

To his experienced eyes the opportunities looked promising, so on April 24, 1824, he set up operations in two spots rented from William Rowe and Thomas Oakes. As an associate Bates attracted Quincy's William Torrey. They had "20 men and vessels." When Bates withdrew, Torrey persisted by himself, encouraged by contracts for Fort Warren in Boston Harbor. As a short-term venture, Torrey branched out to Folly Cove for the flagstones and capstones required at the fort. He and his sons concentrated their efforts at the "Torrey Pit," adjacent to the present Rockport Granite Company bridge. By 1840 virtually all the granite used at government installations in Boston Harbor and the Charlestown and Portsmouth Navy Yards came from there.

Torrey was not alone, however. About 1827 he was joined by Beniah Colburn and Ezra Eames, who became partners in Pigeon Cove. For an eight-month work period they reportedly paid $12 per month plus board. Although at the end of their first year they are said to have had a deficit of $15, they quickly became solvent. High profits came from cutting down the ledge between today's 143 and 151 Granite Street and selling it, "dressed" for cemetery purposes. Their quarry ran until about 1840 and provided granite for the chain bridge over the Merrimack River at Newburyport. In 1830 William Rowe sold land to the Boston and Gloucester Granite Company for the purpose "of procuring, hammering and cutting Granite Stones." Regrouped in 1841, that firm commenced the wharf and breakwater later developed by the Rockport Granite Company, whose stone house and barns they also built.

Opening Up

Isolation receded at an accelerated pace under the influence of the Jacksonian era. The residents themselves saw the impact as they moved about. Take 1825 to 1830 as an example. A post office was opened just off Dock Square in 1825 and a Pool (Winthrop) was commissioned postmaster by President John Quincy Adams. Mail came and left twice a week; within three years the service became daily (except Sundays). Mail was carried in a two-horse stage, driven by a man named Fellows. An announcement informed the public that "commencing on Monday next The Sandy Bay Stage will leave J. Mason's Tavern, Fore Street, Gloucester, every day (Sundays excepted) at 5 o'clock P.M." The return trip left Josiah Haskell's tavern at Sandy Bay (the present Rockport Art Association) "every day (Sunday and Monday excepted) 7 o'clock A.M. and Saturday also 7 o'clock P.M."

By 1828 Rockporters-to-be could ride to Gloucester, devote the day to business or pleasure, and return home in time for supper. Those who wanted a Saturday night on the town were also provided for, though they would have to find their own way back to the bay.

Prior to this period, "but some half dozen newspapers were taken in town." In 1827, however, enterprise produced Cape Ann's first regular newspaper, the *Gloucester Telegraph*. Like nearly all papers of the era, it was politically oriented—Whig in this case—and carried many partisan reports. Since local news traveled so fast by the grapevine, most space was allotted to state, national, and international developments—and of course to the advertisements, which abounded.

By 1829 it was obvious that Sandy Bay could no longer rely solely on the leather buckets of its volunteer fire brigade. Its first engine probably came from a public subscription which raised $315 to buy a hand pump (tub). It required about thirty to man it and was appropriately christened—either the "Independence" or the "Enterprise." The crew received appointments from the selectmen in October, and the equipment was probably stored in a barn at the Front Beach opposite the old cemetery. A town meeting on December 11, 1830, appropriated $400 to build an "engine house" 18 by 20 feet and two stories high down on Dock Square. Into this was placed a town-purchased engine similar to the other. It was named either the "Enterprise" or the "Independence"* and eventually became the property of independent Rockport. A company to take charge of it was appointed on February 25, 1831, with Richard Choate, foreman; Nehemiah Knowlton, Jr., assistant foreman; and Abraham Goldsmith, clerk. The tubs came to Sandy Bay none too soon, for the town's first blaze of consequence broke out in June 1830 when the South Street farmhouse of Deacon Solomon Pool and his brothers caught fire and burned.

Spiritual and Spirituous

There was no extinguishing of religious fires, however, in that period of prodigious ecclesiastical enterprise. Chronologically, development went thus. At the end of the War of 1812 the Congregationalists still had the only meetinghouse in the fifth parish. In the autumn of 1820 the Baptists called their first pastor, James A. Boswell. Following the lead of the Congregationalists, who had begun a Sunday school in May 1818 and were to have 250 scholars by 1836,

---

*Whichever name the first engine did not have.

Enterprise

the Baptists started their Sunday school in the loft of Haskell's grocery store near Dock Square. In 1821 they purchased land from Caleb Pool and, with money advanced by Deacon Ebenezer Pool, began construction of a church building. The first service, on September 1, 1822, the collection totaled $4.50. In 1828 the structure was finished and pews were put up for sale. A belfry was added in 1832 and a bell bought for $180. They had a Sunday school of one hundred by 1836, and Mr. Boswell had had five successors by 1840.

The Universalists had held services at the fifth parish meetinghouse until February 1807. From then until 1829 they met in the schoolhouse. On February 11, 1821, some thirty people signed a compact for the Sandy Bay Universalist Benevolent Society. In 1825 they hired their first semisettled minister, Mr. Lafayette Mace, and on June 24, 1829, laid the cornerstone for their meetinghouse. The dedicatory service was held on October 8, with Masonic rites. Formal incorporation of the society occurred on April 6, 1839.

Next came the small Methodist community. In 1831 a "class" of twelve was established by the Reverend Mr. Aaron Lummus of Gloucester and met in the home of Capt. Levi Cleaves and his wife "Nicy" at 47 Mt. Pleasant Street. After seven years of services on alternate Wednesday evenings, the group was set off from the main Gloucester church and began independent operations in the Methodist chapel, which had been built on Jewett Street where the town hall parking lot is now located. At the time of Rockport's incorporation, the Methodist flock consisted of thirty-five members and sixteen "probationers."

Although their physical bodies had more physicians to tend to them—Dr. Charles Bolles Manning (1822), Dr. Adams Nichols (1830), Dr. Joseph Reynolds (1833), and Dr. Benjamin Haskell (1839)—the ailments of some Rockporters required watching beyond the ministrations of preachers and Sabbath school teachers. One sufferer needed both physical and psychological treatment for "sleeping sickness." From December 1833 until the first week of February 1834, ten-year-old William Blatchford, Jr., occasionally dropped into a state of somnambulism. According to Ebenezer Pool, who observed the spells, the "fits soon became more powerful and wonderful than any ever known of before." Three years later Dr. Benjamin Haskell provided comments for a medical journal.

Many sober Sandy Bayers were troubled by a widespread blight—violations of the liquor licensing laws. On June 14, 1814, five worthies (among them Sandy Bay's James Goss, Solomon Pool, Francis Norwood, and Timothy Riggs Davis) reported that sixteen people were "in the constant habit of selling liquors mixed and drank in their shops in open violation of the statute laws of this Commonwealth." They called for summoning all future violators to court.

At Sandy Bay a group of agitated residents led by the Reverend Mr. Jewett met on February 13, 1815, and initiated "The Society for the Suppression of Intemperance and other Prevalent Vices." Initially the twenty-seven men met at members' homes; later, at the office of the Mutual Marine Insurance Company. From assessed dues of 50 cents they purchased temperance publications and awarded "premiums to the best Scholars for their improvement in Learning and good behaviour." Other efforts were expended on "the due observation of the Sabbath" and counteracting "all vice in whatever form," including profane language, slander, and gambling. Their only specific monitoring act was against Thomas Rowe and a Mrs. Phipps, who were "guilty of cohabitation," living "in a very illegal and indecent manner," and who had "become exceedingly addicted to using very profane and obscene language." Mrs. Phipps was denounced to the overseers of the poor. When the moral society dissolved itself in March 1829, it turned over its remaining assets to the fifth parish church; only fourteen members were left.

A move to restrict the serving of "ardent spirits" on the occasion of funerals received attention by 1825, but in the fall and winter of 1827 there was extra ardor at the bay—a great wave of religion. During the revival, recalled Ebenezer Pool, "more than 200 was supposed to be subjects of renewing grace." Elsewhere he raised the score to three hundred converts and wrote: "Some joined the Baptist then." All this encouraged new attempts to suppress the selling and imbibing of liquor. At the beginning of the 1830s a fresh society was formed with pledges not to indulge in distilled spirits. When members were found who cheated with hard cider, wine, and malt drinks, the pledge was strengthened. Thirsters responded to all these "gag acts," as they called them, and on one occasion demonstrated in Dock Square, "where a barrel of New England rum was tapped and the stars and stripes waved above it upon a staff whose base was in the bung hole. The day was spent in riot and drinking."

The period 1815-40 had its sobering aspects, too, including yet another enlargement of the cemetery. In 1818 Capt. Benjamin Tarr, Solomon Pool, and Ebenezer Pool, Jr., raised $250 by subscription and in February 1819 bought land from Benjamin Soper Marshall for $175 to expand to the south and west. Murder and sudden death hit in May 1821 when Ebenezer Davis, Jr., a boy of about twelve, was killed with an ax by seventeen-year-old Gorham Parsons in the Squam woods. Though tried at Newburyport, Parsons was not condemned. Instead, he went to sea, only to disappear overboard, taking a small grindstone to weigh him down. Slow death in 1822 took a monarch elm which had "stood for ages as a landmark" in Pool's pasture. Said to have been 100 to 110 feet tall, it had a circumference of 18 feet and produced five to six cords of wood when sawed. Rarer yet was a gooseberry bush growing in the crotch of its trunk twenty to thirty feet up, "which was transplanted and bore well." To meet the needs of a growing, scattered population, Sandy Bay required a wheeled hearse. Shoulder biers would no longer suffice. In 1836 a public subscription extracted $96.35 from 147 donors whose names and contributions are still to be seen on the list. The low, four-wheel framed cart they purchased had wooden wheels and was trimmed with black broadcloth.Thanks to another public-spirited campaign, in 1962, it survives in its house on Beach Street below the graves of the many it transported in its thirty-six years of service.

As Rockport-to-be expanded in many directions, fresh roads and connectors were initiated: High Street, then a cowpath called Pasture Lane, was opened as a road in the early 1820s. In the mid-1830s Pleasant Street was laid out, the upper portion of School Street was developed across Capt. John Gott's land, and Prospect Street was opened across Andrew Lane's property. The part of School Street from Main to High streets was laid out about 1837, and Gott Street became a town way in 1838. Two years before, the road between the Front and Back beaches was sharply regraded by Azor Knowlton. Maps began to appear. Jabez R. Gott made one of the roads around Cape Ann in 1823; another was the attractive survey of the Cape made by John Mason in 1830-31.

Sandy Bay received modest attention in James R. Newhall's *The Essex Memorial for 1836*. The village of about three hundred houses and two thousand inhabitants, he wrote, "is on the eastern end of the Cape, about five miles from the harbor (Gloucester). There is no natural harbor here, but a pier and breakwater have been constructed for the security of the shipping." He noted the two lights at Thacher's and the one at "Starksmouth" Island. He mentioned that one of the town's two lawyers, J. B. Manning, was at Sandy Bay and nodded to the

Town on Sandy Bay

three religious societies, one insurance company, two fire engines, Winthrop Pool's post office, and two public houses: "at Sandy Bay, Josiah Haskell; at Pigeon Cove, Daniel Wheeler."

Yet another change reached Sandy Bay in 1836, a third minister for its fifth parish church, Wakefield Gale. Failing health had brought on the reluctant resignation of David Jewett, devoted pastor for some thirty years, who left behind him a flourishing church. His service to the community is memorialized by the street named for him and by the monument raised by a grateful citizenry at his reinterment in 1856.

As the area moved toward independence, its cultural horizons were also broadened. School services were provided by two school buildings at Pigeon Cove and four in the South Village. In 1830, self-enlightenment sired Cape Ann's Lyceum series. Not to be outdone by their intown brethren, Sandy Bay citizens formed theirs on September 16, 1830. Doors opened at 6:30 P.M., meetings commenced "precisely at 7:00." Some townspeople were cavalier about punctuality. "Inconvenience results from opening and shutting the doors during the lecture." The *Telegraph* even ran an editorial on "Late Attendence at Public Worship," charging that "a very common reason with the fair sex is the time employed in dressing." On that note, ladies attending the Lyceum got this finger-wagging: "We have no objections to huge bonnets or capacious sleeves . . . but we think that were the ladies to dispense with the former on such occasions, it would much improve the general appearance of an audience and could not but materially contribute to their own comfort and convenience." Finally, from 1827 on there was the constant leavening of the lump by the newspapers, carrying articles on far-ranging cultural items.

Small wonder, then, given the amount of energy and enterprise generated during those years that the Cape parish and the Coves grew restive at being but an appendage to Gloucester Harbor. By 1818 foreshadowings were noticeable. A decade later they became highly visible. On December 29, 1827, some Sandy Bay voters asked on what terms their area might be set off. They were supported editorially by the *Telegraph*. Yet once the town meeting agreed unanimously to allow Sandy Bay to withdraw, opposition swelled, especially from some Squam residents who complained that, having no reasons to go to Sandy Bay, they preferred to be left alone. A third town meeting was held on January 12, 1828, at which it was reported no agreement on terms could be reached. The matter would be left up to the Massachusetts legislature; Sandy Bay residents were to pay all costs involved whether separation resulted or not. That proposal resulted in a protest against the division, and some sixty Sandy Bay people signed it. Their taxes would be higher! So the proposed separation was dropped. It was not yet an idea whose time had come. March 6, 1839, would be another matter.

ADDITIONAL READING

Much has been written about the sea serpents, some of it far more fantastic than the beasts themselves. A good brief summary with illustrations of the Cape Ann visitation is L. D. Geller, *Sea Serpents of Coastal New England* (Plymouth, 1979). The two contemporary accounts from August 1817 are the *Report of a Committee of the Linnaean Society of New England Relative to a Large Marine Animal . . . near Cape Ann* (Boston, 1817) and *Letters from the Hon. David Humphreys, F.R.S. of the Serpent of the Ocean Frequently Seen in Gloucester Bay* (New York, 1817). An early spoof was William Crafts, *The Sea Serpent or Gloucester Hoax* (Charleston, 1819).

James R. Newhall, *The Essex Memorial for 1836* (Salem, 1836), and James Carter and William Brooks, *A Geography of Essex County* (Boston, 1830), give illuminating contemporary views of the area, the latter for schoolchildren.

From 1827 on, beginning with the *Gloucester Telegraph*, newspapers of the town are fundamental to anyone really interested in the history of the town. Several of them are available on microfilm at the Carnegie Library in Rockport and the Sawyer Free Library in Gloucester. Some rarer papers not available on Cape Ann are at the Essex Institute in Salem.

John Mason's survey map of Cape Ann made in 1830-31 was attractively published by the Bearskin Press at Rockport for the bicentennial.

12

THE TOWN IS BORN

Separation

THE PERIOD OF GESTA-
TION was more than a quarter of a century. The labor
pangs lasted a year. But the result was a small, healthy, new town. On
Wednesday, February 27, 1839, "the male inhabitants of Gloucester,
qualified to vote in town affairs," were officially notified by the constable of a town meeting to be held on Monday, March 4, at 9:00 A.M. at
Union Hall. For his trouble he was paid $1 from the public treasury. Of
the twenty-nine items on the warrant, decision no. 11 was a petition
from William P. Burns and others asking if "the Town will set off
Sandy Bay and Pigeon Cove as a Town—or Sandy Bay only as a
Town." The petitioners proposed a settlement along "such line or lines
and on such terms as may be mutually agreed upon by the Inhabitants."

Pressure of earlier articles delayed the matter of separation until
the next day, when the voters decided to postpone the whole issue in
order to obtain a fair expression of the sentiments of the people of
Sandy Bay. They had learned their lesson from previous agitations.
The following day, however, there was another gathering of the
neighbors concerned at which they voted 78 to 3 in favor of separation
from Gloucester, "if it can be done on fair and honorable terms." On
March 20 the *Telegraph* reported that a very large majority favored the
project. As further insurance, inhabitants of Sandy Bay appointed a
committee of two persons from each of their school districts to call on
each person in their respective areas to solicit their views on the vital

issue of separation. This canvass decided upon, the voters adjourned until Monday, April 8. Two days after that session the newspaper informed its readers of the results: "There appeared 319 in favor and 54 against it. A pretty decided vote."

The next move was to select a bipartisan committee of ten to draw up a blueprint for the separation. The five negotiators from the proposed new jurisdiction were Reuben Dade, George D. Hale, James Haskell, Nehemiah Knowlton, and John W. Marshall. Agreement on the gritty issues was not to be achieved easily. The town meeting of May 6 postponed discussion of questions about the separation indefinitely, though voters agreed to spend $50 (half the sum requested) to repair the street running from High Street to Pleasant Street in Sandy Bay. Permission was also given to pay for ringing bells at the harbor, Sandy Bay, and Squam at noon and nine o'clock in the evening. Readers of history will ever be grateful that the electorate engaged John J. Babson, Alphonso Mason, and Rockport's Ebenezer Pool, Jr., to take measures for the transcribing and future safekeeping "of the old Town Records now in a dilapidated state."

At the end of May a meeting of the citizens picked a committee to determine the lines for a division of the town, preparatory to the setting off of Sandy Bay. That group submitted its report on June 10 and was heartened to find a receptive audience. The highlights of their recommendations were that there be new geographical boundaries; that town property be evaluated by an independent, three-man board mutually chosen from outside the area; and that all town property be allotted to the jurisdiction in which it lay, except the town farm and woodland, the grammar school house, and all personally owned property. The newly launched grammar school, sustained by public funding, had been the source of sharp clashes over its location, the rival candidates for the position of teacher, the progress (or lack of it) among its scholars, and the June 24 decision "that females shall be admitted to the Town Grammar School." Dr. Lemuel Gott had represented Sandy Bay voters and supported the admission of girls. The negotiators proposed that the population data of the Massachusetts State census of 1837 should provide the basis for apportioning most financial resources. Finally, it was agreed that as soon as the new town received its legal independence it should elect its own representatives to the Massachusetts legislature.

With the approach of winter, persistence and goodwill triumphed among the team of negotiators. Boundaries were fixed much as they are today, giving the projected town an area of some six and a quarter square miles or about two sevenths of Gloucester as a whole. This fraction proved to be a workable basis for determining the allocation of assets, liabilities, corporate property, town landings, clam flats, water rights, and other responsibilities to devolve upon the respective communities. Budgetary and related figures for 1838 provided the base for financial calculations. The new town agreed to pay $687 to Gloucester for the present inequalities of the roadways and to share, proportionately, the costs of laying out roads already planned. Residents of the new jurisdiction were to settle all arrearages in taxes as well as all debts previously contracted by, or to be adjudicated to, them. Other knotty problems were proportional shares for maintaining the Cape's many poor citizens and dividing such surplus federal funds as had been paid by or might yet come from the U.S. government. (As expected, no doubt, John Pool III and his hopeful petitioners were denied their request to have such monies handed over to them individually.) By early December satisfactory compromises had been forged on nearly all issues.

What name should the new town receive at its christening? On December 7, 1839, future voters met and asked for proposals from the following men: James Haskell, Thomas O. Marshall, Ebenezer Pool, Jr., Amos Story, Jr., and Daniel Wheeler. Five suggestions were advanced. "These names were written on a paper circulated for each person to mark against." A total of 63 checks were entered: Rockport (24), Cape Ann (22), East Gloucester (7), and Granite (2). One rather capricious proposal, Brest, possibly tossed in because of its comparable location on the opposite French coast, secured 8 votes. No proposal won a majority, so fresh ballots were taken on the leading candidate, Rockport. This time 36 cast in its favor, but a majority of 43 were in opposition. Back to the committee went the assignment. Their next recommendation was to choose between the names Rockport and Granite, the higher number of votes to be binding. Of the fifty men who finally made the decision, forty came down in favor of Rockport and only ten for Granite. Since every cliff had speculative quarrying value, the name coined was indeed fitting.

The new decade soon saw the legal establishment of the new town, just three weeks after Queen Victoria married handsome Prince Albert. An uncontested petition was submitted to the Massachusetts legislature. Stress was laid on the inconvenience imposed on Rockporters by the lengthy distances they had to travel to transact town business and bear their share of civic responsibility in state and national affairs. Both houses of the General Court promptly passed on the petition favorably. That same day, February 27, 1840, Governor Marcus Morton, a Democrat, signed the bill setting off Sandy Bay, parts of Pigeon Cove, and Annisquam parish as the independent town of Rockport.

Rockport on Its Own

Truly on their own at last, the inhabitants were faced with the monumental task of setting up their town government. As a justice of the peace, James Goss, Esq., was the man empowered to issue the warrant for Rockport's first town meeting. The turnout was a crush, even for the newly refurbished vestry of the Congregational church. On Monday, March 9, at 9:00 A.M., James Haskell called the packed session to order. The Articles of Incorporation and the warrant were read. The initial task, or course, was to elect town officials. Capt. John Davis was declared moderator on receiving 242 of the 373 votes cast. William Pool was chosen town clerk, a job he was to hold for twenty-nine years; he was succeeded by his son Calvin, who occupied the post an additional forty years.

In the interest of efficiency it was agreed to choose the selectmen, town treasurer, assessors, overseers, and school committee on one ballot. When the frazzled tellers finally turned in their figures, the moderator declared that Capt. John Gott had been unanimously elected first town treasurer; that David Babson, Jr., James Haskell, and Thomas O. Marshall were to be selectmen, assessors, and overseers; and that Dr. Lemuel Gott, Joseph B. Manning, and William Mann had been voted in as the school committeemen. Next came the explosive question of taxes. It was evident that the critical choice of collectors required the jam-packed meeting to adjourn to the outdoors, "so that the true state of the vote could be ascertained." John B. Parsons and Michael Walen got the official go-ahead from their townsmen. At its debut, Rockport's total town tax was fixed at $3,506.95, of which at the end of the first year of independence Parsons had been unable to collect $81.37 and Walen $98.94, a default of over 5 percent. Also named at the first town meeting were nine constables, seven surveyors of highways, nine hog reeves, and sixteen fire wardens. Once these officers of government had been elected, approved, and sworn into office about 4:30 P.M., the weary voters adjourned.

Town on Sandy Bay

Nine days later, on March 18, Rockport held its second town meeting. Only some sixty voters attended. Annual salaries were fixed for selectmen ($28) and town clerk and town treasurer ($10). School committee members were to receive $1 per day of duty. To support the poor $1,200 was set aside, and $700 was budgeted for highways. Roadwork, if done promptly, could be credited toward town tax bills at the rate of 14 cents an hour for a man and shovel. Only 4 cents an hour was allowed for an oxcart, but 18 cents could be had for plowing.

Who were the first Rockporters? From the federal census taken in June 1840 there emerges a fairly clear, though statistically shaky portrait. In all, the town had 2,647 inhabitants—all white and, of course, all free. (The state census counted 2,728.) There was a preponderance of males (1,407) over females (1,240). It was a young community; nearly half of the population was twenty years old or less (1,294). Only 56 out of 2,647 people were over seventy, and no one was over ninety. Yet Rockport still had eight citizens drawing Revolutionary War pensions—five old soldiers: Joshua Clark (eighty-four), Joshua Gott (eighty-six), Isaac Rowe (eighty-six), James Story (seventy-seven), Jabez Tarr (eighty-one); and three widows: Martha Abbot (seventy-seven), Betsy Rowe (seventy-eight), and Annis Tarr (seventy-eight). To the genealogist the successive acts of Congress providing pensions to veterans of the Revolutionary War produced waves of documentation, beginning with 1818. Among these are a great many files of Sandy Bay veterans. Lemuel Gott related an anecdote about the aged Benjamin Davis, drummer in the Rowe company; about his need for a certificate of service and the shot of Dutch courage that nearly lost him his chance.

Rockport had one deaf-mute child under fourteen, one "insane and idiot at public charge" as well as another being privately looked after, and one blind resident. The town had six primary and common schools, with a total enrollment of 592 pupils. Finally, how did breadwinners earn their livings at the time Rockport was established? The census of 1840 provided seven general categories of employment and clearly assumed that only males worked. Although no Rockporter was engaged in mining or in the navigation of lakes, canals, or rivers, more than half of the town's men were occupied with "navigation of the ocean," (478 out of the 841 employed). Another 266 gave their occupations as being in manufactures and trades; 80 were in agriculture; 12 in the learned professions and engineering; and a final 5 in commerce— such, then, was Rockport in 1840, figuratively speaking.

In less than fifty years prior to being set off from its parent town it had quadrupled in population. The assessed real estate value determined for the town meeting of September 19, 1840, by the selectmen, assisted by Nehemiah Knowlton and Ezra Eames, was $460,814. There were about 300 dwelling houses and 698 polls or qualified voters, who incidentally paid a poll tax of $1.00 per year. The tax rate was fixed at $7.17 per $1,000.

On March 28, 1840, Rockporters adopted their official bylaws. By Massachusetts statute, however, these had to be reaffirmed six months later after mature consideration. This was accomplished at a public session on September 19, after which the bylaws were duly forwarded for entry in the Essex County Court of Common Pleas. A complete text appeared in the *Gloucester Telegraph* on April 28, 1841. From this one gets a remarkable glimpse into the heart of the town and the lives and values of its citizenry.

The first section was devoted to fire hazards, prevention, and protection, including well and pump maintenance. Next came laws governing road traffic and speed, especially prohibitions against cantering and galloping—"extraordinary occasions excepted." The *Gloucester Telegraph* had editorialized against "a vulgar passion for racing," while only a few months before, Sandy Bay had had a sad accident of its own. An eighteen-month-old baby who was being pulled in "a basket carriage" by an elder sister was dumped onto the street as some children tried to get clear of an oxcart, only to topple under the cartwheel and be crushed to death.

Rockporters passed dog taxes of $1 per year, fines for cleaning fish and leaving the remains above the high-water mark, and penalties against using buildings or vessels on Sundays "as a place of resort for persons to engage in pursuits or amusements inconsistent with sobriety, decorum, and good order becoming that sacred day." Throwing stones, bricks, oyster shells, snowballs, pieces of ice, coal ashes, or other things in the streets or upon any house or store was punishable by a fine of 50 cents for each offense. "No boys or other persons" were allowed to slide downhill on any of the public highways or streets within the town; surely few of the $1 fines were ever collected for that misdemeanor. Perhaps the constables had better luck enforcing the laws against "boys or other persons" who assembled, particularly at night, near dwelling houses or otherwise disturbed taxpayers "by any noise or riotous sports" or by obstructing sidewalks.

The last two sections of the bylaws of the new town covered matters such as advance notice for town meetings, hours for the election of town officers by ballots, methods for appropriating funds, double-checking the voting procedures, the submission of written reports by town committees, and the duties of town auditors. Division 6 of section 9 provided that Rockport should be divided into northern and southern areas and that the North Village should be entitled to one selectman, assessor, and overseer at each election and the South Village to two of each. Finally, the selectmen were charged with annually appointing "a proper person or persons of good moral character to patrol the town, who shall be called the Inspector of Police." That worthy was to carry out the bylaws, levy and collect fines, faithfully discharge his trust, and make report of his doings in January and July. For this he was to receive a suitable compensation. For trespassers and willful, malicious, and wanton destroyers of fruit trees, shade trees, glass, fences, gates, bars, and the like, there was the prospect of imprisonment in the county jail of not more than one year or of a fine not exceeding $100. Buttressed by such statutes, reinforced by nine constables and an inspector of police of good moral character, plus a battery of officials of their own choosing, Rockporters faced their independence with confidence.

The First Seven Years

From the time Rockport emerged as an independent town to the establishment of its first and only large-scale industrial enterprise, the Steam Cotton Mill, only seven years would elapse. They would, however, be crammed with change. To begin with there were notable advances in transportation. The Eastern Railroad inaugurated train service from East Boston to Salem the end of August 1838. By January 1, 1839, it had sold almost ninety thousand tickets and inspired Marbleheaders to contemplate a two-mile branch to link up with a regular steamboat line to Gloucester. By April 1 the timetable offered six daily Boston-Salem trips, with stagecoach connections direct to Gloucester that met morning and afternoon trains. "This is an excellent arrangement," cheered the *Telegraph*. "Our citizens can leave here in the morning, spend six hours in Boston, and be back by eight o'clock in the evening." The Eastern reported a 10 percent profit and some 280,000 passengers for its first year. By the time Rockport became a town in its own right, the railroad had already raced on to Ipswich and celebrated its inauguration with "a glorious clam chowder at the car house."

Entrepreneurs on Cape Ann soon caught the railroad fever. In March 1845 the Eastern Railroad got a bill through state legislature to construct a branch railroad, commencing at some eligible point "in the westerly part of the Town of Gloucester . . . thence running . . . through the towns of Manchester, Beverly, Essex, Hamilton, and Wenham" on to the main line. The company also got leave "to extend said railroad from Gloucester to Rockport." The Gloucester branch began running regular trips on November 2, 1847. Rockport had to wait until 1861 for its own trains, but it cashed in on the railroad boom almost from the beginning by providing granite for construction. For example, in September 1839 the Lowell Railroad contracted for $8,000 to $10,000 of Cape Ann stone for its Milbury branch, and the press announced that bids would be opened to transport some four thousand tons of granite "to be taken at Pigeon-hole Cove [sic], Gloucester" to be delivered to Newburyport or Haverhill, "near the contemplated Rail Road bridge." Fired up by such prospects, the *Telegraph* reprinted an article on Cape Ann in which it was said that strangers had no idea how plentiful, how beautiful, and how readily splittable Cape Ann granite was. "There is enough to build many cities as large as Boston." The very week Rockport was christened, the paper boasted: "There is probably stone enough in this single town to supply the whole of the United States with building material for several centuries." Rockport, especially Pigeon Cove, was doing its part with increasing vigor.

In 1847 the Fall River Line commenced night boat service to New York, but by the summer of 1843-44 the steamship *Telegraph* had already made Cape Ann more accessible by sea. Better still was the steamer *Portland* which had begun its summer excursions from Boston to Gloucester, carrying four hundred to five hundred passengers per trip for a 75 cent fare. Departure from Boston was at 8:00 A.M.; the return trip left Gloucester at 3:00 P.M. A band provided music and cotillion parties were got up on board the boat. More direct still, for those wishing to go to Rockport, were the Boston-Portsmouth boats which pretty much hugged the coast. They hove to off Straitsmouth, where "Brown's passenger-boat" ferried customers from Rockport to and from the steamer and also, on request, crossed the bay to Pigeon Cove. Thus, the combination rail and stage lines and ships opened the town to summer visitors on an increasing scale.

Town on Sandy Bay

Accessibility led to visitors, and visitors published the word of Cape Ann's attractions as a summer place. The *Boston Gazette,* for example, ran a flattering article on the town, "its salubrious climate," its charms as a retreat from the dust and noise of the city now made available "by the aid of steam power . . . in 3 hours." The writer especially commended the fifteen-mile drive around the shoreline and the enchanting walks to be enjoyed through the woods and along the rocks there. Of the inhabitants he remarked: "They are hardy, intelligent, and enterprising, and, as natural consequences of these qualities, they are thrifty, contented, civil and hospitable. There is not a more independent people on the face of the earth." As for the fair sex, "the females are blooming and beautiful." Small wonder that the Gloucester newspaper quickly reprinted the paean of Boston.

Nor is it to be wondered at that in the years immediately following the separation of Rockport from Gloucester such enthusiasm inaugurated the influx of summer visitors which still shapes the life of the town. From the early 1840s the tranquillity of Pigeon Cove began exerting a particularly magnetic charm on fretful city dwellers. Among the earliest of the more prominent sojourners were a group of literati from Boston and Cambridge, led by the elder Richard Henry Dana and his family who made extended visits there until he purchased a seafront home of his own at Manchester in 1845 (for $1,800 plus $75 for the agent). When vacationing at Pigeon Cove the Danas stayed at one of the two village boardinghouses then offering hospitality for a fee: the "Old House" run by the John Wheelers at 188 Granite Street (later known as the "Garrison House" and after 1890 as the "Witch House") or the tavern at 167 Granite Street. From the spring of 1838 until they opened their larger, popular Pigeon Cove House up the hill in 1846, the William Norwoods ran that modest resort dating from 1805. It was to the former that the rising Richard Henry Dana, Jr., carried his bride on their brief honeymoon the end of August 1841, the same year his *Two Years Before the Mast* was launched toward fame.

The younger Dana's diaries contain many entries devoted to the delectations of the cove, including fishing: "Caught about a dosen hadduck[sic], hake and cod." He also recorded with glee an adventure he had on being becalmed, alone at night two miles out. With evident pride the young Harvard man concluded his report: "The Nutsfords, two old fishermen, had told father I could not get in as the wind was so light and I was unacquainted."

The Town Is Born

1908 postcard view of the Babson Homestead, or "Witch House," at 188 Granite Street, the original part of which predates 1690. It was purchased in 1925 by Oliver Williams who restored it to an earlier garrison style. (Hoyt)

It was the Danas who lured William Cullen Bryant to Pigeon Cove, "a wild and craggy nook on the extreme eastern point of Massachusetts." During his three-week sojourn he was inspired to finish his "The Return of Youth" and, later, his "Hymn of the Sea." In September 1842, while Bryant was staying at Norwood's tavern, though the others seem to have been at the Wheelers in the "Old House," Bryant posed for a budding young sculptor named Edward A. Brackett. The mixed reception the bust received from family and friends of the poet's is the subject of a number of amusing comments in surviving letters. For their stay at Pigeon Cove from July 28 to August 16, Bryant paid $26 for "board for self and wife and daughter." In a letter to Dana he wrote: "Mrs. Bryant is all the better for her journey and her residence in your air, though it seemed to affect her unpleasantly for the time. Julia is beginning to lose the little plumpness she got at Rockport."

Some thirty-five years later the aging poet edited a two-volume work entitled *Picturesque America.* Cape Ann came in for brief notices as well as views by J. Douglas Woodward of Norman's Woe, Bass Rocks, Stage Fort Park, Thacher's Island, and Rockport from Knowlton's

Corner. There is a fine view of Pigeon Cove Point from Cedar Avenue with an enthusiastic description beginning: "Pigeon Cove, especially, has in these later days become a noted watering place; for here is not only a noble view of the waters, but the opportunity to enjoy many a delightful excursion amid lovely scenes and marvelous sculpture which nature has provided." It would be nice to think that the venerable editor, Bryant, breathed a nostalgic amen when he reached that page of his publication. From Dana, father and son, Bryant, and others were to follow in the decades ahead a procession of contented summer visitors to Rockport's "watering places."

Home Folks

The local, resident population also took their summer pleasures al fresco. An account remains of the alleged first picnic held in Rockport. The date was July 4, 1841; the place was Jabez Tarr's meadow, southeast of Deacon Abraham Pool's "mansion." The celebration "was got up by the Congregational Society" and was launched from the new meetinghouse by Pastor Wakefield Gale, who gave an address. From the church a procession marched to the picnic site where "tables were bountifully spread on the ground with a sufficient quantity of common extra fare of which invited and uninvited guests were made welcome." The following year a second picnic was held, that time in the vestry but also after an address by Mr. Gale. Gloucester, of course, had its own Glorious Fourth observances, the high spot of which was more than a thousand children in three separate Sabbath school ceremonies, extending from 8:30 A.M. to 9:30 P.M. "It is proper to observe, perhaps, that in all these festivities no wines or liquors of any kind were used."

One attraction on the Fourth in 1839 was a new military company which had recently been organized at Sandy Bay, called the Sandy Bay Rifle Corps with John W. Marshall (captain), Francis Tarr (lieutenant), and Peter Stillman (ensign). Although the officers were all active Democrats, their corps was not politically oriented. The *Telegraph*'s Whig editor, Tilden, had recently reported on the "ridiculous" performance of the Gloucester militia contingents and urged his townsmen to follow Sandy Bay's initiative and even make up a military band. "There is musical talent enough." On September 14 *Telegraph* readers learned that the Sandy Bay Rifle Corps, led by Captain Marshall, paraded on Thursday and marched to Manchester, where they encamped overnight. "It is a handsome corps, composed of a good looking set of men." All the soldiers, handsome or homely, were shaken when Governor Edward Everett failed to veto a bill eliminating the $5 bounty to every member of the Light Infantry Guard because economies had become imperative in government spending. Recklessly, Massachusetts had incurred the enormous debt of $178,000.

Yes, prices were high and the cost of living was on the upswing for residents of the newly separated town. Flour had gone up to $5.77 a barrel. The price of butter had risen so scandalously everywhere that Philadelphians were trying to organize a boycott against it, an example Cape Anners were urged to emulate: "When a soft, frothy substance, dignified by the name of butter, is brought in and 27 or 28 cents a pound is asked for it, we think there is reason for complaint."

Other irritations found their way into the newspapers at the time of the separation. The editor himself was grumbling about the wretched postal service. Copies of his publication printed on Saturday morning and deposited at the post office in Gloucester "long before the morning mail closes" seldom reached subscribers in Boston until Monday noon. They ought, he growled, to be there the same day if it weren't for "gross negligence and inattention to duty" on the part of those supposed to look after the mails.

The prolonged campaign to eliminate bounties to fishermen, however, occupied more tongues and pens and hit more homes than other issues in the early 1840s. From the first days of the republic the Congress had provided for its fishing industry. Later Jefferson admitted that "it is too poor a business to be left to itself, even with the nation most favorably situated." Along with the bounties, which at the time Rockport became independent reached some $42,000 "at this port," there was a protective tariff against foreign salt. Massachusetts alone had some 750 establishments turning out nearly 760,000 bushels a year. Mackerel catches had been poor recently, and the *Telegraph* offered for sale or auction almost each week vessels well calculated for the fishing business. The vagaries of the weather plagued fishermen, as they always have and still do. The gale of January 26, 1839, had washed ashore innumerable fish but then left the waters so troubled that not a fish could be caught anywhere in the vicinity of Cape Ann. Beneath the surface the sea had a thick, muddy appearance. Yet barely a month later the schooner *Majestic* returned on February 24 with upward of one-hundred halibut on what was said to be the earliest winter-spring trip hitherto made to the Georges Bank by a Cape Ann boat. "Since Sunday a dozen or more vessels have sailed or are preparing to."

Thus, caught in a bind between heartening statistics on the meteoric rise of fishing ventures out of Gloucester and Rockport and the necessity of poor-mouthing the situation to prevent any rocking of the boat of federal bounties, press and politicians alike kept a hawkish eye out for troubles. These soon came from Missouri's Senator Benton, described on Cape Ann as "the prolific parent of so many 'experiments' and *humbugs*." All the protectionist arguments were unveiled by the probounty forces locally, at the General Court in Boston, and in Washington. Lightning struck when the port collector of Cape Ann, Col. William Beach, "unknowingly" paid out a bounty subsidy to the *Eagle*, which patently (on investigation) failed to qualify; its cargo was not the mandatory sacred cod but mere unsupported mackerel. Protesting his innocence, the colonel-collector hastened to Washington—too late. Even his fellow Democrats in Rockport had chafed over his third term at the public trough. Although they failed to secure the appointment for their party secretary, John W. Marshall, a fellow Rockporter, George D. Hale, who had been one of the negotiators of the Gloucester-Rockport independence settlement, got the job. When the issue of bounty payments finally ground to a halt after the Civil War, wrote James Pringle, "the Cape Ann fishing interest was secretly pleased . . . as the continuance of the subsidy might prove a stimulus in building a dangerous rival."

If the bounty question was so potent that no coastal political leader would dare support a withdrawal during the 1840s, politics itself was a lively matter. Rockport, like its parent town, was hotly divided between the Whigs and the Democratic-Republicans, who soon dropped the word "Republican" from their name. Election results tell some of the story; much more is to be found in the local Cape Ann press and a surviving book of minutes kept by the Democratic Club of Rockport, 1838-46.

From their meetings, usually held at the schoolhouse of district 8, the Sandy Bay Democrats waged vigorous campaigns for the principles of natural equality and justice expounded by Jefferson and Jackson through their "ward" leaders and eighty-odd members whose names turn up in John Marshall's minute book. With regularity they sent delegates to district party conventions at Ipswich and Salem and to state roundups at Boston. Similarly, they programmed in Rockport guest speakers from Charlestown, Lowell, Salem, and Boston—all this at a time when the nearest train station was at Salem, the telegraph and telephone were scarcely dreamed of, and radio had not even been imagined. A Whig, Edward Everett, was governor; but the town had failed to send a Whig representative to the state legislature—by one vote! On one November evening Robert Rantoul, Jr., "addressed the meeting for about 3 hours with his usual eloquence." The Democrats had grasped the local political reins on Cape Ann for nearly a decade, "never permitting a solitary Whig voice to be heard in the councils of the town," grumbled editor Tilden on March 2, 1839, from his presses.

In support of the ticket of William Henry Harrison ("Tippecanoe and Tyler Too"), Cape Ann Whigs went all out, crying their nautical motto: "We will be there: blow high or blow low; we will be there: rain or shine; we will be there." And so they were, for on the day when the question of independence for Sandy Bay came up for a vote, for the first time in ten years the local Whig ticket was elected. The overjoyed *Telegraph* wrote that the successful candidates went home silently and peaceably, having too much self-respect to imitate "the boisterous shouts and exultings which have ever characterized the opposing party." It was, however, a Democratic governor, Marcus Morton, who signed the legislative approval for Rockport's independence on February 27, 1840. The new town elected two Democrats to its first board of selectmen and sent Democrats as its first two representatives to the General Court in Boston.

"Pernicious Practice"

Like politics, a number of other issues were to become perennial in the life of newly independent Rockport. One of these was alcohol. From the pulpits and the press emanated periodic exhortations to reform. In April 1840 a group of topers at Baltimore formed a "society for our mutual benefit" and pledged to give up spirituous or malt liquors, wine, and cider. Their influence took hold and spread widely. By August 1841 it had even reached Rockport. On August 30 a meeting was called at the Universalist church under the chairmanship of the Reverend Mr. John Allen. More than forty signed a pledge never again to drink any intoxicating liquors or to provide them for their friends or for persons in their employ. Two exceptions were allowed: "when prescribed by a medical attendant, or in the case of wine at communion." In addition, signers covenanted to discountenance the use of them in the community and to give their utmost to reclaim those unfortunates addicted to drunkenness.

Within a fortnight William Caldwell was chosen president; initial lectures were delivered by a Mr. Kimball from Ipswich; and soon afterward seven men and five ladies for the "Female Committee" had been installed. From their surviving minutes in the Sandy Bay Historical Society one can trace the rise and decline of the organization from 1841 to 1848. Meetings were usually held in the Universalist church, but occasionally operations were transferred to "the Orthodox Vestry," the Baptist church, and at least once to the Methodist chapel. The society's public debut was a dud: one Mr. Johnson of Boston, "a reformed inebriate" who was to have produced a "powerful lecture," failed to show up. Subsequent performances were more successful and, as the secretary noted, more spirited. By April 8, 1842, without a vote from the membership, the word "Temperance" was dropped from its name and the title abridged to the Washington Total Abstinence Society.

Already by November 1843 the inner core had found it advisable to check membership lists and note the names of those breaking their pledges. In 1844 a brave attempt was made to call on Rockport's vendors of intoxicating drinks to try to sign them up. A visit from Mr. Mars of Salem, "a colored preacher," was followed by two days of addresses by John P. Gough, a national temperance leader and an author of note on his dry subject. He played to packed houses at both the Congregational and Universalist auditoriums. Within the next fortnight about one thousand names were reported as new signatures or renewal pledges. March 7, 1845, found this item on the town meeting warrant: "That the town of Rockport disapprove of the pernicious practice of retailing intoxicating liquors and would affectionately request any person who may retail these liquors to immediately cease." In 1846 the society dispatched a note of thanks to its convert, Caleb Norwood, because "he has ceased to traffic in intoxicating liquors."

Despite "animating temperance songs," "pithy remarks" and at least one "inharmonious discussion which ended in harmony," by November 30, 1847, the minute keeper grieved that "the manifest march of intemperance in Rockport ... produced a chilly sensation on the assembled few." Nonattendance and cider drinking had become rampant. The society's final record, dated December 19, 1848, sighed: "The Committee who were chosen at the previous meeting made no

The Town Is Born

128 report." Yet during the society's life span 1,139 people, nearly half of the town's population, are said to have signed the pledge. As was pithily remarked of the Washingtonians and some lesser, latter-day abstainers: They did a good work for a season, then passed away.

Even Rockport's children had been recruited for the "COLD WATER ARMY." At a parade on July 5, 1841, they sang rousing texts like this:

> *With banner and with badge we come,*
> *An army true and strong,*
> *To fight against the hosts of Rum—*
> *And this shall be our song;*
> *We love the clear Cold Water Springs,*
> *Supplied by gentle showers;*
> *We feel the strength cold water brings,—*
> *"The victory's ours."*

The program that day had thirteen parts, of which number ten was simply "Refreshment." Was there more to be had than cold water? After "Recess" came another hymn in which the Sunday school children promised to drink no more and to repel any offers from drunkards.

> *Our youthful hearts with Temperance burn,*
> *Away, away the bowl,*
> *From dram shops all, our steps we turn,*
> *Away, away the bowl,*
> *Farewell to Rum and all its harms,*
> *Farewell the wine-cup's boasted charms,*
> *Away the bowl, away the bowl,*
> *Away, away the bowl.*

> *See how that staggering drunkard reels,*
> *Away, away the bowl;*
> *Alas, the misery he reveals,*
> *Away, away the bowl;*
> *His children grieve, his wife's in tears!*
> *How sad his once bright home appears!*
> *Away the bowl, away the bowl,*
> *Away, away the bowl.*

Town on Sandy Bay

Having banished the bowl and "the wine-cup's boasted charms," these earnest young Rockporters of 1841 had a return march to the meeting-house yard, there to sing several tunes.

Passings

Rockport had a series of deaths in its first seven years, some of them noteworthy. During the state's annual fast day, April 2 in 1840, Peter Stillman, shoemaker and ensign of the popular Sandy Bay Rifle Company, was accidentally shot "whilst a-gunning" on Dogtown Common—he who had handled firearms perhaps more than any other person in town. Another veteran slipped away at age eighty-five on November 25, 1844; at the age of sixteen Jabez Tarr had enlisted in Capt. John Rowe's company and marched to Bunker Hill. As a private he served throughout the siege of Boston in 1775, and as a corporal went south with Colonel Glover's regiment. Later he served as prize master's mate on the local *Gloucester Packet,* a letter-of-marque ship of fourteen guns. Though he was not the last surviving Revolutionary War veteran in Rockport, as has been claimed, he was the last local survivor of Rowe's Bunker Hill men. His death stimulated two lengthy press accounts replete with helpful biographical data for future historians and genealogists.

Rockport also mourned the loss of two of its admired clergy. The Reverend Mr. L. B. Hathaway, shepherd of the Baptist flock, died in 1843. Earlier, in July, 1841, the venerated David Jewett had passed away; Jewett had been pastor of the Congregational church for over 31 years and had been in retirement since 1836. By contrast, only minor response at Rockport apparently followed the demise of Presidents Harrison in April 1841 and Andrew Jackson on June 8, 1845. There was, however, considerable concern for potential fatalities from a light case of smallpox which broke out in May 1839 while negotiations for Rockport's independence were in process. Rumors forced Stephen Brown, a local miller, to run an article in the newspaper denying he had ground flour from or even been near the cargo of corn on the vessel at Sandy Bay which had come from New York and was said to have had smallpox on board.

The new town was saddened also by the deaths of two of its veteran medical patriarchs in 1841 (the elder Dr. John Manning) and in 1842 (Dr. James Goss). To the small, closely knit community, the departure of these men who had not only tended most of the inhabitants at one time or another but had served their neighbors in countless other capacities was a historical landmark. Luckily, others followed where they had led. For minor ailments, furthermore, Rockporters wishing to treat their own indispositions had half a dozen vendors of pills and other medicaments touted in each issue of the *Telegraph.*

At Sandy Bay there were William Whipple, Eben Pool, Jr., James Haskell, Reuben Brooks, Jr., and Sidney Smith; Pigeon Covers had William Tarr, Jr., and the team of D. and G. Babson. There were Dr. Brandreth's Celebrated Vegetable Universal Pills, Dr. Relfe's Vegetable Specific, Cambrian Tooth Ache Pills, British Antiseptic Dentifrice, Dumfries' Eye Wash and his "certain cure for the Itch." Other available panaceas were Relfe's Anti-Billious Pills, "for Indigestion, Loss of Appetite, Listlessness, Headache, Costiveness, Flatulence, Cholic, Billious Affections, etc." For those able to spare $1.50 for a box, Reuben Brooks, Jr., had Dr. Relfe's Women's Aromatic Pills, a surefire remedy for "Green Sickness, Palpitations of the Heart, Giddiness, Short Breath, Sinking of the Spirits, Dejection, and Disinclination to Exercise and Society." Caution: those pills were not to be taken by ladies who were pregnant or by "persons with hectic or consumptive habits."

More than pills was required to buttress the health of the new town against the sea and its recurrent menacings. Tragedy floated in the wake of the three storms of 1839. On December 15, the day after some uncommon mildness and perfectly clear weather, a violent storm blew in, destroying a new schooner from Bucksport, Maine, skippered by one Captain Nickerson. Named the *Walrus,* it struck on Flat Ground Rocks southwest of Andrews Point and was stove in. The bow and anchors caught there. The stern portion with the name was driven ashore near Pigeon Cove. The crew, all of whom were drowned, had been carrying a cargo of corn home to Maine from New York. On December 13 Judson Pool, master, set forth in the schooner *Transport* bound for Texas with a mixed cargo of lumber, tubs of butter, and other items. He, too, was hit by the gale of December 15 during which the ship was dismasted and lost Jeremiah Higgins, the mate. Repairs were instituted, but two weeks later the *Transport* capsized in a raging tempest. Pool, Murdock McLane, James Clark, and Richard Cross were rescued by the barque *Globe* and taken to Philadelphia. One crewman was lost, and it was said that parts of the hull eventually washed up on the west coast of Ireland. Ebenezer Pool noted among his papers that the vessel was insured for $2,000, about two thirds of the combined value of the ship and cargo.

Far more harmful was the October 4-5 gale in 1841 which shattered the economy of the entire settlement at Pigeon Cove. No lives were lost, but the extensive breakwater and wharf were swept away and the harbor was completely despoiled. Of the cove's sixteen boats, fourteen were entirely wrecked. Not only fishing was jeopardized: "most of the granite is shipped from this village that is used for building the various fortifications in Boston harbor and neighboring cities." Public meetings were summoned at Rockport and in Gloucester to devise measures "in aid of the late storm at Pigeon Cove." As late as January 1889 the *Gloucester Times* reprinted the saga of that storm and the names of fourteen shattered ships. In 1845 the new town mourned the loss of the schooner *Confidence* with David Parsons, its master, and his crew of eight. Two years later a safety measure was added to the 1835 lighthouse at Straitsmouth, when keeper John Davis succeeded in getting a warning buoy placed near Avery's Rock.

Rockport was jolted by its first great fire in early December 1843 when three dwellings on High Street were burned down along with two, six, or eight barns, depending on which account one reads. Several outhouses and a good deal of hay and many vegetables prudently stored for the long winter also perished in the holocaust, too extensive to be contained by Rockport's two fire engines, "an engine well manned" from Gloucester, and some 150 volunteer helpers. Widow Polly Pool "took a violent cold by being hurried out of bed" and died three weeks later.

A religious blaze inaugurated by Dr. Sylvanus Brown at this period through meetings he held in a stable on Cross Street (upper School Street) was soon extinguished. For a brief time he attracted a congregation from other, organized churches; but having disturbed public worship at the Baptist church and later at the Orthodox church, he was "taken up and imprisoned for disturbing" the peace. More happy, too, was the escape from fire when the handsomely renovated Congregational church with its new pews, galleries, ceiling, pulpit, bell, and steeple, not to forget David Kimball's munificent donation of a new clock, was struck by lightning on Sunday afternoon, July 3, 1842. "The house was surrounded and filled with the intensest light conceivable coming through the doors and windows resembling large balls of fire falling to the ground." Providentially, no one was injured and the work of reconstruction was soon begun.

The Town Is Born

Those early years were ones of constructive effort in many ways. A participant in the events wrote that the business of the town was better than an average heretofore. "About 50 dwelling houses were built in three years in town [1842-44] besides other buildings." Additions were being made to wharves within Long Cove Harbor, the unfinished breakwater of which had been breached by the October gale of 1841. The old wharf there was undermined, too, collapsing at the ell end. Reinforcements soon solved that problem. At a town meeting on April 3, 1843, voters faced the issue of equalizing their school population according to the number of children in the several school districts. Each district, it was proposed should receive a sum of not less than $130. The new school built in 1839 near Joseph Bartlett's on Cross Street had cost about $1,100 (without bell). To bring the expanding commercial ventures of Rockport into more direct touch with metropolitan markets, at the end of the decade Edward Shaw began an express freight service overland to Boston.

Less than a year after winning its independence, the young town of Rockport held a public meeting to decide what to do with the surplus money in its treasury. It was decided to retain a sufficient amount to pay off its indebtedness. Out of the balance, however, augmented by taxes, should come the funds needed for "a Town House." The total estimated costs were to be some $3,000. In a mood of confident pride the voters authorized a go-ahead. Should it prove necessary, their committee was even empowered to borrow on Rockport's nascent credit.

A number of organizations changed their names once the new town was no longer a part of Gloucester. Three such shifts which required approval of the state legislature were ecclesiastical in nature. The Baptists, who had commenced their religious life on Cape Ann at Sandy Bay rather than Gloucester Harbor, were the first to mark the independence of their town. On March 10, 1840, two weeks after incorporation of the community, they changed their corporate name to the First Baptist Society of Rockport. On March 3, 1842, the General Court decided that the fifth parish church "may hereafter take the name of the First Congregational Society in Rockport." Three years later it decreed that the "Second Universalist Society in Gloucester shall be known and called by the First Universalist Society in Rockport."

Rockport was on the march—both in the North Village and in the South Village. Allen Chamberlain's meticulously drafted map of Pi-

Town on Sandy Bay

geon Cove in 1840 well documents his point that quarrying had already upset "the quiet of the hitherto farming-fishing hamlet" which had appealed to rustic-minded visitors. In 1846 Rockport was the thirteenth town in the Massachusetts rank order of barrels of fish sold (Gloucester was fourth). In 1847 it had moved up a notch to no. 12. But by 1847 the quiet of the town was to be far more greatly upset by the building of "one of the greatest enterprises" of Rockport's history.

ADDITIONAL READING

The full text of the act of incorporation of the town of Rockport can be read in the *Journals of the Massachusetts House and Senate* for 1840, chap. 8.

A good account of the separation procedure was given by John W. Marshall in his "Rockport" in Hamilton Hurd's *History of Essex County* (Philadelphia, 1888), chap. 111.

For a comprehensive centennial survey of its activity the Steam Fire Association published a *History of the Gloucester Fire Department, 1793-1893* (Gloucester, 1892). It included material on Sandy Bay and Rockport.

The Town Is Born

Part 3

Victorian Rockport

OR THE TOWN OF ROCK-
PORT and for Britain's Queen Victoria, a new way of life began in the
bleak midwinter of 1840. Both surmounted a shattering trauma in 1861–she
the loss of her adored husband, Rockport the loss of peace and the first of
forty-two sons to war. Although at times both found it vexing to adapt to
improvements, neither turned a back on the future. Firmly they marched breast
forward, never doubting clouds would break, never dreaming wrong would
triumph. Victoria was frequently not amused; Rockport regularly was. On
anniversaries both took pride in reviewing past accomplishments. In Britain the
Victorian era closed in 1901, well after its Edwardian contrast had begun.
Victorian Rockport survived until World War I, surrendering not to a mauve
Edwardianism but to a bully, strenuous Rooseveltism.

In the seventy-five years between 1840 and 1915, Rockporters were confronted by many challenges, not the least of which were civic. Initially they had to
establish a government for their town, draw up bylaws to guide it, elect officials

135

to administer it, and create a tax structure to finance it. For their youth they had to devise a school system and then, generation after generation, restructure the plan to meet fresh demands. For their impoverished elderly they had to provide a shelter and cemeteries for their dead, as well as a hearse to carry them to the grave. For residents of all ages, streets had to be laid out with signs to identify them and lights to brighten them after dark.

How would the illumination be provided? As pumps went dry and wells became polluted, where would the town get its water and how might supply mains be laid? As the population multiplied and with it a rise in crime, what of a police force and a jail for lawbreakers? When bucket brigades and hand pumps could no longer withstand fiery threats, whence would come fire protection? A public library was no luxury by 1871. An ample town hall with a spacious auditorium was a necessity by 1869.

The souls of Rockport's righteous clamored for preachers and preachers for pulpits; the praying required pews and bells to summon them there. Churches were remodeled, expanded, newly built, for Victorian Rockporters were a meeting-going breed—most of them. Tipplers, of course, had to be taught temperance. (For "temperance" read "abstinence"). So, onward, Hannah Jumper! Forward, the Cold Water Army! Upward with ballots for women! That struggle was harder to win.

For Rockporters themselves there was no end of entertainments: fairs, collations, parades, musters, concerts, theatricals, lectures, debates, spelling bees, card parties, dances, hay rides, picnics, excursions, fights, horseracing, bowling, baseball, croquet, cycling, and—as the era drew to its climax—trolley car rides and "motoring." What other towns had, Rockport had, too—even moving pictures at the town hall.

Within the commercial sector, Victorian Rockporters functioned with considerable acumen, though often captained by shrewd out-of-towners. The establishment of a steam cotton mill in 1847 brought the town's first (and last) large factory. Enterprise built a railroad to Gloucester that same year; dogged persistence finally got its extension to Rockport in 1861. The telegraph had preceded it by nearly four years. The telephone arrived prematurely in 1881; not until 1904 would it stand on its own. From 1827 on, Rockporters had relied on Gloucester for their newspapers. By 1872, however, they were ready for a paper of their own, the Gleaner. When that monthly no longer sufficed, the Rockport Review appeared, crammed with advertisements, gossip, and hopes for the town.

As urban America developed, so did the market for Rockport's granite. Company after company dug in from the Back Beach round to Folly Cove and thence through Lanesville to Bay View. Openings, closings, transfers, and

136

mergers marked the decades as building slabs and paving blocks were shipped out by sloops, by steamer, and later by train to meet municipal needs as far away as New Orleans and San Francisco. To fill the needs of the quarry companies came immigrants from Nova Scotia, Ireland, Italy, and Scandinavia. Others arrived to man the cotton mill, the isinglass, shoe, organ, bobbin, chair, glue, and other works. To supply their many needs, in turn, Victorian Rockport sprouted houses, churches, stores, lodges, singing societies, evening schools, and bands. Bands of other types also grew stronger: mutual benefit societies, Knights of Labor, union locals. By 1900, lockouts, layoffs, and strikes had become a familiar phase of town life.

Each summer, from the cities came the hot; from the inland came the ocean lovers–in ever increasing numbers. By the end of Rockport's first decade its North Village, Pigeon Cove, had already achieved fame as a popular watering place. Boardinghouses mushroomed; hotels were constructed; real estate developments were mapped out and sold. The South End followed later: Marmion Way, Loblolly Cove, Paradise Cliff, Penzance-Tregony–and the Cornish corner. Turk's Head Inn loomed above its inlet, as Straitsmouth Inn did over its. Tennis courts, a yacht club, masquerades, lawn parties, artists' easels, carriages for hire, excursion boats–these became as common as Rockport's exuberant baseball teams. As summer visitors paid more fiddlers, they understandably called more tunes.

There were two notable exceptions. From 1884, the year Rockport became the American terminal for the Commercial Cable Company's transatlantic cable, life in Rockport was dominated by the gargantuan plan for a breakwater which would transform the town into a Harbor of Refuge comparable to that at Brest in France. To that harbor should come transatlantic ocean liners, and there would be based the North Atlantic Fleet of the expanding U.S. Navy. No liners ever made it. But for years there were regular summer visits from minelayers, torpedo boats, cruisers, and even battleships from the navy. They and their crews, preceded by the trolley car system and followed by the advent of the automobile, marked the end of Victorian Rockport and its epilogue as "Our Town."

13

INTO THE 1850s

Festive

AS ROCKPORT rounded out the first decade of its independence and moved into the 1850s with a new mill, it acquired a varied coloration: festive, patriotic, somber, industrious, depending on the mood of the moment and the observer's point of view. For many the 1850s brought festive occasions. Take the influx of summer visitors, for example, drawn there as by a magnet. Within but a brief span, the attractions had been touted by word of mouth, by letters, and increasingly by print. In March 1849, to cite one widely circulated account, the *National Pictorial Library* ran "Sketches of Cape Ann," written and illustrated by F. A. Durivage. These proclaimed that the area had become a favorite resort for summer tourists, presenting all the attractions and requisites to be desired. In fact, "no where else upon our seaboard has nature been so prodigal of her charms."

Easily reached by the Eastern Railroad at a fare of 90 cents one way or by the fast sailing steamer *Jacob Bell,* which took passengers for 40 cents, the two townships offered many fine views of waves, sand, bold headlands, pleasant valleys, vast sweeps of woodland, as well as pellucid Cape Pond and bold Pigeon Hill with its prospects "at once delightful and sublime." Up above Pigeon Cove, continued Durivage, lies "Tragabigzanda House," the residence of Mr. William Norwood, Jr., a place full of boarders in the summer season where one can enjoy every comfort "and have the pleasure of associating with an amiable

138

Fish houses at Blubber Hollow, Folly Cove, as illustrated in the September, 1875 issue of "Harper's Monthly Magazine."

and well-regulated family. The walks, rides, and fishing in this vicinity are unsurpassed, and the facilities for seabathing are also unrivalled." The Wheelers had given up the old tavern, built a place of their own in 1846, then enlarged it, and inaugurated the popular Pigeon Cove House.

Across the way stood the Old House, once used as a garrison during the troubled times of early colonial history. Other places selected by the author for comment was the property of John Grover, "a perfect mass of clapboards, shingles, spliced beams, and dilapidated supports." The cattle in the barn had to cope with flooring at a 45 degree angle, with the result that on being turned out to pasture they were unable to stand, having grown "into a sort of bovine kangaroos." For many, Dogtown Common conjured up legends, freaks, pranks, and witch scenes of a Faustian nature. Folly Cove and beyond, on the contrary, he found pastoral, rich, and productive, while the lighthouses of the Cape offered attractions of yet another fashion. No mention of fishing or quarrying sullied the sketcher's account, but he did incorporate six illustrations, including "The Old Garrison House," the "Ancient Barn at Rockport," and a "View from Folly Point and Cove."

Into the 1850s

Great attention, he noticed, was locally paid to education. "One can hardly go half a mile without finding a school-house." Perhaps those accounted for the inhabitants being "intelligent, industrious and moral." Durivage found that many of the Cape's finer specimens "have attained to wealth by industry and enterprise. The local society is agreeable, the social virtues being cultivated to an eminent degree." Eleven years before the fact, he disclosed that a history of Gloucester and Rockport had been for some time in preparation "by J. J. Babson, Esq. and cannot fail to be an interesting and valuable addition to the large stock of our local New England histories."

Yes, the discovery of Pigeon Cove had indeed led many visitors to the old tavern, to the Norwoods, and to the Garrison House—most of them forgotten now. While relishing the hospitable charm of the Garrison House, Thomas Wentworth Higginson explored Dogtown Common and its network of footpaths. In his *Atlantic Monthly* papers he incorporated a lengthy report of his meanderings: "I used to wander in those woods summer after summer," he recalled. Later, down at busy "Oldport" (Newport, Rhode Island) Higginson yearned to exchange the incessant roll of carriages for the peace of Pigeon Cove. "I hear the tinkle of the quaryman's [sic] hammer and the veery's song, and I long for those perfumed and breezy pastures, and for those promontories of granite where the fresh water is nectar and the salt sea has a regal blue." Another literary couple who would be charmed by "Susannah's Cottage" at Rockport's North Village during the Civil War was publisher James T. Fields of the Old Corner Book Store and his talented young wife, Annie. In 1865, however, they shifted to Manchester, where they tried poetically to rename the town Manchester-by-the-Sea, an effort which led Oliver W. Holmes to list his address, waggishly, as Beverly-by-the-Depot.

Two major literary figures took kindly to Rockport in the 1850s: Thoreau and Emerson. The former and his friend John Russell undertook a walking tour of Cape Ann, a description of which is to be found in Thoreau's *Journal* for late September 1858. Having put up in Gloucester, they tramped to the Farms next morning before veering across the marsh to the shore near Salt Island. The wildflowers, birds, sea grasses, and the bare, boulder-covered back of the Cape caught Thoreau's eye: "That would be a good place to walk." Using dead bayberry bushes, the men kindled a fire and cooked their midday tea under the lee of a boulder opposite Straitsmouth Island.

Town on Sandy Bay

"Rockport well deserves its name,—several little rocky harbors protected by a breakwater, the houses at Rockport Village backing directly on the beach." Thoreau smiled at the number and variety of "bevelled" roofs on the Cape. "Surprising!—some are so nearly flat that they remind me of the low brows of monkeys." On the hikers pushed to Folly Cove, "a wild rocky point running north, covered with beach grass." Just before sundown they struck south across the common and boiled their evening tea water with more dried bayberry twigs. "Two oxen feeding in the swamp came up to reconnoitre our fire. We could see no house, but hills strewn with boulders, as if they had rained down, on every side ... we heard a squawk, and, looking up, saw five geese fly low in the twilight over our heads." Back at Gloucester, Thoreau noted in his final entry that there was a scarcity of fresh water on the Cape, "so that you must carry your water a good way in a dipper."

Emerson made visits of quite a different style when he descended on Rockport. Like Thoreau, he had been a lecturer at the Gloucester Lyceum. On August 6, 1855, he wrote to a friend, "I took a pair of holidays to go with Mr. Bartol [the Universalist minister] to Pigeon Cove last week." What he saw must have delighted him, for he returned there with his entire family the following year, "transporting the whole cage, young birds and old." The Reverend Mr. Bartol handled the arrangements, and, wrote Emerson playfully, "has made some kind of cavity, I believe, where we can nest, and the nidification is 15 July. . . . The original charm of Pigeon Cove is magnificent sea beach, which my young things have never seen." In his *Journal* of July 23, 1856, the philosopher-poet-essayist penned one of his many rhapsodic passages—this one on making the acquaintance with the sea at Pigeon Cove. In later years that text was inscribed in metal and placed on a rock at Andrews' Point. Regrettably, fear of vandals made it advisable to move the plate to safety at the Old Castle at the cove, but the Emersonian visit is still recalled by the hotel bearing his name.

To be sure, not all summer visitors to Rockport, then or now, found the place to their liking. Robert Carter, together with three friends, chartered a sloop in 1858 to make an excursion from Provincetown to Bar Harbor. Their narrative, published as *A Summer Cruise on the Coast of New England,* quickly became a minor classic. On Wednesday, July 14, they set their course for Rockport. Off Thacher's Island they encountered a fleet of large sloops, laden with granite from Rockport, being taken to Boston. After the vacationers rounded the Headlands, they anchored "in the middle of this curious little port, which is partly artificial, and will shelter fifty or sixty small vessels." Following a supper of cunners and bread, they retired to their bunks in a dark fog.

Next morning, in a dense mist they rowed ashore for breakfast, cheered by the prospect of meeting local Rockporters described in "the veracious Gazeteer of Hayward" as being distinguished for their enterprise in the fisheries and thereby "serviceable to their country abroad, and fit companions for its intelligent and rosy-cheeked damsels at home." To their annoyance, they found themselves at Long Cove, "on a dirty beach, covered with the decaying offal of fish, the stench of which was almost suffocating." Happily, the center of the large and prosperous-looking village provided a postal service and a chance to buy so much "soft tack" that the baker stared and gasped in amazement. Back on board they found the smell of rotten fish so disagreeable that even their tobacco fumes couldn't smother the fishy odors from the shore. Accordingly, they upped anchor and, encouraged by horn blasts ashore, made it safely across to Pigeon Cove. There the harbor, "partly artificial," was protected from the ocean by a high granite wall. It was filled with vessels taking refuge from the fog. Consoled by their claret, a huge lobster, and many songs, the quartet turned in at midnight, awoke on Friday to sunshine, and sailed off via Halibut Point on their course down east.

On Monday, August 21, 1859, the boarders at the Pigeon Cove House sponsored a "regatta" near the Pigeon Cove breakwater. The course ran from there out around a stake boat about half a mile from the pier and back again. There were three laps to be made by the wherries. The cove was alive with boats, according to the press report, "some of which were rowed by the fair sex with a skill and dexterity that would leave altogether in the shade some of the sterner sex." Furthermore, the pier and the opposite shore were lined with spectators, a majority of whom were ladies who entered into the spirit of the thing "with a right good will." The participants in the regatta were two men, a George Dove of Andover and Emily Dickinson's friend the Reverend Mr. T. W. Higginson, who wore black pants, a red shirt, and a cap trimmed with red. Seated in the stern of each wherry was a lady, dressed to correspond with the gentlemen. The first lap found Higginson far behind, owing, perhaps, to "the bewitching glances of one of Boston's fairest daughters who was seated opposite him." A second, noncompeting rower was Pigeon Cove's own David Babson, who for

Town on Sandy Bay

some reason did not return. At the end the clergyman triumphed, and "the cheers that greeted him upon his arrival were loud and prolonged."

Another popular pastime was the drive around the Cape. The *Advertiser* on September 25, 1858, reported on a "Ride to Rockport" and urged readers to take such an excursion. It spoke of the many improvements, of the town's thrifty appearance, and of the neatness of its buildings and the elegance of many private dwellings. Singled out for approbation were the "beautiful estate of J. Sanborn, Esq." and the nursery of John Parsons, which "reflects great credit on its proprietor." Where once there had been an extremely barren lot, "commonly called Hard Scrabble," by dint of filling and clearing of rocks, the tract was full of fruit and ornamental trees. The rider recommended William Allerton's newly opened oyster and refreshment saloon in Johnson's building near the Front Beach, where there was "good accommodation for parties who are traveling that way and may need refreshments in the shape of one of those oyster stews which Allerton alone can produce."

It was not only out-of-towners who found opportunities for festivities in Rockport during the 1850s. Not to be outdone by Pigeon Cove, Rockport's South End had also geared itself up for hospitality. In 1848 the Mt. Pleasant House opened, primarily for summer visitors, though also as a center for local festivities. One of the more

Lithograph of the Mt. Pleasant House on Cove Hill when it was one of Rockport's early inns. In 1856, it was one of the targets of Hannah Jumper's Hatchet Gang. (SBHS)

Into the 1850s

jovial was a May festival held there in 1852. It commenced down in town with a parade led by the Rockport Brass Band, behind which a banner proclaimed: "Leap Year's coming once in four, Give the ladies one chance more." This was followed by fifty couples, the women wearing white sunbonnets with a wreath of roses, "which were worn upon their heads during the evening." Their swains wore the popular "Kossuth hats, which gave them a very interesting appearance."

After two or three hours "pleasantly whiled away" with the various amusements prepared for the occasion, the procession marched to the Mt. Pleasant House, where several colors were suspended across the street, which greatly enlivened the scene, and the rooms were "very tastefully decorated with evergreens and roses." Of course, the tables "groaned" beneath the foods "at the festal board." A pyramid of cake rose nearly two feet high. It contained four rings, "which created some little excitement as to who would be so fortunate as to find them"—not enough excitement, however, to wrest the secret from the reporter whose account ended thus: "In the evening, several innocent amusements were proposed, in which the company engaged with spirit and animation." Readers were assured that the company broke up at a reasonable hour, highly gratified with the proceedings of the day.

Less jocund were gatherings in churches, homes, and halls, such as the first Sunday school concert held in Rockport. In 1855 Baptist youngsters presented a "happening" at their meetinghouse, which was ornamentally trimmed with evergreen trees and artificial flowers. The young people spoke "select pieces" and "select hymns" were sung. The collection taken up was used to purchase select books for the Sunday school.

Even franker glimpses can be had from the diary kept by Austin Wheeler Story of Pigeon Cove in 1853 at the age of twenty-four. In Boston, where he studied bookkeeping, he saw the play of *Uncle Tom's Cabin* and enjoyed himself very much. More gripping was "the notorious Mr. Forest" in the *Tragedy of Metamora* and the circus at Charlestown Street. So, too, were the lectures on many varied topics he attended. Yet back on Cape Ann he shared the joys of Mr. Stimson's Singing School, however imperfect it was, the Sons of Temperance meetings, and playing his violin. In February he confided, "there was a dance at the hall this evening; quite a crowd was there. I was there and danced two Cotillions. I got home at 10½ o'clock." Another evening

I was at Mr. Rowe's to attend a Party. Quite a large company was there. Among the number was Handsome Dolly who has created such a sensation in town. Her Beauty did not suit my fancy, however it might have pleased others. Although she had a handsome face, yet she was rather too familiar with the beaux to suit my ideas of female loveliness. Virtue beaming from the countenance has a higher estimation in my mind than either Coquetry, or Paint. I did not enjoy myself very well at the Party and left an hour or two before it was done. The most of the company seemed to enjoy themselves highly, and I do not wonder at it, if a plenty of kissing will bring happiness; for there was a plenty of kissing there.

Patriotic

A sense of parochial patriotic pride gripped many Rockporters in the 1850s. Beginning in 1852, the Reverend Mr. Gale, turned his attention to his church's centennial. On March 25, postponed from a stormy eighteenth, he lectured for an hour and a half on the earlier years of the Congregationalists and their first resident minister, Ebenezer Cleaveland.

On March 1, 1853, three days before Franklin Pierce became president of the United States, the venerable Dr. William Ferson made a gift to Rockport. He had practiced at Sandy Bay for a few years after the turn of the century but moved on to Gloucester, where among his many public services he had been town treasurer from 1822 to 1830. There in the files he found the first tax assessment list for the Sandy Bay parish (1754). He donated it to Rockport through his friend and fellow antiquarian, Ebenezer Pool, with a request that "it may be preserved for an Ancient Relic to all posterity." In his letter he reminded that "such epochs are generally noted by a celebration, by a discourse on the events of the century that has been lost in the ocean of Time." Two weeks later, the Rockport annual town meeting voted on a motion of Alfred C. Pool to select a committee of ten to choose a suitable person to prepare and deliver such a history. The members, "consisting in part of aged men," presented a unanimous invitation to Dr. Lemuel Gott to prepare the address.

The great day came but with it such a northeast snowstorm that from Thursday evening, December 29, until Monday evening, January 2, 1854, no trains got through from Salem to Gloucester. Hence, many an out-of-towner was unable to reach the Congrega-

Order of Exercises for the 1854 celebration of Rockport's centennial as a separate parish. Featured is Dr. Lemuel Gott's two-part address. (SBHS)

tional church for the double session. A similar fate befell the guest organist hired from Boston, who had been snowed in while on a tour in Vermont. Blizzard and cold notwithstanding, the observances were held. Dr. Gott's address, which required two and a half hours, would form the first portion of the *History of Rockport* (1888). Perhaps its length explains why those assembled were highly gratified with Samuel J. Giles's "Voluntaries on the Organ" and the singing. Ebenezer Pool had hammered out a hymn to be rendered to "America," some of the texts admittedly "borrowed." Because of the prolonged lecture, however, only four of the seven printed stanzas were sung, "though all read." Two others never saw print, nor did his exegisis on his lines. So Rockporters celebrated their first centennial with patriotic fervor and filial piety.

Charged by the success of their patriotic observances in the deep midwinter, they began to plan in April for a stirring centennial Fourth of July. And what an extravaganza they did mount! By May there were subcommittees, committees, and an executive committee. "The whole people were awake and interested in the work." The money raisers gathered up $600 to $700 for music, fireworks, a speaker, and other necessities. An enormous tent, capacious enough to shelter over six hundred people, was unfurled for placement in William Norwood's pasture on the Headlands, and the ladies had promised a collation.

The day itself was as hot and stifling as the January holiday had been icy and blustery. Beginning at sunrise, church bells, augmented by the pealer of the cotton mill, clanged for half an hour. A patriotic prelude was sounded by booming cannon, as people poured into town. At ten o'clock the parade formed at the head of Broadway, spilling back down along Main Street. Of this a full description was recorded in the *Gloucester Telegraph* four days later and in the town *History* thirty-four years after that. A band from faraway Chelsea; an artillery company from Gloucester; some 150 lodge members in full regalia, one carrying a very elegant silk banner presented by the ladies; a carriage trundling "five of our eldest citizens" (motto, "Our Fathers"); and Engine Company no. 3 (in blue trousers, red shirts, glazed caps) were led by marshals and augmented by the Goddess of Liberty, by Justice, Peace, and the Four Seasons, all riding in carriages "appropriately trimmed."

Schools no. 1 (the "Girls in Bloomer costume") and no. 4 were followed by Stars (nine girls "driven by a negro boy"); Morning, Noon, and Night; plus Faith, Hope, and Charity. All of the Sunday school children of Rockport were in attendance, dressed in a uniform for the occasion. Schools no. 2 and 5 ("Truth is our Guide") were divided by Purity (twelve young ladies) and followed by thirty-two lovely representatives of the thirty-two states. The banner for School no. 1 read, "Tall oaks from little acorns grow." Behind this cantered "Indian and Turk on horseback," "Old Folks at Home" (with a spinning wheel), Flora's Bower, and Modesty (sheltered by a full white veil). Bringing up the rear lumbered a glee club of five ladies "in various dresses" and two gentlemen as troubadours.

The parade marched heroically up and down Rockport's decorated, arch-covered, banner-decked highways until on arriving at the intersection of King and Granite streets it abandoned plans to proceed to Pigeon Cove. A week of temperatures between 90 and 100 degrees in the shade, collapsing schoolchildren, and a number of sunstruck artillery company men (Henry Pearce was "insensible several hours") forced the committee on arrangements to alter the line of march. Hence, about 1:30 P.M. the dripping vanguard staggered into the Pavillion at the Headlands. Over the massive spread the Reverend Mr. A. C. L. Arnold sounded a grateful blessing, after which the attention of the company was devoted to the viands before them, which included beef, meats, tongues, bacon, and more. Yet enough was left over after everyone had been satiated to provide quite a surplus for the needy next day.

More praying, a reading of the Declaration of Independence by Lemuel Gott, an-hour-and-a-half address by orator-abolitionist C. M. Ellis of Boston who received $150 as a fee, and yet another hour of "pertinent and short speeches" were reinforced by at least eight toasts, the last two of which were for Chelsea's hired brass band ("May they live to blow long for the gratification of their patrons") and for the young ladies of Rockport ("May they make better wives than their mothers"). Thanks to generous David Kimball, the local boys had a handsome supply of "Chinese explosives," which they were very discreet in touching off. Finally, during the evening there was a grand display of brilliant fireworks and, from the Chelseaites, "some excellent music, including several very popular airs." According to the newspapers, good order was preserved both day and night. There were only two or three arrests for imbibing too freely—and the boozers' supply had been secured from out of town. Gloucester complimented its patriotic neighbors thus: "The whole celebration was highly creditable to the energy, enterprise and taste of our neighbors."

Town on Sandy Bay

Watercolor by Albert Heinze of the early schoolhouse on the southwest corner of Main Street and Railroad Avenue in 1888. Converted to the home of William G. Brooks, it remains a residence today. (SBHS)

Such a production could be staged in a small town only infrequently. Yet the Fourth of July consistently evoked observances. In 1858 two collections elicited about $50 for fireworks, which were displayed between nine and ten o'clock in the evening, and again, "what is worthy of notice, not a man was seen drunk from liquor bo't in Rockport during the day."

Sober

Sobriety in a number of guises touched the lives of Rockporters during the 1850s. As always, along the coast there were storms and other hardships from the weather. In 1851 several local vessels were driven ashore far above the high-water mark. Sails, lumber, fish-drying equipment were washed to sea; the beacon on the Londoner Rock was carried away; the Sandy Bay pier was damaged at an estimated $3,000; and Pigeon Cove's David Babson was faced with a $2,000 loss. Along the Rockport shore, water reached into houses, obliging residents to evacuate. The wharfinger's office floated off, the barns of Dr. Haskell and James Manning were imperiled, and that of James Parsons crashed and sank. For two days the Gloucester branch of the railroad was out of service because of flooding and washouts near Manchester, while along the Lynn marshes the Eastern Railroad was buried out of sight for nearly a mile.

Only a fortnight before, Oliver Stevens and Jonathan Tarr, both experienced seamen, got caught in a freak "flaw" while returning to Long Cove from Boston, were washed overboard, and drowned. Stevens's body was never recovered, but a moving service was held for the men by Mr. Gale, who remarked solemnly that "they sank like lead in the mighty waters." Before the decade was out, on September 5, 1858, another Tarr fisherman, "quiet, sober" George, was also lost overboard. The death of James Story of Pigeon Cove came on December 17, 1851. At eighty, like veteran Jabez Tarr, who had preceded him the decade before, he was a special link to the town's past. His obituary noted that he was the last person in Rockport or Gloucester pensioned under the act of 1818. A month later, on January 21, the ninety-year-old Isaac Rowe likewise passed on, "the last male Revolutionary pensioner on this Cape." Later that year the schooner *Parkhurst,* John Turner, master, went to the bottom with nine men.

On November 27, 1852, the town was sobered by another "smart shock" shortly before midnight. It lasted nearly a minute, began like distant thunder, rattled windows, shook houses, and then gave a "rumbling noise as though made by a heavy team passing over frozen ground." In 1853 three corpses were brought home to their residences within a few rods of each other on High Street: James Stockman on February 26 (a teacher), Nehemiah Boynton in March (a student at Phillips Andover Academy), and Thomas O. Marshall (a former legislator, selectman, and customhouse inspector who fell into the hold of a ship in Boston and died instantly on April 7, a fast day).

Rockport's original burial ground had finally been fully occupied. Next, the Union Cemetery had been promoted as a private commercial venture. By 1855 the town itself was obliged to acquire additional land for interments. Within two years it purchased for $525 what soon became Beech Grove Cemetery. A similar sum was laid out for improvements in 1856, and in 1857 Pleasant Street was extended to provide ready access. On a cold windy morning in November 1856 the area was consecrated by a choir and the Congregational, Methodist, Universalist, and second Congregational ministers, the Baptist parson being absent from town. On the heels of the service commenced the sale of the fifteen by twenty foot lots. Two years before, the North

Villagers had been "accommodated" by the purchase of land in Lanesville adjacent to a private cemetery. Some 170 lots of eighteen by twenty feet made up the nucleus of today's Locust Grove, additions being made in 1869, 1870, and subsequently. It seems that no formal consecration ceremonies were conducted for that cemetery, however.

Two monumental funereal efforts succeeded in the 1850s, but one failed. The first was the vote of $50 by the town in 1854 to raise a monument to Rockport's first settler, Richard Tarr, donor of the original burial plot. That same year, several descendants of John Pool appointed a committee of seven Pools to raise funds from among other Pools to pay for a fence around the graves of John Pool and his first three wives. That venture was not implemented, though on October 22, 1872, the remnants of those four pioneers were exhumed—"a few bits of rusty iron, remains of nails and metalic trimmings, some bones, soft and crumbly, with fine fibres of roots." Placed in a neat box, they were reinterred in the old burial ground, and John Pool's headstone from 1727 was reset to mark his last resting place.

Rockport's climactic solemnity was the reinterment of David Jewett, cherished first church minister of some thirty years. Retiring in 1836, he died five years later, "probably of softening of the brain, the effect of severe mental labors," and was buried at Waltham. In 1855, however, his Rockport friends pleaded that his body be returned to their keeping like a saintly relic. Jewett's family consented, and on Sunday, July 13, 1856, in the presence of nearly two thousand mourners, "many of whom were affected even to tears," he was reburied in Rockport. Three of the men present at Jewett's ordination fifty-one years before acted as pallbearers; William Choate had been sexton at the original meetinghouse in 1800. Over the grave was erected a fifteen-foot polished granite shaft with a marble inscription. Three years later widow Jewett was laid beside her "relict."

Other grave reminders of life's evanescence were the year-end gale of 1853-54, making roads and railroads impassable for several days, the subzero weeks that followed, and the great blizzard of mid-January 1857 in which stage drivers Levi and Edward Shaw carried mail to Gloucester on foot. For over a week no mail came into Rockport. On Friday, January 23, the brig *Waverly* went ashore on Milk Island in a temperature of 18 degrees below zero. Despite the hazards, a crew of Rockporters got a lifeboat to the stranded vessel and rescued the frostbitten sailors, though many of the rescuers were in turn frostbitten. Much of the *Waverley*'s cargo of coffee was saved in a damaged condition and the brig later refloated. The day after the wreck Rockport Harbor was frozen from Pigeon Cove to Straitsmouth, "as to appear as if in one sheet, the ice cakes all touching together. . . . It was never before so seen."

Industrious

What did Rockport look like at mid-century? The federal census of 1850 added a number of new features, some of which are of particular interest to local historians. The town had 442 dwellings, which in turn housed 680 families—an average of over 1.5 families per house. These families consisted of 3,264 individuals; as a decade previously, males (1,710) outnumbered the females (1,554). The life span had increased somewhat, for Rockport had 17 octogenarians in 1850 plus "Gammy" Rowe, who had reached age ninety-five. An overwhelming number of Rockporters (85 percent) were natives of Massachusetts, but some 180 had moved down from Maine, 61 from New Hampshire, 22 from Vermont. A northeastward migration had brought up 20 New Yorkers, 8 from New Jersey, 6 from Connecticut, and a pair of Pennsylvanians. Canada had contributed 45 from Nova Scotia and 3 from New Brunswick. From Europe had arrived 15 Scots, 8 English, and 1 lone Portuguese. Thanks to the Irish famines, as early as 1850 Rockport had acquired 107 Irish-born inhabitants—an influx which would soon be felt in the schools, churches, and occupational structure of the town. The town meeting that year voted $20 for a strip of land to widen the road and make a wall "between the Irish house, so-called, and the house of Mr. Canney"—up on "Paddy Hill."

Also for the first time, the census of 1850 recorded occupations. In all, 1,080 males over fifteen were queried. To no one's surprise 347 categorized themselves as "fishermen," while another 132 used the term "mariner"—a total of 479 directly following the sea. Closely related to these pursuits were 3 sailmakers, 1 ship's carpenter, 3 inspectors of fish, possibly 2 "graders," 2 lighthouse keepers, and 2 customhouse officers. Thus, 45.5 percent of the employed men of the town that autumn were tightly hitched to the ocean.

The next most numerous category was stonecutter (171, or 15.8 percent) thanks to the quarries, followed by 130 men (12 percent) who gave "none" as their reply. For the most part, these unemployed responders were older men or young teenagers (fifteen to seventeen). Farmers accounted for 58, carpenters for 47, masons for 8, and house painters for 5. Merchants totaled another 40 plus 6 clerks. Already the newly built duckmill was taking on male workers as well as unnumbered girls; 27 men were employed in cotton manufacturing. The town provided a living for 25 blacksmiths, 1 machinist, an iron foundryman, and a tinplate worker (tinsmith?). In addition to 13 shoemakers, Rockport had 7 cordwainers, 6 chair makers and 2 cabinet makers.

The carriage trade, over and above the blacksmiths, was served by 1 wheelwright, a harness maker, and 1 stage driver, coachman, teamster, and expressman each. Six coopers made barrels and 4 tailors turned out clothes, mainly for the men, since most women did their own sewing or relied on dressmakers in 1850. Three bakers, 2 butchers, and 2 innholders attended to inner needs, not to mention the 3 physicians, a "botanic physician," and a surgeon-dentist. Things of the spirit were cared for by 3 clergymen and 3 teachers. Finally, in September 1850, Rockport had 1 jeweler, 1 postmaster, a town clerk, a printer, an engineer, 1 lawyer, a soap manufacturer, a "trader," a pedlar, and for its 1,710 males, 1 single barber! These were the men, together with their sisters and their cousins and their aunts, not to mention their mothers, wives, and daughters, who sent Rockport into the 1850s. It was the distaff side who unflinchingly demonstrated which was the weaker sex. By the time inarticulate Hannah Jumper (spinster, seamstress, seventy-five), Tete Lane (termagant, wife,

Hannah Jumper (1781-1865), instigator of the Hatchet Gang Raid, the temperance assault on Rockport's public and private liquor stocks on July 8, 1856. (SBHS)

Into the 1850s

seventy-three), and their gang of 60 hatchet-wielding women (average age forty-seven) had sung their victory hymn before several hundreds in Dock Square that hot July afternoon in 1856 many a thirsty Rockporter would have questioned which was the fairer sex—in both senses of the word. July 8 was a watershed in local history.

To be sure, attempts had been made to control excessive drinking from the earliest days of the settlement. Vendors of spirits were legally bound to present good-conduct certificates in order to secure their sellers' licenses. The "Bay Tent of Rechabites" was put up on March 11, 1847; it soon claimed membership of over one hundred abstainers. Yet liquor flowed unchecked. Rockport's "Smellin' Committee" of four, appointed by the 1856 town meeting to enforce the statutes, went down in defeat before open defiance. It was estimated that the sale of spirits (legal and il-) had climbed 250 percent in four years. The time for talk had ended.

After some days or even weeks, perhaps, of secret planning, on a dry July morning five angry women, armed with hatchets, flaunting an unbleached cotton banner bearing a black-painted hatchet and crimson velour tassels, converged on the heart of Rockport. They were accompanied by Joseph Griffin with his American flag. Behind them marched their henchpersons. "Up and at 'em" was the battle cry. By the end of their five-hour blitz the mob had raided thirteen illegal vending establishments, houses, barns, a pigpen, and privies; had split fifty barrels; and had destroyed some $700 worth of spirits. In the words of narrator Parsons, Rockport "was like a mammoth punch bowl from which the smell of rum drifted for two miles across the bay." The following day the *Gloucester Telegraph* weazled that though "mob law is *always* wrong" the women in their good work "had seldom been equalled and *never* excelled." It took the Massachusetts bar two trials, two reviews, a bevy of lawyers, hundreds of dollars (much of which was put up by John Stimson, of granite fame), and three and a half years before a jury of the superior court after eighteen hours of deliberation found that the defendants had committed no trespass.

Buoyed up by their initial successes, the women of the gang turned out in large numbers in July 1858, held a procession, and celebrated their victory at Justice Lemuel Shaw's court. The *Advertiser* of August 28 reported that a flag with the motto "Hon. Judge Shaw forever— Justice and Truth" had been swaying in the Rockport breezes for a month. In October, they again assembled and marched to the lockup, where they demanded the keys in order to destroy some impounded casks of liquor. When refused, "a strong minded female" poured out a string of invectives which well nigh overpowered the officer. "We think the Rockport ladies," commented the *Cape Ann Advertiser,* "are acquiring an unenviable notoriety." The town acquired the status of prohibitory, which it still maintains.

In general, the 1850s found Rockporters employing their industry on more constructive projects. Spirits of a different genre, for example, were looked after by the churches. The influx of foreign born meant that Roman Catholics needed to be ministered unto. Thus, on February 17, 1850, the town had its first mass, when Father John McCabe of Salem officiated in Caleb Norwood's "Tavern Hall." When treks to church in Gloucester proved burdensome, land was found on Broadway in 1856 and a chapel erected there. Father Luigi Acquarone was the first priest to serve the community on a regular basis. Protestants, too, went through another infusion of religious revivals. According to Ebenezer Pool, in February and March 1853 some fifty were "born again" when the Messrs. Driver and Gale sponsored several weeks of united meetings two to four evenings per week. At a joint session on April 8 some 140 "rose by invitation to acknowledge their hope in the great salvation, or to express their desire to become subjects of Sovereign Grace."

On the Ides of March 1855, a second Congregational church was organized, when sixteen members from the overcrowded first church were "dismissed" for the purpose. David Bremner, the associate pastor to the Reverend Mr. Gale, was ordained on May 2. Later that year a group of stockholders raised some $4,000 to buy a lot on the corner of Broadway and School Street to build a chapel. Today it serves as a Masonic Hall and senior citizens center. In 1858 the Methodists, who had split with the New England Conference in 1843 on the slave issue, returned to the denominational fold and got a new preacher, David Mason. At the time of his death in 1863 he was chairman of Rockport's school committee. At Pigeon Cove a Sunday school was organized on May 31, 1857, at Woodbury's Hall, above the Union Store. That November it moved to the district schoolhouse. The initial enrollment was forty. Meetings were held in the evening with various clergymen officiating, but with Lyman B. Stockman serving as superintendent and Ellen H. Gott as his right hand.

Less exalted were three organizations of a more secular nature. A Young Men's Christian Association was organized in 1859 and took premises in a hall over Joseph Bartlett's store on School Street for its

The building on the northwest corner of Broadway and School Street was built for the short-lived Second Congregational Church and later became the Odd Fellows Hall as shown in this 1907 photograph. It is now the headquarters of the Ashler Lodge of Masons. (Hoyt)

first decade, after which it purchased the chapel of the disbanding Second Congregational Society. On May 23, 1848, twenty men formed the Granite Lodge of the Odd Fellows (IOOF), "to promote good morals, to watch over and provide for the needy." Initiation cost $10 and dues $3 annually. By 1858 the Odd Fellows had sixty members and had paid out that year $150 to disabled brothers. In January 1851 a group assembled at the home of Eben Blatchford with a view toward establishing a Masonic lodge in Rockport. The charter for the Ashler Lodge was dated March 12, 1852. There were eleven founding fathers, but by 1859 it had forty-two members. Its name means "free stones as they come out of the quarry."

Civic Changes

Another example of good works undertaken by Rockporters of the period was the purchase of a farm for the poor. Proposed in 1846 as a use for surplus revenue, the idea came to fulfillment in 1851 and 1852 when $600 was voted to buy four acres from William Young on South Street. The almshouse was completed and Sylvester Pierce named

Town on Sandy Bay

superintendent at $250 per year, plus free rent, fuel, and food for his family. Nehemiah Knowlton succeeded him in 1855 for $25 per year less, a post he held until the Civil War began.

Several other municipal improvements were effected by the town during the dozen years preceding the Civil War. In 1848 a light beacon was placed on the Headlands at an appropriation of $40. A police officer was charged with seeing that Rockport streets were kept clean of incumbrances and "nuisances"; that dogs should be taxed $1 per year, collared, muzzled, and tagged with the owner's name by April 1, 1849; and that any found loose could be killed by any inhabitant of this town. A bounty of $1 per dead dog was to be paid, though a $5 fine was imposed on any dog brought into town from outside in order to get the fee. By 1855, however, the voters decided that dogs might run at large so long as they wore wire muzzles. Those without muzzles could still be shot by anyone, though the bounty was reduced to $0.50. In 1850 graveyard guardians were assigned to keep out "foot passers and others" and to prosecute trespassers. That same year the police were instructed to carry out laws against gambling. One Rockporter was authorized to sell spirits "for medical purposes or the arts and sciences only and not as a common drink." A list was kept of purchasers and the quantities they received.

Of a more civic nature still were improvements to the water supply in the form of reservoirs for Cove Hill (1850-51) and Main Street near John Thurston's home (1855). In the mid-decade, the townspeople paid for a lockup, courtroom, and a room for Engine Company no. 3, which was to be moved to the place occupied by Engine Company no. 2. This new lockup would be the scene of the confrontation with the Hatchet Gangers in 1858.

A series of damaging blazes took place during those years. The barns of Asa Todd (1855), Andrew Bickford (1857), and Charles Tarr (1859) burned down. Thompson's blacksmith shop by the pier was totally destroyed by fire in October 1858. To the original bucket brigade and the "Independence" and "Enterprise" was added in 1848 a third suction engine, the "Votary." It had a crew of forty-five and remained in service until 1885 when it was sold for $65, the year Rockport bought its first steamer. In 1848, however, voters turned down a new fire engine for Pigeon Cove. In 1855 the engine house which had been built in Dock Square in 1830 was moved to Beach Street across from the cemetery and became the site of a landmark which lasted over a century. So that the North Village wouldn't be

Into the 1850s

unprotected, the town warrant for 1854 did relent on an engine house for Pigeon Cove, not to exceed $600. It was not until the turn of the decade, however, that Rockport acquired its fourth fire engine, the "Pigeon Cove"; it came from a Providence firm and cost $1,171.

In the national election on November 4, 1856, voters gave John C. Fremont, the Republican candidate from California who ran on an antislavery platform, 335 votes; the American ("Know-Nothing") party candidate won 210 votes; and the Democrat's compromise candidate, James Buchanan, came in third with 104 votes from Rockporters but carried the nation.

More Rockport roadways were both improved and developed. In late 1847, Broadway, forty feet in width, was laid out west from School Street by a private consortium which sold lots. These included a restriction that all buildings must be set back at least ten feet from the new street. John Hadlock is said to have built the first house on Broadway. Then in 1852 the investors generously offered to sign over their whole area to the town, streets and all, without any charges. Cleaves Street branched off in the mid-1850s, and Smith Street was opened in 1856 (construction costs, $117). That same year Marshall Street was accepted, while Broadway Avenue was surveyed in 1859 and built in 1860. Beach Street received a sidewalk and curbing at that time, as well as four trees beside the old cemetery wall. "They did not live to grow up." Nor did an elm tree planted in the middle of Dock Square in 1857. A replacement put in on May 2, 1859, on the other hand, when its slim trunk had a girth of only five to six inches, throve beside the pump. By 1888 it had achieved a waistline of over six and a half feet, two feet up from the ground. Ebenezer Pool had paid a mere dime for it, he confessed, but sold it to the town for $2.50.

Over at Pigeon Cove the highways were upgraded to the tune of $410 in 1852, and the main thoroughfare was realigned between the Babson Farm and Folly Cove. About 1855 Eben Phillips, the fish oil tycoon of Swampscott, began purchasing acreage in the Andrews'-Halibut Point area, a harbinger of transformations to come a decade later. To today's Rockport, however, the 1856-57 cleaning up, grading, fencing, and otherwise restructuring of the land adjacent to the Baptist church made perhaps the greatest impact of all the town's improvements. Rarely, if ever, was $208.36 spent for a more gratifying landscaping project in Rockport's history.

Rockporters initially continued the system of district schools, each with its own committee. In 1849, the town inaugurated its own first high school. Benjamin Giles held classes in the vestry of the Congregational church during a two-month fall and three-month winter term schedule. At the town meeting in 1850, debate was heated and lasted two hours. Opponents to the costs were defeated and so—in the words of the town records—"the high school abides." But not for long. After two erratic years it was dissolved. In 1855 Rockport commenced a graded school system. After only a year, the school committee (the Reverend Mr. Arnold, Benjamin Giles, and Austin W. Story) reported striking improvements within the primary, intermediate, and grammar divisions. For several winters, special training was provided for those boys who normally were employed in the spring, summer, and autumn terms. In 1856 the town bought up all the district school buildings, initiated more uniform facilities, and in 1857 built a school on Phillips Avenue at an outlay of nearly $3,000.

In the spring of the same year the town resumed paying for a high school. Again run behind the Congregational church in the so-called Proprietors' School, it had as a teacher an Essex woman, Miss M. A. Cogswell, who was paid $300 for a school year of thirty-six weeks. According to reports, the thirty-nine students had an average attendance of thirty-five. Except for the winter of 1859-60 when the classes met in the Main Street schoolhouse, it remained there until it transferred to the impressive new schoolhouse of 1866, today's Community House. From the remarkably clear, detailed street maps of Rockport issued commercially by Henry Walling in 1851 and 1856 one can trace in detail the progress visible in all areas of life in the community.

Commerce and the Cotton Mill

To Edward Shaw's daily express freight service to Boston, carried on by William B. Haskins, was added in 1859 John Legallee's twice-daily run to the new Gloucester depot. Commercial trade in ice expanded extensively, the town voting as early as March 1848 to rent out Cape Pond in the winters, provided it had the right to do so. By 1853 James Manning was storing over four hundred tons in his own icehouse, which he subsequently sold with his pond and property to Caleb J. Norwood. As anthracite coal became a more generally accepted fuel source, Pigeon Covers were furnished expeditiously by William Marchant, who in 1857 set up a coal-and-wood business opposite Breakwater Avenue, which would warm the neighborhood for close to a century.

Into the 1850s

Granite continued to be a source of revenue and employment to many Rockporters. By the 1850s granite for foundations and paving blocks for roads were being dispatched not only to many eastern cities but as far away as New Orleans, Havana, and San Francisco. In 1853 nearly $250,000 worth of granite (about 80,000 tons) was sold from Rockport and transported in some fifteen to twenty sloops. Ebenezer Pool calculated that forty-five pair of oxen were employed at the quarries and that these consumed 340 to 400 tons of hay besides some 1,500 bushels of meal. About 275 men were toiling in the pits, wharves, and the freighters during an eight-month season that year. To improve quarrying, water pumps were introduced by Lewis Lane about 1854 on his return from the California gold mines. Prior to 1853 pumping had been done by hand or cattle power. Steam took over in 1854. The next step was the introduction of steam-powered derricks for hoisting. In 1857, a stone sloop, the *John Brooks,* acquired its own steam engine for cargo and hoisting sails. Two more sloops were so equipped in 1858.

Fishing was more problematical, as it always had been. At the outset of the decade the town had forty-three vessels employed in mackerel fishing—a seasonal occupation occupying some 280 men and boys. Several of the larger fishing boats and coasters were sold off, though in 1849-50 there was a regular weekly packet sloop of seventy tons which made a Boston run, "employed in part by the Cotton Mill." Much fishing was done in wherries during the winter. In the fall of 1855 herring suddenly became so numerous the nets would often sink. The same year was a bumper one for cod and split catches. The year 1859 was a miserable mackerel year, with only about three thousand barrels landed at Sandy Bay Harbor; yet the very next year that figure nearly doubled. The town had fifty-one schooners of from thirty to ninety tons, one large schooner (Capt. John Giles's *Henry Houston*), eighteen sloops, sixteen stone lighters, and twenty boats. Ebenezer Pool's memoranda contain many reports of fishing vagaries and vessels. His score keeping also included the genealogical tidbit that the voting list for 1855 boasted forty-two Pools and fifty-three Tarrs and that Rockport had had seventeen college graduates among her sons between 1807 and 1857.

To accommodate such expansion, the businessmen of Rockport incorporated the Rockport National Bank in 1851. Capitalized at $100,000 it chose Ezra Eames as its president and Deacon Jabez R. Gott

Houses along Atlantic Avenue circa 1859. The white building at right became the Headland House, an early boardinghouse, and the fish houses of Star Island line the shore. (SBHS)

as cashier. Gloucester banking circles opposed the competition and slowed down investments in the fledgling bank. Nevertheless, on June 23, 1853, there was also incorporated a Rockport Savings Bank by a group of investors including both Eames and Gott; James Haskell was named president and Newell Giles treasurer. It soon proved its usefulness as well as the National.

The rush for gold had led many a Rockporter far afield from fishing banks during 1849 to 1851. In January 1849, according to Pool's recollections, ten left for California by ship around Cape Horn. In the spring others ventured by way of the Isthmus of Panama. By autumn several more followed. Dr. Manning received from his son a specimen nugget. In October 1850 George D. Hale got a ten-ounce lump which his son had dug out there. In the first eleven months following the news of gold in the hills some fifty Rockporters caught the fever and left for the chase. Subsequently, still others took their chances, and "some of them have continued there up to 1859."

Gold of quite another variety was the goal of the entrepreneurs who on February 8, 1847, chartered the Rockport Steam Cotton Mill and

Into the 1850s

on February 18 a rival firm at Gloucester, the Cape Ann Steam Cotton Manufactory. Milling and the profits from cotton were to be seen everywhere. At first waterpower was a prerequisite, but remarkable advances in steam and coal opened other areas to the market. Vital were cheap transportation and ready access to coal and raw materials. Rockport's harbor provided both. To the business eye, it offered the great chance—especially when money was tight.

On January 20, 1847, the *Telegraph* reported on the strenuous and determined effort being made at Rockport at establishing a cotton mill. When $38,000 had been subscribed, editors prophesied: "It will not be long before the vessels of the Cape will be able to proceed to sea with canvass manufactured upon their own shores." The *Telegraph* followed the matter and helped thereby win voter support at the forthcoming town meeting. Proponents cried: "Steam drives the spindles and money raises the steam; we can raise it if we try. This is not so great an undertaking as the railroad and the determination of old Cape Ann will not leave this Project in the ditch; she will put her shoulders to the wheel." The newly opened Gloucester branch meant that "railroad is hand maid to factory by the facilities it will afford to the transportation of materials and fabrics." The factory would create a demand for house lots. Moreover, "it will employ many females and young persons as operators, supposed from 200-300 at 50% higher wages than at present." Construction workers would be required for the factory and for houses. Boarding places would be called for to feed and house the workers. "Maintenance money will be put into circulation throughout the town to purchase food and clothing." So went the rhapsody.

Once chartered, the corporation chose officers and directors: Beniah Colburn, David Babson, Jr., Thomas O. Marshall, Josiah Haskell, George D. Hale, Henry Dutch—all of Rockport—and David Kimball of Boston. Kimball became president; the ubiquitous Jabez R. Gott, treasurer-clerk. Construction proceeded down at the foot of Broadway close to harbor facilities. The architect was Luther Briggs, who by his own published advertisements built several other cotton mills in conjunction with Gen. Charles T. James. At the Rockport town meeting of March 22, 1847, voters agreed that all surplus revenue money should be applied to stocks or shares in "the Steam Cotton Factory about to be established in this town." As an added inducement, all the rough stone was given to the contractor from refuse at the quarries—a donation estimated to be worth $37,000 at 50 cents per ton!

Town on Sandy Bay

The mill as originally built was two hundred feet long and sixty feet wide. Half of the structure was three stories high, the other two. The engines were installed in February and March and the machinery in the spring. Despite hopes for May, it was not until September 1848 that it began functioning. The earnings from the first year were set aside to purchase raw cotton, but the six months from September 1849 to March 1850 declared a 3.5 percent dividend. Overseers and operatives numbered some 160 and transformed 3,000 pounds of cotton per day into 1,500 yards of duck. By 1852 they turned a million pounds of cotton into duck, yarn, and "India Rubber cloth"—about 800,000 yards of the first item. The mill also sold about 30 tons of yarn to be made into fish lines in Essex and more for sewing twine for ducksails. Batting was assembled from the waste cotton. The mill's payroll ran to $29,000, and dividends were over 10 percent a year. As the decade progressed, however, dividends dropped steadily. Trouble was not long in casting shadows on the project.

As if it were an omen, a fire broke out on March 2, 1854, in the area where cotton was cleaned by "willowing" machinery, consisting of revolving drums with long spikes. Friction started the blaze, and the lad who was standing nearby was unable to extinguish it. Fortunately, the room was lined with iron and the doors and windows were quickly closed. The Rockport fire department connected an engine to a force pump which squirted four streams and extinguished the blaze. On Wednesday evening, August 18, 1855, the mill had another fire in the willow area. On July 22 the mill suspended operation for lack of demand for its products. On August 28 an announcement was made that work would halt "for the purpose of making repairs." The stone business, too, was almost at a standstill. In 1858 Rockport's tax rate was $6.30 per $1,000, down from $7.50. A year later, however, the *Gloucester Advertiser* reported that the duck factory was again in operation and paying its way. The stone business was also thriving "and is now the principal business of the town." As of August 5 the summer boarding-houses at Pigeon Cove were "full to overflowing."

Industrious persistence had brought a post office to Pigeon Cove. Readers of the August 28, 1858, paper learned that William Fears, Jr., would be postmaster and operate his service from his home on the north corner of Breakwater Avenue and Granite Street. In December the office moved into Austin Story's store at 154 Granite Street, where it would remain for forty years. The decade had also produced a new lighthouse for Straitsmouth Island (1851), two new doctors (Joseph B.

Into the 1850s

Manning and Oscar Abbott), a burgeoning number of apple orchards (mainly of Baldwins, twenty-five hundred barrels of them in 1850), new safety buoys for sailors and ships at the Londoner and Flatground, a house to protect the new lifesaving mortar to be shot out to foundering ships along the treacherous coast (1858), and an extended breakwater to protect Pigeon Cove Harbor (1859).

The success of industrious townspeople in raising $800 made it possible on January 21, 1858, for Rockport to be linked to the commercial telegraph at Gloucester. The outside world was now at the fingers of Henry Clark, operator of the station for twenty years to come. The first message transmitted was on January 22, to Winthrop Thurston at Montreal. To the Haskins's Express Company's Boston office was dispatched the initial commercial telegram. On August 12, 1858, a far longer cable was celebrated in town, a transatlantic one, later to have a cousin landed at Rockport itself. Those irrepressible boarders at Pigeon Cove got up "a grand cable celebration" for which the Pigeon Cove House was illuminated brilliantly. In September and October the very heavens above the town were illuminated by a comet. Yet despite the festivities, the patriotism, the sobriety, and the industry of Rockport and its visitors, the decade of the 1850s ended, like Casey's strikeout, with little joy in Mudville. "The business of Rockport has decreased very materially within a few years." The railroad terminal still remained at Gloucester, not in town.

ADDITIONAL READING

Among the earlier accounts of the Rockport area after it became independent are F. A. Durivage, "Cape Ann Sketches," *The Pictorial National Library,* vol. 2 (March 1849); pp. 143-47; Y.Q.Q., "Gloucester and Its Summer Attractions," *Boston Daily Evening Transcript,* Friday, June 19, 1849; and Robert Carter, *A Summer Cruise on the Coast of New England* (Boston, 1864). *A Summer Cruise* has been printed several times; it is now available in a paperback (but condensed) edition.

For the adventures of some Essex County forty-niners, including one Rockporter, see Katherine W. Richardson, "The Gold Seekers: The Story of the La Grange," *Essex Institute Historical Collections,* vol. 115 (1979); pp. 73-121.

Edward F. Zimmer, "Luther Briggs and the Picturesque Pattern Book," *Old Time New England,* vol. 67 (1977); pp. 36-56, gives a fine summary of the architect of Rockport's Steam Cotton Mill.

Eleanor C. Parsons, *Hannah and the Hatchet Gang* (Canaan, N.H., 1975), narrates the temperance raid in a comprehensive, spirited fashion.

The Walling maps of Essex County and its various towns are of great interest to local historians. That for Rockport as it was about 1856 was reprinted by Dr. John Bloombergh. Copies are available at the Sandy Bay Historical Society.

14

REBELLION
AND RECONSTRUCTION

Rockport on the Brink

WITH THE 20 / 20 vision of hindsight, one is rather perplexed by Rockport's lack of anxiety over the coming Civil War. Life out at the end of Cape Ann was composed and optimistic. According to the federal census of 1860, there were some 3,195 Rockporters: 1,620 male and 1,575 female. With the exception of Eliza Haskell, fourteen, and Mary Haskell, seventeen, black servants to Susanna and Gorham Babson, respectively, all Rockporters were white, though the percentage of foreign-born residents was mounting rapidly. The town itself registered 819 polls, of whom the North Village had 185 and the South 634. The tax rate was $7.20 per thousand, plus a poll tax of $1.50 per male voter. In true Yankee fashion voters were cautious about expenditures. Their police department spent $154.12 in 1860; their fire fighters drew down $1,509.81, of which $1,120 was for a new engine and hose carriage. On their poor, Rockporters laid out $3,003.51, including $103.85 for smallpox cases. The town farm, however, which averaged fourteen inmates during the year, reduced the outlay to $1,893.85. Other departments of the town spent comparable sums.

Custodial services for the nine schools had cost the town $66.00, fuel and related labor another $166.17, while "fixtures and repairs" (including privy problems) called for an additional $337.16. As for teachers' salaries, the budget the year before the war broke out had reached $2,383.97, but then those thirty-five teachers did have to be paid. By state law the school day opened with a Bible reading and other "unsectarian" religious exercises. Recesses were confined to fifteen minutes. "In no case," laid down a decree from Boston, "shall the sexes have their recesses together." Teachers were also obliged to see that pupils observed habits of cleanliness in their persons, their desks, and about the premises of the school houses. No pupil could be promoted without first passing an examination. Truant officers made "frequent calls at such places of amusement and idleness which youth are likely to frequent."

Life in the community at large was also placid, although those temperance lectures were clearly needed. There was versatile new machinery at the Rockport Cotton Mill producing flannel and "drilling" in addition to the usual cotton duck. John J. Babson's *History of Gloucester, Cape Ann (Including the Town of Rockport)* appeared in July 1860 and was fully reviewed with glowing praise: "The book should be in the hands of every resident." No longer isolated, thanks to newspapers, the telegraph link, regular ship and stage-train service to Boston, Rockporters had a copious array of goods spread before them—in fact and in advertising. In her new millinery store, Miss Godfrey was vending French, English, and American straw and fancy bonnets, velvet flowers, and feathers, as well as elegant fall and winter ribbons, laces, embroideries, collars, sleeves, and veils. For the bereaved, she had "mourning goods constantly on hand." Before the daring, T. S. Lancaster dangled "Valentia" (sic) prints, Homburg plaids, and "Paris corsets!! White and colored, a superior article just received." Ladies' serge Congress boots were procurable for only a dollar.

The local men were by no means forgotten in 1860. Benjamin Giles was attracting customers to his new clothing store. Knowles and Company competed with "white and fancy French bosom shirts," hickory shirts, Russian and American frocks and jackets, collars, scarves, cravats, neck stocks, and suspenders. For those gentlemen who might be going to the Leap Year Ball, Alex. Pattillo had four cartons of Paris kid gloves "in high mode colors and white." Working shirts sold from 37 to 75 cents, fine shirts from 75 cents to $1.60; undershirts and drawers were less at 25 to 50 cents. Handkerchiefs and neckties cost 6 to 75 cents, and half hose ran from 8 to 50 cents.

For household use Rockporters could purchase a wide assortment of products ranging from stoves and tinware, Britannica glass, Japan

Town on Sandy Bay

ware, rosin, kerosene, oleine oils, and lamps to Wait's cooking and flavoring extracts, hair oil, perfumery, and soaps. New pianos fetched $265 to $300, melodeons (on sale) $45 to $75. Sewing machines cost $30 to $40. William Ellery carried India rubber, waterproof paint.

Eben Blatchford advertised medicinal Oxygenated Bitters containing no alcohol, but no references to ingredients were included with such best-selling specifics as Ayer's Sarsaparilla, Cherry Pectoral, Cathartic Pills ("for all the purposes of a family physic"). Rockporters were also purchasing, as needed, Dr. McLane's "Celebrated Vermifuge and Liver Pills," Wistar's Balsam, and Dr. Darius Ham's "Aromatic, Invigorating Spirit—a dyspepsia remedy." If doctors and medicaments failed, there was always Charles Procter, who discreetly advertised that coffins were constantly on hand "at the shop in the rear of my furniture store." February brought Valentines: "the richest and most beautiful designs for young men and maidens, old men and children." Why old women were discriminated against was not made clear. That spring photographs were being touted at 50 percent reduction: "Old Daguerreotypes—photographed and enlarged to size."

In early August 1860 the newspaper gave this succinct summary. The granite business was in good condition. Employment was there for all who wished to seek it, although in the spring the men had been on strike, vainly arguing for higher wages. At the mill, "prospects for duck and other cloth are brightening." The Pigeon Cove House and other private boarding places were filled to overflowing. Even the fishermen were doing well from dogfish, taken for their livers "to make oil of." A number of Rockport's vessels had also made "good trips of mackerel." "When the Rockport Railroad shall be completed, business generally will revive into an animation unknown here for the last few years."

It was against such a backdrop that the drama of the elections of 1860 was played. On November 2 the *Advertiser* summed up the situation: "The campaign has been a spirited one; the two leading parties of the day have been actively engaged and an immense amount of enthusiasm in the way of speeches, processions, and pyrotechnical displays have been manifested." Rockporters gave 358 votes to Lincoln, 128 to Bell (the Constitutional Union party's standard-bearer), 42 to Stephen Douglas (the "Little Giant" Democratic, antislavery, debater), and 52 to John C. Breckinridge, the proslavery Democratic candidate. Rockport's own representative to the General Court that year was

Austin W. Story. Breathing relief, an editorial writer said, "The long agony is over. . . . The President of the U.S. has been elected by the people."

"Ominous Signs of Change"

It didn't take long once the votes were in. On March 8, 1861, four days after the swearing-in ceremonies had taken place on the steps of the unfinished Capitol in Washington, the *Telegraph* editorialized: "No president of the United States ever had so just a claim to the kind consideration and support of the American people." Lincoln will command "the ship of state for the next four years, unless death shall interpose; and on him devolve the responsibility whether she shall go to pieces on the rocks of revolution, or secure a safe anchorage in the port of peace." That, surely, was rhetoric understood by all Rockporters.

The opening days of April burst with rumors. The Confederacy was out of funds and out of harmony. "It appears certain that danger to the capital is apprehended." New York was a hive of secret military movements. "Virginia is becoming the center of attention. There are fears of an approaching collision and bloodshed." "Should President Lincoln astonish the doubting Thomases and the wretched Judases of the nation by some sudden 'coup,' he will go down to posterity with the double honors of Talleyrand and Napoleon," declaimed the Gloucester press. With obvious relish many Rockporters read a Kentuckian's comment on the Cotton States that "in no section of the globe where Anglo-Saxons are predominant does there exist that degree of *ignorance and depravity* which may be found in the South. . . . I think we would gain in getting rid of them forever." Other readers were cheered to be told that 80 percent of the total American tonnage was in the North, which embraced the most skillful and daring maritime people of the world. Then came Sumter, surrender, and war.

On Wednesday, April 17, the *Telegraph* gave out the grim details on Fort Sumter and published President Lincoln's call for 75,000 volunteers. "This is to be a terrible war, and we must make it as short as possible." That very day the people of Rockport showed their patriotism by forming a procession and parading about town with the American flag. "Volunteers are offering themselves." On April 22 a special town meeting was held to plan Rockport's response and how to "assist the families or other persons dependent on them for support of such citizens of the town as may volunteer to serve their country." It would be the topic of many sessions to follow.

The military story has been related at length, together with the names of the 358 men procured by the town for the U.S. Army, 11 of whom were commissioned officers, and the 41 for the U.S. Navy. On April 30, 1861, the town voted to appropriate $3,000 from which to pay a $20 bounty to each volunteer who passed the service examination. The remainder was to be used, with discretion, for soldiers' dependents. A recruiting office was opened, and by the end of May there were enough volunteers to form a company. There were delays at the state level and friction at home when it was discovered "that all could not be captains." However, Cape Pond pasture was transformed into a camp to which the men reported the first week in June. Lack of arms, drills, training, and an excess of plain boredom drove 13 of the men to join the organized Fifth Maine Regiment. One of those was Otis W. Wallace, who died at the age of twenty-six on October 28, 1862, from the strains of the Peninsula campaign. His was to be the name selected for Rockport's eventual GAR post. The town's first real veterans' organization, it was organized on August 19, 1869, and numbered 106.

The remaining members of the initial Rockport company of regulars who did not leave the camp in disgust for other units continued at Cape Pond pasture (by then christened "Camp Kimball") until early July. On Wednesday the tenth they moved on to Lynnfield, armed with an elegant silk flag presented to the company on the lawn of the Congregational church by the Honorable Moses Kimball in person. About one thousand turned out for the ceremonies and the departure by carriages for Gloucester. Each man was given a New Testament. Their regiment left for Baltimore on August 20, where on October 27 fell Rockport's first casualty of the war, Lt. George W. Tufts. His body was returned to Rockport on Halloween. Pastor Bremner "appropriately" noted that although it was not the fortune of the young Tufts "to die on the battlefield amid the shrieks of the wounded," he did die at the post of duty. In his final illness the "kind ladies of Baltimore sent him such delicacies as his case required." In the spring of 1862 the regiment moved south to North Carolina, where George Prior died at age thirty-one in September. Another volunteer, William Gould, would die at Andersonville on May 5, 1864.

Rebellion and Reconstruction

In the summer of 1862 Rockport was called upon to provide 29 more men. Response was negligible until a recruitment meeting, band and all, was held in Dock Square under the leadership of William B. Haskins and Pastor Bremner. Quickly, the quota was subscribed and a farewell service held for the departees in Mr. Bremner's second Congregational church. As the town *History* of 1888 put it: "Mark the change within a few days by the effort of a few men and the right kind of music. Rockport was not sleeping, only halting." It had also hiked the bounty to $125, thereby providing a more substantial inducement to volunteer than mere martial music. Next came the presidential cry for 300,000 men for a nine-month period. With effort the town managed to enroll a sufficient number to satisfy the headquarters in Boston. Each of them received a bounty of $100. Then followed the long-expected draft call, for which Rockport's quota was 63. Although 94 names were drawn only 34 passed the examination and either paid the "commutation" fee (the amount required to enlist a substitute) or provided their own substitutes. Rockporters paid $10,610 to avoid that draft call. Eight men, however, promptly enlisted for three years without waiting to learn if they might be rejected from the draft on medical grounds.

In the middle of August a 36 member group of nine-months men came home, having served in New Orleans and elsewhere. Of the original forty-nine in the company, nine were killed or died. Those who returned paraded to the Congregational church where they were prayed over by Pastor Gale and addressed by Josiah Haskell and Benjamin H. Smith. Former President Franklin Pierce, then spending a few weeks at Pigeon Cove, spoke words of cheer, and Parson Barden "addressed them in his happiest vein." Two hours later returnees and guests proceeded to the engine house where the hour "was happily spent in testing the viands and in social conversation." Two weeks later the men were mustered out.

In October 1863, the draft having proved a failure, Lincoln called for yet another 300,000 volunteers. This time Rockport was asked to provide 79. Then came an appeal for 200,000 more and for Rockport to field yet another 35 men. Soldiers who had served two years were declared eligible for reenlistment, so Selectman Henry Dennis hied off to North Carolina and succeeded in getting several reenlistees for Rockport from the Seventeenth Regiment. Additional volunteers turned up locally, the bounty now being $200 each. Still, Rockport had contributed only half of its assigned quotas. After considerable finagling, the town got 34 written off its demand list, because substitutes had been "purchased," because credit was granted for its 13 naval men, and because the men still eligible for the draft raised $900 among themselves and paid commutation fees to hire the remaining three still required.

Rockporters were shocked by a request for 71 more men for September 5, 1864. Recruits could be had but only at exorbitant prices. It was a seller's market. Each liable draftee was assessed by the town $20, a gouge which brought in nearly $6,000. Then the town itself paid its regular contribution from tax funds, plus raising a second, "voluntary" tax of $3,840. From these scrapings 39 men were found, though Rockport was in debt $1,300. Further negotiations with the state finally gave the town a surplus book credit of 21 men rather than its de facto short fall. Another 8 volunteers were flushed out for one hundred days of service in the summer of 1864. In December, for a $125 bounty figure, the town hired 23 more soldiers. To end it, another $2,000 was anted up by threatened draftees. This paid for 29 more soldiers, the last Rockport had to contribute to the Civil War.

Though numerous Rockport men legally purchased an escape from service, many others did fight for the cause of the Union and all that was implied therein. By the surrender at Appomatox 42 Rockporters had died on battlefields, or in prisons or of wounds and disease. At the town meeting of March 22, 1866, voters were asked to decide "will the town give lots in the cemeteries for soldiers who have died in the late war and been or may be brought home for burial?" After a century, the answer still echoes annually on Memorial Day mornings.

Peace

About nine o'clock Saturday morning April 15, 1865, the telegraph "brought us the saddest news ever to be borne over the wires on this continent. . . . Abraham Lincoln, President of the United States is no more." At Rockport flags were lowered to half-mast, bells tolled, the Congregational meetinghouse was "tactfully" draped in mourning, and all three ministers in town at the time conducted an eloquent tribute. Gale prayed, "lengthy and appropriate," wrote Pool; Wheeler read the lessons; Angier preached "well arranged and to the point." It was truly a day of sadness to all loyal hearts; but even in loyal states all did not mourn. Were there any such in Rockport?

Rebellion and Reconstruction

Ebenezer Pool spoke "of a few who yet sympathize with the Rebellion, as some do." It is well to recall that by no means all the townspeople were unanimously against slavery. Pastor Gale's early denunciations had caused notable commotion in conservative circles, as did those at the Universalist church. During the rather short incumbency of Charles O. Towne, in 1843 the Methodist church was also induced by its pastor to take a strong antislavery stance. Dr. Lemuel Gott, a pronounced antislavery man, distressed his business-oriented brother, Addison, when he shared a local pulpit in a Rockport church "with a colored man." While serving in the Massachusetts legislature, the brother later found it convenient to vote for abolitionist Charles Sumner for senator. The town had had its Free Soil political party with slates of activists and candidates for assorted offices during the 1848, 1850, and 1852 elections. In Rockport, the need to be assured of a steady supply of raw cotton for the mill tempered criticism of the South's "peculiar institution."

One overt step was taken by parties unknown on Sunday, November 1, 1861, seven months after the Civil War had begun. Some seventy people had gathered at the Universalist church to hear a lecture on slavery. A bomb was thrown through a window from Hale Street and landed close to the speaker, Parker Pillsbury. On exploding, it filled the church with smoke and frightened the audience. Once the smoke cleared, however, the hardier souls returned to the church for the rest of the discussion. Some of the Universalists were opposed to the use of the house for such lectures. By the time of Lincoln's death and the northern victory, however, Rockport probably had very few pro-southern sympathizers. On April 27, 1867, the Odd Fellows of Rockport joined the national lodges and observed a Day of Thanksgiving for the return of peace and the preservation of order during the war.

The war was painful in many ways beyond the obvious losses of soldiers. Town meetings haggled over every dollar, especially for roadways and schools. In 1860 the Beach Street School (today's Legion Hall) was constructed for $1,439.71, but a reduced school budget (from $2,500 to $1,500) left an academic year of but two terms. Amid the general war excitement and the awakening of material feeling in the young as in others, it was found exceedingly difficult to engage the attention of the pupils in their studies, particularly during the spring term (1861). The report for 1865 spoke of two terms of twelve weeks and one of ten but complained that "our paper currency has depre-

After recess at the Beach Street School in an earlier day. The building was later enlarged and converted to serve as headquarters for the local American Legion post. (Hoyt)

ciated" and that the price of fuel and stationery "has been enhanced to a fabulous extent." More truant officers were needed to find vagrant children. Another barrier was "the extraordinary COASTING of this season . . . very prolific of interruptions in some quarters." Then, too, many parents were anxious about "a loathsome humor" and kept their children out of school to avoid contagion, only to let them mingle all the more intimately "with the same obnoxious creatures in street scenes."

In 1866 came the new high school on Broadway. Rockport was into an era of reconstruction. It began with a school building; it ended with a new town hall. The former was "of the most approved style, single desks, easy and convenient for the scholar. The teacher's desk is of black walnut, elegantly gotten up, and the room the pleasantest we have in town." And well it might be, for it cost the taxpayers, including lot and furnishings, $4,046.56. In 1869 it was lifted up and a lower story constructed for a grammar school for another $2,609; a furnace and other improvements in 1870 cost an additional $479. The decade came to an end with a decision by the school committee that fewer male teachers could be found for economic reasons, but "female teachers have more patience to present the truth." The high school students

Rebellion and Reconstruction

were commended for collecting funds to build up a school library. That year the committee's report included for the first time the winners of the Kimball book prizes, given to those "who have made the most actual progress, whether gifted or less gifted by nature." The first printed list of high school graduates also appeared in 1869: George L. Elwell, Emily D. Haskell, Romulus Norwood, Adelia Parsons, Emma M. Philbrook, and Aria M. Torrey.

"All Things New"

For the "go-getters"—and Rockport was blessed for decades with yeasty leaven to raise its lump—the future of the town had long been pegged to a railroad. Undaunted when the Eastern Railroad declined to undertake the five-mile extension from Gloucester to Rockport, a group of businessmen led principally by granite interests secured from the Massachusetts legislature an act of incorporation for a railroad "from some point near Broadway, so called, in Rockport to some . . . intersection with the Gloucester Branch Railroad." The date was May 16, 1853. Local interests were to lay tracks and switches; assume risks of accidents; construct a roundhouse, turntable, facilities for water and coal; and provide the ticket sellers and all personnel except the trainmen themselves. For its part, the Eastern Railroad would run their passenger and freight trains through from Gloucester and make all connections there.

When stock purchases moved slowly and capital was not forthcoming, the incorporators turned to the town itself. The matter was debated at two town meetings, on March 19 and April 2, 1860. Finally, the decision was taken (326 to 31) to borrow $50,000, for which town bonds would be issued. Only a month later the suggestion was advanced in all seriousness that instead of a steam railroad, Rockport and Gloucester might be linked by a horse railroad. It would be equally convenient, far less expensive to build and operate, yet still be a sound investment. Any chance to take the steam out of the venture was lost on July 13 when the Eastern renewed for five years its earlier agreement with the Rockport company.

Work began on August 23 and was expected to be completed on May 1, 1861. Like many another project on Cape Ann, however, the railroad fell behind because of ledges to be blasted. By late autumn, however, all was in order. Monday, November 4, 1861, brought fine weather for the festive opening. No fares were charged for rides to and

S. P. Randall of the Rockport Hotel provided tables which "literally groaned under the weight of good things" and over which the Reverend Mr. Gale prayed before the company fell to and satisfied the cravings of hunger. After the dinner came the speeches—ten of them. Moses Kimball, a Sandy Bayer turned Bostonian politician, crowed: "It has always been your aim since you separated from Gloucester to outstrip her, and now that you have your railroad you can do it. You are the grand terminus of the road, and she has become a way station." He concluded with "a popular song":

Glory, Glory, Hallelujah
Rockport is Marching On.

Business began in earnest the next morning. The first published schedule shows three passenger trains per day. Daily freight trains left Rockport at 3:00 A.M. and Boston at 5:00 P.M. Since the terminus of the Eastern Railroad was at Gloucester, passengers continued on the Rockport Railroad at their own risk. Baggage was taken out at Gloucester and then reloaded to cover the legal niceties. Of the railroad's total costs of $91,007.28, the town had paid $75,000 by purchasing stock; private subscribers had put up only $13,400. The remaining $2,600 debt was paid for out of profits. By November 1866 the company was "one of the best paying roads in the State." By February 1868 the Eastern Railroad agreed to buy up the Rockport Company for $91,007.28 and the state legislature approved the reorganization. As the decade drew to its close, the Eastern Railroad improved depot accommodations at Rockport by a 150-foot shed to shelter its cars and protect its passengers in stormy weather. The links the trains offered to the world beyond Cape Ann paid dividends quite incalculable.

To those at sea off Rockport, as well as to landlubbers past and present, another constructive undertaking of the new decade deserves a note in the annals of the town. The old lighthouses on Thacher's Island were removed; the lights were temporarily "exhibited" on wooden structures; and new towers were constructed. Those 123-foot towers were lighted during the first week of October 1861. New keepers were assigned to both Thacher's (Albert Hale) and the refurbished Straitsmouth lighthouses (John S. Wheeler).

Rebellion and Reconstruction

Beacons of another variety were lighted. Soon after the war's end, Rockport churchgoers went on a building spree. Like the First Church of Christ in Pigeon Cove (today's chapel), a Second Universalist Society of Rockport also grew from a Sunday school at the cove. Organized in August 1861, with Austin W. Story as superintendent, a post to which he would be reelected for over a quarter of a century, it migrated to Edmunds' bowling alley, then to Edmunds' Hall halfway up Pousil Hill, where the group commenced preaching services. At the end of February 1866 they received a gift of land from George Babson on the corner of Granite Street and Phillips Avenue for a church.

The Pigeon Cove chapel, which had begun with forty-three Sunday school students in May 1857, continued successfully. In 1868 they, too, decided to erect a building. Having expended $3,966, the worshipers marched into their new home. In 1873 the church's tower, bell, and fencing were added at a cost of another $2,475. In 1866 Rockport's Baptist church was remodeled inside and out, "in modern style," with a new steeple as well as a commodious and well-furnished vestry in the basement. The Methodists joined the procession with a fund-raising tent fair in mid-August which, after expenses of $1,050 had been squared up, netted a profit of $800 toward a building. On April 6, 1867, the Universalists issued a report that they would spend $3,000 in reconstructing their premises. It was the Baptists, however, who won the race, holding their rededicatory services that same week in Dock Square.

The last of the ecclesiastical constructions arising at Rockport during the reconstruction era was that of the Methodists. Their new preacher, the Reverend Mr. J. A. Ames, was described as "abundant in labors." During his four years in town (1865-69) the flock secured two lots of land on Broadway for $900. On these they erected a $16,000 edifice, complete with a sanctuary of seventy-two circular pews, bright oil lamps, two vestries, and an elevated choir gallery facing the pulpit—of black walnut and chestnut. For the dedication on April 14, 1869, reported the paper, a special train would run from Boston to Rockport "for those who want to attend services and return home the same day." Only the first church—apart from the rather new Roman Catholic one—failed to grapple with construction at that period. Early in 1863 the wearied Mr. Wakefield Gale had resigned his pastorate after twenty-seven years of toil. He was followed by the three-and-a-half-year pastorate of William Dunning, who added fifty members during that time and encouraged public lectures. Two of these were

John H. Gough's performance in October 1865 on the tantalizing topic, "Peculiar People," and that given in April 1866 by "Mr. John Parker, a colored man and formerly a slave," who advocated the interests of the freedmen. "A large number were present"— Rockporters, not blacks. It was only in 1871 that the major Congregational resconstruction was undertaken.

"The Stone Business Never Was Better"

The rock of faith was far from being the only foundation on which the town's prosperity was being raised. For years yet to come the Rockport Cotton Mill was to be in the center of Rockport's economic life. Three months after the end of the Civil War the press reported that Rockport's mill was again being put into better running order. By September 1865 a large boardinghouse to front on School Street was to be built for the convenience of factory boarders. The mill was humming, and according to the *Advertiser,* "there is a marked carefulness and tidiness about the premises that gives credit to the superintendent, Mr. Higgins." Even more extravagant was the praise for its entire machinery "not surpassed by any mill in the country." Rockport brown sheetings were "as eagerly sought after on the Cape as duck used to be in the palmiest days of the Corporation." The supply was not equal to the demand. In addition to two new boardinghouses for operatives, the company had erected a fine building to serve as offices for its superintendent and treasurer.

On June 15 Cape Ann newspaper readers were treated to a detailed description of the manufacturing process from the willowing machine to the end product. There were two hundred looms running, and "a smart weaver will take care of six looms and earn near $2.00 a day," they were assured. By September 1866 business was so lively that the mill was running an evening shift and putting curbstones for fencing in front of their "Corporation Blocks." By March 1867, a Boston firm proposed to lease the mill for three years, paying the stockholders 6 percent and one half of all surplus earnings over 10 percent a year. The papers reported in 1868 that recently five shares had sold for $25 each.

If there was a Micawberlike optimism about the upsurge of activity at the Rockport Cotton Mill following the war, the reports from the mushrooming granite business were even more rapturous. The quarries were in full operation. During the winter of 1865-66 the Rockport

View from the Western Wharf showing a cluster of craft ready for loading at the Rockport Granite Company's pier. (Caffrey)

Granite Company, which had been organized in 1864, extended its holdings by buying for $14,000 the granite privileges, land, and wharf which had belonged to Hale Knowlton at the end of the Back Beach. By 1866, estimated the *Advertiser*, Rockport's various companies quarried annually some 100,000 tons of stone and employed only "the most skillful workmen." At Rockport, geologists have found green crystals of feldspar unsurpassed anywhere in the world, was the claim. Opals and rare metals had also been discovered there by Harvard scientists, as well as small agates of great beauty. Shortly before Christmas, 1867, the Cape Ann Granite Company was organized with many familiar names among its officers, including Ezra Eames; W. J. Torrey; Stephen Kendrick; and F. K. Ballou, who had tried his luck in the gold fields of California twenty years before.

Like the cotton mill, the quarries had their share of accidents, though most of them never made the Gloucester newspapers. In December 1868 a worker broke his leg, and in March 1869 James Edmunds miraculously escaped death from a premature explosion. He was blown "quite a distance and landed on his back." In May another premature explosion injured a quarryman's eyes, two more men were hurt in a blast, and a huge block fell from a carriage and

Town on Sandy Bay

nearly hit a worker. Even animals were not safe. A team of oxen backed off the breakwater of the Rockport Granite Company that May. One was rescued and one drowned.

The opening of the quarrying season in 1869 brought reports of eight new granite companies at Pigeon Cove. The paving of Broadway in New York City would require tons of blocks. Several new stone sloops and schooners were being purchased as well as several steam engines to transport stone from the quarries to the wharves and relieve oxen from the strain of hoisting. The Pigeon Cove Harbor Company was also refurbishing its holdings. Issue after issue of the *Cape Ann Advertiser* carried reports of improvements in the stone business at Pigeon Cove: derricks, new tools, new methods, even a canal which the Rockport Granite Company was cutting from the waterfront to its quarries. "The only obstacle to its progress is that they have come into a good quarry which will help pay the expenses of the canal." Like the Rockport Cotton Mill, the granite companies began building houses for their workers.

"Fat as Butter"

The third leg of the stool which supported Rockport's economic health in the postwar years was fishing and the related coastal trade. Then as now, the local press gave generous attention to shipping news of all kinds. At the war's end mackerel was running well. Two vessels in July 1865 sold $1,900 worth of fresh fish and salted down 250 additional barrels. In the late summer of 1866 one vessel brought in 100 barrels in a fortnight, earning for the crew about $75 a piece. The next week the *Advertiser* reported "200 sail of mackerel catchers have been in the vicinity the past week. Most of the vessels did well." Their luck continued into mid-October, when the fish were succulently described as "of good size and fat as butter." In January 1869 local fishermen brought in 60,000 haddock ready for sale. Some of the fishing boats were reported as having made upwards of $1,000 in a week, the crewmen averaging $50 to $60 a share.

With catches such as these, new and replacement ships were regularly being acquired. The news in November 1869 that Joseph T. Haskins and William N. Manning had secured a patent for "an improved traveller for vessels' use" made a stir of sorts. The advantage was that the jib could be drawn by the man at the helm. More newsworthy and certainly more eye-catching along the waterfronts of the town were the several new ships arriving to augment the stone-carrying fleet, sloops and schooners both, such as those bought in 1869 by the Rockport Granite Company. The barkentine *White Cloud* with a load of coal for the John W. Marshall firm docked late in April 1869 and rated a comment in the press, which described it glowingly as long and narrow, with a centerboard and three masts, "which were square rigged on the foremast and fore and aft rigged on the main and mizzen masts."

It was the September gale of 1869, however, which was talked of for generations along the Cape Ann coast. A reporter reckoned that "the loss of the two fishing vessels from our port caused more deaths of Rockport people than was occasioned by the War of the Rebellion." Eleven of a crew of twelve went down with the *Helen Eliza* near Portland; one man, Charles Jordan, battled the waves to survive and relate the story of the wreck. It was his third such experience, and in each instance only he escaped. Eight bodies were subsequently found and brought to Rockport for burial: James Bray, George Clark, Emerson Colby, Joel Fairbanks, David Harris, Frederick Lane, Benjamin Lurvey, and Captain Millett. Of the Congregational service the press reported that the bodies were laid side by side before the altar, "and

Looking east on Haven Avenue, Pigeon Cove, circa 1879. This was Ocean View, the Babson-Phillips development before the area filled with summer homes, and shows the handsome cottage of Mrs. Corinna H. Bishop on the horizon. (Hoyt)

Town on Sandy Bay

their features looked very natural. The scene as the congregation 181
passed around the aisles was one not soon to be forgotten." The crew
of the *Yankee Girl* was never heard from, though divers searched the
hull for any remains. Seven of its eleven were also Rockporters. The
gale made eight women widows and twelve children orphans. Ten
other local schooners were damaged and personnel injured that September in one of the most disastrous gales that ever visited this eastern
coast.

The sea was ever ready to engulf the unwary. A steel cross in the
ledge near Gully Point still marks the loss of young Edwin E. Rogers,
who slipped into the ocean there on May 3, 1866, while gunning for sea
birds with a friend. A local dory incident occurred on October 22,
1869, when three sons of two prominent Rockport businessmen
(Newell Giles and Edwin Pool) were going down with their sinking
boat. The sixty-eight-year-old James Rowe, out tending his nets, spotted them, cleared his dory, and with an almost superhuman strength
and effort bent his oars and rowed to the rescue. For this he was
awarded a diploma from the Massachusetts Humane Society and lived
another twenty years, a pensioner for his service in the War of 1812.

The dry death Shakespeare's comic prayed for darkened four stars
in Rockport's clerical crown: the Methodists' Mr. Elijah Mason on
February 16, 1863; licentiate Capt. Levi Cleaves, on June 16, 1865;
Pastor Stillman Barden of the Universalist church some weeks later on
August 7, 1865; and missionary Walter Harris Giles from the second
Congregational church. Ordained in Rockport on August 26, 1864, he
succumbed at Constantinople on May 21, 1867, at the age of thirty.
Both Mason and Barden were serving as chairmen of the Rockport
school committee when they died.

"An Influx of Sea-Siders"

Like the singers in *Carousel,* Rockporters of the 1860s might well
have caroled "June is busting out all over." For the laity there were
"agreeable rides and romantic, woodland promenades"; for the lovers
of science, especially geology, there were the fascinations of the miner-
als and the seashells. For botanists there were the flora and the sea-
weeds which women pressed in albums with red morocco covers and
labeled "Mosses." Long before the railroad reached Rockport, stages
were rolling in with streams of visitors. Even the war failed to deter
those who sought refuge from the cities.

The decade saw an expansion of two sorts: transients and summer residents. In July 1866 the Pigeon Cove House was being run by the energetic Mrs. Ellen H. Robinson, and Rockport's Sandy Bay House, kept by Mr. Burgess, was having "an influx of sea-siders." At Christmastime the successful Mrs. Robinson parted with $9,000 to buy Anna Norwood's Pigeon Cove House.

Of far more lasting impact were the shrewd maneuverings of Eben B. Phillips, who gambled on the eventual success of the Rockport Railroad Company. Having made his initial purchases in the mid-1850s at Andrews' Point, he and some associates from Boston purchased a five-acre tract at Gap Head in January 1866. In March 1866 the *Advertiser* reported the purchase from the Babson family of another tract of land at Andrews' Point by Mr. Phillips. Six months later John Webber began surveying and laying out some 150 acres into building lots for summer visitors. The property was owned jointly by Phillips of Swampscott and George Babson of Pigeon Cove. Things slid along deliberately but not so rapidly as had been anticipated. In the spring of 1869, though, George Babson did announce plans to extend the new street around the point back of the cove, and in April work finally began along "Ocean Avenue," a stretch to be fifty feet wide and two miles long. "Many building lots are already sold on the Avenue." The hard sell there, however, would come only in the next decade.

At the working level, so to speak, Rockport was likewise a nest of activity. Scarcely a week went by in the 1860s when the *Gloucester Telegraph* or the *Cape Ann Advertiser* failed to include chatty notes about real estate transactions. Property changed hands with startling frequency. Lots and houses were constantly being sold, often at auction. New construction, prices not quoted, was a routine item for correspondents to cover. Texts ran like these: "Jesse Savage is building a two story house on the corner of School and Gott Streets for Phillip Webber"; "Levi S. Gott is building a two story building on South Street for William H. Pool"; and John Hooper was constructing "a cottage house" on Cleaves Street for James Cogswell.

More visitors, more residents, more buildings meant more business and fresh initiatives. Take as illustrations these random ones. The autumn of 1866 saw another "Sound Factory" for the manufacture of isinglass from hake bladders. Competition may have stimulated James Manning into constructing his new isinglass factory in 1867. Its machinery would also provide motive power for Hale and Jones's

The road inside the breakwater of Pigeon Cove Harbor about 1925 with the Hotel Edward up the hill at the far right. (Niemi)

recently established anchor works, which was already employing ten hands by February 1867. Their building (fifty by forty feet) was in good working order down on lower King Street. The Pigeon Cove Harbor Company undertook to put up yet another wharf in June 1867, and that autumn Rockport's Nathaniel Robbins, Jr., came out with a new type of windlass to raise anchors. In the spring of 1869 S. F. Poole relocated near Rockport's post office, where he shrewdly manufactured a variety of tools adapted to the wants of both quarrymen and fishermen, and in conformity with Massachusetts law, Rockport selectmen even got around to appointing one or two dealers in old junk and metals.

Most of Rockport's needs were supplied by smaller enterprises. A number of these changed hands in the 1860s, and several new ones put up their signs. For all of Rockport's burgeoning commercial opportunities there was the reassurance that under new federal banking laws the rechartered Rockport National Bank was even more secure. October 1868 produced the first of the new series of directories published by Procter Brothers. In successive Rockport sections one can find the town officers, businesses, and the names of its citizens.

Rebellion and Reconstruction

At the quarries, unlike the stores and hotels, work was hard. It meant an early breakfast at one of the boardinghouses, off to work, one hour for dinner at noon, then more labor until the late supper. Pay consisted of board plus some cash paid out at the end of the season, though not on a weekly basis. In the earlier days, quarry hands migrated down from northern New England about the first of March. By April the gangs were complete. The season ran about eight months. "Most of them were lively and full of fun." Once the Irish flocked in, however, after the Great Hunger of the late 1840s, Rockport underwent periods of tension. The houses built for the Irish immigrants on Granite Street were "two or three times blown up with powder"; other means were also employed to keep out unwelcome immigrants including, much later, the Swedes and the Finns. For years, all the newcomers created lives and communities for themselves within a larger Rockport. Those stories have yet to be researched.

"To Improve the Morals of Society"

Hannah Jumper went to her Judge and Maker in October 1865, quite suddenly, on a Saturday, at eighty-four years of age. The obituary reported no campaign honors at her funeral. Rockport was, and long had been, dry—officially. Yet scofflaws still had to be watched for. In February 1869 many Rockporters must have been startled by one of the oldest liquor dealers in town. On a Monday morning he suddenly "renounced the accursed traffic" and emptied the contents of his barrels and demijohns into the street. "Every good citizen in the community," cheered one editor, "should encourage this individual in his resolution to lead a better life." It seems more likely that many citizens must have wondered what in tarnation the old tippler had been drinking that wintry weekend.

The virtue of temperance was everlastingly being preached. In addition to the Rechabite Tent there was the Independent Order of Good Templars, (IOGT) organized November 1, 1865, with the Reverend Mr. Angier as "worthy chaplain." Other worthies listed as officers were Levi Cleaves, Sophia A. Poole, Calvin W. Pool, Asa F. Tarr, Henri N. Woods, Moses H. Cleaves, Maggie C. Burnham, John Knights, Eliza Caldwell, Hannah and Fanny Dade, Annie F. Gott, and James J. Gott. Northern Lights would later shine over Pigeon Cove through Lodge no. 240 of the IOGT, descendants of the Sons of Temperance who had earlier taken up residence there. Rockport in

Long Beach in the early days, with Maude Sawyer and her mother strolling in the sand. (SBHS)

the 1860s was offered temperance concerts, temperance lectures (some of them in a series or course), temperance "levees" (two hundred attended the one in mid-March 1867), temperance installations, temperance social gatherings, and temperance visits.

Then there were the temperance picnics. In September 1866, 180 Samaritan Tenters from Marblehead invaded Rockport by train for a basket picnic up on Poole's Hill above the depot. They brought along their own band. The Bay Tent escorted the Marbleheaders through town and on up Summit Avenue, where they partook of their collation. The hillside quickly proved too rocky "for tripping the light fantastic," as a reporter coyly put it, so the more agile members descended to the depot area for an hour of dancing. Even at picnics there were temperance talks. After Rockport's chief tenter, Newell Burnham, came four speeches by out-of-towners. The picnickers were reminded that their goals were "the promotion of temperance, chastity, and every other virtue that adorns the human character." When some restless, alert tenter discovered that the departing train wouldn't leave Rockport for Marblehead for half an hour, the temperance picnic ended with another, briefer whirl of dancing at the depot.

For those less addicted to the town's temperance societies, the 1860s offered other diversions. In warm weather there was the recreation area off Nugent's Stretch known as Schenck's Grove. "There is a nice

Rebellion and Reconstruction

cook house furnished with two stoves, and boilers for chowder and coffee. Then there are swings, a fine platform for dancing, singing, or speaking, and on the pond are sail and row boats ever ready for those who wish to use them. It is easy of access either by carriage or by cars and the proprietor is one of the most gentlemanly men on the cape." Many outings were held there in the years ahead, including a citizens' picnic in July 1865, at which Gilmore's famous band from Boston was engaged to perform, and the Rockport Cornet Band's own mammoth picnic in July 1867.

Bands, of course, and paramilitary groups like the newly organized Cunningham Guards, had long been popular. In the early autumn of 1866 some twenty young Rockport men were rounded up to become members of a brass band. On May 31, 1867, the Cornet Band gave its first "promenade concert" of the season at Dock Square. "There was a large concourse of people in attendance, and it was quite a pleasant time." The players were encouraged to present weekly concerts during the summer: "Undoubtedly they will be well appreciated." As for their July 1867 toot, the cost was a dollar; but a ticket admitted a gentleman and his family. Train service would be available at half price for the "glorious time" to be anticipated. The same phrase was used to advertise a joint Sabbath school picnic at Schenck's Grove that summer.

Cookouts grew in popularity, such as the one in July 1869 when a group of out-of-town visitors were carted over to Long Beach. As a farewell compliment one eater offered this testimonial: "We have eaten many chowders in our day; but summing them all up, it seemed to us that Rockport chowder excelled them all." The sea didn't always present such delectable offerings. On May 13, 1867, the body of a boy about seven, dressed in a dark shirtwaist and pants, was picked up on Long Beach. The head and lower legs were missing. It was taken in charge and buried by the undertaker. For his labor C. S. Choate was paid $6 by the town. More than a month passed before the story was printed. Less gruesome was a large bone about three feet long and forty-two pounds in weight hauled up by a Rockport trawler that same May. "It is supposed to be part of an elephant's leg." As such it was exhibited at the store of J. H. Glover.

On August 26, 1869, the Essex Institute sponsored a trip to Cape Ann. Many members, with local naturalists, took a special train to Rockport. Visits were made to Pigeon Cove and Halibut Point to enjoy the coastal scenery and observe the natural features of the area. Had their visit been made three years earlier, it would have coincided with the many curious spectators who watched forty whales disporting themselves between Thacher's Island and Eastern Point. Science was reaching into the lives of the general public to such a degree that the school curriculum began devoting more time to natural philosophy, as it was still called by the old-timers.

One remarkably generous gesture to improve the town was made by David Kimball in March 1867 when he offered the town sixty shares in the Sandy Bay Pier Company. The income from ten shares was to provide prize books to pupils of good behavior "who manifest a desire to improve, though less gifted by nature." His bequest is still drawn upon annually. From the income of the other fifty shares was to be paid out assistance "to such of the American born inhabitants as are sick and infirm" and hence "unable to procure the comforts needful to their situation." None of the bequest, however, was to relieve any people already supported or assisted by the town.

Among the many lectures given to improve Rockport was that by one "Rev. Ames," who in December 1866 spoke about "Woman." The impact of the women's movement was beginning to be felt even on Cape Ann, but the shake-up would come five years later, one irritated editor announcing that "the Woman's Suffrage Question does not find much favor among us." Women, he declared, were pretty well satisfied with the portions they held, though "a few wear britches." It would be better to continue letting men attend to matters and duties of the state, he concluded.

What did find favor among many Rockporters of the period was a rousing debate. In February 1867 ten people formed a new debating society to meet every Friday to advance its declared object of the mutual improvement of its members. By March 8 the Washington Club had swollen to twenty-four. Debates, compositions, and declamations were conducted at the Broadway School, and the public was invited to attend. One subject announced was: "Resolved that the American Indians have a better right to the American Soil than the White Man."

Another outlet for surplus energy and improvement of the body if not the mind was sports. The latest national craze was cycling. Rockport did not escape. On February 19 the *Advertiser* warned: "The Velocipede mania has reached our town." To satisfy the "many of our young men that have a great desire to learn the science" there were plans for a cycling school at Johnson's Hall adjacent to the Front Beach. A week later came the news that J. E. Stickney had opened his

Rockport's Town Hall was built in 1869 and razed in 1956 to make way for the Town Office Building. There were stores and offices on the first floor, an auditorium on the second, and lodge and banquet rooms under the Mansard roof on the third. (Borge)

velocipede school. Because "there is considerable interest manifested in this mode of locomotion by the young people here abouts," the press predicted that the school would be well patronized. By the time spring was on the horizon the mania was rampant. A third shop was to open in the old Methodist chapel on the site of today's town parking lot. It would be owned by C. H. Cleaves and C. F. York, while John Fears would superintend the operations. Cycling would become the national recreation; and Rockport would become the subject of a paragraph or even a chapter in bicycle manuals and a page or two in cyclers' maps.

A Town Hall

As if to show that Rockport's senior citizens were made of sterner stuff, seventy-eight-year-old William B. Haskins inaugurated the last year of the Civil War decade by skating the entire length of Cape Pond up and back five times, a distance of eight miles. What did he and the twenty-four Rockporters over eighty think about their newly constructed town hall when they saw it? All the women and eight of the men had been born when their town was a parish of Gloucester and

Town on Sandy Bay

had fewer than one thousand residents. George Washington was the president they proudly recalled from their youth.

The matter of a proper town hall for Rockport had been aired repeatedly at town meetings. Repeatedly it had been postponed or rejected. Other needs were greater. Then in 1869 it happened—the first time the warrant for a Rockport town meeting was printed. For a North Village schoolhouse and lot there had to be found $3,000; for the South Village the required sum would be $4,000. There was a cry for roads at "Hardscrabble" (Prospect and Summer streets) and rumors that the town would have to pay heavily for a damage suit. "Tax payers will grumble worse than ever." For a town hall lot came the usual motion for postponement. But it failed! Purchase was approved. A motion for reconsideration was quickly entered; it, too, failed. A recount was demanded: the results were 187 yeas and 96 nays. Rockport was finally to have a proper town hall. The $30,000 payment would be made from a twenty-year loan from the Commonwealth. In October an extra $5,000 would be voted for furnishings, grading and fencing the grounds on Broadway, close to the shiny new Methodist church.

By November itchy improvers were completing schedules for lectures to be presented in the auditorium of the long awaited "Town House." Series tickets would cost $1.50, single events only $0.25. The inaugural program would be the band of Patrick Gilmore, impresario of the monster Peace Jubilee Concert held at the Hub with one hundred Boston firemen pounding authentic anvils during a rendition of Verdi's "Anvil Chorus." Among the lecturers would be Mark Twain, Paul du Chaillu, and a series of clergymen. The first week of December 1869, all was opened, including the auditorium seating "800-1,000" people. The hall was first used on Thursday, December 9, when a "goodly audience" heard several short addresses and listened while the Rockport band "discoursed appropriate music." The next night came Gilmore's concert, "which has been the principal theme of conversation of late." On Wednesday the fifteenth there was a grand ball with music by Hodgkins's Quadrille Band. On Saturday evening, wrote the *Advertiser,* "a precious set of scamps calling themselves the 'Star Troupe' attempted to give an entertainment at the hall. It was a big swindle . . . it was a good lesson for them to learn, and those who have charge of letting the hall will look out sharper in the future." The following attraction was Mark Twain, already well known as an entertainer and writer, though by then he had published only some short

Rebellion and Reconstruction

190   stories and, in 1869 itself, *Innocents Abroad.* His immortal Tom Sawyer, Huck Finn, and other characters lay yet unborn. He "perpetrated" his talk, but it was a disappointment. According to the reviewer, "A good many of the ticket holders wanted a humorous lecture, and they all know now just what a humorous lecture is, and the Rockport market is supplied with that style of goods for the present. The regular lectures are not always weekly, but this one *was* weakly. He is accused of being a humorist, but his hearers here will generally vote for a verdict of not guilty of the charge." Poor Twain was accused of concealing his wit and humor so adroitly that his audience found it very difficult to detect them. "In short, his lecture was remarkably satisfactory, only with an emphatic *dis* before it." He was housed at the home of temperate Dr. Sanborn on Broadway, next to the town hall. Despite the packed auditorium, the committee asked Twain to cut his fee by ten dollars. His refusal to do so and his brusque manner, especially at being called for breakfast too early, so angered his hosts that the children of the family were forbidden to read later Twain books, however diverting they were.

As Rockporters proudly moved into their new official home at the end of the decade, one familiar face was missing in the new office for

Col. William Pool (1796-1871), a private in the Sea Fencibles during the War of 1812, was the first Rockport Town Clerk from 1840-1869. (SBHS)

Town on Sandy Bay

the town clerk. In his thirtieth year of service, William Pool, direct descendant of both Richard Tarr and John Pool, decided to put down his pens. He had served his town from its incorporation in 1840. The time had come. "For the precision and neatness of the records and his admirable correctness in detail," ran the resolution voted at the town meeting, "we tender to our retiring Town Clerk our expression of good will for his future welfare." With them went the grateful hopes of his community that the closing years of his life "may be crowned with health, peace, and contentment," and that "hope's radiant bow" would "illumine his pathway to the better land beyond." As his successor, Rockport elected the "son of a worthy sire" to the office. Calvin W. Pool would occupy his father's post for over thirty-nine years.

ADDITIONAL READING

To supplement the story of Rockport in the Civil War as related in the *History* of 1888 one should check individual records in the eight volumes of *Massachusetts Soldiers, Sailors, and Marines in the Civil War* (Brookline, 1931-35).

For risible reading on Twain as a lecturer see Paul Fatout, *Mark Twain on the Lecture Circuit* (Bloomington, 1960). The lecturer's own view of his Rockport sojourn is in Dixon Wecter, ed., *The Love Letters of Mark Twain* (New York, 1949).

Rebellion and Reconstruction

15

"LOCAL IMPROVEMENTS FLOURISH"

THE EMERGENCE of Rockport from a hamlet on the outer edge of "ye Cape" into the world beyond the Cut had been taking place for a century and a half anyway. It was not until the 1870s, however, that Rockport finally began publishing its own newspaper, that symbol of communal maturity. To be sure, Rockport had had a newspaper of sorts in the summer of 1868. On June 6 the *Rockport Quarry* made its debut from Salem. Part of an Essex County chain, it carried a few items of Rockport and Pigeon Cove news, plus four local advertisements, but the rest of the paper dealt with other communities and their affairs. July 18 saw the end of the *Quarry*.

Not keen at the prospect of competition, the Gloucester press mentioned in late February 1872 that Mr. Levi Cleaves would be starting "an advertising sheet" for Rockport. Volume I, number 1 of the *Rockport Gleaner* was dated March 1872 and consisted of four pages with five columns each. Initially, copies sold for 3 cents each. Far more than an advertising sheet, it appeared monthly for fifteen years and lived up to its publisher's stated desire to be lively and local. He also made it a point not to run ads from other than community stores, with a handful of exceptions. By December the paper was issued as an outsized folio with eight columns per page, which virtually doubled the amount of material printed. Although the *Gleaner* was but a monthly and therefore passed over the purely ephemeral, its news stories and

The town as a whole rounded a corner during that decade. Christmas had been celebrated by all the churches. Services had not been thronged, however, perhaps because of poor weather. On Christmas afternoon skating offered the principal diversion, despite the poor state of the ice.

The new year opened with a week of prayer and with a confrontation. Sexism and suffrage came to town. On Friday, January 7, Rockport's newly opened town hall played host to an all-day Women's Suffrage Convention. Crowds heard a roster of proponents, including Julia Ward Howe (Boston's poet) and the renowned Anna Dickinson, whose pointed evening lecture on "Whited Sepulchres" brought down the house as well as many listeners from Gloucester. A special train was added to take them back afterward. "She is decidely the best female lecturer that has ever spoken here." The whole vexatious question of women burst like a skyrocket over the town, leaving reverberations and flashes for weeks to come.

The popular Universalist minister, George Vibbert, had announced a sermon on women's rights, adding: "The opponents of Women's Suffrage are especially invited to attend." They took him literally. His own church was locked against him and the lamps made inoperable. As a substitute, he tackled the issue of dancing, also highly controversial, with a sermon entitled "Young Women and Balls." At a special meeting fourteen Universalists rose to justify their action, including "a large number of females also." The following Sunday, Mr. Vibbert did set forth his views of equal rights at the ballot. His text was Galatians 3:28 ("there is neither male nor female"), and his final point was this: "It is said that if women vote, they will hold offices. Why not? Women are needed in public affairs." The provocative Mr. Vibbert stuck to his guns in a sequel on "Obedience of Wives." Over at the Methodist church a woman evangelist held forth for more than a fortnight in February 1870. The reporter described her as a good-looking, hearty, substantial woman, who was a very forcible, earnest speaker. She did, however, appeal "like a woman, almost entirely to the emotions."

Temperance also offered a vehicle for the women of Rockport, and in the spring of 1876 one campaign culminated in a Rockport's Women's Temperance Movement, with Olive P. Bray president and Mrs. Janette Parsons secretary. Churches and schools cautiously added

194   women to their various boards. At the Universalists, Susanna Torrey
became treasurer in 1870, and in 1872 "a vote was passed that females
be allowed to vote in Society Affairs." In December 1877 the *Gleaner*
noticed that "it is becoming very common now to have women as
members of the School Committee—a very sensible movement, since
girls as well as boys fill the schools." The Congregationalists on January
14, 1880, voted that their church committee should consist of three
males and two females. Mrs. Nancy E. Brooks and Miss Fanny Dade
were the pioneers. The fact that "Mr. John Rowe's corset manufactury
lately moved to Boston," as reported in 1878, should not be inter-
preted as a breakthrough for Rockport women, however. They would
continue to be straitlaced for quite some years to come, their improving status not withstanding.

The more visible improvements of the 1870s testify to an upsurge
of energy. Perhaps the most enduring was the library. The winter
lectures of 1869-70 cleared $200 as seed money for a Rockport public
library. The annual town meeting took a reciprocal step, adding nearly
$250 more from dog taxes which by state law were for library use. A
room in the town hall was set apart; shelving was acquired; some 350
books were purchased; and in December 1871 the library was opened
under the aegis of Thomas F. Parsons. A fee of 50 cents a year was
charged. In January 1872 the YMCA deposited its collection of 64
items in the town library—to be kept on separate shelves, however.
The press noted that there were already 150 subscribers and a printed
catalogue was available. The following January the *Gleaner* remarked,
playfully, "Rockport dogs, to their credit be it recorded, contributed to
the Public Library a tax of $105 for the past year. Who else in town
does as much for the library as that?"

In July 1870 a new post office was erected on Main Street next to
William Manning's jewelry store, and the old one was sold for $150 to
make room for the solid new National Bank. In September 1871 the
postmaster found it necessary to add another dozen post office boxes
to keep up with the demand. A twice-daily mail service between
Rockport and Gloucester was instituted in January 1874. Far more
rapid was the telegraph system which stretched its wires from
Rockport to Pigeon Cove in 1871. An office was opened at the Pigeon
Cove House at the end of August. In April 1875 the telegraph wires
between Rockport and Gloucester were replaced by "a brand new
galvanized one." At the same time a new telegraph station was opened
at the depot for the use of the Eastern Railroad Company.

Town on Sandy Bay

Cottages at the northern end of Halibut Point. The Moorish dome just visible behind the large building at left center belonged to "Way Villa," the second structure built by John M. Way about 1880. (Hoyt)

Telegraphy provided a vehicle for a far-reaching improvement at sea, so in 1874 the lighthouses on Thacher's Island became a storm signal station by connecting the island to the Rockport telegraph office through a submarine cable. The system enabled the island to run up beacons to warn ships of approaching storms. In the tempest of January 1878, not one wreck occurred within forty miles of the Thacher's Island station. By February the cable telegraph was able to give mariners a twelve-hour advance alert. Less efficacious were the telephones mentioned in the *Gleaner* as being experimented with by several Rockport tinkerers. All the devices were "home made," but some were also "home-maid," thereby inaugurating a new if not improved technique for courting.

Other maritime improvements included a thirty-foot-high tripod beacon on the Salvages (August 1873) and a beacon for Half Tide Rock just east of the Rockport Granite Company's breakwater in 1878. In November 1877 the Massachusetts Humane Society donated an eighteen-foot Swampscott dory to the Rockport lifesaving station. A previous rescue dory had been moved from Dock Square to Fish Avenue in September 1872 for quicker availability.

"Local Improvements Flourish"

Although most Rockporters of the 1870s were pedestrian, they took steps to improve their mobility. Two residents of Main Street put down sidewalks in September 1870; the next August a number of enterprising merchants in Dock Square had their sidewalks tarred. "Such a sidewalk is very appropriate in this town, where there are so many Tarrs," joked the paper.

To illuminate several ways and walks, existing and being constructed, streetlamps were supplied during the 1870s. At the outset these were one more example of Rockport's private initiative, the *Gleaner* first commenting on their appearance in November 1874 when a number were placed on Main Street, on Dock Square, up Cove Hill, three on Broadway, and one at the foot of King Street. By July 1875, some twenty to thirty streetlamps had been erected at Pigeon Cove, and in August came the word of more for Rockport and for the road to Pigeon Cove through the North Village. These were not oil or kerosene burners but used a kind of naphtha from a Boston firm on a contract basis, the cost being $20 per lamp per year. Economy trimmed the lamps in November 1875, with the decision to burn them only twenty nights each month and never during a full moon. Other lights came with the years, including sixty-four new lamps in 1878 for the avenues at Pigeon Cove to make things pleasant for the summer visitors. Almost every cottage was open there; hotels were crowded; and at Hoop Pole Cove, to the west of Andrews' Point, "proprietors are clearing away rocks and erecting bathhouses which when completed will make one of the finest bathing places on the Cape."

Rockport streets would be further enhanced as a result of bids, in October 1878, for forty-five new street signs to identify public roads. Less than a year later even Beech Grove Cemetery blossomed with road signs and "never looked better." Back in 1872 Rockport had bought a new hearse, then added a new harness, a house for both, and a loading platform—all for $1,151.23. Azor Knowlton had the questionable honor of being "the first corpse to occupy the present hearse." Subsequently, Pigeon Covers pooled funds and bought a hearse for the North Village, which the town repainted for $30 in 1878. For riders still able to enjoy their jaunts, there was Mr. Randall's shiny new stagecoach (March 1872) and Mr. Woolford's new "barge" to bus people from the depot over to Pigeon Cove. One of the popular cove barges was the *Pinafore* named for Gilbert and Sullivan's sensational new comic opera.

The "Duck Pond" at Dock Square, located at the site of the present pumping station, served as a source of water in case of fire before mains were installed. (Mrs. Elizabeth Knowlton)

Waterworks first became a concern to Rockporters principally for fire protection purposes. Although they had reservoirs, including a large and costly one near the hotel in Pigeon Cove and the 29,000-gallon one at the intersection of Pleasant and Summer streets, the question of drinking water for humans and horses came up at town meetings. In July 1875 a Rockport Water Company was organized to draw from Cape Pond, primarily for the use of fire fighters. According to its charter it could construct a suitable works, lay pipes, and establish rates. The town itself was empowered to take stock up to $5,000 worth. The *Gleaner* decided that that proviso was probably valid, though at the time there was "neither any vast demand for water nor any serious want of supply." Formal incorporation did take place in the early winter of 1876, with John D. Sanborn as president and Henry Dennis, Jr., as treasurer.

At this period the town also undertook to improve its fire-fighting equipment. A special town meeting in December 1875 authorized a hook-and-ladder company, the purchase of a truck for $1,500 (later reduced to $750), and an additional twelve hundred feet of hose and a

Rare view of the keystone arch Granite Bridge built from start to finish during the summer of 1872. Ground on the quarry side had not as yet been graded, and the buildings above the bridge were later removed to make way for Wharf Road. (Heslin)

Town on Sandy Bay

hose carriage. In late March 1876 the company of twenty-six men proudly exhibited the new equipment; the truck bore the name "G. P. Whitman" and the hose cart "C. H. Parsons." Two new engine houses were constructed. As a do-it-yourself system, Rockporters voted in March 1875 to encourage portable fire pumps by allowing a tax reduction of $1 per year for five years. Many extinguishers were purchased, and in October 1877 residents enjoyed a public muster in which eleven men competed. Levi Parsons threw a stream fifty-nine feet, six inches, and Alfred Parsons was runner up at fifty-seven feet, eight inches. Following the serious demonstrations, "there were playful exercises in reciprocal squirtations," which failed to amuse innocent, drenched bystanders. As further protection, the town hall acquired a fire escape and doors which opened outward.

At this time Pigeon Cove was also the scene of several major improvements, beginning with the tunnel and arch bridge constructed in 1872 over the passage between the Rockport Granite Company quarries and its wharves. A truly noteworthy feat of engineering, its sixty-five-foot span became one of the largest in the state. Then came the railroad from the Pigeon Hill Granite Company's pits across Granite Street and down to its waterfront pier. A gravity line, it relied on horses to pull the empty flatcars back up the hill. The extension of the Eastern Railroad from Rockport to Pigeon Cove, for which the *Quarry* had pleaded, sporadically roused optimism. In November 1879 railway officials even climbed Poole's Hill to see the prospects from above, but like Keats' stout Cortez at Darien, they remained silent on the peak. The company did, however, erect a loading derrick at its freight terminal in the spring of 1871, and in June 1877 the Rockport Granite Company began the novelty of shipping paving blocks to New York by steam-propeller-driven freighters rather than by sailing sloops. "Delivery is more prompt and sure, there being no delay for wind or tide."

North Village children, as well as an overflow of bright youngsters from the Beach Street School, had a new schoolhouse at Pigeon Hill, today's residence at 107 Granite Street. At its opening in September 1872, the school enrolled some fifty to sixty pupils. For Rockport as a whole there were the church bells, all improved; even the struggling Cotton Mill bought a replacement in May 1871. A journalist jibed: "There will be no excuse for any sinner in Rockport who does not obey the summons of the church-going bells."

Four horses pull a granite car uphill from the Pigeon Hill Granite Company wharf against a backdrop of paving blocks. (C. Swan)

Inventions, Inventiveness

Yankee ingenuity certainly demonstrated its vitality in Rockport during the 1870s, as a string of townspeople secured patents for a wide array of devices: Ebenezer Rowe's method of recycling icewater for cooling the cylinders in the manufacture of isinglass, Levi Thurston's gadget which enabled ship rudders to be moved more easily or be fixed in position, Thomas Fitzgerald's patent for an improved trolling hook, and John C. Knowlton's patented Metallic Ratline Clasp for wire and hemp rigging. Transportation was helped by Sylvanus Holbrook's imaginative railroad track gauge and by Jacob Goldsmith's invention for detaching a horse from the carriage shafts instantaneously and his improved wheelsocket to grip spokes. In early 1874 Oscar E. Wait invented a machine for manufacturing horseshoes rapidly, and in 1878 he patented a system of spools and bobbins for use in spinning mills. Nathaniel Robbins had already patented a safety stop for sewing machines and protected his "chalk-line holder." Women rejoiced at Asa Frank Tarr's ingenious clothesline pole (1874)—"easily adjustable, secure when on, and readily removable."

Town on Sandy Bay

A stone sloop under way with a deck load of granite blocks destined for a construction project. (SBHS)

Three sets of patents launched substantial enterprises in Rockport, each of which would plummet to disaster within the decade. First came the American Hide Seat Company to construct woven chair bottoms from hide. It purchased land below the old anchor works on King Street and went into business. By September it was employing thirty men; by December its "vast" new building was finished. At its first annual meeting in May 1872, prospects were very satisfactory and encouraging. Orders were heavy. February 1873 found the company no longer turning out seats at all, only cord and a hide heel stiffening for shoes, for which a patent had also been secured. By October the Hide Seat Company was in trouble. February 1874 saw its collapse, and in March the building was sold at auction.

In May 1872 the versatile William H. Manning devised his improved method for building parlor organs, claiming these could be taken apart in less than a minute and without unscrewing a screw. Prices would be half of the usual amount. The Manning Organ Company began manufacturing in March 1873 in the rented upper stories of the Hide Seat Company building. Orders poured in far faster than the factory could turn out the instruments. For a period, salesmen

The Haskins Block, now 37 Main Street, was built in the 1870s and was then occupied by Butman & French's Dry Goods and Gents Furnishings stores. (SBHS)

were withdrawn in order to dampen enthusiasm. In December came a new patent for a reed piano-organ action, which almost produced the rippling effects of the piano. Yet all was over in a year and a half, though the local press loyally soft-pedaled the sour notes. In April 1876 the company held an auction of its products. In May the patents were disposed of to Rust and Marshall of Manchester and the factory taken over by yet another star-crossed improvement.

Oscar E. Wait's patents for bobbins and spools produced another new hope for the town and a reinforcement for the Rockport Cotton Mill. The Bobbin Company acquired the previous hideseat and organ factory on King Street in June 1877, the very month the bankrupt Rockport Isinglass Company was sold at auction for $2,925. By September the Bobbin Company employed twenty men. By December it was already in difficulties and was being reorganized. That same month, however, the newly housed Cape Ann Isinglass Company near the depot on Railroad Avenue commenced operations, also with twenty men. Its manager was Henry Dennis, Jr. In February 1878

bobbins and spools rolled out of town forever, moving to Gardner,
where wood was so much more plentiful that costs would be reduced
by one third.

In April 1878, when the insolvent Pigeon Cove Granite Company
was being subdivided and auctioned, the Russia Cement Company of
East Boston leased the empty bobbin factory. The following year the
company was running night and day "filling large orders for their
celebrated liquid fish glue and isinglass." Yet it, too, would find the
factory a Jonah and in time move to Gloucester, closer still to fish
supplies. Lewis Nickerson's new and ample gristmill came into being in
June 1878, adjacent to the all-important railhead. A survey team came
to Rockport testing for pottery clays in January 1879. They met with
success and formed the Pigeon Cove Pottery Company. "The latest
novelty is to have your dishes made of this ware, and the cups, mugs,
and other such articles nicely marked with the name of the owner . . .
bean pots with covers and family names are finding their way into
town."

There were also the moss gatherers who collected, dried, ground
fine, packed, and sold Sea Moss Farina. By 1879 William Day was
working three men and shipping out seventy barrels a month. The
process took about three weeks from raking to packing. To cope with
rough weather and fishing conditions, the local firm of York, Saville,
and Company started manufacturing waterproof clothing in the
spring of 1870 under their own patent. By 1872 Rockport had seventy
stores, one for every 50 inhabitants.

Thus, with new industries rising (and falling), new shops opening
up, two new hotels being built for Pigeon Cove (the new Pigeon Cove
House and the Ocean View on the Avenue), new homes for mill
operatives, company housing and buildings for granite operatives, a
veritable epidemic of summer cottages at Pigeon Cove and the South
End, and even more cells at the lockup for Rockport's expanding
"tramp hotel" trade, townspeople cheered for still better times ahead.
The *Cape Ann Advertiser* wrote enthusiastically that in Rockport "local
improvements flourish."

"Not by Bread Alone"

How many Rockporters of the decade went to lectures in order to be
improved and how many went to be entertained or just to have some-

thing to do is a matter for speculation. But how they did flock to be talked to! During the decade the press covered talks on such topics as these: "The Adirondacks," "California from Missionaries to Today," "The Future of our Country," "Prison Life" (by the warden of the Charlestown jail), "Life in the Army," the "Orders of Nobility," "Locomotion of Animals," and "The Man Who Laughs: or Good Nature." Two Irish evenings reflected the newer immigrants: "The Last Days of the Irish Parliament and Ireland's Chieftain—Patrick Sarsfield," "Muscle and Brain, Napoleon and Bismark, Washington and Grant—our Military Reformers" provided sets of contrasts. Rarely did the newspapers ever criticize the performers negatively. One exception was a parson, H. W. Warren, who explored light in December 1870 but "was over most people's heads." As for temperance talkers, they seem never to have run out of breath. Methodist Mr. Merrill reported in April 1874 that during the past year he had delivered forty addresses on temperance under the auspices of the Good Templars.

The entertainments which Rockport supported so enthusiastically at the time included concerts by the churches, the schools, the Sabbath schools, and several bands. The famous Hutchinson Family Singers included Rockport on their itinerary in 1872, as did the London cornet virtuoso, Page, in March 1873, and Spaulding's bell ringers, who presented a "chaste and elegant concert." Local organist Mr. Ryder in a recital in December 1871 roared out "A Stormy Ocean" and tweeted "The Mockingbird." At the YMCA chapel in August 1878, John Carter of Gloucester gave "Sweet Geneveive" (sic) (well rendered) and "Rocked in the Cradle of the Deep" (with excellent effect). Sparkling melodies poured from the Pigeon Cove House in September 1871 when Signor Giovanni brought his "charming exhibition of trained canaries" to town.

Rockporters were astonished by the Royal Japanese Jugglers and their "unexplainable tergiversations" that September 1871 and in November 1870 (at Dock Square) by a small "wax opera" with "captivating figgers of murdered maidens and assassinated victims, displaying lovely gashes and pleasant streams of blood." In August 1872 Buffalo Bill galloped into Rockport on a Monday and "drew a good many small bills from the pockets of the dear people," who went in crowds to the town hall to witness his delineations of wild life. A frank journalist reported that the Morris Brothers' Comic Troupe brought in more people "than the ten best preachers and their ten best sermons."

Town on Sandy Bay

Rockport had its share of theater from both out-of-town companies, which usually played at the town hall, and local groups. In February 1870 Meyer's Dramatic Company gave "good satisfaction" in *Rip Van Winkle*. In the spring of 1878 the Pigeon Cove Dramatic Club performed that beloved tearjerker, *East Lynne* (followed by a social hop with a "capital" orchestra) and Goldsmith's comedy *She Stoops to Conquer* in November. The following year on April 1, *Uncle Tom's Cabin* made yet another reappearance at the town hall, and in November the Pigeon Covers mounted *Ten Nights in a Bar Room* before a rather slim house because of wretched weather. Debating clubs continued to attract interest. A new one was formed in the South Village in March 1872, and in March 1875 Pigeon Covers formed a club to discuss questions, give readings, and "discourse music." The craze for spelling matches appears to have hit Rockport in 1875. Reading clubs followed by 1877, in both the South and North villages. Each issue of the *Gleaner* helpfully ran carefully prepared summaries of new books, comments on new music, and interesting articles in the nation's better magazines.

By the 1870s nearly everyone was having dances. In the winter of 1871-72 the Pigeon Cove House was the scene of "a gay dance every Thursday." There were antique balls, Thanksgiving, Christmas and New Year's Eve ones, calico balls in both centers of town. Countless masquerades were reported gleefully by the press. In March 1879 a wag wrote in the *Gleaner* that "dancing is forbidden during Lent but fish *balls* are allowable." A reverberation of the antidancing stance of some church members was echoed among the alumni of Rockport's schools, where a division occurred "as to the propriety of dancing at the annual reunions." In January 1877 a compromise and reunification were negotiated.

Rockporters made some desultory attempts to form a Natural History Society in 1871 and put exhibit cases in the library room. An Agricultural-Horticultural Society was founded in February 1874, to "embrace" agriculture proper, gardens, trees, flowers, domestic animals, and fish. In October 1874, 168 people exhibited vegetables, 60 contributors showed 40 varieties of apples, 55 offered 200 specimens of pears, 30 contributed grapes, and a round 100 brought flowers. In May 1872 the *Gleaner* called: "We need a village shade tree society, voluntarily clothing our streets in the delightful beauty of forest verdure." Birds also emerged as a subject for the press to write about and for people to study and collect. Henry C. Leonard spoke to the Rockport Scientific Club in March 1877 on "Voices of Birds." The

Southern shore of Rockport Harbor in 1878 showing the wharf and fish houses at the public landing off the Headlands. The long white building on the uphill slope was the "bowling alley," part of which later became a residence on Norwood Avenue. (SBHS)

newspapers made much of the arrival of some twenty English sparrows at Rockport in November 1876 and again in 1878. The Steam Cotton Mill people put up houses for the colony of "useful little busy bodies," expecting them to eat up the canker worms, grubs, and caterpillars infesting trees and gardens. A flying rarity of a different species was a hotair balloon, which floated down on Saturday, July 20, 1872. Some overly experimental Rockporters tried to inflate it by burning whiskey but succeeded only in burning up the balloon. Two weeks later it was discovered that the "fire balloon" had been sent aloft at Amesbury the same day it had landed in Rockport.

The sporty members of the area also indulged their hobbies. Walking became so popular that by the end of the decade the town hall auditorium was the scene of several walking matches. Rowing, like sailing, attracted enthusiasts, particularly Reuben Brooks with his elegant little single scull, imported from England. The regatta of September 10, 1878, proved to be a failure because of an absolute calm. Only sixteen yachts entered and only nine sailed. In 1871 six or seven boys "of large growth" were caught in the act by the police on the

Town on Sandy Bay

swore never to do it again, at least never on Sundays. Skating and
sliding was for everyone whenever the weather permitted, but on
Christmas Day, 1877 it was so mild that "a party of young ladies played
croquet."

Baseball arrived. The first local mention may well have been the
Advertiser's note of June 16, 1876: "Rockport has a lively base ball club,
whose brisk exercise may be witnessed almost any evening in one of the
ample fields on Norwood's Head." By July, the *Gleaner* said the town
had two teams, the Granites and the Quicksteps. In a letter the same
paper carried the first known published grievance: "It is a pity if we
cannot have good honest ball playing without swearing." By August
the teams had doubled to four, and "entire games have been played
with hardly a profane utterance." The 1878 season began on May 11,
at Bottle of Rum Rock Pasture: Clippers, 16; Our Boys, 28. In June,
yet another team was formed, the Eckfords. Once the virus took hold,
it spread. For over half a century summer Saturdays would never be
the same for innumerable Rockporters.

Also in the second half of the decade, fishing parties, picnics, and
excursions were "all the rage now." As one summer visitor wrote in
1877: "One is remote from fashion and nonsense, can wear old clothes,
and go without gloves." Boats, he went on, could be hired for rowing
for 25 cents, a dory seating four or five with a fisherman and tackle for
half a day's deepsea fishing cost only $2.50. "It is rare fun, when the
fish are not on strike." He himself had caught thirty large cod and
pollock in two hours.

For a long while large parties had been invading Rockport, especially its North Village. In 1878 one irritated resident counted 202
teams passing his home between 8:00 A.M. and 8:00 P.M. one Sunday.
Nearly all were "idle pleasure carriages and buggies, and the occupants were bent on mere recreation." On another Sunday in August
1878, the steamer *Cambridge* of Boston landed some seven hundred
passengers at Pigeon Cove. The *Gleaner* remarked: "We think it would
be better if our town authorities should prevent such parties landing
on the Sabbath Day." The paper also observed that the encampment of
Penobscot Indians on the Avenue would not desecrate the Sabbath by
selling their baskets but kept their tents closed. Also on an August
Sunday in 1878, the *May Queen* from Haverhill brought in "a rather
rough crowd." So by September two hundred Rockporters had signed
a petition to bar the landing of excursion steamers on Sundays.

The town had also become a popular camping site, especially for the Lowell-Nashua people. The *Gleaner* was forecasting that the South End might become more than a match for any other part of "our goodly town." In 1878 there was a tent village near Loblolly as well as a colony of cottages there. More campers were at Gully Point enjoying themselves and fostering two baseball teams, the Chowders and the Biled [sic] Onions.

The Lord Moves

Against such a secularization, Rockport churches had to intensify their efforts. Statistics in April 1872 noted that the town had five religious denominations, seven church buildings, aggregate seating for twenty-three hundred worshipers, yet only about thirteen hundred townspeople or one third of the population, attending services. Although the percentage was about the general average throughout Massachusetts, the writer declared that "something is wrong." Revival meetings were intensified to lift up the fallen, espe-

The First Congregational Church, built in 1804, continues to be an outstanding landmark of the Town. The steeple was struck by a cannon ball during the British attack in 1814. (Hoyt)

Town on Sandy Bay

cially among the Methodists and Baptists. In 1873 the latter declared pews to be free. Everyone was welcome to sit where he pleased. Their minister, too, had no fixed salary, but relied on regular contributions. "This is a mode of sustaining public worship somewhat novel here," wrote a journalist of the time; "its success will be observed with interest." In April 1875 the Baptists were free from debt. Other churches, however, continued to rely heavily on annual rental fees. Two lasting improvements came in 1873. In August the Congregational church was lighted with gas for the first time. And Pigeon Cove got its own Universalist church, on the corner of Granite Street and Phillips Avenue. Its style, reported the *Advertiser,* would be one of the most elegant churches of its size in the state. When dedicated on June 12, 1873, it had cost $10,540 and had sixty family units as members. In 1878 it changed its name to the Second Universalist Society of Rockport. In September, 1874, the Pigeon Cove chapel, consisting of nineteen members, was recognized as a fully constituted Congregational church under the title of the First Church of Christ at Pigeon Cove.

Back in October 1870 Rockport Catholics rejoiced that they would finally have a fulltime priest, Father Thomas Barry. In December he purchased a rectory on the court off Smith Street from its Bostonian owner. Six months earlier the Methodists had bought their parsonage for $1,600. In 1872, for several months, the few Episcopalians of Rockport held services at the YMCA building on Broadway thanks to the ministrations of the rector of St. John's in Gloucester. Nothing more seems to have been done prior to July 1878, when thanks again to St. John's, "services peculiar to the Episcopal Church" were held at Eureka Hall. After October regular services were again dropped for several years, though during the summer a mixture of clergy and laymen held forth in Pigeon Cove.

In November 1876, the year in which 534 Rockporters voted for Hayes and 277 for Tilden, the fragmented church community formed a Union Bible Class. Faith was far from dead. The handsome church of the Methodists, however, was destroyed by a great conflagration on Sunday morning, May 2, 1875. The cause of the blaze was never determined, and the lapse of an insurance policy left them, once the mortgage was paid off, with only $3,000. With Joblike patience they cleared the rubble, recommenced fundraising, and on the old site erected the church which still stands on Broadway. The cost was about $9,700. The Congregationalists had also been dispossessed of a meeting place as a result of their overly ambitious renovations in 1871, which expanded the body of the church at its center with a kind of gusset insert of twenty feet and left a bill of $28,000. With a business recession the members were unable to cope. When the Rockport Savings Bank foreclosed, the YMCA opened the doors of their chapel and bade them a hearty welcome. Herculean efforts made it possible for the bank—itself in receivership—to reopen the doors of the church.

The YMCA itself purchased the ill-fated second Congregationalist church in March 1870, with W. W. Marshall, Addison Gott, and Nathaniel Pool as trustees, and in 1871 gave to the town a few feet of their corner lot, so that School Street might be widened. Each summer they held outdoor meetings every Sunday at 6:00 P.M. on the green near the Baptist church, and they, too, organized a series of public lectures.

With the rapid rise in population and the influx of a wave of immigrants used to hard drinking in their countries of origin, Rockport expanded its already staggering capacity for booze. In addition to the two IOGT societies and the Rechabites, who numbered about one hundred, was added a WCTU chapter which in no time had one hundred members. The centennial year produced an extensive temperance revival during which the auditorium of the town hall was filled "to utmost capacity." Hundreds of enthusiasts donned the blue-ribbon badge of membership, and many were reclaimed from their cups. During the upheaval, it has been said, saloon keeper Greer heaved his stock of liquors into the gutter and closed out his business.

A Youth's Temperance Union was also formed in 1876 and soon had fifty members. Did the Cold Water Army dry up, one wonders? Also in 1876 began the Temperance Reform Club, which held weekly meetings. In March 1876 a Pigeon Cove branch was formed and a bonbon party was held to help furnish its rooms. At their first anniversary, the Reformers had an enrollment of about 250 in the South Village alone. The thirtieth anniversary of the Rechabites came in 1877. Two of the founders were still members. During its three decades the Rechabite Tent had paid out over $4,000 in charities, sick benefits, and funeral funds. Yet before Christmas of 1877, the Reform Club closed up and turned down its empty glass. The next month, though, the stubborn Rechabites dedicated their own new hall, the walls of which were festooned with mottoes and pictures, and decided to carry on the Monday weekly sessions of the defunct Reformers. But all these movings and shakings failed to dry out an officially dry town.

Town on Sandy Bay

This Procter stereo view of granite quarry workers from the 1870s clearly indicates the barren nature of the surrounding land.

Issue after issue of the papers ran pleas for tighter enforcement and tales of drunkenness and even of death. November 1870 brought the news that "the usual number of police arrests have occurred during the past week for assault and battery, head cuttings, and nose biting, all of course the result of whiskey."

Like a stuck record the tunes of intemperance played on. So, too, came the reports of shipwrecks and drownings. In addition to fishing vessels, Rockport stone freighters also sailed perilously. In 1872 James W. Bradley was appointed Essex County commissioner of wrecks and shipwrecked goods. June 5, of that year was talked about for months because of the storm which drove ten vessels ashore, most of them wrecks. February 20-21, 1879, brought a gale during which a dozen Gloucester fishing vessels were lost with their entire crews, including four Rockport men, all married and fathers of twelve children in all. One of the men was "John Hakanson, a Swede, who has resided in Rockport the past two years; he leaves a wife and three children."

Hardest hit by accidents were not seamen but quarry workers and even passersby. Week after week poured forth grueling stories of cables snapping on hoists; falling blocks of granite; toppling machinery; landslides; runaway flatcars; slipped derricks; and blasting incidents taking an eye, a finger, a hand, and not infrequently a life. Yet it took only the slight drop in business in 1872 to remind selectmen, taxpayers, shopkeepers, and workers who met the town's chief payroll. By 1877 Rockport had 211 acres of quarries with a capital investment of $259,000 and an annual sale of $475,000, produced by 258 men between fifteen and thirty years of age. Granite, not cotton, was king by the 1870s.

Several other accidents involving Rockporters of the era occurred in the Rockport Cotton Mill, on the trains (which had two wrecks in the 1870s), in houses and barns, and on the streets (usually from balking horses). Townspeople took up collections for victims of both the Chicago fire (1871) and the Boston one of 1872.

There were also lively rejoicings in much of Rockport in November 1872. The presidential election had elicited 479 votes for Grant and 126 for Horace Greeley. The election torchlight procession, led by Thomas Parsons, Jr., and the Cornet Band, marched from the South End all the way to Pigeon Cove, serenading houses and making speeches along the line. Daniel O. Marshall, the oldest man in town at over ninety, had proudly voted in his eighteenth presidential election, only to die a month later, leaving two sisters aged eighty-four and eighty-eight, eleven children, seven grandchildren, and three great-grandchildren. When his counterpart, Mrs. Sally Clark, Rockport's oldest woman died, that same month at ninety or so, she left seven children, twenty-two grandchildren, thirty-two great-grandchildren, and three great-great-grandchildren—sixty-four living descendants.

Like most American communities, Rockport observed patriotic holidays with assorted activities. The Fourth of July still took a back seat to Bunker Hill Day. Usually there was an "Antique Horribles Parade" with at least some bands playing. In 1870, following the march, Henry Dennis, Jr., the orator of the day, "delivered a side-splitting oration in Dock Square which abounded in numerous local hits, and was received with great applause." On Washington's birthday in 1872, a reporter remarked: "So many good, honest, people had their naps cruelly tattered and torn by yesterday morning's eternal bell ringing that they were sorry that famous Washington baby was born." With the arrival of the Irish in increasing numbers, St. Patrick's Day was observed by them. It was June 17, though, which generated Rockport's jolliest celebration, primarily because that was when all the fire companies turned out their equipment, their uniformed crews,

Hose 1 in front of the Fire Station in Dock Square. From left: Charles A. Poole, Frank Jordan, George Hobbs, Benjamin F. Burns, John R. Tarr, and Franklin Jordan. (SBHS)

their "pretty ladies," their most stuffing collations, their friends among the bands, and the paramilitary groups. There was intense competition at the musters, staged in three or four different parts of town, and then during the "Trial of Tubs" for the hand pumps.

With Decoration Day, May 30, 1870, the town commenced its annual observance of Memorial Day, a custom still practiced. The leadership was taken by the newly formed GAR post; official funds were appropriated; cemeteries were visited and graves were decorated by schoolchildren, Good Templars, and other patriotic societies. At one cemetery or another (the town had four by then) all of the clergy had an opportunity to function. In its report, the *Advertiser* noted that the Odd Fellows were very well represented and that "the young misses who assisted in flower ceremonies" were unique and attractive. The choir singing of "The Soldier's Dirge" was "touching."

In the 1870s, the War of 1812 was to townspeople about as remote as World War I was to observers of the bicentennial in 1976. Yet there was a special aura about it all which surfaced at the obsequies in November 1871 of veterans Col. William Pool and Capt. Charles Tarr at the age of ninety-three. Their passings and the discovery of two

"Local Improvements Flourish"

Capt. Charles Tarr (1778-1872), captain of the Sea Fencibles in the War of 1812. (SBHS)

6-pound cannonballs in 1871 and 1872 while men were excavating in the yard of the Rockport Cotton Mill gave the *Advertiser* and many older Rockporters an opportunity to reminisce and write about that war and especially the encounter with the *Nymph* in 1814.

In 1877 Rockport again recalled its invasions of 1814. The annual town meeting voted to remove from the seashore rocks the small cannon captured from the British raid and have it repositioned with a suitable historical inscription. On Saturday, September 8, a proper ceremonial occasion was held at the town hall, where the relic had been mounted on the west lawn on a neat frame and a pedestal of granite. Town Clerk Calvin Pool gave the principal address, the two Dartmoor Prison survivors rambled on about their wartime experiences, and the band tootled "Yankee Doodle." The recently passed veterans' pension bill approved payments for Joseph and Abner Tarr, Isaac Dade, Aaron Pool, Samuel Saunders, Thomas Thompson, William T. Abbot, Francis Tarr, John Parsons, William P. Clark, and Amos Story, as well as for thirteen widows, including those of Daniel and Timothy Riggs Davis.

Bad Pennies

No account of the decade would be complete without some acknowledgment of Rockport's bad pennies, so to speak, some of which had been circulating with disconcerting frequency. With increasing population and prosperity came increased vandalism and crime. Of both, the newspapers made all they could, frequently linking liquor to the perpetrators. There were reports of stolen horses and of speeders, "people from Gloucester riding their horses at breakneck speeds through Rockport. They should be arrested." On June 23, 1871, from the *Advertiser* came this: "The city fathers of Rockport would do a good thing if they should put a fence every Saturday night across every highway leading into this town, and blockade the flash Sunday teams that tear over the roads to the annoyance of quiet people, and the distress of stable keepers." There were graffiti on the rocks. At Folly Cove on a smooth rock "a love-lorne driller" had carved the name "Mary Jain" and added a "highly artistic profile of the dear."

There were the robbers who stole a $12,000 draft from the post office and then tried to cash it, the three boyish lawbreakers of December 1872 who were "fined moderately," the "chivalric" gentlemen who smashed windows in November 1871 and were obliged by Judge Dennis "to pay some hundred dollars for their lively entertainment," the unknown vandal who threw an empty whiskey bottle through a window of the Baptist church, and a breakout from the lockup to rescue a drunk named Keefe (rearrested the same evening, however). More cells were added to the Rockport jail, "so that people will not be afraid to venture out nights," and a stronger safe was installed in the town hall. The newspapers of the 1870s tell of store thieves, safecrackers, yacht stealers, muggers, and a vandal who sawed down a beautiful cherry tree on King Street in 1878 out of sheer hellishness.

The *cause célèbre* of the decade was Rockport's sensational murder in 1877 of a pedlar, Charles H. Gilman, killed at the reservoir on Poole's Hill by his companion, Albert Joy, whose death sentence was commuted to life imprisonment. Several other rendezvous with death were not commuted during the 1870s. Three in particular left all Rockport sadder but grateful for the services rendered to the town. First went Jabez R. Gott, public official, church deacon, businessman, at the age of eighty-two in March 1876. At his funeral the pulpit was decorated with leaves; his remains were followed to the cemetery by the Sunday school, the Odd Fellows, the Good Templars, and many mourners from Gloucester. On January 26, 1878, pneumonia took off Dr. Benjamin Haskell, a skilled physician, agriculturalist, and man of commerce. After a crowded meeting at the town hall, where tributes were paid for his many contributions, he was given a massive funeral from the Congregational church in a raging blizzard. Hundreds stood at the obsequies, which "exceeded in magnitude and impressiveness" anything remembered in Rockport.

Rockport was fortunate in having a young, devoted successor to Dr. Haskell. In 1870, on his graduation from Harvard Medical School, Dr. Augustus M. Tupper came to town, bringing his bride, Frances, to their new home in Pigeon Cove's "Old House," later known as the Witch House and Garrison House. In 1872, they moved to the South Village in order to be closer to the town's senior practising physician. On the death of Haskell, Dr. Tupper, originally from Woodstock, New Brunswick, purchased the home of his departed colleague next to the First Congregational Church and continued to practise medicine there for fifty years. A lover of horses, he made his rounds with a horse and buggy and often just on horseback. When need called, he would be rowed out to Straitsmouth and Thacher's Island. On one occasion he nearly lost his life in a storm, and later treasured the one oar which had saved him. During an emergency, on a Pigeon Cove kitchen table he performed a tracheotomy. He was active at the Leander M. Haskins Hospital, once it became a reality, and served as an examining physician in World War I. Among his civic-minded activities was his support for establishing St. Mary's Episcopal Church and the Carnegie Library.

On April 10, 1878, death claimed the venerable Ebenezer Pool, aged ninety years and nine months. A descendant of the first and second settlers of Sandy Bay, he began school in the very first schoolhouse at "ye Cape" and later attended the new Proprietors' School which opened in 1797. Of his seventeen children, eleven marched behind his coffin. The compilers of the Rockport *History* of 1888 wrote: "He left a large number of pages of valuable memoranda to which we are indebted." Nine decades later the compilers of this history are still more in debt to that remarkable rescuer of things long gone.

ADDITIONAL READING

In addition to the files of local newspapers on microfilm at the Carnegie Library and the Sawyer Free Library there is a file of the *Rockport Quarry* and a nearly complete file of the *Rockport Gleaner* at the Essex Institute in Salem.

Railroad buffs should consult Francis B. C. Bradlee, *The Eastern Railroad* (Salem, 1922, reprinted by the Essex Institute and Panorama Publications, Melrose, 1972).

"Local Improvements Flourish"

16

"NOTES OF THE BUGLE"

CONFINED TO HIS SMALL HOME, James Parsons Davis was fretful when they brought him his January 1880 *Gleaner*. Despite his sixty-eight years he was still an energetic, up-and-doing sort. Like most Rockporters, he turned to the second and third pages for the local news and the bits of gossip in the column of "gleanings." Suddenly, he stopped. With the stentorian voice of a seaman used to shouting above the winds, he called out: "Listen to this!"

James Davis, 70 years of age, was at work on his vessel in the dock; he slipped from the rail and fell into the dock, the tide being out, and received a severe fracture of the shoulder. He is being attended by Dr. C. B. Hall.

Muttering, perhaps, that he was not seventy, Captain Davis was no doubt pleased to see his name in print. People like him rarely made the news. But they read the paper with enthusiasm, as it rolled from the presses on Dock Square the middle of each month.

The opening of the decade provided the press with many statistics of household interest, such as the fact that 1879 had been "very healthy," with only 87 rather than the average 100 deaths. (Nearly a third of those were of children under five years of age.) Rockport had had 85 births, 38 marriages, and a shrinkage of 57 polls. Clerk Calvin Pool noted that 34 of Rockport's new babies had been born to foreign-born parents, 10 to those of mixed backgrounds, and 39 (fewer than half) to parents of native American stock. The origins of two babes were not known. Of Rockport's foreign-born residents, Canadians excepted, the federal census of 1880 reported that 186 were from Ireland, 60 were from England, 34 from Scotland, 24 from the Azores or "Western Islands," 17 from Sweden, 11 from Finland, 2 from Germany, and 1 each from Denmark, Fayal, France, Portugal, and Spain. In the presidential election Rockporters as a whole voted two to one for Garfield.

The town had a public debt of $22,585. In the year just passed, reported Police Chief J. W. Bradley, his department had made 21 arrests: 12 for drunkenness, 4 for assault, and 5 for larceny. Some 116 tramps had been cared for at the lockup at a cost of $49.75 for food; 65 dogs had been licensed. The library owned 1,540 volumes by 1880, of which a new catalogue had been prepared. In March the town meeting voted to abolish the 50-cent membership fee. The trustees, however, objected that since the demand for books already exceeded the supply, larger appropriations would be required. Free it did become, though; free it survived.

Some other figures appeared from federal census takers. They counted a population of 3,907 (three more than in 1870 but 573 fewer than in 1875, when Rockport had had precisely 2,240 males and 2,240 females listed on its records). Rockport in 1880 had 6 residents who were blind; 8 who were deaf and dumb; 20 insane; 25 "maimed, crippled, bedridden or otherwise disabled"; and 5 who were categorized as idiotic. Washington Davis was the only Negro, but there were 5 mulattoes in town. There were also 2 nonagenarians (Olive Bickford and William Atwood) and 30 octogenarians.

Residents read that their town had 760 dwelling houses, 150 horses, and 148 cows. The tax rate was $13.60 per thousand, and the total tax assessment was $28,790.24. Pigeon Cove had 263 polls as against 709 for the south precinct. Corresponding figures for real estate valuations were $485,721 to $1,060,894; those for personal property, $106,575 to $254,694. Just who paid what and who was delinquent in tax payments was being printed annually in town reports by then. A local census in 1880 indicated that Rockport as a whole had had a summer influx of at least 2,500. In 1881 Pigeon Cove alone boasted accommodations for 450 in its hotels and boardinghouses, "while the Avenue population is about 150."

"Notes of the Bugle"

For James Davis and other newspaper subscribers, however, the papers' chief attraction was the chitchat which filled the columns of Cape Ann's inside pages. Readers with a seaward orientation would have noted that Nehemiah Knowlton, for fourteen years keeper of Straitsmouth lighthouse, had died at seventy-three, that John Griffin had opened a new fish market opposite Moffatt's provision store, that the trawl roll invented by Coleman Manning about 1852 ("an uncooth-looking affair") had been presented to "the National Museum of the United States," that Rockport had 165 active fishing boats in its harbor one October day in 1880, that Pigeon Cove catches of mackerel were almost more than could be handled, that herring were numerous, and that one vessel out at New Ledge had caught twelve thousand pounds of cod during a Friday-Saturday trip.

It was news that John Parsons and Charles Hodgkins had bought Milk Island in May 1881, to run "a brisk fish business" there. Swordfish made their appearance off the coast and in the press in September that year. In one week, three schooners brought into port seventy-seven specimens. The prize fish story of the entire decade was a nine-foot horse mackerel caught by Pigeon Cove's Adin Story in August 1883; it weighed some nine hundred pounds. When he put it on exhibition, "large numbers invested their dimes in a wondering view of the novel inhabitant of the deep." A far weightier exploit was George Tarr's purchase for $180 in May 1883 of a ninety-foot dead whale, "killed by a bomb lance." From it he squeezed four hundred to five hundred gallons of oil before setting the carcass adrift, eventually to wash ashore on unsuspecting Rye Beach. October 1886 brought a bonanza of herring to Rockport exceeding anything for twenty-five years. More than fifteen hundred barrels a day were landed at Sandy Bay and Pigeon Cove harbors, while the Milk Island "trap" was completely filled and had to be closed to prevent the nets from sinking completely. Rockport fishermen hoarded their herring, though, until Boston offered more reasonable prices.

The building of a sixty by twenty foot shed on Bradley's Wharf to be used as a workshop for repairing vessels was received with special warmth in January 1887. The installation of a set of blocks to hold boats while being repaired or painted met a long felt need at the harbor. That February, George McClain's model for a new type of vessel for the Georges Bank fisheries was highly commended "for the common sense embodied in the design." Rockport mariners were gratified to read in April 1886 that the Massachusetts Humane Society

This family snapshot at Long Beach shows in the background the best extant view of the Ballast Loading Platform at the southern side of Cape Hedge. Popples from Witham's Beach were loaded into the holds of empty vessels needing ballast for the return voyage. (Hoyt)

had presented a new lifeboat to the town and that George Elwell was planning in June to build a lifeboat station down on "Emerson's Point." That was to be the new "official" name for what had been Emmon's Point for two and a half centuries. A new brick building was projected for Thacher's Island for the steam-powered foghorn; but winter set in before the materials had been delivered, so the superstructure was delayed until the spring of 1887.

Rockport sports fans had a new, if somewhat limited competitor to baseball during the 1880s. Yachting, sailing, regattas—all popular among a selected few in the postwar decade of the 1870s—received a fresh impetus during the 1880s, culminating in the founding of the Sandy Bay Yacht Club in 1885. To fishermen like James Davis and professional coastal mariners, the club and its activities may well have further divided the "them" from "us." Yet yacht club activities were by no means the private preserve of summer visitors. In August 1883 four local yachts participated in a regatta, the course of which was around Thacher's Island. By July 1886 the club had thirty-five boats and new ones were being added. By August the Sandy Bay yachtsmen

"Notes of the Bugle"

Mooring stone uncovered at Long Beach by the blizzard of February 1978, some forty feet from the location of the Ballast Loading Platform. First used under water by the Norwoods in the early 1800s, mooring stones were large blocks of granite with center holes into which tree trunks were inserted roots down. (Photograph by William D. Hoyt)

were entertaining the club from Hull in what newspaper readers were assured was "the most prominent event in town this week."

"Sociables" were held in the winter at places like the new Haskins Hall. The club balls in the spring proved to be good money raisers, music being provided on at least one occasion by the Salem Cadet Band. The enthusiasm of Rockport yachtsmen and their fellow townsmen led the *Advertiser* to comment towards the end of the decade: "Few clubs along our coast can or will show a better lot of prizes than the Sandy Bay has now on exhibition." In 1887, the year in which a sailing dory club was formed to "increase the interest in this pleasant sport," August 1 was declared "Rockport Day" and the Sandy Bay Yacht Club sponsored events worthy of a July Fourth celebration, even to fireworks.

In 1886 Capt. James Davis and his fellow seamen learned that the storm-warning signal service on Thacher's Island was to be dismantled. Late in April, "the last act in the piece of folly of the chief signal officer" occurred when the office building, underwater cable, telegraph wires and poles—even the flagstaff—were auctioned out at the

Town on Sandy Bay

island. Then in late December 1887 Customs Inspector Prior was
abruptly relieved because some "big wig" in Washington wanted to
save money. Press excoriations against the bureaucratic "whim" of
some officer "who probably never saw the station" was a high-water
mark of editorial indignation.

Five months previously the whole town was treated to a marine
event when the U.S. frigate *Richmond,* the first ship of war to enter
Sandy Bay since the War of 1812, rounded Straitsmouth Point and
then crossed the bay under full sail. About halfway across, it put on
steam and veered off toward Portsmouth. With a combination of
vision and optimism, the editor reflected: "It was an odd sight to see
this war vessel with her row of portholes in our quiet bay, but probably
the years are not so many when such a sight will be a common one in
the grand harbor they're constructing."

The Breakwater

The 1880s brought a number of lasting changes to Rockport, some
of considerable magnitude. None, however, exceeded the scope of the
breakwater and "Harbor of Refuge" project, spread out as it was over
some three decades before technology and Congress abandoned it. To
the James Davises and most Rockporters, hard news and rumors,
however soft, stirred their imaginations and evoked visions of hitherto
undreamed-of grandeur. To newspaper reporters, editors, and publishers almost every event had potential links to the breakwater.

Take the *Rockport Review,* for example, one of the most significant
additions begun in the 1880s. In December 1881 H. C. Cheever of the
Essex County Review came to Rockport and began publishing a weekly
newspaper from "the Low's Building" in Dock Square. The format was
four pages of six columns each; the price was $1.50 per year or 3 cents
per copy. From its inauguration, the editor-publisher beat the drums
for a breakwater. The second issue included an impassioned plea by
"Seacoast": "Why, sir, there is not a ship harbor in the world that would
compare with it." The paper of December 24 carried a long editorial
asking why business, especially fishing, in Rockport had been falling
off ever since 1876. The answer was clear: the harbor needed a
breakwater. Cheever called for a citizens' meeting to discuss the project.

By February 4 readers of the *Review* were admonished to collect
thousands of names on a petition and to find a "shrewd, skillful

"Notes of the Bugle"

diplomatist to manage the game for us in Congress." An editorial against "croakers" who claimed that Rockport had seen its best days cheered that "we have men unwilling to give old Rockport up yet." A letter from "Triton" renewed the call for a citizens' meeting; a breakwater would set all right with Rockport. Thanks to extensive line-storm damage to the old harbor and Long Cove breakwater, public meetings were held in March 1882. Ladies looked down from the town hall gallery while the town meeting voted $1,000 for use by the breakwater committee.

Rejoicing that the ball was finally in motion, editor Cheever enumerated eight viable foundations for Rockport's economy—though each was admittedly not without its weaknesses: the National Bank, a railroad, the Annisquam Cotton Mills, the quarry companies, one oilcloth and two isinglass factories, hundreds of indestructible sites for seaside cottages, sea fertilizers for farm produce, and the harvest of the seas—fish. Every one of these would benefit from a good, protected harbor, he insisted. The *Review* shouted triumphantly: "The movement has begun, the first notes of the bugle have been sounded for the advance, and the battle has commenced on the right of the line. There must be no retreat, and victory will crown the banner of the brave."

Out of such rhetoric Rockport's breakwater was born. Petitions were circulated up and down the coast from Maine to Maryland; Congress agreed to a survey; by the end of 1883 the U.S. Engineers had recommended construction of a V-shaped, 9,000-foot breakwater to run from Avery's Ledge across toward Andrews' Point, leaving two broad entrances to a harbor some 60 feet deep and over 1,660 acres in scope. The first contract was signed in November 1885; two more would extend the operation halfway through 1890. The stone, hundreds of thousands of tons of it, came from the Rockport and Pigeon Hill Granite companies. At 12:26 P.M. on November 12, 1885, the first load of granite was dumped—to the shrieks of steam whistles on the sloop named the *Screamer,* of which Albert Pittee was captain.

Week in and week out the newspapers reported the progress: new scows for transporting the rubble, new tugs to pull the scows, a new engine for hoisting stone out of the pits, alterations and improvements to the scows to insure that the loads would be dumped in dead center instead of to the side. There was chagrin when a scow's release lever was accidentally opened and a whole load of granite was dumped at the wharf of the Rockport Granite Company. There were anxious weeks in the spring of 1886 when the Congressional Committee on Rivers

Fishing vessels, dories, and a barge in Pigeon Cove Harbor, a typical scene of the period and a fine collection of masts. (C. Swan)

and Harbors failed to include an appropriation for this project, "whose completion is so much desired by our seafaring men"—not to mention our commercial men—yet did include large appropriations "in the interest of the South and West." A group of lobbyists was hurried to Washington to demonstrate the "necessity of funding the breakwater again." Great was the relief in August, when $100,000 was appropriated "for this most important undertaking."

There was persuasion to be exerted by tug trips, quarry tours, and dinners at the Pigeon Cove House whenever congressmen came to town to inspect the progress. There was ridicule when the U.S. Engineers took bids for a concrete cylindrical block for Avery's Ledge to mark the southern boundary of the breakwater, "an absurd undertaking." There were invidious comparisons at the disparity in costs between a concrete block and a granite pier, which would stand "forever," and obvious delight when the cement washed away through a leak: "It lasted as long as the Rockporters expected it to." By mid-June 1886 nearly forty thousand tons had been dumped for foundations.

Before the decade was out, the harbor-breakwater received its third appropriation. Although its supporters had hoped for more than another $100,000, on learning in March 1888 that most projects had

"Notes of the Bugle"

been cut by 25 to 50 percent, they hastened to express their appreciation to Congressman Cogswell for his efforts on their behalf. In late September 1889 newspaper readers on Cape Ann were startled to learn that a Miss Grace Hale of California had become the first woman to dump a load of stone on their rising breakwater, "that vast, though yet hidden, monument of Rockport's grit and brains. . . . The work has now gone so far that it is as good as insured." In the words of the *Cape Ann Advertiser,* "It is already attracting the attention of some of the great men of our country, and all such we are pleased to note endorse the great undertaking."

More Grit and Brains

In addition to a weekly newspaper of its own and the beginnings of a vast, protected harbor, Rockport made a few other advances of lasting importance during the 1880s. A telephone line from Gloucester to Rockport would be "a paying institution." By May 1881 posts were installed to Rockport and part way to Pigeon Cove. In August it was announced that the telephone office would be at Alfred Parsons's store, that a call would cost 10 cents, but that patrons could phone all over Cape Ann for that price. In November the service was in operation, and after three weeks nine private homes and offices had been connected to the central. By the spring of 1882, however, Rockporters read that because of inadequate support their central facility would be discontinued after April 1. A common "transmitting instrument" would be maintained at a store in town, but the central transfer office would be back at Gloucester.

In the meanwhile, during part of the summer of 1881 Pigeon Cove had numbered among its summer visitors the vacationing Mr. and Mrs. Alexander Graham Bell and their children. The *Advertiser* of August 12 reported Bell and his assistant, Schuyler Johnson, as being at the Pigeon Cove House. As late as August 8, Mrs. Bell was still in Cambridge, but on the fifteenth at the cove she gave birth prematurely to a boy who lived just three hours. Reports of the birth and death, datelined "Pigeon Cove, Massachusetts, United States," appeared in the *London Times* on September 3. By September 19 the Bells were on shipboard and in sight of England. Their sojourn in Rockport had been very brief and not felicitous. Legends to the contrary, there is no hard evidence the inventor was experimenting on his already successful telephone or hawking stock shares in his company.

Town on Sandy Bay

The American landing of the Atlantic Cable at the southern end of Witham's Beach, from an illustration in "The New England Coast " (1891)

In his January 1880 *Gleaner,* James P. Davis probably read that the American Union Telegraph Company had come to Rockport, had appointed a local agent named G. T. Margeson, and was running poles from the railroad station down Main Street to his office opposite the Rockport Savings Bank. The new line was to be ready in about a week. In fact, the first telegram was not sent by the office until March. Tucker Margeson would usher in a new development for Rockport far more enduring than a telegraph office. To him would go the palm of being the harbinger of generations of Rockport artists. By the early 1880s the press was favorably reporting on his output, which attracted admirers and purchasers. At the outset, however, it was the telegraph and his store which paid him a living. A second telegraph office was to be opened by the Western Union Company at Pigeon Cove in 1881. Soon telegraphy proved to be a vehicle for women's skills, as demonstrated by Althea Mason at Pigeon Cove in July 1889 and by Bertha Tarr, who went to Taunton "to study telegraphy" that October.

The United States and Europe had been linked by an underwater transatlantic cable ever since 1866. Others had been put into service afterward, notably by the ship *Faraday.* After months of surveys the

"Notes of the Bugle"

firm of Bennett and Mackay determined on Rockport as the American terminus for its cable. Cape Hedge was to be the landing place and house the office of the Commercial Cable Company on the shore above it. Another bugle note would soon sound. Such festivities the town did organize to welcome the ship when it rolled out at the South End the final feet of the largest ocean cable laid to date!

But the best-laid plans, like the best-laid cable, came acropper. To begin with, the *Faraday* was spotted off Thacher's Island at 4:20 A.M. on May 22, 1884, a full twenty-four hours ahead of schedule. By 5:00 A.M. it had come to within three quarters of a mile from the landing spot and fired a salute. The town replied with a cannon of its own and the pealing of church bells. Three Rockporters, N. F. S. York, Nathaniel Richardson, Jr., and Town Clerk Calvin W. Pool, boarded the ship and extended greetings on behalf of the eager town and an invitation to an inaugural dinner.

That was when they got the bad news. Some 250 miles from Rockport, the *Faraday* had been obliged to cut the cable, buoy the end, and sail directly for Cape Ann to work backward until the two ends could be spliced. There would be no time for festivities for the 220 officers and men of the *Faraday*. Undaunted and unknowing, the crowds poured down toward the South End in a long procession escorted by bands from Rockport and Gloucester. Four rafts carried six hundred fathoms of cable (twenty tons to the mile) toward the shore, laid it in the deep trench, and poked the end through the hole bored in the wall of the cable hut.

Eager spectators sat in their dories; others lined the shore and stood by the Stars and Stripes run up on a pole by the beach. Representatives of the company, the state, town, and the press swarmed all over. In its account, the *New York Herald* (James Gordon Bennett's own paper) wrote:

Just as in the days of ancient Rome, when warriors returning from a successful expedition, were met with an assembly of city fathers and a procession of garlanded virgins, so in Rockport a procession of school children and firemen, heralded by a band of music, was provided to do honor to the Faraday. *The inhabitants of the town flocked down the beach; old men and boys, blooming girls and strapping matrons were there in scores, thronging around the cable hut, seeming anxious to explore the prospective mysteries within.*

The bands played "Hail Columbia!" and "Rule Britannia." A
38-gun salute (one for each state) booming across the water, cheers
from shore and the crew, and blasts from the "heavy steam whistle" of
the *Faraday* ended the affair. The men returned to their ship, and the
Rockport delegation raised a toast to the officers and electricians:
"Without their skill and able efforts our gathering would have no cause
to exist." About 11:00 A.M. the *Faraday* steamed away, trailing her cable
behind her, to make the spliced link 250 miles away.

Back in town on Main Street near School Street John Swett's Abbott
House, "gaily decorated," offered hospitality to many lively guests and
spectators. That evening some eighty people participated in a dinner
served at Haskins Hall at which the waiters were "seven of the finest
young ladies of Rockport," all dressed in white. Following the edibles
came what a reporter called the intellectual feast: nine toasts, nine
speeches, nine responses. Dr. Sanborn's was even in rhyme. Two of the
replies politely alluded to the Harbor of Refuge which with the new
Atlantic cable would soon make Rockport famous. Many participants
then returned to the Abbott House, "where the festivities were continued until a late hour." The more prudent or less mobile took the
special train to Gloucester or Boston. On May 26 at 2:00 P.M. the first
message was received at the Commercial Cable office, a greeting from
the *Faraday* thanking Rockporters for their welcome.

One doubts that the spirited celebrants returned to the inn to sing
"Drink to Me only with thine Eyes." Yet Rockport continued to be
officially dry. Temperance meetings continued to be held on Mondays
by the Rechabites. Liquor continued to be seized, including three
quarts of whiskey found in the skirts of one Mrs. Davidson in October
1889. Fines continued to be levied, such as the $50 fine slapped on
Stephen N. Tarr in January 1880 ("the smallest the law admits") for
keeping and selling cider. The *Advertiser* carried a story of an under-
cover spotter who came to Rockport, made friends with drugstore
employees at Andrew Mason's and D. B. Hoyt's, where he bought
many cigars, only to inform on the storekeepers for illicitly selling
spirits, offenses for which they were convicted in October 1886.

At a head-counting of the faithful from the Rechabites, Rechabites
Junior, Sons of Temperance, and the Good Templars of Pigeon Cove,
taken at a rally in February 1883, the first group numbered 82, the
second 50, the third 40, and the last about 105. They were reinforced

in March when the Massachusetts Temperance Union organized a Pigeon Cove chapter with Caroline Babson, Phoebe Hale, Florence Story, and Serena Tucker as officers. In May 1885 the Rechabites disbanded their Bay Tent but organized a Rechabite Temple of Honor to replace it. In January 1886 Rockport schools distributed diplomas of some sort to students who were members of the Massachusetts Total Abstinence Society. The summer of 1886, however, introduced a shift of emphasis with a Sunday observance committee which had thirty vigilantes to see to it that the Sabbath was arid and not secularized. In mid-June several Rockporters formed a branch of the National Law and Order League, their purpose being to enforce the nondrinking, nonworking Sunday laws. The Rockporters' first shots were aimed at halting the landing and selling of fish on the Sabbath.

Services

Most Rockporters had other concerns on their mind. Once the Commercial Cable Company became operational, it established an intown office at what is still called the "Cable House" on Norwood Avenue. The company showed sensitivity for public relations. Early in 1886 it constructed a billiard room above its offices and opened it to anyone wishing to play. In April, when the schooner *Addison G. Proctor* lost its anchor on the cable offshore, the superintendent made restitution for the loss. In July 1887 Fred Choate, who had been "learning the mysteries of cable-telegraphy" there for more than a year, was promoted to the Boston office. The practical use of Rockport's cable operations had been dramatically set forth the year before when it transmitted medical information from Victoria, British Columbia, to London so that a celebrated physician in England might diagnose the ailments of a British peer in Canada and prescribe treatment for him more than six thousand miles away.

More immediate benefits enjoyed by Rockporters in the decade included increased street lighting. To the fifty-seven lamps in operation, an additional forty were approved in March 1882. The new ones were installed on iron posts with a wooden base and burned kerosene. In 1882, $450 was set aside for another public service, a new three-dialed town clock for the tower of the Congregational church. The rental fee was to be $1 per year, provided the clock was kept in constant repair by the town. To everyone's delight, it was in place by early July.

Several new lamps were placed in the cove in time to shed their glow for the Christmas season in 1889. Yet by September there had been

The Boston and Maine Railroad's Engine No. 202 with crew at the depot. (Peckham)

press speculation about the installation of electric lights. Back in January 1880, the *Gleaner* had run an article on "Edison's Electric Light," saying "the inventor's claims are very lucidly set forth; and in spite of some newspaper reports, we are inclined to believe that he has been successful in his endeavors to provide a cheap, endurable light." In 1882 the *Review* had assured its readers that their eyes would benefit from the new electric lights and colors would seem brighter.

Still another service offered to Rockporters was the establishment of the Granite Savings Bank in December 1884, John G. Dennis, president, and Nathaniel Richardson, Jr., treasurer. The failure of the Rockport Savings Bank had made depositors skittish, but the first sum was placed in the Granite on April 11, 1885. Accounts began to draw interest on January 1, 1886, as business improved. The first dividend was two percent. The American Express Company extended its operations into Rockport in January 1886, where it was run by Daniel Mahony, stationmaster, at the depot. As for Rockport's post office, which was open from 8:00 A.M. to 8:00 P.M., it had grown so extensively by the opening of 1888 that it was raised to a "presidential" category, and Walter G. Peckham received his appointment that January from Grover Cleveland, soon to be succeeded by Benjamin Harrison for

"Notes of the Bugle"

Children's Day at Long Beach about 1910 with the outdoor theater at the left and restaurant at the right. Trolleys carried visitors from Gloucester over the marshes at Good Harbor Beach. (Hoyt)

whom Rockporters had cast 537 votes to only 161 for Cleveland, a Democrat.

Town highways new and improved continued to absorb energy and funds. Main Street at the upper end of Dock Square was widened in 1880, and a culvert was constructed under Railroad Avenue five feet wide and high enough for a man to walk through. In 1882 the "road from Main to High Street" was built at a cost of $3,348. Summit Avenue was laid out in 1885 and improved the next year. The same dates brought Curtis Street to "Lurveyville." It was named for Jason L. Curtis, who had already completed the northern end. In May 1887 Thomas Gaffield set out 134 shade trees along his development in the Halibut Point area, thereby adding much, commented the *Advertiser,* "to the comfort and pleasure along those drives." A February flood in 1886 did some $600 in damage to Granite Street, High Street, and Broadway, all of which were "pretty well washed out." When the floodgate at the mill pond gave way, the factories on today's Millbrook Meadow had their basements flooded. So in the summer George Elwell dredged the pond, which had been badly silted up with gravel from the brook running down into it.

Town on Sandy Bay

Railroad developments were at least indirectly matters of concern to most of the town. For August 1880 the sale of train tickets at the Rockport depot had exceeded by $400 the sales of the year before. Perhaps some of the increased patronage was attributable to the fast trains the Eastern had set in operation that summer. A morning train ran express (after Salem), arriving in the Hub at 8:50. Another left Boston at 2:15 P.M. for Rockport and arrived there in one hour and twenty minutes. There was even talk of a parlor car "with comfortable chairs," the price of which would be $36 above the regular fare for the three months of June-August.

The perennial railroad dream, an extension to Pigeon Cove from Rockport, repeatedly appeared in local newspapers. In January 1880 a survey would shunt the tracks around the eastern side of Poole's Hill, in the rear of the quarries, and out near the upper end of the North Village. The next month that route was abandoned as too expensive, but "another survey would probably be made." In December 1884 the Eastern Railroad leased its lines to the Boston and Maine. In the summer of 1886, the new firm inaugurated a day-away-from-Rockport trip departing Sundays at 5:00 A.M. returning at 5:00 P.M. That autumn the mounting number of Rockporters commuting to work at Gloucester petitioned to have a train arrive there at 7:00 A.M. instead of 7:30 A.M. In August 1886 Boston and Main officials met with representatives of Pigeon Cove hotels and the major granite companies to discuss an extension to the North Village. Nothing came of it, as usual. Yet optimism was still high in January 1887: "We are informed that the surveyors have been at work this week at Pigeon Cove laying out the proposed route for the railroad through the village. The people of that section of the Cape seem very sanguine of the road being built within the very near future, and we hope such will be the case."

Instead of the North Village, however, railroaders turned their eyes towards the developing South End. By the end of 1887, there were plans for a rail extension down to Long Beach for summer visitors there. Agreement was reached for construction within the next four years, so long as the road did not interfere with the regular rail line, with the beach itself, or with access to Long Beach by the residents of Rockport. Over the horizon lay the era of Cape Ann trolley cars.

Farm news became rarer in the 1880s, the decade during which silos came into local use. The first three were on the Babson farm at Pigeon

Cove, on James P. Merridew's property, and in October 1887 on the Dodd farm on the Gloucester road. The annual exhibitions of the Agricultural Association continued to be well attended.

Local housewives were offered the opportunity of buying improved clothespins locally inspired, which would hold their washings firmly but free from contact with clotheslines themselves. A real luxury was a two-closet refrigerator described by the newspapers in January 1888: "The recepticle [sic] for the ice is at the top, which has a faucet for an outlet to furnish ice water. It is surmounted by a high, nicely sawed back on which is a neatly designed shelf. It is all the work of Mr. Daniel G. Keene, who made it to suit his own taste." To attract wives, husbands, and children, the YMCA exhibited "Mr. Edison's phonographic talking machine" in October 1882.

Music took hold more firmly in the 1880s, what with more concerts by out-of-town artists, trains to carry Rockporters to out-of-town concerts, the formation of a local singing society and the Mozart Orchestra, and the publication of compositions written by William Manning. Masquerades, as described by the newspapers, indicated a broader familiarity with current cultural trends. At one party in February 1882 there were three Oscar Wildes in "black suits, sunflowers, etc." This was the time Wilde was currently making his sensational American tour. Lecture topics also broadened in scope with firsthand reports about Italy, China, Japan, Eskimos, and oil production in Pennsylvania. Recitations and public readings brought many aspects of literature, past and present, to enthusiastic audiences, as did an increasing variety of theatrical performances, including *The Drunkard* (1882), *The Flowing Bowl* (1886), *Under the Laurels,* and *Fun in a Boarding School* (1889).

Intellectual stimulus was also roused by the formation of the Chautauqua Circles, which got started in the South Village in September 1883 with fifteen to twenty members. It was from the Pigeon Cove group, however, begun in 1887 and spearheaded by Maggie Dwyer, that the Pigeon Cove Improvement Society was launched in May 1889 in the parlor of Mrs. Henry L. Story. Alonzo Tuttle was chosen president; Chester Story treasurer; and Maggie Dwyer, secretary, a task she held for over forty years, never missing a meeting "special or annual." Their noble goal was to improve and beautify the place.

For the younger set, in October 1883 Rockport opened a roller-skating rink in a new building on Broadway, which also supplied music for the skaters. In addition to the many attractions of the yacht club, there was the Ladies' Pedestrian Club of 1880, organized to "ramble through the woods." In March 1881, hobbyists formed the Amateur Natural History Club of Pigeon Cove. In 1883 they possessed "a creditable collection of curiosities and objects of natural history." In August 1882 newspaper readers learned that "the game of lawn tennis is being naturalized in Rockport, upon the grassy expanse of Mr. Haskins' isinglass premises." By the summer of 1887, tennis had become so well established that a group of younger men had hired the grounds in the rear of the burned-out cotton mill to serve as lawn tennis courts. That very October a tennis court was being built at the home of George Everett on Pigeon Cove's Gaffield Avenue. The summer of 1888 found the Rockport Croquet Club meeting every Thursday on the grounds at Camp Sans Souci. In 1886 Dock Square's Lowe building acquired a poolroom. Wrestling and shooting matches also attracted a few supporters, as did one "Professor Miller," who magically freed himself from a cross to which he had been locked by bracelets about the neck, waist, wrists, and feet.

Baseball continued to draw large audiences and even more eager participants. Toward the end of the 1880s the town had teams with names such as The Picked Nine, The Pigeon Hill Starters, the Methodist Nine, Captain Garlick's Nine, the Stars, the Dogfish Nine, Old Bill's Nine, Old Hook Nine, and a summer residents' nine at Pigeon Cove. The season began in mid-March, and by May 1889 Rockport had joined a league with other towns, including Annisquam, Gloucester, Magnolia, Ipswich, Newburyport, Beverly, Nahant, Lynn, two Boston teams, Newton, Stoneham, Medford, Rockland, and even Taunton. Home games were very rare because of a lack of a suitable diamond. In September 1889 second baseman Slade, a local "Mighty Casey," was given a gold watch for hitting a home run over the center field fence on the Woven Hose grounds at Boston, where Rockport won a game 19 to 3.

The bicycle mania of previous years intensified in the 1880s with cycling groups regularly swishing through town, some of them making

View of the ruins of the Annisquam Cotton Mill from the steeple of the Congregational Church. The Corporation Houses, where mill workers lived, and the spire of the Baptist Church are immediately beyond. (Hoyt)

a day of it, such as the "Ladies Eastern Tricycle Tour," which invaded Pigeon Cove just after Thanksgiving in 1888. To facilitate such excursions publishers and cycling clubs printed guidebooks for would-be travelers. At least two from the mid-1880s have pertinent accounts of Rockport. From the *Wheelman's Handbook of Essex County* (1884) one learned that "there is not a wheel owned in town, and all information locally must be obtained by inquiry. The roads are in good condition most of the year. There is no sand, but the roads are hard, and in some cases, border on the rocky." More practical was the tip that the Pigeon Cove House was "first class and makes a discount." A charming set of narratives of several bicycle trips, replete with attractive drawings and poetic, purple-prose descriptions, was John Webber's *In and Around Cape Ann* (1885), in which all areas of Rockport were described.

Unlocked Stables

James P. Davis had long recovered from his shoulder injury by the time the *Rockport Review* came out with a dark speculation on April 15,

1882. Noting that almost every paper reaching the editor's desk carried grim reports of fires and asking if Rockport was just lucky or if Rockporters were extracautious, editor Cheever queried: "Suppose a fire should get fairly started on Main Street or Dock Square, where would it stop? Have we a fire department that could successfully oppose its progress, or would it burn until there was nothing for it to burn? These are questions which should be considered now. It is safest to lock the stable door while the horse is inside." Despite new reservoirs at the head of Broadway, the foot of King Street and, too late, on South Street, the town got a burning reply to his query in early December 1883. On a Sunday morning at 7:00 A.M. fire broke out in the engine room of Rockport's large Cotton Mill. Working in a dark area to put a safety guard around the main belt, a laborer happened to touch his lamp to the belt. The cotton fluff caught fire, and "flames flashed like gun powder up into the weaving room overhead." The estimated loss after the two-hour holocaust was $250,000, despite the rescue of the buildings south of the burned area; the huge chimney; the gashouse; the storehouse with ninety bales of cotton; and five valuable "burners," three of which were nearly new.

Owned originally by local men, for the most part, the mill had suffered many vagaries since 1847 but was declaring a 6 percent dividend when destroyed. Some 235 operatives were profitably turning out corset jeans and sateens and earning a monthly payroll of $5,600. Rockport's fire department, aided by steamer engines from Gloucester and distant Salem, did save some structures but not the jobs. Within a week, agents from other towns hurried to Rockport to lure workers to other factories in other cities. By December 14 the *Advertiser* announced that "it is painful to record that Mr. Theophilus Walker, the heaviest owner, says it will not be rebuilt, as the cost of restoring it would far exceed the amount of insurance." There, in the heart of town, the ruins remained, stark and desolate, year after year. Sporadic efforts were made to revive and rebuild them. None succeeded.

Rockport businessmen felt other setbacks, too, some of which were fortunately softened. For example, the hide seat, organ, bobbin factory was bought in May 1880 for $5,540 by the Haskins Brothers, fish dealers in Boston, for use as an isinglass factory. Production, always seasonal, commenced in December, the price of isinglass being $2.75 a pound at that time. The town's only other surviving producer was near the depot. On May 22, 1880, the glueworks at Beaver Dam burned

"Notes of the Bugle"

The Cape Ann Isinglass Factory and Fred Nickerson's Grain Mill on Railroad Avenue. The former, with top story removed, is now the Rockport Rope and Twine Company, and the latter houses the J. Raymond Smith lumber firm. (Hoyt)

down at a loss of $1,000. In 1881 Mr. Lepage's fish glue works, of which Reuben Brooks was manager, moved to Gloucester, a loss mitigated by Elwell's new glueworks built at the eastern end of Cape Pond, which added a structure measuring thirty by eighteen feet in the summer of 1883. Competition from the isinglass works for fresh fish heads and skins was a real problem. Both the Sheridan House hotel and the Seacroft House at Loblolly Cove were totally destroyed by flames; but the area between Loblolly and Long Beach finally caught the eye of developers. In October 1887 Nathaniel Tarr and some Boston associates of his purchased an impressive expanse of seashore property there for $25,000, about which more would be heard in the Gay Nineties. The town's prestige suffered wounds when the local court was closed down in 1887 and Rockporters were obliged thereafter to plead their cases in Gloucester.

Efforts were made by the new Rockport Business Improvement Association to attract fresh, significant industry to town. Publisher Cheevers urged tax breaks as an inducement. When a shoe factory at Danvers burned down, he focused on that project for Rockport. At the

Town on Sandy Bay

Derricks lifting huge blocks of granite from a quarry which had not yet been worked deeply. (Caffrey)

longest town meeting in Rockport's history, lasting one day and eight nights, with only one negative ballot, voters agreed in March 1887 to allow a shoe factory to set up operations for a ten-year period so long as it relied on the fire-fighting facilities of the Cape Ann Isinglass Company's factory on Railroad Avenue. Press reports promised employment for about two hundred workers. From then on, newspapers issued spotty bulletins about the shoe factory. In March 1889 a construction contract was let and work begun just when rumors flew through town that the cotton mill might be revived. In November the engines were fired up for the first time, and there was an announcement that about fifty people (not the anticipated two hundred) would be hired, initially. Abraham Tucker was to be engineer. On November 28 owner Hollis's shoe factory at Lynn burned down, providentially just after he had secured his Rockport property on which to fall back.

Although the quarry companies found themselves in reasonably satisfactory shape throughout the decade, there was a strict separation of labor between those providing stone for the breakwater and those engaged primarily in cutting paving blocks and other construction stone. Once the ten-hour working day law had gone into effect,

"Notes of the Bugle"

quarrymen—mainly foreign born by 1880—decided that they, too, deserved the benefits. Petitions were signed and presented as of April 1, 1880, to the Rockport Granite Company and to the Pigeon Hill, Cape Ann, and two Lanesville companies. The Lanesville duo soon gave in, "for the present." At the two main Rockport quarries, on the contrary, the signers were called in, paid off, and fired. By April 10 there were 340 men on strike, holding meetings, collecting whatever supplies they could get for their families, but remaining adamant. Stonecutters and hammerers already worked a ten-hour day; the recalcitrants were quarrymen, blacksmiths, teamsters, and other laborers who were putting in eleven or more hours daily. By late April the Lanesville companies, with over 100 employees, were rushed with orders.

Orders also came in to both the Rockport and Pigeon Cove granite firms. After six weeks of strikes many of their best workers had headed for the Quincy quarries. Several new, smaller operations or "motions" were begun by the unemployed. Months passed. The modified strike was maintained. In February 1881 the ten-hour men met and petitioned on behalf of their fellows, only to find themselves paid off and discharged. At the end of the year-long stalemate on April 1, all the quarry companies capitulated to the ten-hour-day demand except the giant Rockport Granite Company, which had lost most of its trained workers by then. When only one was left, the bitter directors gave way. By April 29 they had fifty men back at the pits.

The legacy of conflict remained, and from 1880 on organized labor in various guises began to develop strength in Rockport. That first year the Labor party locally nominated the popular Democrat Jason Curtis as a representative to the Massachusetts legislature. He got 312 votes, only 40 fewer than the winning Republican, Nathaniel Richardson, Jr. In 1881 a cooperative life insurance venture was established as the United Order of the Golden Cross. Secret sessions of the Knights of Labor were held periodically, and in 1886 a bevy of Lanesville Knights drove to the town hall in "barges and stages." In March 1887 a sick benefit association was reorganized in Pigeon Cove. The group had started a year before as the Pigeon Cove Mutual Benefit Association with 54 members, from the Knights of Labor, Joseph B. Dunahue, president, and Edgar L. Waite, secretary-treasurer. By 1888 it had grown to 110 members.

In the South Village in February that same year, 91 men formed the Sandy Bay Mutual Relief Association. Not an offspring of the labor movement, it was more closely related to the various lodge groups of the community. To that array had been added a new and highly colorful one: the Improved Order of Red Men, instituted on June 10, 1886, with 106 charter members. Initially christened the Tragabigzanda Tribe, the men soon opted for the "old" name of Annisquam, "Wonasquam," and promptly followed the lead of other fraternal organizations operating in town by holding social occasions for themselves, their wives, and their families.

As would be expected, public awareness in Rockport of its expanding ethnographic composition took several forms. First of all, perhaps, it was the religious manifestations that came to the fore. The *Advertiser* in June 1883 reported that the Reverend Mr. H. Olsen of the Swedish Mission of Boston was making "a sort of missionary visit to the Swedes in this vicinity and will hold a meeting in Pigeon Cove Chapel to promote evangelical work." Swedish services were held each Sunday evening from 1883 on at the hospitable chapel until the immigrant groups established their own churches. In 1888 some other Swedes rented space for services from the Rockport Granite Company. Reports of the unremitting toll taken in quarry accidents increasingly referred to the immigrants, such as John Peterson "a Swede, single, 22," killed in February 1882.

The *Advertiser* on March 5, 1886, quoted with irritation a Lynn paper stating that Rockport had about fifty Scandinavians and Siberians who earned only 50 cents a day. "This is false!" The reason it was false, wrote a Gloucester reporter, is that "there are no Scandinavians or Siberians only a few Norwegians and Finns and they earn at *least* double that for ordinary labor." Furthermore, they would get a 10 percent raise in the spring, concluded the article. In July 1887 a press report stated: "To be sure, we are a small town, but we are known even in Sweden, where people intending to come to Rockport buy their tickets direct."

Even exotic food began to be noticed in the land of the bean and the cod. The Congregational church's Evening Circle just before Christmas of 1881 held a Japanese supper. Japanese articles were for sale, and Japanese tableware was used, along with other "oriental decorations" and Chinese lanterns. "The attending ladies" (waitresses, not geishas, one can assume) were in costume. By October 1887 D. B. Hoyt's store in Rockport had been transformed into a Chinese laundry by one Sing Lee from Boston; East and West had met on Main Street, Rockport. In a long article on macaroni, the *Gleaner* wrote in January

"Notes of the Bugle"

1883: "Neither are our Italian citizens the only consumers of this healthy and slippery diet. Americans especially are taking lovingly to its consumption."

The decade of the 1880s was marked by one phenomenon which still defies categorizing and which still evokes spirited comments from Rockporters and their visitors whenever the subject is mentioned: the sea serpent. Cape Ann had received its first visit from the leviathan in 1817. Decades were to pass before a return visit of the mighty one took place in the area, though summer hotelkeepers up and down the coast periodically caught "well authenticated" glimpses that made them (and their paying guests) less forlorn. A detailed narrative of the event, written by Granville B. Putnam of Boston's Franklin School was printed in the *History of Rockport* (1888). It should be read and savored with other newspaper reports, such as those in the *Cape Ann Breeze* and the *Boston Journal*.

About 1:15 P.M. on August 12, 1886, Deacon Calvin Pool, Rockport's town clerk, roused his friend Putnam from a tome on algae with word of a strange creature some thirty-six feet offshore about an eighth of a mile away. With the help of binoculars the men watched its undulations for about ten minutes. Their report, and those of some forty others who saw it that afternoon, calculated its length as not less than eighty feet, its head about the size of a nail cask, its body larger in girth than a man. Its head was never above the water level, though the body had ten to fifteen convolutions in evidence at a time. The mottled brown body had a whitish head; its tail was never visible; its speed was about five miles per hour. For a brief moment its body was extended along the surface prior to contracting to dive. One week later the assistant minister of Boston's Park Street Church, his wife, servants, and several friends also saw the serpent off Andrews' Point at Pigeon Cove. In the spate of articles which appeared in the serpent's wake, there was "a substantial agreement" of descriptive detail. Despite a $20,000 offer to anyone who could catch it, the creature disappeared as freely as it had arrived.

On September 10, after the Rockport board of trade had enjoyed a fish fry at Gully Point, they touchily assured a reporter they wished to have it distinctly understood they had *not* seen the sea serpent. Eight decades of other board members and thousands of other Rockport residents and visitors, however, have yearned in vain for even a glimpse.

Fishermen's Memorial and Record Book and Fishermen's Own Book (Gloucester, 1873 and 1882).

Ellen D. Hale, "The Cape Ann Quarries," *Harpers New Monthly,* vol. 70 (March 1885); pp. 547-60.

John Webber, *In and Around Cape Ann* (Gloucester, 1885).

By the 1880s a number of maps of the area were being commercially published, several of which are quite detailed and consequently of real use to genealogists and local historians. Among them are the "Balloon View—Cape Ann to Boston," copyrighted by J. H. Daniels in 1879; "Cape Ann, Mass., 1881," published by the Eastern Railroad Company; the "Driving Road Maps, Essex County," copyrighted by the George H. Walker Company in 1884; Walker's "Village of Rockport, Mass." and "Town of Rockport, Mass." (1884); his aerial view of Pigeon Cove (1886); and successive maps of Rockport and Pigeon Cove in the Sanborn insurance map atlases beginning in 1885. The Walker map of Rockport Village (1884) was reproduced in 1975 and is available at the Sandy Bay Historical Society.

"Notes of the Bugle"

17

THE GAY NINETIES

ROCKPORTERS SLIPPED into the new decade almost imperceptibly. Most of them were at home asleep. Some, though, were on their toes at a watch dance in the town hall: "They danced the old year out and the new year in and enjoyed it very much." By contrast a few reverent townspeople were on their knees, at least figuratively, when the 1890s arrived. Beginning at 8:45 P.M., the Methodists held a watch night service in their vestry. It was followed by a prayer meeting. At the Pigeon Cove Congregational chapel, the members held an ordination service. Among the stay-at-homes that December 31, many were ailing, for as the press commented ruefully: "A large number in this vicinity have had or have la grippe." Among the robust, however, was the William Hunter family on Broadway, who had a large number of friends in to make fancy and old-fashioned molasses candy.

One topic for conversation had appeared in the *Times* that very day: skirts and what was and wasn't worn under them. "There seems to be the greatest possible curiosity about the Divided Skirt. Everyone wants to know what it is like," remarked an informed journalist. Her revelations continued: "Imagine a full petticoat gathered to a yoke, which yoke buttons on to a Union Suit. The skirt is divided from the hem to the yoke, the garment being put on like drawers." A divided skirt never wobbles, nor interferes with locomotion, nor slops in the mud, she claimed. "Now a word about Union Suits. The woman who once wears these easy, bandless, adaptable garments will never go back to the old vest and the drawers tied with a string or fastened with buttons that are too loose sometimes and uncomfortably tight at other times." "What will they think up next?" was the question in many minds as Rockporters entered upon the Gay Nineties.

Just how pleasurable would the new decade be in reality? Reasonably so. It would not be a period of marked upheavals, let alone cataclysms, though on the national level it would produce American imperialist ventures in Cuba, the Philippines, and Hawaii. Even Rockport itself would expand, principally in the South End and Pigeon Cove, but the growth would be gradual. Two innovations would alter most local life-styles: the advent of trolley cars and electricity.

Although there had been skating at the rink at Edmunds' Hall on Christmas afternoon and evening, the weather held mild. On Saturday, January 4, the *Review* editor wrote: "Today our desk is adorned with a bouquet of pansy blossoms picked out of doors yesterday by U.S. Eng'r. Williams from his garden." In the new decade townsfolk would continue to find pleasure through many avenues, including lectures and talks on widely ranging subjects. By then, though, most would be illustrated, thanks to the simplified camera and better reproduction facilities. The improved stereopticon offered increasing opportunities for lecturers treating material other than travelogues. For example, current events of a sort were taken up in an August 1890 lecture by Professor W. A. Briggs on the Johnstown, Pennsylvania, flood the previous May. On October 6, 1890, the GAR Memorial Association sponsored an historical lecture on "The Great Rebellion." The show was "magnificently illustrated by a powerful oxy-hydrogen stereopticon with 150 illustrations."

There were private camera delights, too. In July 1894 Herbert Low opened "a small ferrotype and tin type room at Sandy Bay near the Humane Society's boathouse." He advertised pictures made and finished in fifteen minutes, sharp, bright and clear. Babies were welcomed on Mondays at a special rate of eighteen tintypes for 30 cents or thirty-six types for 50 cents. Not to be outdone, James J. G. Tarr rushed into print announcing his new "Electro Photography" made with the help of some fast German equipment. He, too, welcomed the baby trade at his shop on Mt. Pleasant Street, taking youngsters instantaneously, "before they have time to move." He also made flashlight photographs of evening parties, proclaiming: "This invention operated by electricity is my own, nothing like it in America."

The Gay Nineties

A charmingly fresh view of the gaiety enjoyed by so many of Rockport's summer residents was given in the *Review* in early August 1894. It described a new summer cottage at Norwood's Head:

It commands a magnificent view of the ocean and harbor and the cool bracing breezes from the ocean keep the temperature enjoyable even in the hottest days. The cottage is pretty and commodious. It is two stories in height and surrounded by broad, inviting piazzas. Upon the first floor is a large general reception room, two dining rooms and a roomy kitchen, fitted with a range, ice chest, cupboards, etc. Upon the upper floor there are seven sleeping rooms, roomy, light, and airy. The guests, many of whom are from the busy, dusty city with its noise and confusion, find much to interest them and time passes rapidly.

The reporter became rhapsodic on the diversions available in town. "Those with artistic tendencies find many 'paintable' things in quaint old Rockport: the odd shaped houses and buildings with their soft colors, the streets, and the rocky cliffs ever battling with the grand old ocean, making admirable subjects for the painter's brush." That line pointed the course Rockport would be taking in the new century. "If you want a plaque or a panel to paint something on for your friend, call at Margeson's where also may be found a good assortment of artists' materials, easels, paints, brushes, etc. Also pictures framed in latest styles." So wrote the *Review*.

For those less artistically orientated, there was the joy of fishing off Cunner Rock, a sail upon the water, a ramble about the rocks, a dip in the surf. For algae lovers, there was the Sea Moss Club. To become a member one had to display twenty-five mounted varieties. For the plain lazy there was "a comfortable chair or hammock with a novel or paper on the verandahs." J. E. Stickney bought a powerful telescope in 1890 to set up in his Villa Breakwater View so he could watch the granite being placed on the slowly rising protector.

Rockporters began to catch up on bicycles in the 1890s. The papers reported a group out on May 16, 1890: "Their flashing lights and merry whistles rendered it quite a jolly and pleasant occasion." By July there were sixteen wheelmen in town. The wheelwomen were not left behind, for in June 1891, "Mrs. Frank Foster, Miss Kate Hale, and Miss Lizzie Butman enjoyed a cycle trip around the Cape Saturday." Soon the newspapers were running extensive advertisements for cycles of all kinds. In late May 1895 some twenty young men organized the Rockport Cycle Club. One year later appeared Procter Brothers' cycle

Procter stereo view of the 1870s shows summer visitors on the rocks at Andrews' Point with the Ocean View House in the distance and its Bath House to the right. (Hoyt)

manual, *Pleasure Drives Around Cape Ann,* and the Cape Ann Tool Company was busily engaged in making bicycle parts.

For those Rockporters who were content with less strenuous thrills, there were the usual local picnics, box suppers, donkey parties, and excursions. In September 1890, "Barge riding and the hay rack rides are in order and in full blast now." Card playing became so popular that scarcely a day passed without one or more whist games being noted, such as: "A very pleasant whist party was held at Mr. F. E. Pool's, 27 Beach Street on Friday evening. Mrs. Maggie Murphy and Mr. Elmer Crage won first prizes and Mr. J. Cameron the booby." There were masquerades, grand hops, a dance at Edmunds' Hall with "the prince of waltzers." The Village Improvement Society had a dance for members of the society "who have reached the age of 30 years." Benjamin N. Tarr was "raided" at a surprise costume party of friends who "looked like a detachment of the Salvation Army." The Priscilla Lodge arranged a tug-of-war one mid-February between Pigeon Cove, Sandy Bay, and anyone who'd like to try. That same week the new Rockport Athletic Association also played lightweight and heavyweight tug-of-war. For Emma Cleaves's birthday, there was a

The Gay Nineties

Jack Horner pie with many, many ribbons fastened to it. When they were pulled, each child got a bagful of candy.

The Christian Endeavorers played Quotation Match; Martha Hale won her lodge's china fruit dish prize for having driven 108 tacks into a board in five minutes; Dr. George Lowe won his lodge's award of a mustache cup and saucer for sewing twenty-six buttons on a piece of cloth in ten minutes. One can but speculate on a "slave party" held by the juvenile Templars in October 1890, the slaves being sold to the highest bidder without reserve. A good sum was realized, and "a grand social time enjoyed until 10 p.m. when the young people dispersed to their several homes, well satisfied." Today, also no one seems to know what the Methodists' old-fashioned "Love Feast" was when it was held in late August 1890. Then, too, there was that July lawn party one Monday evening at the base of Pigeon Hill. "Hammocks were suspended under the orchard trees, while Chinese lanterns and colored fires produced a nice effect. Several excellent voices enlightened the occasion and a variety of games beguiled the happy hours."

December 1890 witnessed two unusual Wednesday evenings—first a *Cantata of the Pilgrim Fathers;* next a husking bee. "Nothing like this has ever been given here." The corn was imported from Essex. There were band concerts, Johnnie Garlick's caged young owl, and Willie Welch's "very beautiful fantail doves, the only ones of their kind in these parts." At the end of the first year of the Gay Nineties, the *Advertiser* revealed that there were 114 widows in Rockport: "Get going bachelors; here's your chance!"

Sporting life in Rockport flourished in the 1890s, injecting a few novelties. Baseball, of course, became the town as well as the national sport. By July 1890 at a basket picnic during which "Mr. A. Smith amused the spectators with his organette," there was a coed baseball game in which the Priscilla Lodge beat the Granite Lodge and Blanche Burnell won a $1 prize in a running race. An uncommon surprise developed when a group of black waiters imported from the South to serve at the new, luxurious Turk's Head Inn proved to be first-rate swatters. Tennis had become so well established that the Ocean View House had its own spacious tennis grounds and held annual invitational tennis tournaments during the summers with prizes. The 1890 tournament lasted four days and got full press attention. That summer, a bathing pavilion was erected at Land's End to balance Pigeon Cove's long popular facilities. The Rockport Athletic Association, organized the previous February, also began sponsoring other events.

Town on Sandy Bay

Pugilistics soon emerged as a spectator sport. In February 1890 a fighter named Kearney stirred up interest when he gave a sparring exhibition at the town hall. By November, "devotees of the fistic art" were agog over the impending battle of two lively lightweights of 131 pounds each and 5 feet, 5 inches in height. The reporter hinted the battleground would be either "on a certain island not far away or among the solitude of the neighboring woods." It was also down at the Southern Woods in 1890 that a new attraction appeared, a coon hunt. Fall gunning for wild seafowl, mainly duck, always lured a quota of townspeople. One Wednesday in October 1890 Dr. Maguire of Pigeon Cove brought down seventy-six birds. The next month, though, some Rockporters were far from gay: "Mr. Forrest Batchelder is creating havoc in the skunk line in our neighborhood, having shot one each morning for six successive mornings."

Horseracing drew many spectators in the lively 1890s. On Thanksgiving Day, 1890, some five hundred gathered at the avenues in Pigeon Cove and saw baker Knowlton's horse win twenty-five bushels of oats. The Christmas race was "one of the greatest events of its kind that ever took place here, fully 1,500 people watching it." The purse was $100 and there were four races. By September 1896 Rockport was having a "Hare and Hound Chase" every Saturday afternoon. For the more pedestrian athletes there were walking competitions inaugurated in August 1890 by guests at the Pigeon Cove House. The course was the fourteen-mile Cape Ann tour; the gait was "square heel and toe as in sporting circles duly prescribed." The phalanx departed at 10:10 A.M., took an hour's break at Gloucester, and the winner crossed the line at 3:05 P.M.

Theatrical presentations always drew crowds. Among the productions presented in 1890 were *Alice in Wonderland; We'll Have to Mortgage the Farm,* "which was very finely rendered and was highly appreciated, the performers being Messrs. Will Parsons, George Rowe, G. N. Pettingill, Mrs. George Witham, and Mrs. Daniel W. Knowlton"; a children's *Mother Goose,* which "must have required much time and patience"; *Kit, the Arkansas Traveler;* and a display of living "Greek Statuary" by ladies of the Congregational church: "It proved to be superior to our most sanguine expectations. The movements were graceful and the grouping and poise were perfect." William Manning continued to compose songs, Oliver Ditson bringing out his "National Hymn—The Banner of the Brave" in January 1890, but also continued to sell pianos, the finest in the world for the price. A shift in the

William Pool (1829-1913), known as "Cumberland Billy," was a member of the crew of the U.S.S. "Cumberland" which was sunk by the C.S.S. "Merrimac" at the battle of Hampton Roads, Va., in 1862. (Hoyt)

Town on Sandy Bay

popularity of instruments was reflected in the benefit concert for Will
Parsons presented at the town hall in June 1891 by the Lynn Banjo,
Mandolin, and Guitar Club. More women appeared on local stages,
too, including the Land's End Ladies Glee Club, which donated its
proceeds to the sick of the GAR.

A recent invention of the period made the late 1890s still gayer for
ever widening audiences—the phonograph. On January 10, 1899, the
Ladies' Sewing Circle of the Universalist church at Pigeon Cove had its
annual meeting. "What added very much to the evening's amusement
was the graphaphone." A week later there, Emerson C. Collins of
Gloucester gave one of his Graphophone entertainments before the
Bachelor's Club, "which was greatly enjoyed by all present." On that
same January 18, 1899, the Boston and Maine Railroad inaugurated
its "Theatre Train," carrying 150 passengers, including Rockport's
William K. Simpson family, express from Gloucester to Boston. It was
to run experimentally every Wednesday evening for twelve weeks.
Departure from the Gloucester depot was at 6:20 precisely; the return
trip pulled out of Boston's Union Station at 11:10. The running time
in both directions was exactly forty-five minutes. A slight signal delay
caused the inaugural express to reach Boston a regrettable thirty
seconds late.

Rockport was indeed on the move in the 1890s. The proposed Civil
War Veterans' monument emerged from the planning chrysalis as a
Memorial Hall. Monitored by newspaper and visual evidence, the
project took shape in a year from Nathaniel Richardson's sale of land
on Main Street for $250 in April 1890, to the final occupancy at
Memorial Day, 1891. This structure "will be architecturally an orna-
ment to the town and show in a modest way that the services of the
heroes of the Rebellion are not forgotten here." Commenting on the
dedication, the *Advertiser* wrote flatteringly: "We doubt if there is
another town of its size in Essex County that could have turned out
more fine looking ladies, both young and old, than did Rockport on
Memorial Day." Lest anyone think the building might be used flip-
pantly, however, the covenant of sale provided that the Memorial Hall
"is not to be used for dancing or for any gambling or games of chance
whatsoever, or for any other purpose inconsistent with the purpose for
which said Hall was designed."

There were fewer religious revivals as time moved on and more
emphasis on social events, including concerts, readings, and plays. The
trend toward joint services continued, notably for such occasions as

Thanksgiving. The annual observance of Children's Sunday became an established practice among the Protestant community. The opening year of the decade initiated sporadic contacts with disadvantaged children from the city. In April, "the services at the Universalist Church Sunday were made very interesting by the singing of four little orphans from the Little Wanderers' Home in Boston." In August, "Mrs. Henry S. Story has been kind enough as to take one of the orphans from the Boston Home for a week or more."

Activity among the lodges continued to be vigorous, notably with the Red Men: "The Wonasquam Tribe of Red Men have refurnished their wigwam with elegant plush furniture which adds much to the appearance of the hall and will render it much more comfortable to the members." November 1890 saw the formation at Edmunds' Hall of yet another fraternal organization, Ocean View Lodge no. 84, Knights

A Rockport theme on the sheet music cover of "Our Cape Ann Home," composed by William N. Manning and published in 1885. (Hoyt)

Town on Sandy Bay

View east on Main Street about 1915. Amazeen's Ice Cream Store is at left, with the brick Memorial Hall beyond, and the ancient elm of Dock Square at the right. (Hoyt)

of Pythias. There were ninety-two charter members, many of whom hailed from Pigeon Cove's Scandinavian community. Another group got a pat on the back from the *Gloucester Times* in its Rockport notes: "One of the places in town which it gives one pleasure to look upon during these winter evenings is the Young Men's Christian Association. Plenty of wholesome reading matter is provided and appropriate games are enjoyed." As the flamboyant 1890s got under way, the sober Rechabite Temple was reshingled, perhaps a symbol of the group's wavering vitality.

An energetic array of more worldly Rockporters organized on March 13, 1891. "La Tosca Club is the very pretty name adopted by a coterie of young men in Rockport, who have fitted up their rooms in Lowe's Building, Dock Square, with all the comforts of home.... Their rooms are furnished with excellent taste and have quite the flavor of elegance about them." As an indication of cultural awareness at that time it is worth noting that Puccini's opera, *La Tosca*, was not written until 1900. Thus, the Rockport club took its exotic name from Victorien Sardou's recent play, *La Tosca* (1887), which was described as "a prolonged orgy of lust and crime." Few townspeople knew about that.

The Gay Nineties

Life was far from being all fun, games, and parades even in the Gay Nineties. A scarlet fever epidemic hit Rockport, shutting Sunday schools and day schools alike. Other ailments struck and struck again throughout the decade, children being frequent victims. In the middle of the summer of 1894, there was a wave of sickness among youngsters. "Cholera morbus predominates this season." One local physician reportedly treated more cases in one day than a whole season during the previous year. For babies, "Groder's syrup cures colic" was the refrain. Poole's pharmacy had decided that Chamberlain's Cough Remedy was the thing for "La Grippe," whatever the age of the victim. Another popular tonic was Hood's Sarsaparilla. "It makes the weak strong, gives strength to the nerves, elasticity to the muscles, vigor to the brain, and health to the whole body." If that failed, Mrs. D. D. Nason at 3 Summer Street was vending "Oxien, the great food for the nerves and all other ailments." She had it in large boxes for $1.00 and small ones for $0.35. One scourge threatened all age groups. Consumption (tuberculosis) carried away little eight-year-old Lizzie Parsons of South Street at the New Year season, as it had her sister a year or so before.

For Rockporters unable to withstand the hazards of church-lodge-club suppers, the *Times* started running advertisements headed "Fat Folks Reduced." Patients would be treated by mail, confidentially, in a harmless fashion and with no starving inconvenience or bad effects. From fifteen to twenty-five pounds per month would vanish, and women were comforted that "no wrinkles or flabbiness follow this treatment, endorsed by physicians and leading society ladies." More confidential still were the discreet remedies for unmentionable gaieties. "Delicate diseases of either sex, however induced, promptly, thoroughly and permanently cured. Send 10 cents in stamps for large illustrated treatise, sent securely sealed in plain envelope."

To some residents the continued emergence of women on the public scene was regarded as a social ill. By February 1896 Rockport had 60 of them on its voting list (but offset by 990 males). The spring of 1895 witnessed a spirited public session on equal rights. Alice F. York spoke affirmatively, claiming that "women having a right to the gallows, jail, and tax list should not have their rights abridged at other points, not even at the ballot box." Samuel Murray argued that women had a right to the cares, sufferings, and duties of home, and that was

One of the Village Improvement Society's contributions to the well-being of Pigeon Cove was this watering wagon which dampened the dust of the dirt roads. (C. Swan)

enough for them. Pastor Dolloff's point was that women already had more privileges than they could use and cited Mrs. Henry Ward Beecher, the preacher's wife: "God made men and women as they were and it would unsex them to grant equal rights and destroy the charm of home."

The crimes, accidents, heartbreaks, and other griefs besetting quarry workers and their families continued to remind some Rockporters the Gay Nineties were the grim nineties for other residents. Each winter, workers were laid off or their hours reduced. By spring their ten-hour days resumed, though in March 1891 petitions were circulated calling for a nine-hour workday for quarrymen. Yet in June, while the $3 day demand was being negotiated, at a town hall meeting a cry "that the importation of labor from Finland, which was driving the native workmen to the wall, be stopped evoked the greatest applause of the evening."

By the end of 1895 quarrying was in a depression, and the Rockport Granite Company led the general cut in wages by reducing its paving cutters by $2 a thousand blocks. With their backs to the wall, many quarrymen went into the woods and began cutting blocks wherever

The Gay Nineties

The granite sloop "William H. Moody" loaded with rough stone to be used as footing for the Sandy Bay breakwater. (SBHS)

they could find the granite. These "motions," as they were called, still dot the landscape of Cape Ann like pockmarks. By May 1897 things were looking up again; a ten-hour day was enforced; and the Rockport "stone fleet" comprised ten vessels, all powered by steam. There had not been one steam sloop in 1885.

The Sandy Bay breakwater rose slowly from its submarine depths. Appropriations from Washington got raised to $150,000 annually. By January 1899 the government had appropriated $900,000 on the Rockport breakwater-Harbor of Refuge. Some six hundred feet were complete; twenty-four hundred feet were complete to low water, and sixteen hundred feet had been built up to twenty-two feet below low water and with a width of forty feet at the top. Over one million tons of stone were in position at the end of the decade. Even under the revised plans of March 1892, however, the *Advertiser* wrote: "At the present rate, taking into consideration the decreased cost of stone, the work will require about 25 years before it is finished." Yet the impossible dream lived on: "Having already expended so much on this work, it seems certain that the government will push it steadily to completion."

Town on Sandy Bay

Other businesses in Rockport also had their ups and downs at this period. In November 1895 the Cape Ann Oil Clothing Company was running in good shape, employing twenty-five to thirty girls, only to be burned to the ground, after two previous fires, at the end of August 1897, probably through an arsonist. Mr. Hollis's shoe factory did finally produce shoes. At the opening of the Gay Nineties, William Parsons displayed "a pair of very pretty and substantial women's button boots." The paper marveled that they showed no signs of having been made by local hands hired in Rockport within about two months. The boots were neatly packed in a paper box which was also made in the factory. A week later the editor smiled: "The Rockport Shoe Company is the name we like to hear." In May 1891, though, the *Advertiser* soberly reported: "The shoe factory was decorated in mourning Wednesday, the southerly end of the building being draped in the form of a diamond, with the inscription 'Died 5/17th' and the time the factory closed. This is carrying the thing a bit too far."

One sooty Rockport enterprise had begun, in a sense, back in the 1850s as Dyer Poole's blacksmith shop, only to be sold to a young chap from Maine named Henry Pingree, who expanded the works into a factory for equipping the quarry workers of the area with the tools of their trade. By 1890 he had installed six steam-powered hammers and was producing an extraordinary line of products, when he died suddenly at forty-nine. His foreman, twenty-five-year-old John M. Tuttle, took over briefly, and a new company was organized in February 1891, to be called the Cape Ann Tool Company. A young man named J. Judson Dean became manager. By April the newspaper noted that "most of the force is to work nights at the Cape Ann Tool Company for the present in consequence of the increased demand for their goods." From that time on the Cape Ann Tool Company grew to become the keystone of the economic structure of Pigeon Cove.

The Fuller 1890s

Rockport in the gay-sober 1890s strove to make life fuller for its inhabitants. The Pigeon Cove Village Improvement Society took up the challenge of beautifying the landscape, often scarred by quarry operations, by planting shade trees, an effort which inspired several individuals to follow the example. In February 1891 the members began raising money for a watering cart to lay the dust of Rockport's

Laying the first water mains on Cove Hill's Mt. Pleasant Street. The man leaning on the bicycle in the center background is Harrison P. Wires. (SBHS)

unoiled summer streets. Flower seeds were given freely to children in 1895. An Agricultural Fair was rewarding. A children's improvement society was projected at the cove in the autumn of 1899, but the Children's Street Cleaning Brigade proved a complete failure.

The two libraries in town grew by leaps, especially the fledgling at Pigeon Cove, which was furnished with officers, readers, bylaws, and 432 books by the spring of 1891. Repeatedly, the local press acknowledged gifts of books to the Pigeon Cove "Free Library" from summer guests. Located in a room in the Harris building on the corner of Granite Street and Tenny Court, it formally opened on March 1, 1889. In November 1895 Rockport received a $4,000 bequest for the town library from the estate of Gloucester's Samuel F. Sawyer.

There were a number of other civic advances made to make the 1890s fuller. Written or printed ballots known as the Australian systems were voted for in February 1898. From then on written nomination papers had to be filed, properly signed, prior to the town's election day. At the opening of the 1890s a number of roads were up for rebuilding. Halfway through the decade at a town meeting taxpayer J. L. Woodfall quoted:

Town on Sandy Bay

These roads are not passable,
Not even jackassable;
And the persons who travel them
Should get out and gravel them.

At the beginning of the 1890s an addition was made to the high school, and the school committee agreed to a protracted one-session day for the older young people from 8:30 A.M. to 1:30 P.M. There was also some new fire-fighting equipment.

The great work was the implementation of the new town water system in January 1895—first with the testing of hydrants and the quality of the water, then with the opening of supply pipes to businesses and private homes. To make the hydrants more visible and to reduce the dangers of sideswiping from carts, hydrants were painted bottle green with white caps. Because of pollution the state board of health ordered the Rockport water commissioners to seize all the land around Cape Pond and to arrange for the destruction of several houses and summer cottages. An even greater threat were the adjacent glue factory and Gloucester Isinglass Company.

By then, public water was everywhere available from Cape Pond. As the decade drew to a close, Thurston and Hale, plumbers, were receiving plaudits for their magnificent work at the new Hale cottage on Land's End, where "all the exposed piping is of brass or nickel and throughout is a fine piece of workmanship." The Mt. Pleasant Street School got running water in July 1899; at the opening of the year, the new $3,000 schoolhouse at "Montrose Park" (Pigeon Hill Street) was opened with Helen Canney as teacher. The reporter commented that "the new school house is very pretty and is fitted up with all the modern improvements, the sanitary improvements being particularly so, which is of great need in a school house." No doubt school committee member Austin Story would have cried "Amen!" to that. The surviving memoranda of his labors during 1892-94 indicate that one of his principal chores was checking on school privies and the janitors who seemed loath to keep them in order, graffiti and all.

Crime and Inspiration

Then, too, there were the boys who surreptitiously sprinkled cayenne pepper on the school stoves and so forced an evacuation of their weeping classmates and teachers. Far more serious than this,

Austin W. Story's Pigeon Cove grocery store and delivery wagon in 1907. H. Carleton Story (center of group at left) had just taken over management of this family business which operated from 1856 to 1969. (Hoyt)

than throwing snowballs at girls, than forging excuse notes from unsuspecting parents, or than using obscene language was putting kerosene into a lighted school stove, a prank which endangered many lives. Rockport in the 1890s continued to be plagued by pranksters, vandals, and thieves; reports of their depredations were fully printed in the newspapers. Among the assault-and-battery cases which made the papers were some involving immigrants, such as one between "rivals for the affection of a comely Swedish girl," and one in the spring of 1898 over "an attractive Finn girl named Lena."

The larger issues of crime and punishment was the subject of a debate held before some 250 people in Pigeon Cove on some three weeks before the United States declared war on Spain over Cuba. The topic was "Resolved: that capital punishment should be abolished." The Gloucester YMCA defended the proposition; a group from the Young Men's Club of Pigeon Cove took the negative side. The *Gloucester Times* gave the story well over a full column in which all the points were summarized. The judges, who based their decisions on weight of argument and manner of delivery, declared the Pigeon Cove team winner.

Town on Sandy Bay

The original Turk's Head Inn, which opened in June, 1890 on the site of the old Asa Todd Farm, before fires required structural changes. This is the view which hung in the lobby until the hotel was closed. (Hoyt)

By the 1890s the Scandinavians were becoming increasingly well acclimated to Rockport, and Cape Ann papers mentioned more and more of their activities, especially at church and temperance meetings. In 1891 at Edmunds' Hall "four ministers from abroad" conducted Swedish services, and more reports were issued concerning a Swedish church building on Pigeon Hill Street, land for which had been given by Messrs. Cleaves and Goodwin. That same Sunday at the Good Templars' Hall the Finns had a service with the Reverend Mr. Frank Erik Ohds of Michigan as preacher. At the end of April 1891, the grounds for the Swedish Lutheran Church were dedicated and the cornerstone laid. By May the building at Montrose Park was rapidly advancing, "and gives promise of being very pretty." Talk was then beginning that the Swedish Methodists, who had organized back in 1883, would build a church for their denomination "near the old Rowe farm." In 1891 this building was erected on Granite Street and served its people well.

On June 7, 1895, the Council of Congregational Churches granted recognition to the Swedish Evangelical church (Mission Covenant) at a service in which the singing was in English and Swedish. In reporting

The Gay Nineties

the occasion the *Advertiser* wrote: "This church is the result of the preaching of the gospel in the Swedish language by the missionaries of the Massachusetts Congregational Home Missionary Society, who were the first to begin work among the Swedish population of Rockport." It had sixty-one members at that point and "a pretty and convenient meeting house" (at 111 Granite Street).

The Episcopalians had renewed their services on October 31, 1885, at the home of Otis Smith on High Street, then with a service in Haskins Hall conducted by J. S. Beers of Natick. Next came regular services in the Rechabite Temple of Honor. On May 7, 1886, St. Mary's mission was organized with nineteen members and Otis E. Smith as warden. A room in the town hall served as a chapel. Then, on August 6, 1892, the Feast of the Annunciation, St. Mary's church on Broadway was opened for divine service for the first time.

Homes Away From Home

Spectacular Turk's Head Inn captured the attention of virtually all Rockporters as the Gay Nineties began. Compared to the GAR Memorial Association's molehill, F. H. Nunn's inn would be a mountain.

-of Cape Ann" on Thatcher Island.　Looking South we have the broad expanse of Massachusetts Bay, dotted with its wealth of commercial and pleasure craft; to the right, the pleasant and cosy town of

VIEW IN THE PARLOR.

Rockport, and the dome-like summit of Pigeon Hill, velvety and green, with its rich back-ground of grand old woods, in whose cool groves and along

Front and back covers and interior illustration from Pigeon Cove House promotional brochure issued in 1890. The second building depicted on the front cover was built in 1872 and became a popular resort hotel under the management of Mrs. Ellen S. Robinson. The back cover and parlor illustrations reflect to perfection the Gay Nineties atmosphere and Victorian style of seaside resorts of the period. (Hoyt)

Rockport had had nothing comparable and never would again. From the preliminary sketches, news reports poured forth steadily. By mid-June nearly all the furniture had arrived. So had proprietor Nunn with a dozen servants, and thirty more of the latter were expected in a few days. Prior to opening, puffed the *Advertiser,* the demand for rooms far exceeded the most sanguine anticipation, "and if the hotel were as large again as it is, it could be filled easily." By the end of June a long-distance telephone was in operation and nine more "colored" waiters had arrived—soon to achieve local eminence as baseball players. The paper for July 18 counted 150 guests on Sunday. Harvey Tarr had imported several horses from New York to set up a livery stable at the inn for the benefit of its many guests. For those who weren't able to wander through the superlative hotel, the *Advertiser* of August 22 gave a detailed, guided tour of the place in superlative fashion. Then, in September, proprietor Nunn hosted Rockport town officials at lunch.

Closer in to town was the development at Gap Head and beyond. Soon after Turk's Head Inn opened this note appeared in the local press:

The Gay Nineties

Stonehaven–How does that strike you for a name? Well, that is the name by which the new Phillips property will be called. The principal road which encircles the entire property along the shore is Marmion Way, which commences at South Street in place of Estes Avenue, which name will be abandoned. Shetland Road and Gap Head Road are completed and Straitsmouth Way, the latter leading from old David Smith's homestead to the beach. Over 70 beautiful lots have already been laid out. The hotel site has been situated on Gap Head. The whole estate comprises about 70 acres, every inch of which is eligible for seaside cottage lots.

Half a century of hospitality lay ahead down at Land's End. That summer the *Advertiser* noted: "There is not an unoccupied cottage on the shore."

Other Rockport hostelries hurried to prettify themselves. Mr. Harding added "some valuable improvements to his popular establishment," the Abbott House. One of these was an eight-foot piazza along the full length of the front, shaded by a fancy duck awning which would insure "a very pleasant promenade" for his guests during the summer. In June 1891 came the word that Pigeon Cove would have "another fine new hotel directly across from the Ocean View House." Work began at once. Then, in 1897, the heart of Rockport got the Adams's reconstructed hotel, the Granite Shore on Main Street with forty rooms, each with steam heating, electricity, and call bells. The whole first floor and the spacious verandas on two sides were lighted by electricity. Just next door to Mr. and Mrs. Adams's new inn, made from the Abbott House, Rockport's expanded post office was opened, it, too, being equipped with electricity. The town's other federal installation had been built the year previously, the new lighthouse on Straitsmouth Island.

Rockport Electrified

By the turn of the century Rockport had been electrified—in both senses of the word. In February 1891 people were spellbound by the "instructive" lecture given by one W. C. Haughton on "Electricity in the Household." The newspapers reported that a large variety of practical instructions were given. Among the marvels displayed were an incandescent lamp which was lighted. An electric clock was shown and an electric gong struck. "A sewing machine, burglar alarm, organette, etc., made the whole very interesting." Probably the two show-stoppers were a fire, lighted in a stove by electricity at a given time by the clock, and a miniature electric bed, "which dumped a little occupant out."

By April 1891 the *Advertiser* was optimistically writing that an electric railroad around the Cape "lies far inside the range of probability." At the end of May, the Gloucester Street Railway Company petitioned to run electric cars from Dock Square to the Gloucester line through the South End. Technicians quickly objected that because of induction the current for the Rockport trolley cars would so interfere with the operations of the Commercial Cable Company that the company would have to leave town. Discussions at town meeting grew heated indeed. Proponents claimed the electric car people were coming to make Rockport "bloom and blossom as a rose." Opponents charged that the franchise requested was for an experiment and would not benefit the townspeople but only the summer residents for a few months.

Before any trolley car system could be organized, the area had to have electric power. On August 10, 1893, the Rockport selectmen made an agreement with the Gloucester Electric Light Company to light the streets of the town with electric incandescent bulbs of 25 candlepower each. In all, 125 lights were to be used for 252 nights during the year (21 nights per month) until December 15. Service finally began on January 23, 1894.

It was in November 1895 that a Rockport Street Railway Company was formed to run through town, on to Pigeon Cove, and so to the Lanesville line. The stock was capitalized at $125,000, with the Rockport directors being Leander M. Haskins, C. N. Cleaves, A. Goodwin, and Henri Woods. There was a delay caused by an alternate plan to run the cars down Broadway and up Main Street. The fare from Rockport to Gloucester was fixed at 5 cents. Those traveling beyond the junction of Granite and Beach streets (Knowlton's Corner) would pay 10 cents. Work moved forward rapidly. On July 3, 1896, the trolleys were put to the test. Service began on the Fourth, at 4:07 A.M., when three fully loaded cars left Gloucester for Rockport. Every half hour afterward cars departed, "strings of five cars being run most of the time during the day." In addition, large numbers of trippers traveled "by the steam cars." By the first week in August, the "electrics" were running through to the cove and giving great satisfaction. By October, Rockport merchants generally were complaining that retail trade was going to Gloucester because of the convenience of the electric cars. By the end of the decade, trolleys had become so much an accepted part of the Rockport scene that entertainment programs were timed to meet their schedules. Real estate advertisements were quick to point up the convenience of the trolleys: "To let—in Rockport, a very desirable estate situated on Broadway, stable connected with entrance in rear. Three minutes walk from depot and electric cars pass the door." Even friendly jokes were cracked on the subject: "Why was the snow of yesterday like the electric cars? Because it went so fast." Its success was rapid, too, for on November 19, 1897, the papers reported that the Gloucester and Rockport Street Railway "is one of the highest dividend paying roads in the state."

Grumbles were sounded periodically at the doors of the Boston and Maine, first about a need for a new depot. "The present one is so dark at times that one is not always sure of his footing while boarding or alighting from the cars." Work finally began in the last months of the decade. Meanwhile, another complaint had become pressing— smoking. In a letter to the editor in October 1899 a *Times* reader urged: "Give the smokers and tipplers a car by themselves for the ladies' sakes."

The 1890s were not historically oriented in Rockport, at least to judge from surviving evidence. Perhaps people were too busy living and enjoying the present. The few stories which turned up in the newspapers largely served as filler. One published record of interest even today was Charles E. Mann's *In The Heart of Cape Ann, or the Story of Dogtown,* with its helpful map and attractive sketches by Catherine Follansbee. His account of the deserted village ran serially in the *Cape Ann Advertiser* in the autumn of 1895 prior to being issued as a hardback book for 50 cents by Procter Brothers. A hurried and rather careless narrative was James E. Pringle's *History of the Town and City of Gloucester,* privately printed in 1895.

The Stormy 1890s

The 1890s, like every other era in Rockport's history, had its share of storms, literally and metaphorically speaking. There was a record breaking gale the first week of February 1898, when at least twenty Cape Anners were lost and twenty-five vessels went ashore in Gloucester Harbor and half a dozen more at Rockport and Pigeon Cove. All trains from Rockport to Boston were suspended, and the electric car system was badly damaged. The entire roof of the Bass Avenue carbarns was lifted off, crashed down, and demolished a dozen trolleys parked there. Successive blizzards and storms inevitably tied up trolley service and, to a lesser degree, the Boston and Maine. The most famous gale of the decade, the Portland gale of November 26-27, 1898, named for the loss at sea of the Main-bound steamer *Portland* with all hands and passengers—some 176 in all—took its toll in Rockport only in property, not in lives. The imperiled ship *Portland* was last sighted about midnight some twelve miles northeast of Thacher's Island by Capt. Reuben Cameron of the fishing schooner *Grayling* as the ships raced for shelter in Gloucester Harbor. Seven vessels were wrecked at Pigeon Cove, and one resident, then a boy of five, never forgot having his family's henhouse whipped into the sea from the bluff at Pigeon Cove. With it went his loved pet rooster, named Dewey, after the currently popular hero of the Battle of Manila Bay.

The squalls of the Spanish-American War made more of an impact on Rockport through the newspapers than on the lives of its residents. With war still undeclared, defensive measures began to be called for. In retrospect, they seem all but laughable. On April 8 the *Advertiser* announced: "It is said that six guns will be placed in position on the point of land just beyond Gap Cove and that C. L. Dunlap will be in command. The number of men needed is estimated to be over 100. Some of the Sons of Veterans have already been asked to hold themselves in readiness." The *Advertiser* of April 22 ran an interview with a very aged resident of Folly Cove as he reminisced ("through a glass darkly") about the attempted British invasion there during the War of 1812! On April 25 war was declared, and the names of 187 men from Gloucester (but none from Rockport) appeared in the paper as enlistees in the U. S. Navy.

Five army officers from the "signal service" arrived at Rockport on Saturday morning, April 23, but immediately hiked up Poole's Hill, where they set up their tent near the residence of Representative Leander M. Haskins. They were supplied with firearms, provisions, and instruments used in signaling. "They will establish there a signal station." Thus, warning could be dispatched of any potential Spanish or Cuban invaders of Rockport.

In addition to those five men (whom the *Advertiser* categorized as coming from "the most intellectual class in the service" and who would soon warrant a building, not a mere tent), Rockport would be further protected by the auxiliary cruiser *Prairie* as it patrolled the coast. On July 1 Rockport's postmaster agreed to accept canned goods and other imperishable dainties to be sent "to the boys who have gone to the

The Gay Nineties

front." In mid-July the Women's Relief Corps of the GAR undertook to collect items for the combatants. Their first effort resulted in "a large box" filled with bandages, canopies, sheets, pillowcases, stockings, reading matter, and so on. Their second shipment, "hospital shirts," went to the Volunteer Aid Association the next week. Then came an announcement that the signal station on Poole's Hill would be discontinued on or about August 1. The Spanish American War ended on August 7.

It was a different type of storm which hit a few men from Rockport in 1898. The rage for Klondike gold and its excitement blew up in January. "One of our Swedish residents, Nels Carlson," wrote the *Advertiser's* Rockport reporter on January 28, "started for the Alaska Gold Fields on Monday. His family will remain here." Of the ten members of the Cape Ann Mining and Trading Company who left town the second week of May 1898, there were five Gloucestermen and Martin Evans, Andrew H. Lane, Haley Lane, George F. Parsons, and G. Edward Wendell from Rockport. Their route was to be via the Boston and Albany to Chicago, then by the Northwestern Railroad to Seattle, thence down to San Francisco by steamer. As soon as the ship *Woodbury* had discharged its cargo of coal at San Francisco, it would carry the whole Cape Ann contingent to the new gold fields at Kotzebue Sound, where the boat would be sold.

At the end of May, Nels Carlson returned from Alaska, intending to go again equipped to work his claim there. Less than a month later Martin Evans was back in Rockport, because "some unforseen accidents" had prevented the Cape Ann Company from sending more than fifteen members to the gold fields, the others therefore being obliged to return. "They retain their interests in the company, however." By mid-August all the Cape Ann "Klondike" vessels were sold or up for sale at San Francisco, and disagreements raised bitter rebukes throughout the company.

A late footnote to the Alaskan gold rush appeared in the *Gloucester Times* of September 20, 1906, which mentioned the return of P. M. Olson to Pigeon Cove from the gold region at Rampart, north of the Yukon River. The onetime quarry worker "took the gold fever" in 1897 and went to seek his fortune. "During his absence of nine years," noted the writer, "he has been quite successful taking several large nuggets out of his claim."

The dreams of showers of gold came much closer to town than the Klondike. Three days before the Spanish-American War was declared, the *Advertiser* informed its readers of an erroneous rumor that the small building being erected on Halibut Point was to be a fort built by the government for protection from the Spanish. "Its purpose is really to set up a plant to obtain gold from salt water." On May 13 it announced that work had been begun on the gold-producing plant on Saturday. Then on August 12 came the report that the Halibut Point gold plant, "is now in full operation. The tents in which the men lived were burned down by an explosion of an oil stove." To head off any assumptions that the venture might involve skulduggery, the paper announced: "This is not in any way connected with the Lubec plant, notwithstanding rumors of its connections with the other unfavorably known concern." As may be surmised, however, the only gold Halibut Point produced was goldenrod and ragweed.

To Rockporters of the 1890s the prospects of gold lay in the Harbor of Refuge. The new century would see numerous naval visits there. A harbinger of things to come took place during the last summer of the decade with a report on Saturday, July 8, that the North Atlantic Squadron was to visit Rockport. Its presence would "probably bring out as many people as Rockport ever had." Six battleships and cruisers were involved: The *U.S.S. New York, Indiana* (10,288 tons; speed, 15.5 knots), *Massachusetts, Brooklyn, Texas,* and *New Orleans.* There were silent regrets that the visit would be under a captain (Taylor) rather than an admiral (Sampson, who would be on a month's leave) and that because of the brevity of the sojourn the navy had declined the town's offer of a banquet for the officers. Some Rockporters ventured to sniff that the visit was only "a fitting tribute to the past achievement of Rockport in the wars of our country."

The realists saw it for what it might be worth—vast appropriations for the breakwater-harbor project, already dragging along for fifteen years. "Let everyone display bunting and flags and thus help to make this a gala day for our town." T. T. Hunter Harwood was a committee of one to provide fireworks. He had also secured a load of tar barrels for the evening's bonfire. As a special appeal the Rockport committee had pleaded the cause quite unabashedly: "It means very much to the success of our Harbor to have an official visit from the North Atlantic Squadron by order of the Secretary of the Navy." The call, therefore, was: "Make every effort to receive them in a manner befitting the magnitude of such an undertaking as the Sandy Bay Harbor of Refuge."

They came, they saw, and they were conquered—after a fashion, as the new century would demonstrate. For most Rockporters the Gay Nineties ended as they had begun. A few were in church, others were dancing, and most were in bed when the town clock rang in January 1, 1900.

ADDITIONAL READING

Hermon Babson, "The Building of a Breakwater," *New England Magazine,* new series, vol. 11 (1894); pp. 163-73.

Paul Kenyon, "Cape Ann Trolleys," *The Gloucester Magazine,* vol. 1, no. 3, pp. 6-11.

John L. Cooley, *Voice of a Village* (Pigeon Cove, 1964), sketches the V.I.S. story, and his *Granite of Cape Ann* (Rockport, 1974) offers a short summary of the quarry epic. The definitive treatise will be Barbara Erikkila's forthcoming volume.

Charles E. Mann, *In the Heart of Cape Ann, or the Story of Dogtown* (Gloucester, 1896).

Mary T. Falt, *Pleasure Drives Around Cape Ann* (Gloucester, 1896), describes the area in preautomobile times.

On the gold of Halibut Point see Joseph E. Garland, "Cape Ann had its own Great Gold Rush in 1898," *Gloucester Daily Times,* May 19, 1962.

18

OUR TOWN, ROCKPORT

A NEW YEAR, a new decade, a new century. Rockport ushered them in with fire and ice, those elements which Robert Frost thought might sometime end the world. The fire in question gutted the house of Nels Carlson near the corner of Main and Beach streets, breaking out at 2:30 A.M. As for the snow, it was so heavy as to tie up the trolley cars to Pigeon Cove and the railroad to Gloucester. At the cove "walking was simply fearful." Turn-of-the-century Rockport might almost have served as a model for Thornton Wilder's play, *Our Town,* so serene was its life. Yet a dozen years later, much of that tranquillity had become a memory. On the eve of World War I, townspeople looking backward could have put down signposts marking Rockport's new directions: in schools, social services, transportation, industry, daily living in all its ramifications.

"School life is a pleasure today as it has never been before," commented a Rockporter in 1901. That June, a senior class of twelve was graduated; Norwood H. Knowlton won first honors, Leonora Dillon second. President Capen of Tufts came to give the address, "with an occasional touch of the facetious." Music included the "Soldiers' Chorus" from *Faust.* "Never in its history has such fine chorus work been done by the school." Although the weather was "hot, hotter, hottest" all week, at graduation the "air was laden with the breath of many flowers," evergreen, laurel, and roses. "The beautiful dresses of white, the toilettes of the graduates, the happy bright faces of the school vied with one another." Our Town at its best.

271

The Jewett-Tupper House, built in 1806, home of the second pastor of the Congregational Church. The Choate house at the right was later moved to make way for the Carnegie Library. (SBHS)

But all was not so pastoral in the school department. The state had condemned the classrooms in the town hall. For awhile there was a plan for a new high school; firm decisions were made, then unmade. By September 1904 the existing high school had been renovated, its privies removed, and plumbing installed in the basement; all talk of a new high school was over.

All schools were crowded; the ratio of female to male teachers was far too great; only one building was "correctly lighted"; records were insufficiently detailed; Rockport teachers were paid far less than the average in Massachusetts; and the textbooks in use were comparably cheaper. The statewide average cost of education per pupil was $26.49 in 1902. In Rockport it was $16.52. In the winter of 1904-05 voters decided to create a school for elementary grades out of the remains of the machine shop of the Rockport Cotton Mill, and George J. Tarr gave the town the remainder of the mill property for use as a playground. At that point there were 834 children in Rockport at between five and fifteen, an increase of 33 in two years. "No wonder the schools are crowded." The new school was finally opened with the new term at the beginning of 1907. Seventy years later it still nurtures several elementary grades.

Town on Sandy Bay

Leander M. Haskins (1841-1905), businessman, public official, and philanthropist. (SBHS)

The town did respond to several educational deficiencies, though. New privies were built at the Beach Street, Pigeon Cove, and Pigeon Hill buildings in 1908; in 1909 a new science laboratory was set up; common drinking cups were eliminated and drinking fountains were installed in 1911; and medical examinations were inaugurated. Homework was required of grammar school pupils "for the purpose of furnishing occupation for the evening hours." In response to requests from Swedish and Finnish residents for an evening school, one was opened in 1911 at the Temperance Hall on Forest Street. Two teachers held classes twice a week for about thirty adult students.

Education through a proper library took a striking new departure with the new century. The present site was purchased in May 1904 for $2,000. At the end of June the town received a welcome gift of $10,000 from Andrew Carnegie. The cornerstone, laid on December 3, included a box of souvenirs for the future. At the end of January 1906 the Carnegie Library, as it was named, was opened with a fanfare. Public approval was instant.

On the social welfare front, Rockport had done reasonably well in the nineteenth century. One serious gap remained, however. Rockport's six physicians issued a call on December 22, 1900: "We believe it is feasible to start and carry on a small hospital even in this small village." Pointing out the distance from their town to the Addison Gilbert Hospital in Gloucester, the lack of any appropriate medical facilities in Rockport, and the number of quarry workers and sailors being injured—often critically through accidents—they appealed for a Rockport hospital association. Their urgent request touched enthusiastic tinder. Within a fortnight, "our foreign born citizens are filled with a commendable public spirit and are easily aroused to determined and persistent effort," praised the *Rockport Review* in an item reporting "Finns and Swedes working hard for the hospital scheme." By mid-February a hospital corporation was under way. "Here is something everyone can rally around, for there are no class, social or other lines of demarcation here." The annual town meeting approved the plan.

The crucial step, however, came with the death of Leander M. Haskins at age sixty-three on August 1, 1905. In his will he left his residence, accompanying buildings, and two plots of land totaling seventy acres to the town for a hospital and park. Strangely, the *Review* urged voters to reject the offer, since the town did not require a hospital, could not afford one, was already levying excessively high taxes, and badly needed the $800 tax money produced by the Haskins property. The March 1906 town meeting voted 242 to 19 to accept Haskins's gift. C. C. Amazeen was named caretaker, and trustees were appointed. Dr. Tupper received funds for supplies, and on October 1 the hospital admitted its first patient—a youngster with a compound ankle fracture suffered during a school recess. During the last year of the decade, Rockport's hospital treated eighty-four registered patients.

Better Communications

Although Our-Town, Rockport, was not ready for the telephone when it was first introduced, by 1900 it was eager. Commercial firms had blazed the trail. By early 1904, the *Rockport Review* was thumping the tub for a municipal gasworks and a telephone central. Soon a company representative informed the town that local services would be available for $18 a year. Rockporters watched telephone poles being placed in late July and the switchboard in August. In the final week, telephones rang through Our-Town's own central. Only a week later there was a petition for a public phone at the depot, and on September

The Foster-Manning Beaver Dam Farm on the road to Gloucester about 1900, with the Nugent family, its last occupants, at the left. The stone summer kitchen is now the Babson Cooperage Shop Museum. (SBHS)

10 the *Review* loftily proclaimed: "Telephones are now a necessity." On April 29, 1905, Dr. R. L. Carter listed in the newspaper a telephone number for his office in Savage's block. Six weeks later, also on Main Street, Clark's Cash Market followed suit. By the end of the spring of 1905 the telephone company reported having ninety regular and thirty summer subscribers.

Early in the new century the veteran Commercial Cable Company was given a run for its money when the enterprising Roger Babson quietly acquired Milk Island in September 1901. Three and a half months of suspense slipped by before the cagey young enterpreneur unveiled his scheme in an open letter:

You may be interested to know that I am corresponding with Sig. Marconi relative to a Wireless Telegraphy Station on Milk Island. If Sig. Marconi makes Newfoundland his American-terminus, he may desire to repeat his messages from Newfoundland to Milk Island, and use said plant as a distributing center.

One Marconi message did reach Our-Town at the year's end, but via the Nantucket lightship. Sig. Marconi preferred Cape Cod for his

Our Town, Rockport

eventual station, and the Babsons generously decided Milk Island was better for birds.

Electricity, on the other hand, sparked Rockport from the moment it came to town. By the spring of 1901 the town was already "littered with unsightly poles." In 1904 poles were added along Breakwater and Phillips avenues in Pigeon Cove, and that May an ordinance was issued levying a $10 fine for putting up personal signs or advertising on telephone or telegraph poles; defacing trees was added for good measure. Newspaper advertisements assured readers that the convenience of "press the button, we do the rest," made electric lights a household necessity after they were once installed. Store owners flaunted the news of their electrification, and local gossip columns long carried items like this one of December 22, 1900: "Mr. Benjamin Tarr, Granite Street, has had his house wired for electric lights recently."

Electric cars and railroads were something else again. Once rolling, the electric cars soon became the target of complaints. Service was poor, equipment substandard, derailments too frequent. In the interests of safety, in June 1901 a slower schedule was inaugurated. The response was an irritated "Gloucester is now fifteen minutes further away." Improvements brought more riders. "Wait till the line is connected at the Lanesville and the Pigeon Cove end. Then, you will see the rush around the Cape." When in 1902 the joining was completed through Langsford Street, there began a rush the momentum of which lasted a dozen or more years.

The railroad also maintained its momentum. The new century welcomed our town's new depot—"one we may well be proud of." It would be a benefit to the town, "in the summer business especially." For the 6:05 A.M. to Boston, Charles Rowe purchased the first ticket from the new station. The Boston and Maine was next petitioned for an intermediate station between Gloucester and Rockport. A simultaneous petition to transform dry Rockport into a licensed town was rejected, but the Boston and Maine purchased from Benjamin Randall a strip of land beyond the foot of Great Hill. Although its Bass Rocks station along Nugent's Stretch has long since disappeared, the location may still be spotted. Patrick Nugent himself never saw the shelter, for he had died suddenly at fifty-one at his Beaver Dam Farm in December 1900; "a practical farmer and a good mechanic, sturdy and thrifty." He had managed his farm well and "was restoring the old historic place to its old time appearance," commented the *Gloucester*

The Straitsmouth Inn in 1908. This popular seaside hotel was opened in 1907 by Mrs. Everett R. Wilkinson and managed by her until it burned the night of December 31, 1960. (Hoyt)

Times—"old" meaning the barn built in 1833, not the alleged Babson coopershop.

The *Review,* the short-lived board of trade (April 1901-January 1904), and other promoters of a new Rockport clamored for more, wider, and better roads. "Manchester roads half make Manchester." June 1901 had already brought the Waite family from Cambridge to Rockport for a few days "over the road in a locomobile." Shore drives became essential "to meet the demands of the time and cater to the wants of these guests who make up our town life" and pay "no inconsiderable part of the tax burden." By April 1904 plans were aired to link up Jason Giles's ambitious real estate development at "the Headlands, formerly Norwood's Head," with the already bustling Marmion Way area. The *Review* had begun a column of "Marmion Way Notes" in July 1901, with trivia of transient interest such as news of tennis courts marked out in response to the reawakened popularity of that pastime; the lures of the public lifesavers' drill held Mondays and Thursday mornings at ten; and reports of the new Straitsmouth Inn, opened by Mrs. Everett R. Wilkinson on June 22, 1907, to the anxiety of some of the neighbors. "The watering cart at Marmion Way is a

Our Town, Rockport

View south on Eden Road from Cliff Hall, the home of Joseph P. Reynolds. This photograph illustrated a promotional booklet issued in 1905 by Reynolds' Paradise Cliff development. (Hoyt)

luxury we can ill afford to dispense with," cautioned the editor of the *Review.*

By August 1905 Our-Town laid down a speed limit of fifteen miles per hour. The *Review,* however, warned that "something should be done to stop reckless automobile speeding in town before any accidents happen." The following week Police Chief Sullivan and his stalwarts stopped six violators. Hazards were increased in 1906 when the state highway was favored with $5,000 for the stretch from the foot of Great Hill to the Gloucester line. During the inaugural North Atlantic Fleet visit that summer an estimated five hundred automobiles came to Rockport in one day. That same year local hotels stocked automobiles for guests to hire, while local newspapers instructed readers where to write in Boston for automobile road maps. By the spring of 1911 three Rockport grocers bowed to the inevitable and secured automobiles for handling deliveries during the summer rush.

All was far from mechanized, however. When William Hodgkins bought Alden Bray's milk route, he also bought a fine new delivery wagon. Another horse-drawn addition to Our-Town was the hand-

A two-masted schooner and smaller craft moored at the Bradley Wharf in 1906. Motif No. 1 is at the left, T Wharf and its coal pocket at the right, and Atlantic Avenue in the background. (Hoyt)

some new fire engine with its extension ladder, chemical fire extinguisher, and rubber coats and helmets for the crew of volunteers proud to man it. Confident of the future for carriages, Elmer Burgess took up the local agency for Kelly-Springfield rubber tires. "They will wear longer than any other and cost no more." He was also confident of human mortality, for he advertised caskets, coffins, monumental works, robes, and "everything pertaining to the dead," including a "lady assistant when desired."

Communications would soon be changing in the harbors as well as on the roadways. Mel Rich, looking ahead, built a gasoline-powered small boat for fishing in the spring of 1902 to the praise of the *Review:* "This kind of power in conjunction with sails has a great advantage over the ordinary boat and we think will play an important part in the fishing of the future." Only a decade later sailing trawlers along the entire North American coast would be fighting for their very survival against steam-powered foreign ships. And as unglamorous a craft as a scow would be powered by gasoline. Hodgkins and Tarr bought such a thirty-footer from Lawson and Knutsen in October 1911.

Our Town, Rockport

In June 1911 several submarines appeared in Sandy Bay Harbor and went through maneuvers. "They would be seen gliding along with hulls out of water and then gradually sink from sight only to appear later, perhaps miles away, and at other times only a short distance from where they disappeared from view." By then, though, a whole series of U.S. naval visits had conditioned Rockporters for almost anything maritime.

There had been little local conditioning for air transport, however, so "Rockporters were somewhat baffled at the appearance of the town's first "UFO." On July 15, 1911, "something that was taken for an air ship was seen crossing Sandy Bay from southward." It flew over the breakwater, "and on approaching it dropped down as if on inspection of the work. It then rose and went flying across the Bay, rising and falling, but steadily and rapidly gliding past Andrews' Point. The novel sight was witnessed by quite a number along the shore."

"Water, Water, Everywhere"

Although most of the concern shown for water had been directed to the sea, fresh water had come increasingly to Rockport's attention in the decade before 1900. Early in the new century, mains were extended even as far as Babson Farms, but Long Beach's request in July 1904 was rejected as an unprofitable venture. That year the *Review* spoke of noticeable improvement in the quality of town water, but by Christmas, 1905, the euphoria ended. Our-towners were told by state officials that Rockport's water was "the most impure of any in the State." Yet they were not shaken. On Christmas their paper reflected that the question of a remedy would probably be considered at the March town meeting. Restrictions against garbage and other offal were laid down, and the board of health also tackled water pollution along the Front Beach, caused by open drains. "Bathing is engaged in to a greater extent that ever before, so our beaches should be taken care of, the rocks removed, seats, etc. built to make them more attractive." Naked bodies, though, were not deemed attractive. So from 1901 on, John S. Eaton, constable of Rockport, covered the waterfront with this notice: "All parties are forbidden Bathing on the Beaches, Harbors or Piers unless properly dressed. Nude bathers will be prosecuted if detected." By July 13 the *Review* told its followers that nude bathing "has been practically stopped." Unconvinced, Constable Eaton continued to post his warnings.

View west from the Congregational Church steeple over Front and Back Beaches. Observatory Point is in the center and beyond lies the hulk of the wrecked Schr. "Hattie Page." (Borge)

Although taxpayers were unprepared to finance retaining walls and etceteras for the Front Beach, they thought differently about their houses. In April 1904 Thurston and Hale were doing the plumbing of the Charlesworth House on Main Street. "They are putting in hot water and a bath room." In an advertisement the plumbers assured doubting Thomases that "your cigar bill for a year or two would give you all the comforts of a modern bath room in your house."

But it was the salt water which occasionally gave the "Push Rockporters" attacks of megalomania. In June 1901 an overnight stop by the navy's one-thousand-ton gunboat *Newport* inspired a dream of the time "when Rockport sports a complete harbor large enough for the entire navy of the country and a large fraction of the shipping besides." In 1904 boosters developed a scheme to provide for the oceangoing vessels then berthing at East Boston: "Think of the opportunity that is ours. Push until Rockport is the terminal of ocean liners, the rendezvous of the U.S. Navy, the great harbor of exits and entry from the European ports of commerce."

No potential influence wielder was safe from an arm-twisting for the breakwater project. By 1904, $1,305,000 had been appropriated.

Our Town, Rockport

Congressman Lawrence was confidently quoted as hoping for $500,000 in the next appropriation, though he would have preferred $5 million in a lump sum to finish the job. Just after the shattering gale of January 26, 1905, which damaged Rockport far worse than did the Portland gale of 1898, Congress handed out another $200,000. That July a New York-based firm purloined the breakwater contract from the Rockporters. After a troublesome hiatus during which the pork barrel had provided for other dippers, the Rockport and Pigeon Cove granite companies did get another turn and resumed work in May 1911.

The quarry workers, though usually weak in English, had grown strong in a knowledge of what they and their unions felt were right and rights. The details of their sporadic conflicts would require too much space in a history such as this. A strike was averted in the late winter of 1900 by the granting of a half cent an hour increase in wages. Business boomed at the quarries and at the Cape Ann Tool Company that summer. In 1905 another showdown was bypassed, but 1906 brought trouble. The breakdown occurred on March 22, and a final settlement was not reached until June 15. The next walkout lasted seven weeks in March and April 1908, following which an uneasy truce held until March 1, 1911. By then some seven hundred men were involved. After twenty days a state board of arbitration hammered out an agreement. On Monday, March 27, all hands were back on the job. Compressed air for the drills was being paid for by the companies.

To Our-Town the password for the future was "The Fleet." Eager promoters spread rumors of warships to visit Rockport soon at every appearance of a naval ship, however small. In 1906, and for years to come, though, the *Yankton*'s forecast proved that summer in Rockport would not be the same. Ships arrived and went and with them officers, crews, bands, payrolls, and prospective husbands. Some officers even found quarters for their wives and families in Rockport. The admiral set up his lady in Pigeon Cove's Ocean View House. There was a glorious moment when the town thought it would entertain Admiral Dewey himself and Secretary of the Navy Bonaparte. It cheerfully settled for a lesser hero, Rear Adm. Robley D. Evans who, on being queried, replied promptly that he "admires the harbor as one of the best in the country." Menus from the monstrous dinner at Turk's Head Inn at which he was guest of honor are still cherished family souvenirs.

Town on Sandy Bay

Certificate for five shares of Rockport Granite Company stock issued in November, 1908. (Heslin)

At the word of his flotilla's approach church bells pealed and quarry whistles shrieked. The entire shoreline was quickly covered with excited spectators. Our-Town had already tricked itself out with bunting and flags and the Rockport Granite Company's enormous scow had been towed to T Wharf to provide landing facilities. At the critical moment a 12-pounder boomed out nineteen salutes. In charge was Civil War veteran John E. Stickney. The new flagship *Maine* courteously responded with thirteen. In all, thirty-five vessels of various tonnages made up the force. The battlewagons were open to visitors daily from 1:00 P.M. to 5:00 P.M. On the night of July 18, eight to ten thousand people lined the Rockport shoreline to marvel at the searchlight display. There were receptions, dances and baseball games. Rockport's team defeated the *Maine's* 4 to 3 and the *Iowa's* 5 to zero. Nevertheless, according to the *Review*, the gobs declared Rockport was "the best place they've been."

Anxious townspeople sighed with relief at the "fine appearance and gentlemanliness of the men" and later did some statistical reckoning: 263 lodgings had been registered; 1,500 men had used the YMCA setup in the town hall; 2,500 sheets of writing paper had been con-

Our Town, Rockport

The Str. "Wilster" aground on Long Beach in March, 1902. Her cargo of sugar was salvaged and the vessel hauled off successfully. (SBHS)

sumed; 250 articles stored and checked. Some 60 sailors had relished "hospitality at Sunday dinners." On August 12 about 20,000 people had visited Rockport, with the "largest number of motor vehicles ever seen in town." On learning that an athletic field would be purchased for the sailors from contributions by the men, the *Gloucester Times* on August 20 announced with certainty that the fact meant "Rockport will be the regular summer rendezvous for the Atlantic Fleet." After the flotilla's departure, the editor of the *Review* warmly wrote: "Now that the fleet is gone we can find how large a place they filled in the social life and activities of the town. . . . We hope they'll be back next year." They were, and for several summers afterward.

Debits and Credits

For many older residents the death of Queen Victoria and the assassination of President McKinley symbolized the passing of an age. Both events were locally observed by appropriate tributes. Before the decade slipped into history, there would be many other losses. Some would have compensations, especially the commercial ones. Throughout the period the *Rockport Review* would chide, scold, goad: "Boost

The Linwood, a popular hotel on Andrews' Point at the corner of Point de Chene and Linwood Avenues built by James Hurd in 1877. It was expanded a year or two later. (Hoyt)

Rockport!!" Attacking the "folly of 'paying as we go,' " it clamored for lower taxes to induce new industry, new people, new construction to come to town. "Pigeon Cove people are clannish—in the good sense of the word. They care about their neighbors. Pigeon Cove is for Pigeon Cove." How the *Review* howled in 1901 over advertisements reading, "SALEM is the rallying point for Christmas shoppers."

In a number of areas, Rockport did develop in the new decade. Noteworthy advances took place in summer expansion. The Pigeon Cove House incorporated a five-story addition, which, however, burned in January 1903. The cove's Linwood Hotel, which had been dispensing hospitality since 1877, went up in flames in April 1906. These losses were to be offset in due course by a luxurious modern hotel, the Hotel Edward, which opened in 1913. At the New Oakdene, the proprietor boosted her "ideal summer home, especially restful for brain workers." In the South Village the Turk's Head Inn kept turning away trade until its new proprietor, C. B. Martin, undertook to build a thirty-room wing in 1905. At Gap Head the Straitsmouth Inn was built in 1907. Carpenters were all busy; "Rockport has room enough and charm enough for thousands more visitors." At his Headlands, Jason

Giles had provided for "a mammoth hotel." It was never built, but lots for cottages which "will bring much taxable property to the town" were readily sold. Week by week there were progress bulletins in the press. "Rockport has passed the day of doubting that the summer people are a benefit."

Two new express companies began providing daily runs to Boston and intervening towns. Everett Lane opened a cold-storage plant next to the Baptist church and provided jobs for a dozen men. In 1906 the Rockport Cold Storage Company began manufacturing ice—at times five tons of it per day—from artesian well water. The Hodgkins family set up their grain enterprise by the depot in 1907. The complete destruction by fire of the old gristmill beside the mill pond in late August 1907 closed that chapter and carried with it the adjacent, defunct ironworks. The ironworks at Pigeon Cove, on the contrary, had become one of the largest plants in Essex County. In 1906 the corporation added forty feet to its already tall chimney. The Cape Ann Tool Company was unquestionably Pigeon Cove's most striking landmark. Soon J. Judson Dean would buy out the Hawkridge brothers and become president-treasurer of the flourishing firm.

Fishing clung to its hold, but as of January 1906 Rockport's total investment was only $105,318. There were 35 Rockport "vessels," 19 boats other than dories, and 143 dories. The trend was to lobsters, initiated when Chase's "fish trap" was tested off Turk's Head Inn in the summer of 1901. "It is a sure catcher and many poor people can get a good living with one to six of these cages." By late October a dam was being built at Hale Knowlton's dock to create a huge pool for live lobsters. Watching the shift from fishes to crustaceans, a commentator wrote: "This is a new industry for Rockport, and we hope it will prove successful." So did the gourmets.

Finally, the town went into the new century still manufacturing isinglass, its own contribution to American life. By January 1905 a fifty-eight-hour workweek was fixed, and factories closed at 4:00 P.M. on Saturdays. For Christmas, 1906, the union secured for its workers a $10 paycheck for that fifty-eight-hour workweek.

It was in the homes, schools, churches, lodges, clubs, and engine houses that the tranquillity of "Grover's Corners" persisted longest. Although the *Rockport Review* changed crews and formats a number of times during the new century, Charles M. Stevens was never far from the editor's pen. In the daily columns of the paper and in its countless advertisements are to be found myriads of items still redolent of the

Rare photograph of two fishermen tarring nets on Bearskin Neck in preparation for another trip to sea. (C. Swan)

"Our-Town" long gone. There were the eternally recurring fairs, entertainments (including some profitable ones for the new hospital), firemen's musters, lodge meetings, concerts of all types from Professor Marshall's organ recitals and the colored Mendelssohn Quartet's renditions to the Harvard Male Quartet (which brought laughter and tears), the mandolin clubs, and the hurdy-gurdy man with his dizzy music. ("Rockport is not so 'high tone' as to prohibit him from dispensing his music on her streets"). And, oh, such dances as the firemen's ball with its waltzes, quadrilles, a polka, schottische, Virginia reel, the Lancers, and novel two-steps. The popular Swedish masquerades at town hall always lured "a good number of Americans" plus eager observers who paid 15 cents to watch from balcony seats. There were endless rounds of whist parties and even townwide tournaments, and the shattering disappointment when ice cream for the Village Improvement Society's fair got misdirected to Rockport, Maine.

Captain Strople ran boat excursions to the Isles of Shoals for $1.50; including dinner; other groups made outings to Thacher's Island to climb the lighthouses and inspect the steam-powered foghorns. St. Mary's took its choirboys for a "merry day" at Salem Willows; the

Young Men's Lyceum ventured to Boston by the steamboat from Gloucester; others found diversion at questionable Revere Beach or safer Norumbega Park. After some years of mutual standoffishness, the Sunday schools of the North and South villages managed a union picnic at Centennial Grove. Circus day in Gloucester meant closed schools in Rockport.

The chronicles held darker pages, too, such as the attempted strangulations and butcher knife attacks by the deranged James Woods, the suicide-hanging at Babson's Field by the insane Edwin Frost, and the numerous accidental drownings in quarry pits. Death also took its conventional toll, including James P. Davis, "one of our oldest and best known citizens"; baker Knowlton, beloved for his hot, dark, secret recipe loaves for breakfast; and Sanco Dennis, at eighteen Rockport's oldest dog. Incendiary activities brought untimely ends to a number of buildings during those years, notably at Long Beach and Pigeon Cove.

To some folks few pages were darker than the successes of the Law and Order League in closing all stores on Sundays, even foodshops. In 1905 only the drugstore and waiting station could get licenses, but the league was vexed that Sunday yacht racing was increasingly common. From crippled bastions temperance militants struggled manfully, reinforced by Christian Endeavorers, the Methodist Sunday school's White Shield League (Lester Stevens, president; Ernest Orne, secretary; Ralph Silva, treasurer), and in 1905 the Pigeon Cove Juvenile Temperance Club. Joint temperance meetings between North and South Village churches included exhortations by Pastor Isaakson in Swedish. The public library was given the "Hatchet Flag" carried into battle by Hannah Jumper fifty years before. Today it adorns a wall in the Sandy Bay Historical Museum. As for Hannah's house, it was identified by "a sign bearing the name Hatchet Cottage, surmounted by a pretty hatchet."

At the end of 1901 Thaddeus Tatterstall knowingly assured readers of the *Review* that there was "more wickedness to the square inch in Rockport than in small cities, Gloucester excepted." In March 1905 Pigeon Cove's Pastor Easton charged that there were twelve places "where liquor may be obtained" between Babson Farms and his chapel. The "Rambler" jibed in August 1905: "In any town or city you will find it so, but I do not believe there is any town in the country where so many unmarried men live with unmarried women as in Rockport. Of course, the women are housekeepers and this covers the law of the country."

Town on Sandy Bay

The baseball craze led to a movement for regularization and plans for a Rockport town team. In March 1905 Herman Poole became "manager elect," Fred S. Moore the secretary-treasurer, and the White Sox were launched on a wave of enthusiasm. Football was still in doubtful repute, however, and it would be some years before the roughhouse aspects of contests were brought under control. Press pressure helped:

The foot ball game between the Bay View and Pigeon Cove elevens has been the topic of discussion for some time. It is to be regretted that the game which attracted more attention from the townpeople than any other for some years should have been attended by such rough playing. Many had never seen a game before roughness was the main part of it and thus an almost irreparable injury to real sport was done. We hope that next year our boys will arrange a game with a team of Gentlemen *and that the noblest game ever invented will clear itself of the stigma which the last contest placed upon it.*

Thus, the adolescent years of the twentieth century were times of confusion and calm, of rejection and acceptance, of harvest and seed-time for Rockporters.

ADDITIONAL READING

By all odds, the best insights into Rockport life in the new decade are to be had from the files of the *Rockport Review* and the town reports. Two commercial brochures are also revealing: *Handbook of Rockport Massachusetts, 1902,* published by the *Review,* and a richly illustrated promotional folder from Jason Giles entitled *Ye Headlands of Cape Anne* (c. 1902).

19

FADE-OUT—1912

LIKE THE LEGENDARY old soldiers who never die, Our-Town-Rockport simply faded away. The process was gradual and, to some extent, is happily still incomplete. To no single year can the tag "the end" be affixed, yet 1912—at least in retrospect—marked many an ending as well as a host of new beginnings. The new year was ushered in by a storm, which brought out town plows for the first time that winter, thus enabling the faithful to get to church. And on January 13 Rockporters wakened to their coldest morning in forty years, with thermometers dipping to from 5 to 15 degrees below zero. Out on the level, beyond their windows, lay a three-inch snowfall to boot. At the Leander M. Haskins Hospital there were five holdover patients plus six new ones, four Americans, one Swede, and one Italian.

At eighty-three, James W. Bradley died, the last survivor of the town's recruiters for the Civil War. In May, Capt. John E. Stickney closed his popular tobacco shop cum meeting place called the "Senate," next to the Rockport National Bank, struck out for home and dropped dead. He fought to the end to secure the Harbor of Refuge and breakwater. As the town's oldest resident when death came, he proudly possessed the gold-headed cane which the *Boston Post* had donated to Rockport on August 7, 1909. John R. Thurston had carried it for less than a year before death passed it to Fears. In 1912, ninety-year-old Robert Tarr of South Street received the local mace of longevity.

This rough shelter at Loblolly Cove was a very popular seafood restaurant operated by Emerson and Francis Haskell early in the twentieth century. President Taft, while summering at Beverly Farms, drove down for lunch one day in August, 1909. (Hoyt)

If Rockporters saw many curtains being rung down in 1912, they were soon to be surrounded by startling overtures to dramas opening up. Women were already taking over the limelight. On January 1 the papers quoted the superintendent of the Boston Hospital: "We have noticed that girl babies are getting taller and that they are appearing in this world lately with more real vitality than formerly. The boy babies continue on the average." Mrs. Craig Biddle of Philadelphia's ultra-smart set displayed outrageous vitality when she "openly smoked a cigarette" while dining with her husband and a woman guest in the public dining room of the Quaker City's most exclusive hotel. "What next?"

There would be quite a string of nexts to shake up the more stodgy. In 1912 U.S. courts would decree that wives could legally extract money from their husbands' pockets. Mount Holyoke would prove the falsity that college "unfits or indisposes" girls for marriage. Over 45 percent of Holyoke's graduates had married and borne children, and not one wife had been divorced. Yet a nostalgic piece on "The Home Loving Young Woman" sighed: "There are many who believe this type passed and gone." On July 27 the *Gloucester Times,* speculating on "Why

Fade-Out–1912

Servants are Scarce," decided that "many women refuse to do house-work at any price." Two weeks previously, Rockport readers were informed that coed colleges were disappearing. Girls developed sooner and thus were a source of embarrassment to their male counterparts at coeducational colleges. A lively local discussion developed on the wisdom of senior class trips to Washington. Pitfalls lay everywhere, opined an editor, so take no girl on such a journey without her mother. Another issue was allowing women to receive mail through general delivery rather than at home, a growing practice "detrimental to good morals, especially among young girls." The females lost their mail skirmish, but 1912 departed leaving a press feature on "The Mannish Model," asserting that "young girls are finding the mannish shirts made of striped or plain washable silk or crepe de chine very much to their liking. Most of the models are absolutely masculine in the severity of their lines." What next, indeed?

Women's suffrage, of course. It was like the moving trains in the motion pictures, hurtling down on a victim bound helplessly to the tracks. By 1912 Rockporters had long been thrilled by the movies, both in town and at Gloucester's Union Hill Theatre offering films "absolute flicker-less and non-tiring to the eyes." Orchestra seats were 10 cents, balcony ones a nickel. By early August 1912, Rockport's town hall was crowded with "our best people and a liberal sprinkling of summer people." Thus, Rockporters were thoroughly familiar with *Perils of Pauline* shows.

Defeated by the Massachusetts legislature, some two hundred members of Rockport's summer colony rallied in August at the Straitsmouth Inn to discuss women's suffrage. A working girl had to vote, else "she has no way to determine whether her water supply, milk supply, etc., was good, unless she has some way of expressing herself politically." Rockport women were perhaps too absorbed with a naval visit to go out to Straitsmouth that day. But on August 29 a group of Gloucester hearties did found a suffrage society. Soon the waves would crash at Sandy Bay and Pigeon Cove.

The drive for the vote was heightened by the election campaign. So far as Rockport itself was concerned, the Democratic party and Wilson scarcely existed. In town the contest was restricted to the Republicans. By spring the division between President Taft and former President Roosevelt had become irreconcilable. From the outset, the Roosevelt forces proved more energetic. To be sure, the newspapers ran almost chummy accounts of President and Mrs. Taft's summer sojourns at

A schooner on the ways at Waddell's Boat Yard on Bearskin Neck about 1918. Motif No. 1 is at the end of the Bradley Wharf just to the right of the vessel. (Niemi)

Beverly Farms and their motor trips throughout the area. At Loblolly Cove, Capt. Emerson B. Haskell and his son Frank, proprietors of Haskell's Camp, "famed for its fish dinners," proudly satisfied the massive maw of the president. But summer was not for politicking—in Rockport.

On November 1, however, both political groups were to stage mass meetings in Rockport with a parade and band concert at Post Office Corner. The *Gloucester Times* avowed correctly that Rockport had had the liveliest campaign in years but wrongly that Friday would be "a vigorous, old time rally" with the usual accompaniments of music, fireworks, and excitement. Instead, the evening was a literal washout. Some two hundred did brave the rains to support their respective candidates. But both sets of campaigners were overwhelmed by the Wilsonian deluge on election day. In all, Rockporters cast 786 ballots—all male. Wilson squeezed out a meagre 178 votes, Taft got 222, and the roaring Roosevelt 312. At least locally the Bull Moosers could be "naturally jubilant." They also returned Republican Congressman Gardner to Washington. His competitor had accused him of not supporting appropriations for the Harbor of Refuge project.

Fade-Out–1912

View south on Bearskin Neck from the far end of the principal roadway about 1900, when the area was devoted entirely to fishing operations. (Hoyt)

Gardner's direct reply was that he always had pushed for funds but that currently no additional funding was called for.

Behind his honest answer loomed yet another end-of-an-era omen. The loss of the contracts by local firms was handwriting on the wall. Having the Breakwater Construction Company import stone from Hurricane Island, Maine, was truly a coals-to-Newcastle reminder, wrote the *Times*. Some shipments were slow, "the project has no appropriation in the Rivers and Harbor Bill just passed." On December 7 the newspaper grimly intoned: "It is a great disappointment that there is no recommendation for an appropriation for Sandy Bay." With funds still unexpended, for the second year Rockport's breakwater had been bypassed. For some other labors, it was heartening that the Cape Ann Tool Company was working overtime to fill its orders. Down at the wharf David Waddell pursued his modest shipbuilding operations with contracts for two new gill netters, for a large "bathing raft" with springboard for the old Garden Beach, and for two sixty-foot lobster smacks in November.

Town on Sandy Bay

By 1912 the brave new world was the automobile. New car registrations published in March included a Pierce touring car and a Chalmers runabout for the Rockport Granite Company, a red runabout of 28 horsepower for Dr. Tupper of Main Street, and a dark blue Oakland with "gray gear" for Fred S. Moore of 6 Union Court. Rockporters were being assured that "now one finds the motor car is an all the year around vehicle." The *Times* divulged nineteen hints for automobile care and an entire article on "Gasoline and How to Handle It." Sargent Carter was lauded for his new shop with large doors "especially for repairing automobiles." Only three days afterward, however, appeared this: "Is the Horse Vanishing?" Reassurance was given. Not yet. "There are still many uses for horses . . . there will always be people who prefer to feel the horse's tug at the other end of the reins."

Once the automobile invasion began, there were problems for all seasons. Only by a hairbreadth were several coasting accidents averted in January. "Now there are so many automobiles running about the town with a brilliant light on either side, the road ahead of them is dazzled by the twin lights." Animals were no longer safe. Dr. J. J. Egan's new 1911 Cadillac roadster (four cylinders) was stolen by "Joy Riders" and smashed in Lanesville. "Rum and gasoline are not a good mixture," decreed Judge York as he sentenced a man for running over a twelve-year-old girl. By the end of June 1912, so many automobiles and carriages were parking without drivers as to interfere with traffic and be "a menace" to the safety of the public. In an attempt to reduce the safety hazard at the foot of Broadway, a one hundred-foot-long white dividing line had been chalked on the oiled street. Big businessman George Harvey drove down on the wrong side in August, was halted by the constable, and ordered to make the approach correctly. That he belligerently refused to do.

Yet automobiles had come to Rockport to stay. C. B. Martin had built a forty-five car garage at his Turk's Head Inn, "a very popular place for automobile tourists." The new Hotel Edward promised private dining rooms "for automobile parties," a chauffeur hall, and a fireproof garage for thirty cars. Stores were already advertising touring capes and bonnets of rubberized fabrics, "rain proof, dust proof

Fade-Out–1912

Bathers at Old Garden Beach in 1919, with the impressive houses of the Harvey development beyond. (Hoyt)

for the motor car." The newly elevated William Cardinal O'Connell traveled to St. Joachim's in his new automobile to confirm nineteen boys and twenty-five girls. It was the first time any cardinal had visited Rockport. On August 1, 1912, the *Times* ran an informative account about "motor driven fire wagons."

It was also a time of far-reaching change for labor and management in many fields. In April 1912 the local carpenters' union asked for a forty-hour work week with Saturday afternoons free. For this they sought an hourly wage of $0.50, or $22.00 per week, not the current $21.60 for forty-eight hours. Memorial Day brought up the question of scheduling of Monday holidays. Managers stoutly objected that their workers would be useless on Tuesdays under such a scheme. Better, conjectured the press, would be to have Saturdays off and get over holiday effects on Sunday. By June housewives were paying $6 for a market basket of products which had cost $5 in June 1911. Halfway between those market-basket trips, Rockport housewives could have bought from Frank W. Tarr lamb forequarters at 10 cents a pound, roast beef at 12.5 cents, and pork roasts at 13 cents. Fatima brand cigarettes sold for 15 cents for a pack of twenty. On October 3

Town on Sandy Bay

local coal prices were raised 50 cents a ton: $8 for furnace size and $8.25 for nut and stove coal sizes. The trolley car fare from Boston to Gloucester was $1; the fare around Cape Ann, a trip of one hour and forty minutes, was 20 cents.

By 1912 the electric cars were attacked for being cold. In November Rockport women inveighed against "rattlebang cars," charging that there was "one general shakeup from the time they got on till they leave the car." In early December 1912 the Boston and Maine reported with pride that it had ordered one hundred new locomotives, yet on December 31 crushed its student passengers by the decree that with the New Year special student rate tickets would be a thing of the past.

The long and bloody strike at the mills in Lawrence, which had opened the year and elicited donations from the Gloucester Socialist Club, encouraged many Rockporters to move leftward in their economic thinking. A series of five socialist lectures was conducted at strategic places on the Cape. On August 22 some 150 persons "from every nationality in town" attended a socialist rally in Dock Square. "The Socialists from Squam Hill were present and made up a good part of the crowd." (The same period, however, had 80 children enrolled in the Sunday school of the Finnish church on Forest Street.) To the open-air rally, the Finnish community brought out its brassy Aalto Band. While one Samuel Levenberg stood on an express wagon haranguing for an hour and a half, an adherent patiently held aloft a three-burner kerosene torch. The *Times* did point out that there were many Rockporters present "who do not believe in the Socialist doctrine." But the old economics were changing.

So, too, were emergency health services. As Clara Barton of Red Cross fame went to her reward, Maj. Walter Hale secured from Boston a fine carriage ambulance for the Leander M. Haskins Hospital. Refurbished with rubber tires; repainted with a gold cross and gold letters saying "Rockport Ambulance"; reequipped with a new harness, mattress, and a completely restocked emergency chest, it was stored at Sheahan's stable close to the steeds who would pull it on call. A reporter forecast that it would last for years. Another welcome security for the town was a new ground-floor vault for the National Bank with fifty safe-deposit boxes for those for whom the old sock or mattress was no longer safe enough. Voting would be clarified by an ingenious voting machine invented by Rockport's Gustaf Johnson. The papers proudly and in detail described the "clever and accurate workings" of the device.

Fade-Out–1912

The old system for the telephone was revised in 1912 by the installation of a new central office in the Grimes building (second floor), having been squeezed out of the waiting station (today's Curtis News Store). On July 29 the larger quarters were opened, with Mrs. Harvey Jodrey as chief operator. She and two assistants by then had 260 regular subscribers and 300 during the summer. (For the new Hotel Edward there were to be 50 more, one for every sleeping room, advertised the builders.) Up the way on School Street was the new two-story warehouse, fifty by fifty feet, built with metallic siding for the L. E. Smith Company. Old ways were changing.

Not all the harbingers of things to come were blessings. On March 6 the townspeople voted $1,000 to oil, not water, their dusty roads. Having observed the work, the *Times* decided that the new equipment, which had been affixed to the rear of the watering carts, was better and more economical. All main thoroughfares had been brushed and covered with oil—"a bit of a nuisance but a blessing." To farmer Thomas Latoff on the northwest side of Main Street, however, it proved a hardship. The state had raised the highway several feet; once the road had been oiled, rain flushed the scum over his farm, ruining his crops. His suit for damages was one of Rockport's earlier exposures to the price of progress.

Other symbols of the fading age of innocence were to be read about. There was the alarming decrease in lobsters, with resulting cries for regulation on catches. There was the bill to regulate clamming. There was the campaign to shift the controls on catching migratory fish from state to national hands. Pioneer ecologists were charging that "we even defile the air and make it unfit for human beings to breathe." On February 3, 1912, the *Times* asked its readers: "What are you going to do about the ten billion cigarettes?" One writer advised that those people who objected to having public school children going into the statuary room at the Museum of Fine Arts had better redirect their complaints to the menace of advertising billboards. Canned movies with rampant shootings through the Wild West were spawning gangs of toughs in American schools, charged other parents.

Inventions

But there were gains, too. On April 17 Cape Anners read that Marconi had arrived in the United States, bringing with him a new type of wireless equipment: "The day of terror on account of fogs is

Town on Sandy Bay

about over on the sea." On June 5 Rockporters heard that sixteen-year-old Richard Swanson of Hale Street was erecting a small wireless at his home and his expense. He had been studying electricity for several years and had already made several experiments. Other boys were also putting their time to profitable use. Some had banded together to become Boy Scouts. In the Memorial Day procession one contingent paraded. At Pigeon Cove in September a troop of thirty-six Boy Scouts was organized at Pythian Hall, with Lt. Lindley Dean in charge. They "planned to have cordial relations between the Boy Scouts of Rockport and the scouts of Pigeon Cove."

For most of the town's young people, especially the boys, the future meant the airplane (then commonly spelled aeroplane). A list of new library books in October 1912 included the *Aeroplane at Silver Fox Farm* and the *Boys's Book of Model Aeroplanes.* To be sure, Amundsen's triumph in reaching the South Pole excited readers and there was a copy of the new *Boy Scouts in the Maine Woods,* but most of the boys preferred aviation to woodcraft or at least grabbed *Motor Car Operations.* Even the girls had *Patty's Motor Car.* Young and old alike turned out in record numbers on August 14 to observe Gloucester Day, 1912, and see a "hydroaeroplane" fly in from Marblehead in twelve minutes. For thousands of curious people, ran the account, "this great wonder of the air" made two thrilling exhibition flights over the harbor and Eastern Point. Then, too, there was a huge balloon ascension; two thousand feet was "the dizzy height" it reached. From there, using three parachutes in succession, a one-armed "professor" chilled and thrilled an adoring audience. Rockport's few combat veterans were roused by a summer press photo story of an invention being tested by the army at College Park, Maryland. It was captioned "An Aeroplane Gun that may Revolutionize Warfare."

By 1912 local life was faced by a different threat—the great steam trawlers which, by their ruthless methods of dragging, menaced all fish and schooner fishermen. Soon the entire American and Canadian fleets were campaigning to purge the coast of such predators. In mid-November an article appeared which created only passing concern, yet seen in retrospect, it forecast an end to our-townism, not only for Rockport and Cape Ann, but also for international fisheries. It counted that Japan already had 125 steam trawlers and in two to three years would have several hundred. Another forecast from the Orient had been made the first week of 1912, as Sun Yat-sen took office as president of China. "It would be well," cautioned a writer in the

Gloucester Times, "for the United States to understand that when the Chinese people thoroughly awake, this country is likely to be profoundly affected." Eleven months later, Pigeon Cove's Pastor Owen was also concerned: "Do you realize that the Oriental religions are in our country? The mysteries of these religions are peculiarly attractive to women. Their teachings lead to insanity and death."

It was in sports that Rockport really prolonged its our-town character. Thanks to the genuine appeal of athletics and to the rousing responses of newspaper correspondents, sporting events of all kinds received unflagging support. When the winds blew victoriously, their columns fairly glowed. Adversity could often be overlooked. Those were the years when Harold Grover, Rockport's nineteen-year-old pitcher, had been signed up by the Pittsburgh Pirates, and hope was expressed that he would be to them what Gloucester's John "Stuffy" McInnis meant to the Phillies. It was the time when Trafton Gott left town for the Lawrence baseball team, and manager Arthur Leman began beating the bushes for recruits to fill the vacancies in the Rockport White Sox. "They will be missed."

Other diversions were also changing the town by 1912. "Power boat racing enthusiasts are to be paid more attention this year," advised one reporter. When Maurice Olson became high roller against the Brunswicks, the *Times* admitted that "that Rockport team can bowl." Then there were the girls. Basketball had become an accepted sport for them, thanks to a teacher of French, Miss Neville, who also doubled as coach-referee. On April 9, having played all season for themselves, the two Rockport High School teams (junior and senior girls) admitted the public to watch them at Murray Hall. All the seats and the stage as well were quickly filled. Lest anyone have concern for proprieties, the paper observed the next day that "all the girls were neatly and appropriately attired for such work."

In the summer of 1912 a schoolgirl won a small prize for a perceptive essay on the "Passing of Old Gloucester." The *Times* found it worthy of publication on July 20. That same week artist Cecilia Beaux bluntly warned against the fading of our-townism and forecast an exodus of artists from Cape Ann

if a few ambitious and unthinking real estate men persist in destroying the natural beauty of this famous shore. By erecting large and unsightly sign boards in conspicuous places, allowing people who buy land from them to put up small and crude looking cottages and dumping dirt at many points along the shore,

Battleships of the North Atlantic Squadron at anchor in Sandy Bay during one of the fleet's periodic visits between 1906 and the outbreak of World War I. (Hoyt)

they are ruthlessly defacing that which has been admired by artists from all sections of the country.

Not yet ready to leave, however, was Harrison Cady. In fact, he came late in 1912, at least it wasn't until September 6 that the papers noted that "the 'Stage Master of Bugdom' was in our midst."

In May 1912 the Congregational church installed a new five-ton organ, brought in by truck from Salem. Funding had come on a matching basis from Andrew Carnegie and local donors. The dedicatory recital was given by Professor John P. Marshall and a harpist and violinist from the Boston Symphony. A soprano rendered Gounod's "Ave Maria." Another feature was "the famous 'Handel's Largo' . . . one of the most popular pieces at the Pop Concerts." Only a few weeks later, that distinguished organist dramatically demonstrated the changing times. The press was excited to tell its readers—"Met Rockport Boy in Paris" ran the headline. "Prof. John P. Marshall, son of Selectman John W. Marshall, who is now in Europe, was greatly surprised while in a store in Paris to meet another Rockport boy,

Fade-Out–1912

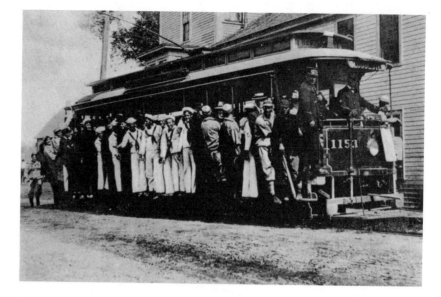

An open trolley loaded with sailors from the fleet moves up Broadway about 1908. They were headed for a baseball game at Webster's Field on Nugent's Stretch. (Hoyt)

William H. Colby." The description of their encounter predictably concluded: "The world after all is small."

Ships Once More

The great world in all its symbolic power had been coming to Sandy Bay Harbor summer after summer. Hence, there was joy all around when word came that a division of the North Atlantic Fleet would visit Rockport once again from August 10 to August 16. The initial response was blatantly materialistic: "Fully 3,500 men will be brought here by the crafts, and as pay day comes about that time, business will probably be lively, for Uncle Sam's sailors are free spenders." Once again the large room at the town hall was turned over to the Women's Auxiliary to be "fitted up with beds, reading and writing materials, etc., so that the boys will feel at home." On arrival men commenced rotational shore leave at once, some going to Boston, some to Gloucester, some staying in Rockport to see friends from previous visits.

On Monday thousands of people lined the shore to look at the largest fleet of naval craft ever seen at Rockport at any one time. In the

Visiting Day on a battleship anchored in Sandy Bay in 1906. Launches carried the visitors from T Wharf and back, and when seas were rough the transfer from launch to platform was difficult. (Hoyt)

evening every ship was illuminated by electricity, and searchlights were crisscrossing the sky. They alone were "worth going miles to witness." The trolleys were jammed, with sailors clinging to the running boards and dashers; some were even on the roof. Since so many remained overnight in Gloucester, extra cars were put on in the mornings to get the boys back on time. The bed count at Rockport's town hall for the four nights was seventy-seven, eighty-four, eighty-nine, and eighty-nine. Old-timers recall Town Clerk Byron Russell reading poetry aloud to the sleepy sailors.

Each night a band from one of the ships played in Rockport. The Congregationalists capitalized on the visit to hold their fair, at which musicians from the *Ohio* performed. It would be harder to find a better example of our-town life outside a Norman Rockwell portfolio.

Autos and vehicles of every description were lined along the streets. The popcorn man, the sherbert and ice cream vendor were on the School Street side in opposition to those serving these articles on the green. The sidewalks were crowded and the church lawn was like a bee hive with its throngs of people.

Fade-Out–1912

Tim Sheahan's Christmas party on Broadway, date unknown. The old Broadway Garage is at the right.

Deacon Frank Elwell was kept busy serving ice cream. There was fully as large a crowd around the punch-and-cake table. The hot dogs were in charge of George Cushman, who kept a corps of small boys busy selling them in the crowd. The candy table was "a credit to matron Mrs. Albert E. Tuck." (She had been a member of the church quartette for four years and possessed "a rich and powerful contralto voice which has been much enjoyed.") At 6:00 P.M. supper was served and every conceivable seat was taken. "One man was heard to say that it was a treat indeed to taste a piece of home-made pie. The sailor boys said it was the best supper they had eaten for years. Those who made the coffee certainly knew how to make it to the queen's taste." At the concert there was a cornet solo by the bandmaster. The grounds were brilliantly illuminated by "strings of colored electric lights which were festooned from tree to tree."

Thursday the Gaumont Company had a representative from New York securing pictures of the battleships in Rockport "for moving picture shows." It was also the night of the naval ball at the Ocean View House in Pigeon Cove. The *Times* lavished half a column on the gowns of the ladies in the "beautiful-creation-of-spangled-net-over-lavender-silk" style. Five lines were given to "Among the Gentlemen."

Town on Sandy Bay

That night fifteen sailors rode back from Gloucester on the roof of a trolley car in a downpour. On Friday some eight hundred guests streamed out to the *Ohio* for a reception. Every available launch was pressed into service. There were light drinks and punch, "a delicate and dainty luncheon of sandwiches, salads and ices," the sailors acting as waiters to the ladies. Each lady also received an armband reading "U.S.S. Ohio." Two other bands provided music "in a profusion of floral decorations" until ten-thirty, when the final waltz ended.

Admirals Wilson and Fletcher expressed their regret at being unable to accept the selectmen's invitation to take an automobile ride around Cape Ann. They were busily occupied "studying out the war game" of taking New York Harbor in the dark at night. On Saturday, commencing at 8:00 A.M., the four battleships sailed away and "made a pretty picture rolling up dense volumes of thick black smoke." That spring a Rockport High School group had debated if money for battleships might not be spent to better advantage. The verdict seemed to be that it was "unwise to lessen the size of our Navy so long as other countries, Germany for instance, continued to build 'Dreadnaughts.' "

The year 1912 drew to its end leaving a vision of an our-town way of life still cherished by those who remember it and envied by many who do not. Thanksgiving was a day of thick snow from forenoon to early evening—a truly over-the-river-and-through-the woods scene. Christmas brought a repeat, as well as a coal barge that made port on the twenty-fourth and relieved the "famine." The local newspaper stringer clearly felt Dickensian—the author's centennial having been observed at the high school with a talk, exhibition, and readings. "It was the old time snowy Christmas, bright and clear," he began. From early morning, sleigh bells could be heard jingling merrily. At nine-thirty the distant bugle call rang out.

Riding in the middle seat of a tallyho coach came Santa Claus, drawn by four white horses, each with a red saddle blanket, with Osborne Eaton driving. Charles E. Fears blew the bugle as the tallyho raced over the snow and through town. Along South Street and down Mt. Pleasant, up Main, across Beach, up King, back along Granite, down Forest, and across the Front Beach they sped, finally reaching Main and School streets and the benevolent Tim Sheahan's store. There seven helpers guided eight hundred children around the Christmas tree to Santa Claus. Every child in Rockport from Folly Cove to Long Beach received a remembrance. Elmer Burgess took pictures. When that excitement was over, Santa Claus on horseback

Fade-Out–1912

visited the shut-ins at home. Remembering the old and needy, he also took gifts to the almshouse, to which Major and Mrs. Hale had already sent two plump Christmas geese. That night countless Rockporters went to bed with Tiny Tim's "God Bless Us, Every One" in their hearts.

New Year's Eve would bring to Cape Ann glimpses of the future. At Gloucester's Olympia Theatre a novel program, combining films and colored slides, would open. Its topic: *On Russia.*

ADDITIONAL READING

There is little pertinent material to recommend for the immediate pre-war period other than the town reports, the *Gloucester Times* and the scarce *Rockport Review.* The *North Shore Breeze,* printed in Manchester, carried some social and historical tidbits. It also published for years a rather pretentious *Who's Who Along the North Shore.* There was also a *Cape Ann Summer Directory* from 1910 to 1913 issued at Salem by Albert W. Dennis. McKenzie's *Hand Book of Gloucester,* an annual through 1913 has a good deal of revealing advertising as well as trolley schedules. One very readable novel which includes this era is Naomi Lane Babson's generational story of her family's experiences at Pigeon Cove: *The Yankee Bodleys* (New York, 1936).

Map of Rockport, Geo. H. Walker & Co., 1884.

Fade-Out–1912

Part 4

Rockport in a
Time of Unrest

OCKPORT HAS SURVIVED
*through adaptation. From the day
the first white visitors came ashore in
1605, sniffed a sea change in the air, and so sailed away safely ahead of a
potential Indian ambush, it has been blessed with at least a few lookouts who,
sensing breakers and shoals, kept her pointed into deep water. Before all the tall
timber which attracted the first settlers was despoiled, alert pioneers turned to
harvesting the oceans. Although hardship was their garment, the parishioners of
Sandy Bay endured. Until World War I, in fact, few towns more consistently
practiced the adage they preached: "Eat up, wear out, make do." Native Yankee
parsimony was reinforced in the Victorian era by the cautious heedfulness of new
arrivals from a niggardly Old World.*

*As fishing and coastal trading began to lose out to the competitive advan-
tages of more efficient port facilities at Gloucester and Boston, Rockport made*

do with the granite ledges on which it lived and moved and had its being. Some were adapted to provide watering places for jangled city nerves. Others were quarried to supply blocks for buildings, monuments for the departed, pavement and curbing for streets. For a century they solidly supported the town. But technology overtook granite, and with it breakwaters and Harbors of Refuge. The internal-combustion engine changed the course of history for Rockport and its residents.

Though the town found itself hard-put to cope with the demands of here and now, it also found it had much for people whose interests lay more in the then and there. Painters, sculptors, teachers, and collectors discovered in the coves and byways of Rockport what they sought and what they could sell. So as quarries were abandoned, easels opened up. Toolsheds and fishing shacks were transformed as if by magic into studios and galleries.

For the last half century or so Rockport, like the nation as a whole, oscillated uneasily between conflict and quiet, four global wars interspersed with periods of chilly détente and fragile peace. Each crusade exacted sacrifices from the town through its dead, wounded, and disillusioned. In 1918 there was also the awesome influenza epidemic. Both world wars created shortages. With the Korean conflict came queries of "Why us?" From Vietnam rose anguished doubts and divided houses.

On the local scene Harding's normalcy and Coolidge's prosperity were followed by the Great Depression. Rockport was quite transformed by a Roosevelt it never voted for and the successive "Deals" which Washington spawned. Physically there came a new post office, fire station, police headquarters, town hall, water supply, and schools and more schools. Social services blossomed; philosophies were rethought. As never before, Rockporters came to realize that no man, woman, or even a child could ever again be an island.

The metamorphoses were accelerated by automobiles, buses, airplanes, boats, by better roads and superhighways, by improved harbors and new marinas. Summer boarders became summer cottagers. The flight to suburbia brought added transformations. Summer cottages were winterized; vacant lots were snapped up; new housing was constructed. A happy combination of accessibility to the attractions of metropolitan Boston and the relative tranquillity of Rockport made the community an ideal location for retirees, with all that is implied by that word.

Simultaneously, accessibility to traditional centers up the line and to the explosive developments along Route 128–factories, decentralizing business enterprises, and the staggering array of shopping center plazas–provided once unimagined job opportunities for Rockport's mobile breadwinners. Those same commercial attractions have drastically altered Rockport's Main Street.

310

On the other hand, that very mobility began luring droves of out-of-towners to Rockport's beaches, boutiques, and facilities. Day trippers flock by train, by car, and by busloads. Gone, for the most part, are the expansive hotels. In their stead are motels, overnight lodges, and myriads of rooms to rent. Restaurants, snack bars, and souvenir shops blossom and die annually. Perennially, though, the town stays dry—officially. To meet all those and countless ancillary needs—especially sewage disposal, water reserves, landfill areas, and conservation sanctuaries—Rockporters are increasingly confronted with difficult choices at their town meetings.

The bicentennial came in the middle of America's "Me Decade," some 370 years after the first stranger visited Cape Ann's shores. It provided a time for residents and visitors alike to halt and reflect a bit on the question, Whither Rockport? Much will depend on the answer.

20

WAR AND PEACE

I N THE WORLD beyond the Cut, trouble had been brewing. More would come, beginning with income taxes. The postal savings hurt local banks. The parcel post hurt private express companies. Minimum wage laws for women and children hurt businessmen. Winning the Lawrence textile strike encouraged unions in the quarries and factories of Cape Ann. The U.S. Merchant Marine was shrinking. Militarily and diplomatically, America was speaking less softly and carrying a bigger stick, especially in Cuba, in Nicaragua, in the Dominican Republic, in Haiti, in Panama and its Canal, and more especially in Mexico from 1913 on. Rockporters, oblivious in 1916 of a military commander known as "Black Jack" Pershing sent south to prevent Pancho Villa's raids, would be serving under him as their commanding general by 1917.

All those excursions and alarms in China, Manchuria, Korea, and Japan seemed as remote as the moon. To most Rockporters, China meant their laundryman, Harry Goon. At a time when their Swedish-American neighbors like Mrs. Charles Carlberg were taking a trip to Sweden and Irish-American ones like Edward Maguire were going back to the old sod, many residents were pleased that Mr. Goon, who had come to Oregon as a boy in 1882, was off to China to see his old mother, to whom he had been sending money all those years for her support. "Few of the Chinese become so popular and are regarded so kindly as the genial proprietor of the Main Street laundry." For continued good service he had provided his cousin Goon Wing and two brothers for the year or so he would be away.

Rockporters knew more about the troubles in Europe. After all, the town had large numbers of residents from there, and the Balkan Wars of 1912-13 did attract editorial concern: "Constantinople is now a sink hole of suffering and starvation. . . . This is a time when the people of America can give effective expression to the brotherhood of man"—through relief money. By and large, however, it was not before 1915 that anxiety over the war in Europe surfaced in Rockport.

Life in town proceeded without momentous ups and downs. The *Rockport Review* again altered its format and improved the quality of the paper and the photographs it reproduced with increasing regularity. It assumed that most of its readers depended on Gloucester or Boston papers for news beyond the North Shore. Local news became the principal reason for its weekly appearance. Every Thursday Rockporters could read who had been where, entertained whom, acquired what—all for $1 a year. There were "Rockport Locals," Pigeon Cove, Lanesville, Annisquam notes, editorial comments, theater and opera news from Boston and Salem, observations by the "Rambler," church and legal notices, plus a feature article or two. From early June well into September there were "arrivals at the hotels and boarding houses" and the "doings of the summer cottagers on Cape Ann."

Rockport grew more dependent on those peripheral residents. Well before the summer influx of 1913 came this safety proposal for "an absolute maximum speed limit, say 25 miles an hour . . . no sane operator would care to go much faster." In April some businessmen gathered at the *Review* office on School Street to form a board of trade. Much time was devoted to discussing the benefits of the summer industry, and the need for new businesses. Fears were expressed at rumors the Cape Ann Tool Company might move to an economically more congenial climate. Charles H. Roffey was named president of the board, William O. Blatchford secretary, and Frank W. Tarr treasurer. One proposal was to foster a baseball team "which would cause no one to blush." A "hitch" had brought an end to the peak standards of 1907-8, yet a baseball team offered many inducements—so they were told. The White Sox did resume their games at Webster's Field in 1913 and won the Cape Ann championship. The usual Memorial Day observances were held, and except at Gloucester "A Sane Fourth!" in

1913 "brought pleasing diversions into the lives of the townspeople and the birds of passage—the Summer Folk."

The event of the season, of course, was the June opening of a nest for those birds—the looming, luxurious Hotel Edward. It boasted a long-distance telephone, furnishings of white inlaid mahogany, and featured seven rooms on the top floor "exclusively for young ladies"—one more indication of the emerging liberation of women. From the verandas patrons could enjoy fine views of the naval vessels behind the Sandy Bay breakwater, attracting hundreds of visitors daily. At the South End arose another amenity largely for summer visitors, the Rockport Country Club. When proposed in the autumn of 1911, it was to have included a golf course, tennis courts, a baseball area, and a clubhouse. Costs and "facilities" would run an estimated total of $20,000. As with most ventures in Rockport, realities failed to keep up with press speculation. The summer of 1914, with its "Guns of August," proved to be a poor year for transients. Boosters pinned their hopes for 1915 on the golf links and the country club to attract more visitors. Thanksgiving brought word that the club's foundations were in. Finally, on July 3, 1915, the Rockport Country Club was formally opened, but by then the tempo of summertime life at Rockport had quickened noticeably in some quarters while it ground to a near halt in others.

On the livelier side, "new" was the adjective. The Rockport Granite Company had produced a new store; Pigeon Cove had its new spot for its post office (with Charles Andrews still in charge as he had been since 1901, when the office was opposite the forge shop), the Cape Ann Tool Company built its "mammoth new structure" of steel and concrete to make room for which the Pigeon Cove library had to be moved to a new site. The town had finally been permitted to construct a public float in Long Cove Harbor, and townspeople had won right of access to it over property of the pier company. Dredging the harbor and removing rocks, though a welcome idea, was estimated to cost $15,000. In August a $12,500 appropriation was received, however; and on September 4 dredging began to produce new depths. Waddell's Ship Yard could launch still larger lobster smacks than the *Reliance* of April 1914. William Hobbs, vice-president of the Boston and Maine, spoke at the Congregational church of railroads generally and the problems inherited by his new but progressive management. Also in 1914, Rockport was to benefit greatly by a new Speedwell "auto-combination" fire engine—an unwelcomed arrival so far as the livery stables were con-

The quarry engine "Nella" hauling a flatcar loaded with granite blocks from the Fitzgibbon quarry in Lanesville. The route crossed Granite Street to the pier in Pigeon Cove Harbor. (Poole)

cerned. Like the egocentric railroad managers resisting progress and the funds required, the liverymen had vigorously fought even attempts by the town to purchase fire horses of its own rather than to hire them when needed.

Quarry production had fallen and business was stagnating in some offices. The *Gloucester Times* in January 1914 ran reminiscences of four decades of brighter years. In April the Rockport Granite Company's Bay View polishing plant burned to the ground, though stone for Providence was loaded in Pigeon Cove by the *Eureka,* which had brought in thirteen hundred railroad ties and three cars for Fitzgibbon's quarry. After some months of rumor, a "consolidation" was effected in November between the Pigeon Hill Granite Company—inoperative for months—and the slowed-down Rockport Granite Company. Bonds for the sale running to $100,000 were guaranteed by the latter works, which had won a bid for the new South Boston drydock, "the largest in the world." Contracts were not signed until October 1915, however, though employment forecasts then were for about three hundred quarrymen. Ever optimistic, the *Review* reported almost gleefully the problems being encountered with concrete, brick,

War and Peace

and macadam roads and rejoiced in September 1914 that "this revival, throughout the country, of granite as road material, will ultimately mean a boom to Rockport." More specific consolation was a government contract for granite for the monument at Richmond, Virginia, for President John Tyler.

But the spring of 1916 blew in another of the grubby strikes at the quarries. It dragged on for over nine weeks. Nearly nine hundred workers were involved. At the outset, the engineers settled for an hourly increase of 2 cents. Not so the stonecutters, then getting $3.25 per day. They held out for a $4.00 daily wage and a three-year contract; the company wanted a five-year one. By early May a compromise had been negotiated, again with different benefits for the quarrymen, stonecutters, and paving cutters, respectively. Two months later, as the last peaceful summer began for Americans, came the discouraging report from Washington that Engineers for the Harbors and Rivers Committee of Congress no longer felt that the costs to complete the Sandy Bay breakwater would produce sufficient commercial benefits to warrant further appropriations.

William E. Parsons, Postmaster of Rockport between 1898 and 1914, and manager of the theatrical team of Parsons & Pool which traveled widely to put on performances of "Uncle Tom's Cabin." (SBHS)

Town on Sandy Bay

The assassinations at Sarajevo touched no sparks at Rockport during that momentous 1914. Rather, townspeople were interested in the debate over compulsory smallpox vaccinations, meetings of the local antisuffrage association, lawyer Teresa Crowley's prosuffrage meeting near the post office, the lack of a baseball team for the new summer season, and the seriously low water pressure in town. In the twenty years since the mains had been installed, 565 water users had become 1,100 and 83 hydrants had grown to nearly 150. That October, the whole of Cape Ann was plagued by forest fires, especially once the "gunning season" commenced in the woods. The Sorosis Club of young ladies went on a joy ride in Elmer Burgess' power boat.

Lester Stevens, the local artist who in June became editor of the *Review* managed by his brother Charles, had a painting accepted by the Pennsylvania Academy of the Fine Arts. The subject was *Quarry at Rockport*. The Honorable A. Piatt Andrew donated to the GAR a painting entitled *High Water Mark of the Rebellion, 50 Years after Gettysburg*. It showed veterans of the Blue and the Gray shaking hands over a stone wall where Pickett's charge had been checked. Soon new veterans would be off to new charges. Another veteran, long popular as a "first class man in a third class office," was "Uncle Billy" Parsons, reappointed Rockport's postmaster. Finally, there were all the fairs, particularly those for the Haskins Hospital and for the new Esty organ at the Universalist church. December found some Pigeon Covers remembering native son William Wadsworth, "star of stage and screen," who had made his theatrical debut twenty years before but had just been written up in *Moving Picture Magazine*. His newest film role was the part of "Wood B. Wedd." Christmas Eve found even the *Review* ominously reporting Adm. B. A. Fiske's statement that it would take five years to bring the navy "up to fighting efficiency against a strong enemy." Bids were being opened for eight new submarines—of the long-range, seagoing type.

It was 1915 that marked the real turning. Although the *Rockport Review* continued to editorialize on local issues such as sidewalk improvement, cleaning up the Front Beach, and—constantly—the need for new industries, it did run a column of national and international news. Into that were lumped such items as "the State Department was warned by the German Government that American vessels should avoid the north and west coasts of France" (February 12) and "the corner stone of the $2,000,000 Lincoln memorial structure was laid at Washington" (February 19). There was a full account of the thirty-three day imprisonment by the British of American sailor Reinhold Swanson, a crew member of the *George Hawley* bound for Copenhagen with oil and grain (March 26). Then came May.

In Rockport, at Webster's Field, the resuscitated baseball team played its first game. At the town hall Charlie Chaplin played "Mabel's Married Life." Off the coast of Ireland a British liner named the *Lusitania* played into the hands (or torpedo range) of a German submarine and sank, leaving 1,198 persons dead among whom were 128 Americans. The war of words began. On Monday, May 24, two submarines and four torpedo boats invaded Sandy Bay Harbor. They were part of the "coast-defending fleet taking part in the war games." Graduation came and went, adding seven girls and three boys to the roster of the alumni. Another six Rockporters graduated from Gloucester High School. The Rockport Country Club opened; the projected "Rockport Day" fizzled; and on July 23 the warships *Virginia, Nebraska,* and *Georgia* were anchored at Rockport—reminders of past pleasures and impending anguish. For many Rockport women there came another anguish, having women's suffrage defeated by 108,000 Massachusetts voters in early November.

A week later James E. Bryan, "whom many will remember as a member of the local baseball team this summer," left for Canada, joined a Canadian regiment, sailed from Halifax, and on November 2 was in England, preparing to go to the front. "Young Bryan was formerly a sailor in the U.S. Navy and was a member of the crew of the torpedo boat destroyer *Ammen* when the boats were here two occasions. He married a daughter of August Mattson of this town." Thus, by Christmas, 1915, as carolers paraded through town and gathered at the "electrically illuminated municipal Christmas tree" at the George J. Tarr Park, arranged by the Women's Club, the shadows of World War I had darkened Rockport.

The New Year began with a meeting of the Brotherhood of the First Parish Church, at which the Universalist minister spoke on the "Ethics of War." In the light of things to come, the town was fortunate in having an unusual contact with the outside world. Never strong on security considerations, the *Review* proudly told one and all on January 14, 1916, that Rockport probably had the only two licensed women wireless operators in Massachusetts "and, it is thought, in this part of the country." Each evening, ran the report, "while seated in their own completely furnished laboratory, [they] are in communication with the outside world and learn the events of the day"—an advantage the

editors themselves lacked in those preteletype days, "They are the
Misses Margaret Campbell and Gertrude Tarr, who have a fine station
and are experts." Built with their own money, it had "all the latest
attachments." After attending school in Boston, the women had fitted
up the commercial station and were following the news from the
wireless station at Wellfleet. That same month, Rockport reached 363
"working" telephones, an increase of 136 in five years. A few other
increases disclosed the police chief's salary as $250, the busy town
clerk's as $468, and the annual budget of the Carnegie Library as
$1,000.

Belaboring President Wilson for allowing all of what America had
once stood for in being trampled in the dust by Mexico and Germany,
the local paper—run by Bull Moose, Progressive Republicans—
decided that the fearless Theodore Roosevelt "is the only person who
can restore American pride." He called that spring for a 225,000-man
navy. Rockport, as a "naval" town, was urged to vote for him and for
protectionism. Late in April the town learned of Wilson's sharp warning to the Germans against submarine warfare, given in an address to a
joint session of Congress. In time for some sailors to participate in the
annual Memorial Day parade came a small contingent of battleships.
From May 24 to June 15 the officers and men "enjoyed the hospitality
of Cape Ann and the people of Cape Ann have been pleased to have
them here." By late July war had come closer to town, when a letter
from Gilbert Everett, a member of Company G, 85th Infantry, Massachusetts militia, was quoted in the press. Writing from El Paso,
Texas, on the Mexican border, Everett was serving under General
Pershing. In November, Wilson was reelected on the grounds that he
had kept the United States out of war. At the dawn of 1917, Rockport
and the nation once again hovered on the brink.

War

Then it happened. On April 4, 1917, the U.S. Senate voted 82 to 6
to declare war. Two days later the House concurred, 373 to 50. Thus,
the Great War—the war to make the world "safe for democracy," the
"War to end Wars"—began for the Americans, a year and seven
months after it had begun for the Europeans. It would be another year
and seven months before it ended, in a railway car in a forest in France.
For Rockporters, as for millions of other Americans, the interval
would be grim, the losses painful. In all, nearly 4,800,000 American

War and Peace

320 troops were to be called up; 2,084,000 would go overseas. Rockport school pupils prepared an honor roll with a star for each alumnus summoned to the colors. There would be more than 250 before they finished, 96 high school graduates, though the armistice did come before a few left for duty. Of the total, 6 would lose their lives. One, Pierce N. Hodgkins, lived to produce and publish one of the town's few autobiographies. His account of the war years and his overseas service is doubly illuminating, for he was an aviator at a time when so few were so intrepid.

On Rockport's home front, wartime activities were largely coordinated by the committee of public safety appointed by the governor early in 1917. The draft aside (it was initiated May 18), the first order of business was to prepare for emergency aid. A call went out to the town's religious, social, and fraternal societies to survey all buildings and supplies available for use in a crisis. The estimate calculated that 906 people could be cared for overnight. There were also 200 church cushions which could serve as mattresses, in a pinch. Food was available for 766 people, temporarily. Hospital supplies were soon inventoried and made ready. That spring a committee on food production and conservation secured vacant land and divided it up for the planting of Victory gardens. Canning and cooking classes were instituted for the uninitiated, since shortages surely lay ahead. One of those shortages was to be flour and would require Food Administrator Herbert Hoover to declare meatless and wheatless days. For countless civilians their meals were made somewhat less austere thanks to the Hodgkins family mill beside the Rockport depot. There, a new process was devised and put into production. It ground out "all-of-the-wheat flour." With the direct intervention of Hoover, Hodgkins's mill worked three shifts daily to supply carloads of whole wheat flour to hungry Americans.

Thanks to the perennial home-gardening projects of Rockport's school department, a foundation had been laid back in 1911. In 1912 over four hundred school children had accepted free vegetable and flower seed packets, and more than one hundred young people had exhibited their produce in the harvest show. It became an annual event. In 1918 the outlay for seeds was $35.71. On the other hand, pest control against gypsy and brown-tail moths cost the town $2,863 in 1918. All enemies were by no means overseas. Some four thousand pounds of arsenate of lead were purchased as ammunition. Even so, tree warden Alfred Blatchford was anxious about "the ravages of the leopard moth, which I think is increasing rapidly and should be taken seriously."

For physical security, Company M, the Rockport company of the State Guard, was mustered into service and assigned to the Fifteenth Infantry Regiment on June 7, 1917. Its complement was seventy-five men and three officers. Five were discharged for industrial reasons, however; four moved out of state; two were released on disability claims; and one died. Weekly drills were quickly initiated and a power boat was berthed at the waterfront for emergency use. Guards from the U.S. Marines arrived and were posted strategically to protect the operations of the Commercial Cable Company. As for the breakwater, a lamentable decision had already been taken not to continue funding its construction. Clearly, the U.S. Navy was far more in demand elsewhere than in Rockport's unfinished Harbor of Refuge.

Other security was being developed in Pigeon Cove. The Cape Ann Tool Company, whose wooden shed had burned in 1913, replaced it with a new metal structure. In 1918 still more land and wharfside property was acquired for the expansions needed to meet the demands created by a nation at war. By then accessories for the granite quarries had become a minor part of the tool company's output of forgings.

Once chemical warfare was unleashed overseas, prompt countermeasures were taken to provide gas masks for "our boys." From Washington emerged an appeal from the Treasury Department noting that "poison gas was one of the fruits of *Kultur*. It stings, blinds, kills. Charcoal or carbon made from fruit pits and nut shells is used to neutralize it. The Government needs carbon." To the Rockport Boy Scouts fell the chore of organized collecting. They managed to gather "a sugar barrel of nuts and shells," mainly peach, plum, prune, cherry, and apricot pits, plus walnut, hickory, and butternut shells.

Older residents bundled up and endured the coal shortages and price doublings as best they could. Fortunately, the town schools secured a sufficient supply to be able to maintain operations, which many Massachusetts communities did not. To add to the fuel shortage was the bitter cold, the plumbing freeze-ups, and the heavy snow that often hindered transportation. A burial agent was added to the list of Rockport officials. His duties were "to carry out the provisions of law relative to the burial of soldiers and sailors." In 1917 the town paid out its first "Mother's Aid" ($423.50); in 1918 the sum jumped to $1,060.

322   Shortages of oil for roads and runaway inflation staggered the town accountant.

In some ways the children outdid their elders. The town's schools responded to the many challenges in a laudable fashion, as Superintendent Eldredge's annual reports reveal. During the war Rockport had eight school buildings with 29 rooms, including the two for manual training. These were staffed by 28 women teachers and one man, Principal William Woodward, all poorly paid, though. In 1917, for the first time, the town had over 900 registered pupils, but in 1918 registration dropped to 869. Attendance was compulsory for children aged seven to fourteen, but any child who had reached age five by October 15 was permitted to enter school in September. The total budget for schools and salaries reached $25,352, of which $23.75 was spent for athletics.

Throughout the war Superintendent Eldredge, his teachers, and the school committee maintained a skillful balancing act of engaging the town's student body in the vast conflict yet not losing sight of the longer-range goals of society. Interestingly, class attendance records were better even than usual: there were only fifteen problems for 1918 in the South Village (of which six were truancies) and thirty absences in the North Village (with nine truancies). One case revealed a condition where the pupil could not come "on account of inadequate clothing." This was promptly remedied by the helpful PTA. At the high school thirty-one pupils were neither absent nor tardy the entire academic year 1917-18. Lower schools had even better records, all in the higher 90 percent range.

Among the wartime efforts conducted by or with school personnel were the Junior Red Cross "work pledges." Some 260 pupils got these either by paying 25 cents for materials or, more generally, by working. Among their jobs were printing "Welcome" cards, cutting thread reels, making Red Cross stencils, selling tickets, cutting leaves for needle cases, or collecting old rubbers for sale. Ruth Tuttle's pupils drew many posters for war-work groups, "an excellent and commendable adaptation of drawing instruction to practical needs." The schools also encouraged students and their parents to learn and study William T. Page's "The American's Creed," the prizewinning result of a nationwide contest. Some of the townspeople were frankly nervous at having so many foreign-born neighbors.

Prior to the four drives for Liberty loans, Rockport participated in the Canadian Halifax Relief Fund, collecting almost $800. Then when

Town on Sandy Bay

The Leander Haskins Hospital at the top of Pool's Hill, shown here about 1908, was left to the town by Leander M. Haskins at his death in 1905. It was closed in 1919, and the land is now a town park. (Hoyt)

the American appeals began, schoolchildren joined their parents in the national effort. During the four successive Liberty loan campaigns, the town raised $659,950, including $211,655 from summer residents. Rockport exceeded its quota in every drive, despite having "no men of large wealth and few large business enterprises." By December 1918 some 340 pupils held $2,250 worth of war savings and thrift stamps, while the high school had 11 "Liberty Boys" and 27 "Liberty Girls" who had pledged and paid a total of $70. Rockport was one of only twelve Massachusetts towns whose pledges were fully paid up.

As an indication of how the war penetrated Rockport homes, one need only look at the graduation program for 1918. (The ceremonies cost $70.10 that year, including $10.00 for the orchestra and $1.50 to tune the piano.) The fourteen who received their diplomas on June 19 had an idealistic class motto: "To the Stars Through All Difficulties." Their essays, though, coped with mundane matters. "American Aid to Stricken Europe" was Ellen Jensen's topic; Edward N. Bailey spoke on "American Marksmanship"; and Gertrude Upham reflected on "War and Thrift" and Edna Welch on "The Use of the Cartoon in Politics and War." Surprising for that era and for Rockport's ethnic composition was Esther Pearson's "The American Negro as a Soldier." There were timely recitations of works by Lloyd George, "Through Terror to Triumph"; Marshal Joffre, "The Battle of the Marne"; Secretary Robert Lansing, "Democracy and War"; and Henry Ward Beecher's rousing "The National Flag." Students and their assembled well-wishers joined in singing "Keep the Home Fires Burning" and "After the War is Over." One of the few pacific touches that evening was Edith Mills's piano rendition of Schubert's "Hark, Hark the Lark!" It was to be a summer of slugging. Then came fall.

In many ways Rockport's most severe testing arose not from the battlefields of France and Flanders but from the flu. In a four-month period in 1918, influenza became pandemic, exacting more lives than the four years of World War I. The disease entered the United States through the port of Boston. By the end of the year, 929 cases had been reported to the Rockport board of health, 18 of which were fatal. Eighty-six cases of other diseases also hit the town in 1918; 9 of these were also mortal. The selectmen, doubling as the board of health, held their fifty-two appointed weekly meetings; during the epidemic; moreover, they often found both daily and evening sessions mandatory. High above town on Poole's Hill the Leander M. Haskins Hospital was reopened for emergency cases on October 4, following a meeting of concerned officials and citizens the day before. Schools were closed for four and a half weeks. In response to an urgent call for personnel and food issued by the local committee, three nurses arrived from the state committee on public safety, another from Gloucester, and one more from Rockport itself—"all without expense to the town."

An army major named Thompson in charge of the military hospital in Gloucester assumed command of the Haskins facility but quickly placed it under Capt. George Strople and a detail of the Massachusetts State Guard, an arrangement which continued throughout the epidemic. A veritable village of tents had to be erected on the lawns to care for the scores of victims too ill to be looked after at home. Canteen service was organized for all sick and needy families unable to provide for themselves unaided. The Red Cross established an emergency committee of district nurses to assist the stricken who remained in their own homes. Women learned to drive automobiles, and teachers became volunteer nurses; two popular teachers died: Rachel Hodgkins and Ora Trudeau. Fortunately, the committee on public safety also had some success in securing sugar, fuel, and other scarce supplies, so that throughout the war Rockport was saved from the suffering which

Town on Sandy Bay

Dock Square, looking toward Bearskin Neck, from an old stereopticon view. Harvey Tarr's livery stable is at left facing the town pump. The elm tree was nurtured by Ebenezer Pool, sold to the town for two dollars, and placed in the Square in 1859. (Wires)

occurred in many communities. As the suffering drew to its end locally, so did the carnage overseas.

Peace

"Armistice is Signed—Fighting All Over this Morning," proclaimed the *Gloucester Times* on Monday, November 11, 1918. Its editor had been routed out of bed before 6:00 A.M. by news which "caused him to hotfoot for the office," he cried. Bells rang, work stopped, and there was dancing in the streets. By evening parades had been spontaneously whipped up by Boy Scouts, Red Men, veterans, and others. Everyone wanted to go somewhere, anywhere, to celebrate. One of many armistice temptations offered Rockporters was this: "Dancing! Patriotic Novelty Party. Tonight at Jazz Land, Now and Then Hall, Salem. Come Down and Go Wild!" By Sunday, six days later, however, calm had been restored; special services drew the grateful to their respective churches. There were seven in Rockport and five in Pigeon Cove. Then, in the weeks and months which followed, the townspeople faced up to readjustment. It was not going to be easy.

War and Peace

Twin Lights on Thacher's Island
Oil painting by G. Tucker Margeson
(Mr. and Mrs. Story Parsons)
Courtesy: Granite Savings Bank

Town on Sandy Bay

Cape Ann Tool Company at Work, 1923

Oil painting by W. Lester Stevens

(Cape Ann Tool Company)

War and Peace

328   There was anxiety as well as humor in the current hit tune, "How Ya Gonna Keep 'Em Down on the Farm After They've Seen Paree?" (Although far from being rural, at the end of the war Rockport residents had among their 1,266 dwelling houses 205 cows, 198 hogs, 100 horses, and 749 fowls, according to the tax assessors. Furthermore, 273 calves and 87 pigs had been butchered that year.)

One wag has defined history as a record of what never happened, written by someone who wasn't there. Rockport's sixty years between World War I and the bicentennial were crowded with people who were there and many who are here still, who well recall what happened and in some instances even made it happen. Accordingly, it seems prudent to reconstruct only the framework of the period and leave it for others to complete the structure, to add the trim, and above all to reassemble the furnishings of that more than half century.

The months following armistice brought back "the boys." Pigeon Cove's Alden Anderson was the first returnee from France, where he had lost a foot and been taken a German prisoner. In mid-January he was tendered a public reception. A week later the town had its first memorial service for sons killed in action: Harold T. Grover and Edward R. Everett. Hjalmar Mackey, who ran away at fifteen to enlist, returned at the end of January, bringing his Distinguished Service Cross. March found many Rockporters mourning other veterans which could never be brought back: the old elm tree planted in Dock Square on May 14, 1857, and the surviving horse-drawn fire engines. The annual town meeting voted $10,000 to motorize the department. Another moribund veteran was the isinglass factory, which made but a short run in the winter of 1919. Its passing bell was tolled by the dry law, so called. Nearly 90 percent of the isinglass company's production by 1919 was used in clarifying ale and beer. The closing of breweries resulted from the passage of the Eighteenth Amendment, ratified on January 29, 1919. By December 1917, nineteen states had already adopted statewide prohibition, and the Volstead Act of October 1919 defined as intoxicating any beverage containing more than half of one percent of alcohol. Prohibition commenced nationally on January 16, 1920, and with it the era of bathtub gin, speakeasies, and rumrunners, which some Rockporters came to know rather quickly. One ironic touch came on March 2, when Rockporters fell "off the water wagon" and voted for liquor licenses—the first time in eighty years.

March 1919 brought another departure—the squad of marines who had been guarding the Commercial Cable Company's property

Town on Sandy Bay

for twenty-three months, at the landing place and the office itself. April brought home more returnees, including Gilbert Everett, Antonio Contrino, David Babson, and J. Warren Main. It also brought another drive for money, this one a Victory loan, aided by the fly-over of a dirigible dropping literature. Rockport subscribed $260,150, some $88,000 more than its quota. Although the Memorial Day parade honored the town's World War I veterans, it was July 4 which became Rockport's official homecoming welcome to some 250 sons who had gone off to the services. By then about half had returned and participated in the noon procession, the presentation of service medals, a "Salute to Service Men by the Young Women of America," a band concert, a banquet for 400, and finally dancing.

With that behind it, a week later the town felt almost like its old self when the battleships *North Dakota* and *Delaware* put into port. Except for short cruises, they remained two months. The destroyer *Bancroft* was also in port for ten days in September. As before the war, thousands of visitors came to inspect the ships and share in the entertainment, some of which was supplied by Rockport's own cornetist, Harrison Fears, who had been in the *Delaware's* band two years by then. In the decade ahead the town would have occasional other naval visits; for example, a group of minelayers spent a week in port in August 1924. The band of the *Shawmut* provided music for the carnival known as the "Rockport Rinktum," held for the benefit of the Health Association. From nine to midnight the lower end of Broadway was roped off for street dancing. In late July 1928 the *USS Utah* made a visit, and on June 27, 1929, the *Cincinnati* cruised into the harbor.

A mid-August storm and an early September tornado, in 1920, producing a temperature drop from 90 to 56 degrees in two hours and a tidal wave to boot, failed to damage the naval vessels or a three-masted schooner then riding in the harbor thanks to the shelter of the breakwater, or so its supporters claimed. A number of vociferous campaigners refused to believe that "Journey's End" had been reached for the Sandy Bay Harbor of Refuge. Admitting that "very little, if any, progress has been made upon this project during the past year" because of wartime higher priorities, and grudgingly nodding over two adverse reports by the Board of Army Engineers, the town's triumvirate exhorted: "Now is the time to fight harder than ever in a well directed effort to get the national Government to complete the work which it started off our shores in 1884. . . . If Rockport does not work with all her might to bring this desideratum about, it will have missed a

Flat Ledge Quarry, 1921
Oil painting by Aldro T. Hibbard
(Rockport National Bank)

Town on Sandy Bay

Main Street with Elms
Oil painting by Anthony Thieme
(Mrs. William P. C. Smith)
Courtesy of Cape Ann Bank
and Trust Company

War and Peace

The fire engine Speedwell No. 2 which operated out of the Pigeon Cove Station. (Hoyt)

golden opportunity to do something for posterity and the future, not only of Rockport, Cape Ann, and Massachusetts, but of the entire nation as well." The Essex County Association of Boards of Trade voted support for the project which had received $2 million by then but still required $5 million more. A new tack was devised: in its incomplete state, it was considered "a dangerous menace to navigation." Congress, however, saw things differently from the Essex Boards of Trade and Selectmen John Henry Dennis, Eli L. Morgan, and John Marshall. In the 1920s and the decades to follow, Rockporters had to search elsewhere for golden opportunities.

The search was already in progress, though many Rockporters had failed to realize it. In increasing numbers, artists were looking for places to paint, for locations to set up studios, for sites for schools. As John Cooley put it: "When those mainstays, fish and stone, went the way of change in the period between the two World Wars, the village had a well-established, built-in substitute at hand." At the end of the first war, however, parochial issues still claimed the prior attention of Rockport residents, matters such as the fire which might have destroyed the town hall but for the alacrity of some navy men roused by the wild ringing of the Congregational alarm bell, when the fire signal had been put out of commission by the storm. Back in February heavy snowstorms had crippled the town. Electricity failed not only in homes but also on the streets. Trolley cars could not move and automobiles were stuck. Grocery stores suffered shortages, since by 1920 trucks were carrying most produce. The "auto chemical" of the fire department got stuck at the head of Forest Street and had to be hauled out by a team of horses and a chorus of "I-told-you-so's." The next month it was an electrical storm in the heavens, an aurora borealis, which garbled telegraph and wireless operations worse than at any time since 1870.

The "Salem Willows Waltz" of 1919 claimed that "You don't mind the trolley because you can jolly the nice little girls by your side." For Rockporters the jollification was about over. Storms, automobiles, maintenance costs, and acute losses of passengers meant only one thing for the electrics. A final attempt to keep them running was made in the spring of 1920 with the one-man safety cars. The innovation failed. The first week in June the trustees of the Eastern Massachusetts Street Railway announced that service would be discontinued in the Gloucester district as of June 20. The board of trade supported such a move on the grounds that the local unit could carry on by a pay-as-you-go system. The municipalities involved, though faced with many irate riders about to be deprived, voted overwhelmingly not to use money to aid the trolley companies. In the wings, motor bus promoters were lined up asking for licenses. The last trolley cars ran in Rockport on the night of June 19-20. The next day a special town meeting authorized the selectmen to issue temporary licenses for buses. (That same meeting appropriated $3,000 for maintenance of the ailing Leander Haskins Hospital, which had been closed for three years, except during the flu epidemic.) The temporary license expired on April 30, 1921, but by August 1 the Gloucester Autobus Company had newer vehicles carrying passengers to and from Gloucester.

Other matters of local interest that opening year of the decade included big guns of a variety other than the battleships, which had been so much a part of Rockport's summer scenery. Early in August spur tracks were laid down at the depot area in anticipation. By the twenty-fifth all was in readiness. In rolled the 42d Regiment of the Coast Artillery, which set up its great cannon and then engaged in extended target practice, firing at floating targets pulled along at sea

War and Peace

Mobile coast artillery cannon ready for target practice behind the Rockport railroad station during the summer of 1920. (SBHS)

by tugboats. The whole town reverberated to the blasts, and people living near the cannon area had their windows shaken and ceilings menaced.

The week those explosions were taking place brought the end to another drawn-out siege. Tennessee became the thirty-sixth state to ratify the Nineteenth Amendment. Women won the right to vote. On September 7 they voted in Rockport primaries for the first time. On October 13 Abbie Gott, aged ninety, registered to vote in the forthcoming presidential election, on November 2. At the town meeting in March 1921 the Rockport voters elected a woman to a salaried office for the first time. Lois F. Sherburne became treasurer-tax collector. Harding and Calvin Coolidge swept the nation with a campaign program of "normalcy." Coolidge emerged from relative obscurity at the State House in Boston through his call in September for volunteers from the State Guard to enlist for duty there during the hitherto unheard-of strike by policemen. Lieutenant Quinn took charge of the Rockport contingent, which in its way helped catapult Coolidge into the White House.

Although Rockporters were jocular about voting for liquor licenses when there was no danger from the results, they felt otherwise about the matter of Sunday baseball. The issue was defeated on a vote of 77 to 76 after an intensive campaign. The same session turned down a money request to purchase a chunk of the Headlands property for conversion into a memorial park. Undaunted, the next year found volunteers working for a baseball field behind the railway freighthouses in a park since known as Evans Field. One veteran, who had been in the Spanish-American War, was belatedly memorialized in December 1920.

School Days

Beginning with the school committee and superintendent of schools, many townspeople wished to memorialize their neighbor heroes, not with a park, but by a living monument. Some 750 citizens, parents, PTA members, and taxpayers in general signed a petition generated by committee members Louis A. Rogers, Walter Campbell, and Fred M. Full: "We believe that the most suitable and fitting form of a permanent memorial for those who participated in the World War would be a new and adequate High School building for the boys and girls of Rockport." Such "a civic center" would be "a constant reminder of what 'our boys' did." That year Rockport was spending only 28 percent of its tax money on schools, a remarkably poor showing in comparison with other towns in the state.

By 1923 it was recommended that the town appropriate $95,000 to construct such a building adjacent to the George J. Tarr School, since there was a growing support in America for a high school education for all the children of all the people. Despite statements that the building then in use was "outgrown, out-classed, and behind the times, illy adapted for work, and is said to be the worst example of a high school building in a town of this size that is to be found in the State of Massachusetts," voters rejected the recommended appropriation. By 1925, however, a sum of $125,000 was voted, a building committee appointed, and bids accepted. No Rockport firm submitted bids, so construction was carried out by Gloucester firms. As soon as the building was occupiable, pupils were moved in—in February 1926. Thanks to intercessions from Professor Marshall Saville of Rockport and Columbia University, a generous New Yorker named James Ford presented the entire library equipment for the new high school.

War and Peace

As Miss Ida Manning and Miss Mary Lurvey, veterans of some forty-five years of service in Rockport schools, retired, they saw at last the long, long anticipated new building, were honored at a reception, and may have attended the first public speaking contest in the new auditorium, when Alice Peterson won the first price ($5). They also observed school baseball being reorganized with happy results and the introduction of football with caution, since "in spite of the modifications of the rules in recent years it is still a rough and more or less dangerous game." In 1927 Rockport High School was placed on the approved list of the New England College Entrance Certificate Board, and in 1929, as the decade ended, it achieved for the first time a Class A rating. For the first time, too, a graduating class of Rockport High School had a week-long celebration consisting of a baccalaureate service, banquet, class day, prom, final assembly, and the graduation exercises themselves.

Spurred by the improvements at the new high school (today's school administration building), a group of Pigeon Covers set wheels turning for a new school building in their part of town, as there had been no new construction since the Reed School was erected on Pigeon Hill Street. The spot selected was adjacent to the Pingree Memorial Park, that "improvement" for which the Cove Village Improvement Society had toiled so valiantly to achieve. Lindley Dean took up the burdens of chairing a committee, and by 1929 that new $48,000 structure was also complete.

Not putting their faith in bricks and mortar only, concerned Rockporters implemented a number of academic projects, including a higher pay scale for teachers, the appointment of a physical education director (in response to a state law), a two-platoon system, a four-term school year, physical examinations for all pupils in grades one through eight, carried out by the school doctor and nurse (627 defects were found in the 608 children examined in 1924), the commencement of standardized tests in silent reading and arithmetic, the addition of a dental hygienist (paid for by the Red Cross), the institution of a school savings bank system to foster habits of thrift ($2,115.85 was deposited by the first eight grades in five months), and the introduction of milk for the lower grades at below-cost prices (1927). By 1928 more music was heard in the schools, including the glee clubs and an orchestra. From funds raised at a pageant in the spring recordings were bought for study-listening and a "club night" was held in the new auditorium. In 1927 a polio epidemic hit the area, though luckily in those pre-Salk vaccine days only one case occurred in Rockport. The next year 150 pupils were given immunization shots against diphtheria, and first-aid classes were started for the high school.

Art Came to Stay

Among its legacies the war left an uneasy feeling that the nation had too many "foreign" elements in its midst. The Russian Revolution, antiwar demonstrations, the start of a Communist party in the United States, radical actions of the IWW, the Boston police strike, and the Sacco-Vanzetti Case—strung out from 1920 to 1927—all contributed to a far-reaching "Red Scare." Added to this gallimaufry was the severe recession of 1921, brought on by the immediate return to civilian life of over 4 million veterans. Rockport rolled with the storm reasonably well, though many older immigrants and their children still recall being taunted occasionally as "Bolsheviks." In 1921 the Massachusetts legislature passed an act insisting that all elementary and high schools teach courses in American history and civics. Pamphlets outlining such courses were issued by the state. Rockport dutifully resumed its evening school projects, aimed largely at Americanization. The first year there were thirty-eight adult students and two teachers. Reports from 1922 showed the project working well, and the state paying half the costs.

An ancillary educational service was the town library system. In 1921 circulation rose to 18,000 books, and 354 titles were added. By 1925 the popularity of the institution began to call for fitting up the basement of the Carnegie building as a children's room; the next year came preliminary recommendations for enlarging the whole library, once again a pressing need. Rather than subsidizing brainwashing, Rockport voters decided their tax dollars should be used to augment their town's water supply by sinking tubular wells near the upper Millbrook in the meadow belonging to F. W. Poole.

By the time of its centennial in 1940, lessons of quite another variety than those administered in the public school system had revolutionized Rockport. G. Tucker Margeson opened the town's first known art studio in 1873, followed by Parker S. Perkins, another immigrant from Maine. "Sunday painters" and summer dabblers moved in before long, including Ellen D. Hale and Gabrielle de Vaux Clements. Some of them stayed; others—like illustrator Harrison Cady of Peter Rabbit fame—bought property and settled down as

War and Peace

The Old Tavern, built before 1787 and long a public house, was purchased in 1929 as headquarters for the Rockport Art Association. (RAA)

perennial summer residents. W. Lester Stevens was the town's first native painter to achieve prominence, though in his earlier years he worked on the *Rockport Review* to insure a livelihood. Other pioneer arrivals on the Rockport scene were Charles R. Knapp, Eric Hudson, the Norwegian-born Jonas Lie, Galen Perrett, and Harry A. Vincent. By 1920 there may have been a dozen year-round artists in Rockport.

That summer brought Aldro T. Hibbard to town, fresh from Provincetown. With him a new era commenced. After a preliminary sojourn on High Street and at Margeson's former workshop on Atlantic Avenue, he acquired space in a deserted livery stable on the waterfront behind the waiting station on Main Street. There he opened the Rockport Summer School of Drawing and Painting with a "student body" of eight World War I veterans. In addition to serving as an art school. Hibbard's home evolved into a club. By July 1921 some fifty Rockport artists gathered there and planned what the *Gloucester Times* described as "the first exhibit of the work of professional artists ever given in Rockport." Ebenezer Cleaveland's first Congregational meetinghouse found itself playing yet another role in the life of Sandy Bay when its vestry walls displayed nearly one hundred pictures in late August 1921. At the end of the season the artists and their friends, sweethearts, and wives donned fancy-dress costumes and marched to and from Dock Square to the Hibbard studio, accompanied by mandolins and a trombone. Rockport was marching to the music of a different drum.

The little town witnessed a phenomenal flowering of art in the decade of the Twenties; it then began to realize that the men and women who painted and etched were changing its economy and that the fading granite and fishing industries had a vigorous replacement in the production of pictures, prints, sculpture, and handcraft work.

Old houses began to undergo renovation and new ones were built. Fishing shacks and old barns "now faced new adventures as studios and homes." Art came to stay, and with it came a flock of artists. Their story has been told in a delightful series of narratives assembled in 1965 by John L. Cooley, who took to heart the advice of veteran art lover Ruth Spoor that if a book is to sing, it must have stories. His *Rockport Sketch Book* abounds with them.

Yet even that volume could not encompass the full story of the Rockport Art Association, which after exhibitions at the Congregational church, then in the old Murray Hall on Jewett Street, and subsequently on Main Street, was formally incorporated in August 1928 by Hibbard, John M. Buckley, Kitty Parsons Recchia, Richard A. Holberg, Charles R. Knapp, Antonio Cirino, and W. Lester Stevens. More than two years would pass before the association was able to acquire its own property in 1930, one of the few rainbows in a decade of clouds which overhung Rockport and the nation.

Three other undertakings of that period continue to bring joy to Rockporters today: the establishment by Rockport's native son, George Harvey, of the landscaped park at the junction of Broadway and Mt. Pleasant Street which bears his name. He purchased the land, tore down an eyesore factory, transformed the Baptish church to which he had already given an organ in memory of his mother, and then laid out a park. In the process, wrote one journalist, "the dumping ground of yesterday has become the garden of today." Preserva-

340   tion and edification were also the underlying motives in the establishment of the Sandy Bay Historical Society in September 1926, the year of the American sesquicentennial, and of the Rockport Community League in 1929, which later rescued for adaptive use the present Community House.

Buffetings

Rockport also had its share of destructive experiences in the 1920s, including a shattered romance which led a Pigeon Cove woman to sue her wealthy lover in August 1922 for breach of promise. She priced her broken heart at $2 million. In 1924 there were the incendiary fires which burned down Pigeon Cove's Edmunds' Hall, then used by the Woolfords as a garage, and on April 16, the Bass Rocks railroad station. In November 1928 the Woolfords' own home was destroyed, and in 1929 there were fires at Land's End and the Babson Farm plant in June. Four firebugs were captured and confessed, but in October Pigeon Cove lost another landmark, Parsons's Ice Cream Shop and the adjacent building, formerly Mason's Drug Store. During the Prohibition period, Pigeon and Folly coves both endured a series of fires, generally believed to have been set to conceal activities of bootleggers. More dramatic damage was that from the automobile which on December 3, 1928, glided through the huge plate-glass window in the Haskins building in downtown Rockport.

The sensation of the decade, however, was the railway train which just didn't stop for Rockport station on the evening of October 26,

Signatures of the seven original incorporators of the Rockport Art Association in 1928. W. Lester Stevens, N.A., was the only native of the town to achieve national recognition; Antonio Cirino is now the only survivor.

Town on Sandy Bay

1926. A brakeman apparently forgot to throw the switch for a side track, with the result that an incoming train plowed into a line of empty passenger cars, which in turn rammed a freight car across Railroad Avenue and into a small restaurant, which was knocked off its foundation and caught fire. The engineer and firemen were badly scalded by steam, but fortunately no one was killed. It was late the following afternoon before derricks were able to lift the cars back onto the tracks, clear the debris, and open the road to traffic. A whir of camera shutters occurred on that day.

For many families, Rockport's most deleterious experiences of the decade came from the quarries. Constantly blighted by strikes—in 1919 the workers had battled for a 10 cent raise but finally accepted a 3 cent one, which gave them 43 cents per hour for an eight-hour day— the industry was also being pushed to the wall by changing technologies. Fewer and fewer were the calls for paving blocks. December 1921 brought orders for grout to be shipped to Coney Island for jetty work. In March 1922 there was an accident at the Rockport Granite Company when a railroad car broke loose from its locomotive, careened down the tracks, and crashed into other cars. Far more of a crash was the dragged-out, bitter strike of 1922-23.

The manufacturers' association decided that the time had come to resist the encroachments of the unions. Accordingly, the Rockport Granite Company—which virtually was the industry on Cape Ann by then—refused to permit a closed shop or allow collective bargaining. "Any American has the right to work at what he wants without intimidation," was its position. The strike began and lasted more than a year. Scab workers were imported, many of them illiterate and untrained. Somehow contracts had to be honored, for midwestern limestone was proving to be a convenient substitute. The former Pigeon Hill Company store was renovated to board strikebreakers. Guards and a cook were brought in from Boston in early April. Mass meetings, fortunately orderly, were held at the town hall, at Lanesville, in Gloucester. Guards were posted at the Rockport depot in August. Both sides of the conflict appealed to the public through the press and the pressure on families squeaking by without paychecks.

The strike failed to break the unions. On May Day, 1923, representatives of four of them met in Lanesville to celebrate the pyrrhic victory. One of the talks was in Finnish. Work resumed, though orders fell off. In 1928 stone was shipped for construction work at Boston's North Station; grout went to Miami, Florida; and more granite went to

War and Peace

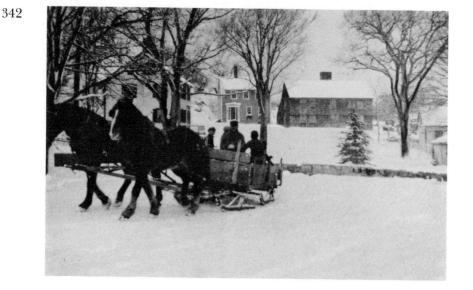

Early winter scene: David Philbrick's sleigh with "Old Castle" in the right background. (Hillier)

Providence for its war memorial. But also in 1928, the air compressor plant was dismantled and shipped from Pigeon Cove to Jonesport, Maine, on the Company's ship, the *Moody*. That June the paymaster went down to the dock and took a picture of a five-master and a four-master loading grout from Rockport. He would have few chances in the future.

The Calm Before

The era known as the Jazz Age and the Aspirin Age came to an abrupt end in the autumn of 1929. Rockport did not escape the "capital chop." The year began, on the other hand, in a mood of buoyancy. To be sure, the country was troubled with another flu epidemic, but it was nothing like the one of 1918. By January 30 the town was given assurances the peak had passed. Snow had been heavier than usual, and on January 17 Pigeon Covers saw that "sleighing is good, but very few here abouts have either sleighs or horses." Automobiles had taken over, so much so that the Boston and Maine was running specials of various kinds to stimulate railroad travel. One success was the "Garden Special," trains to carry passengers to the Boston Garden for athletic and other events. (The blight of rock

Town on Sandy Bay

Procter stereo view from the 1870s showing vessels awaiting cargoes of stone at Granite Pier. Gull Island lies behind the masts at the right. (Hoyt)

concerts had not been dreamed of in those dry days.) In 1928 passenger traffic from North Station had fallen 1.5 million. Since 1920 the decline had been a third.

Rockporters from both villages were as occupied as ever with their lodges and clubs: the Masons, Odd Fellows, Red Men, each with its distaff associates; Vasa Order's Spiran Lodge (chartered in 1906 with 36 members); the Knights of Pythias; Court Svea Companions of the Forester; the Women's Relief Corps; the Peterson Post of the American Legion; the DAR; Boy and Girl Scout troops, the latter having been formed in 1916 in both land and mariner troops; and the Firemen's Association. The Finnish Temperance Society at its hall on Forest Street was observing its thirty-ninth anniversary. The Rockport Women's Club was charged with good humor and energy, while the Pigeon Cove Singing Club was making melody under the leadership of Bessie Story Rogers. Ernest Nelson's Swedish Glee Club was in great demand, singing "as always with feeling and emotion and a fine sense of tone." On January 28 came the news that a community chorus was planning an old folks' concert for early April.

There was also live drama in town that month, when one company staged *The Burglary at Browns,* the Alpha Delta Club put on a three-acter called *Apple Blossom Time,* and the American Legion sponsored Mrs. J. Fletcher Burnham's two-act comedy, "full of mirth, dancing, and song," entitled *In Hot Tamale Land.*

Despite midwinter weather, sports were being encouraged. Deficits incurred the previous year were wiped out by the baseball carnival, which grossed $502 and left a net profit of $211 in the kitty. Basketball at the high school had been roused from a long hibernation by Coach James T. Quinn and Miss Richardson, who had 150 girls working out. The *Times* pointed out, however, that "it requires time and patience to revive a sport which has been dead, so to speak, for a decade or more and restore it to a healthy spot in the scholastic sun." Another touch of optimism at the high school was the initial issue of a school magazine, *Rocks and Pebbles,* the first to appear since 1922. Not only the school but the whole town rejoiced that January to learn that the president of the senior class, honor student J. Zoltan Reday, had been named by Congressman A. Piatt Andrew to the Naval Academy at Annapolis—the first Rockport graduate to achieve such a distinction.

The Rockport churches were hustling to keep in the running, as the three Congregational ones show. Rockport's first church had begun a rather startling novelty on Sunday evenings at seven—showing moving pictures. On January 20, for instance, the film was *Dog of the Regiment,* featuring Rin-Tin-Tin. The newspaper ad frankly said: "These services are arranged to meet the needs of all, and they strive to present religion with a smile." At the Pigeon Cove chapel, which had joined forces with the Universalist church there in 1921 and adopted the name "Federated Church," the Reverend Mr. Donald B. Howard was headlining a series called "The Rainbow of the Abundant Life." Interestingly enough, the Swedish Congregational church, with Pastor Harrold, organist Florence Larson, and Sunday school superintendent August Olson, was still able to maintain a morning and evening service, Sunday school at 11:45 A.M. and a youth group at 6:00 P.M.—without films or rainbows.

As the final year of the decade opened, Rockport was also bright with hopes in other areas of community life. The board of trade was preparing "a larger and better booklet than ever before." George Todd found the ice on the mill pond in good shape for cutting. The state legislature voted to allow the police department to be placed under Civil Service, provided Rockport voters chose to do so. The legislature also proposed to end the jurisdictional conflicts over town landings jointly owned by Rockport and Gloucester by permitting each

Putting ice in Reuben Norwood's ice house at the Mill Pond in 1908, with the Haskins Isinglass Factory at the left. (Borge)

community to take full possession of the landings in its own territory. Once again the Cape Ann Tool Company was working overtime. Even the Rockport Granite Company put up a good front when President C. Harry Rogers and his wife set out for the week-long national convention of granite companies at Atlantic City—their last.

Back in 1927, carried away by developments in aviation, a committee had been established to study the matter of an airport for Cape Ann. Rockporters had vicariously shared in the accomplishment of "Lindy" in May that year. The *Spirit of St. Louis* was powered by a single engine, parts of which had been forged at the Cape Ann Tool Company. The *Gloucester Times* hailed the work of Lindley Dean's company thus: "All Cape Ann should feel proud of the connection of this concern with Captain Lindbergh's marvelous feat which will go down in history as one of the world's greatest events." In 1928 Medford's Amelia Earhart flew her *Friendship* to Wales. Air transportation, even for Cape Ann, was believed to have a practical, commercial future. So proponents pushed vigorously, and by January 1929 they rallied 133 to a dinner at Gloucester's Savoy Hotel. There the recommendation was laid out on the table to build a commercial field on the Annisquam marshes. Instant counterreactions shot up from summer and year-

War and Peace

round residents alike. Complaints about noise were met with stories of new "silencers" for planes, but opposition continued to mount. The sanctity of Armistice Day also fell to commercial opponents, who complained that business was being jeopardized by holiday restrictions. Eleven years had passed since the eleventh hour of the eleventh day of the eleventh month of 1918. Less than eleven months lay ahead before Black Thursday. Yet on January 25, 1929, some Rockporters must have pondered an article in their *Times* which read: "Investors Should Have Good Bonds. Babson shows fallacy of ignoring sound investments in the Speculative Craze."

Between the warning and the debacle, Rockport did acquire two more lasting monuments. On March 6, 1929, the historic old house in Pigeon Cove dating back to at least 1715 was formally transferred to Pigeon Cove's Village Improvement Society by H. Chester Story, Bessie Story Rogers, and George L. Story, whose family had acquired the property in 1892 and 1893. At the conveyance it was mutually agreed that the Old Castle, as it had been known for at least seventy-five years, would be permanently preserved and maintained as a New England antiquity and a community center in memory of Abbie F. Story, a

Abbie Story (1844-1918), founder of the Village Improvement Society, Pigeon Cove. (VIS)

Town on Sandy Bay

founder of the Village Improvement Society in 1889, "who for so many years labored . . . for the uplift of Pigeon Cove." It was also in 1929 that all of Rockport had an uplift through the purchase of the five-acre summit of Pigeon Hill. That seamark, voted in 1713 to be a perpetual piece of common property, had been sold in 1819 and in due course passed into the hands of Ezra Eames. It was from his heirs that the town bought the site at the top of Landmark Lane for park purposes for all the people.

On October 24, to many Americans who had never read Shakespeare, "chaos is come again."

ADDITIONAL READING

For some contemporary materials one could read, with a grain of salt, Solley and Dummer, *Alluring Rockport* (Manchester, 1924), and Arthur Morley, *Rockport, A Town by the Sea* (Cambridge, 1924). Pierce N. Hodgkins, *That Is the Way It Was* (New York, 1977), is more an autobiography than an "autobiographical novel."

War and Peace

21

"THE LAMPS ARE GOING OUT"

WITH A HEAVY HEART, on August 3, 1914, Edward Viscount Grey, Britain's foreign minister, looked at the world he had known, loved, and served so long. Sadly he concluded, "the lamps are going out all over Europe; we shall not see them lit again in our lifetime." Grey died in 1933 in an age when other, brighter lamps were being extinguished, not just in Europe but in the New World, too. Even Rockport was to lose many between 1929 and 1939.

Quite literally there was the loss of the northern lamp on Thacher's Island. From the time of the first twin lighthouses there in 1771, successive lamps and towers had faithfully sent forth their glow to countless mariners and landlubbers alike. For a century and a half through fair and foul weather, there had been few interruptions. By January 1922, however, word filtered out that changes lay ahead. Somehow they were kept at bay until 1930. That January, Congressman Andrew warned his constituents of the contemplated discontinuance of one light and the electrification and strengthening of the other. On July 17 the commissioner of lighthouses doomed one of the Thacher twins. Conversion plans moved slowly, and so the lamp shone until February 1, 1932. Under the new system, the southern tower would no longer shine steadily. Rather, it would flash for two seconds with a one-second interval and be visible more than twice as far as its combined predecessors. The Straitsmouth lighthouse, white until then, was replaced with a more brilliant green one, and a gas buoy was positioned near the Salvages. Another replacement at Thacher's was a new telephone cable from Loblolly Cove. Since the personnel assigned to the island would remain, the fraying line got a substitute during a visit from the *Pequot* in July 1930.

Figuratively speaking, Rockport was plunged into darkness along with the rest of the nation on Black Thursday, October 24, 1929. From the Stock Market Crash and the Great Depression of 1929-33, followed by the New Deal of 1933-40, would emerge a town significantly altered in appearance and outlook. First to fall was the granite business, once believed to be as strong as Gibraltar. Although Indiana limestone provided increasing competition for granite, the quarries on Cape Ann maintained production until the late 1920s. On April 1, 1927, however, the Rockport Granite Company suspended operations for ten days. It was no April Fool's joke. The company's New York office had discovered that more than a majority of the three thousand shares of stock had been quietly purchased by an unknown buyer. After more than two years of trying to operate with a minority bloc, with "no knowledge of what the future plans of the majority stockholders may be and since said majority holders are unknown to

Charles S. Rogers (1840-1926), Treasurer of the Rockport Granite Company from 1914 to 1920. (SBHS)

"The Lamps Are Going Out"

the directors," the Rogers brothers announced through the *Boston Herald* on January 23, 1930, that with the completion of their remaining contracts the company would be dissolved. Since by then the Rockport Granite Company held a near monopoly on the business, its liquidation spelled the end of an era for the entire area. Activities at Lanesville and Bay View were shut down, along with those in Pigeon Cove. Ironically, the *Gloucester Times* of January 27 reported that "the granite paving-block quarries of the United States met in convention at Norfolk, Va. last Thursday, and reelected their entire board of officers and directors. Rockport's C. Harry Rogers was president.

By late March unemployment had become grave. "As yet very little work is being done hereabouts in the granite works," though fortunately the Cape Ann Tool Company had worked full-time that week. Speaking on behalf of the entire community, the *Times* on March 28 urged: "It is hoped that everyone having work planned will make every possible effort to commence same early. Several men, out of employment for the last five months, are seeking work of some kind." The opening of June brought news of negotiations, and hopes rose. "The people of Pigeon Cove are anxiously looking forward to adjustment of the Rockport Granite Company's affairs in hopes of a reopening of their works." But ten days later the real and personal property of the company was sold at public auction at the Boston Realty Exchange for the benefit of the mortgage holders. The price was $11,000. On June 20 the properties were taken over, the mortgages foreclosed. In six months more than three hundred men lost their jobs in the granite business. A few people left; most of them remained and faced the Depression in Rockport.

Early in April 1930 the fifteenth federal census was taken. Local figures were released on May 13. Rockport's population was given as 3,591—a loss of 287 since 1920. There were still 20 farms in town; but 166 residents were listed as unemployed. Gloucester had 358, Manchester 42, Essex 14. Those numbers did not include people temporarily laid off because of weather, strikes, sickness, or lack of materials. The town tax rate was trimmed $4, to $30 per thousand, the lowest since 1923. In an attempt to offset stagnation, the paper printed an article, "More Things to Do Around Home." November 4 was state election day. Rockport went Republican all the way. On the matter of repealing the Volstead Act defining alcoholic beverages, however, when Massachusetts as a whole voted overwhelmingly for repeal,

Rockport voted 475 for repeal and 452 to continue the stringent law.
There were 203 blanks.

Temperance was by no means a dead issue in town during the depression years. As with many quiet coastal communities, Rockport had had its share of rumrunning and rumrunners throughout the era of Prohibition—some of the latter were tactily known to the community. Occasionally hauls were made in police raids. One at Pigeon Cove in January 1932 netted two truckloads of "hooch" and a bustling crowd of spectators at the Dock Square police station. Having gone wet as a joke in 1920 (325 to 268), Rockport had to grapple with the licensing issue once nationwide Prohibition was repealed in 1933. On January 16, 1930, the tenth anniversary of Prohibition had been observed everywhere. Local church bells were rung at noon, and midday services were widely sponsored, though less enthusiastically supported. The Wickersham Report was much discussed in 1931. President Hoover's stand against Prohibition in August 1932 shook his faithful followers. In Rockport after the national repeal a special June election favored beer licensing 531 to 239. The results proved uncongenial to the residents. In 1934 the vote was close—698 to 654. For 1935 the verdict was switched. The *Times* of January 5 reported: "Rockport dry as the Sahara since the New Year," the town had reverted "to an official alcoholic desert."

As the economic situation declined month by month in 1930, the governor requested municipalities to set up local emergency committees on unemployment. On November 21, at the request of the chairman of the board of selectmen, Roy H. Lane, the Rockport group decided that residents seeking employment should register at the town clerk's office and that some immediate local aid might come from unexpended balances in various departmental budgets. Only a week later eighty-three men and three women had signed up, including thirty laborers, fifteen quarry workers, fourteen paving cutters, and one (each) lobsterman, bookkeeper, and blacksmith. By December 4 the total reached ninety-nine men and four women.

A barebones view of what was done during the succeeding dozen years to help Rockporters in time of need can be had from the annually published town reports. The ERA (Emergency Relief Administration) and its successor, the WPA (Works Progress Administration), provided assistance until 1942, by which time the town and the nation were again darkened by war. Month after month, newspapers carried stories of relief projects begun, in motion, terminated. The devastating effects of penury and poverty on families, however, survive in a few personal letters, in fewer diaries, and in the recollections of individuals who endured.

Initially, the town tried to meet its own crises. In April 1931, to cite one instance, the American Legion planned a dance at the town hall to benefit the unemployment fund. Outside help was soon needed— from public and private sources. In October 1932 the town's welfare board received 120 bags of flour from the Red Cross. Rockport alone could never have met the emergency. Its own welfare payments for 1933 were $50,000, recipients being employed on road and other construction projects, by the park department, and elsewhere. Every employee of the school department returned 5 percent of his wages for welfare assistance. The sum was $1,252. The board of public welfare spent $34,164 in 1934. In 1935 food and other commodities were distributed to 210 families, and the town appropriated $36,364 for welfare, old age assistance, and soldiers' benefits. By 1936 there were 96 families (321 individuals) on welfare ($25,682) and 83 people collecting old age benefits ($16,684). From the WPA Rockport received $37,330 in 1934, $51,292 in 1935, and $72,845 in 1936. In January 1938 there were still 62 WPA men on the payroll, several of them working at Evans Field.

Despite the make-work nature of many of the relief undertakings and the often justifiable criticisms of the workers and their output, Rockport received many rewards from which it still benefits: the water main system at the Millbrook Valley beyond the depot, sewer lines for Main and other streets, the grandstand and other improvements at Evans Field, expansion of roads and lots at Locust Grove Cemetery, the extensive cataloguing projects at the high school library and the Sandy Bay Historical Society (three to six people on an off-and-on basis made a typewritten transcript of five volumes of Ebenezer Pool's papers), reforestation on town watersheds, clearings of roadsides, grading of land to make a playground for the Pigeon Hill School, the landscaping of Mill Pond Park given to the town in 1936 by the estate of George Todd, and both murals and paintings for public buildings.

When funds became available for the buildings as well, federal money was added to a town appropriation for alterations and substantial additions to the George J. Tarr School. The new quarters were opened in September 1939, as Europe went to war. In 1934 a federal emergency relief nursery school was established with a teacher eligible

The two almost identical fish houses which came to be known as Motif No. 1 and Motif No. 2, in 1925 when sizable fishing vessels were still in evidence in Rockport's harbor. (Hoyt)

for public assistance. First run at the Baker home, it later moved to the Legion Hall. In 1935 seven students received $4 to $6 monthly from the National Youth Administration for work at various clerical tasks in the school system. The money was used for lunches and in some instances made it possible for the recipients to stay in school.

At the beginning of 1939, the WPA issued a status report on its activities in Rockport. In five years it had spent $265,720. At that date it had 86 people on regular work assignments and 793 Rockporters enrolled in recreational programs including basketball, puppetry, music, accordion classes, and dramatics. The five recreation supervisors operated at Haskins Hall, the Pigeon Cove School, the Pingree Memorial Athletic Association (once the Pigeon Cove Universalist church), and the Legion Hall. Of the 793 enrollees, 514 were under sixteen years of age. And so the figures went, gradually tapering off as the age of economic anxiety passed into that of military concern.

More Gloom

The decade of the Great Depression was a time of gloom in other ways, too. The winter and spring of 1930 brought the deaths of four

354   pillars of the community in their time: the pastor of the Congregational church, W. W. Campbell; schoolteacher to three generations,
Eliza Caldwell; minister, author, town clerk, Byron G. Russell; and
Charles S. Pittee, popular captain of the tug *H. S. Nichols*. Throughout
the anxious spring of 1932, Rockporters shared the nation's agony and
outrage over the kidnapping and murder of the Lindbergh baby.
Many a throat caught, too, at the passing of Rin-Tin-Tin at fourteen
years of age from paralysis of the legs and back. In April 1936
Rockport lost its last surviving Civil War veteran, Addison Haskell,
though in February 1938 it rejoiced over the one hundredth birthday
of its native son Thomas Addison Knowlton of Framingham, who had
served in the Union navy during the war. In recognition of its departed colleagues, the American Legion created and dedicated a new
plot in the Locust Grove Cemetery for veterans. At the old parish
cemetery, thanks to a substantial group of public-spirited
townspeople, the old hearse house was given a thorough restoration
in 1936 by carpenter Lewis Eaton. The next summer two teenage boys
were killed when a grout pile at the deserted Halibut Point quarry
broke loose and hurtled down.

Fires took their toll, too. In addition to the widely reported ones at
the Capitol in Washington on January 2, 1930, and the July 1932 blaze
at Coney Island with its $2.5 million loss, there were at least two
Gloucester fires to which Rockport responded. First was the combined
Police Court-Fisherman's Institute conflagration of January 28, 1931,
estimated to have destroyed $50,000 worth of property. When the
Cape Ann Anchor Works went up in flames in October 1936, the train
trestle was damaged. Mail, baggage, and passengers had to be taken by
bus and truck from West Gloucester over the Blynman Bridge to the
Gloucester depot. Luckily, there was a train on that side of the Annisquam River. On the local scene, April 1930 witnessed yet another
Woolford burning. "Believed to have been of an incendiary nature,"
about 3:00 A.M. it totally destroyed the "small summer hotel" on Granite Street, Pigeon Cove, of Clara W. Bangs, leaving only the chimney
still standing and a $20,000 loss. The L. M. Haskins Isinglass Factory,
tinderbox that it was, was ruined on the evening of July 1, 1932. A
providential rain kept the flames from spreading to adjacent buildings
in the present Millbrook Meadow area. Smaller fires hit the Tarr
School, already badly overcrowded, in January 1936 and the haybarn
of Clayton Gott on November 3, 1939—the work of some young boys
playing with matches. Playing, dancing, and dining were all ended

The Schr. "Col. Lindbergh" just after launching from Waddell's Boat Yard on Bearskin Neck in 1927. (Niemi)

right after Labor Day, 1939, when the popular restaurant, the Rendezvous, at Folly Cove Wharf went up in flames. Druggist Poole had an unwelcome Christmas present that year when fire damaged his home and store.

Two sets of forest fires darkened much of the town at this period. On April 19-20, 1931, Rockport resembled the "Smoky City," wrote the *Times*. A series of forest and brush fires extending over a six-mile front burned some one thousand acres. Forest Warden John C. Martin had thirty-five fighters on the scene, and Fire Chief Levi Thurston dispatched all the town's equipment and forty more men to assist the weary firemen. The blaze began on the Rockport end of Dogtown Common but spread toward Lanesville and the South End simultaneously. It was finally contained behind the Haskins Hospital and at Beaver Dam. October 28, 1935, was the date of the fire which roared from Squam Hill across to Pigeon Hill, leaving an autumnal scorched earth of five hundred acres.

Given losses such as these, Rockport was fortunate in having concerned citizens on the lookout for woodlands for conservation. On initiatives of the Garden Club taken in October 1935, the next town

"The Lamps Are Going Out"

meeting warrant contained an item calling for "town forests" at Cape Pond and the Haskins Hospital grounds—some 370 acres in all. The plan passed the following March and made a welcome addition to the twelve-acre reservation the Pigeon Cove Improvement Society, under Charles H. Cleaves, had persuaded the trustees of reservations to buy. That permanently secured eight hundred feet of ocean frontage beyond the old Gott house. No sooner was that project completed, though, than further pressure in 1936 won strong support from local State Representative Frederick H. Tarr, Jr., to get the state to acquire an adjoining sixty-five acres at Halibut Point, previously owned by the defunct Rockport Granite Company. That plan remained a vision, however.

For some losses there were compensations; others proved irreplaceable. In the latter category was the old fire alarm. In May 1930 a new whistle began screeching from the town hall. According to the papers, some people heard it and others did not; "but all who did agree it possesses a most weird tone and might be called a number of things." Soon to go was another town institution: the sounding of the curfew at 9:00 P.M. Discontinued at the end of July, it left as the only time signal the blasts of the fire alarm each noon. Although no alarms were sounded, two days later at noon on July 31, Rockport was scrutinized from the dirigible *Los Angeles*. Floating across Sandy Bay, it cut over the town and headed inland on a northwest course. Some six months later townspeople recognized their transient summer visitor in a photograph from "gay Gotham" showing the "giant of the air" harnessed to the mast of the Empire State Building.

Another loss, far more widely mourned than the old fire whistle was 2 cent postage for letters, which expired on July 5, 1932. By way of comparison, it is worth noting that halibut was selling for 19 cents a pound, but pork, a bit earlier in the season, had dropped to 14 cents.

Also lost for good were appropriations for the still unfinished breakwater. After a lull of twenty-five years with only an occasional murmer, a corporal's guard of townspeople resumed efforts to complete or at least repair the damaged hulk. They were rebuffed by a double rejection in March 1936. In reply to the selectmen, Congressman A. Piatt Andrew wrote that to reinforce the structure and restore it to its prestorm condition would cost $100,000. Such funding was not available "at this time." Two weeks later, the acting chief of engineers, General Pillsbury, confirmed the lack of money. There the matter was dropped until the opening of 1938. Then Selectman William Reed and his cohorts descended on Washington, returning with a report that Army Engineers were now more favorable. Some buck-passing went on behind the scenes, and word leaked out that "Washington" had returned to the authors in Boston the negative report which the latter had submitted. The *Times* fairly glowed with praise for Miss Hilda Olsen, chairman of the breakwater committee of the board of trade: "A Victory Has Been Won!" A scant year later, on January 5, 1939, the dejected *Times* wrote: "Thumbs Down." After a year of further study, the engineers had estimated that $8 million would be required to complete the structure. Such sums for such projects were unthinkable. Harbors of Refuge were no longer in the scheme of things. That once master of oceans, the *Leviathan,* which had so often sailed past Cape Ann, sailed by on its way to be scrapped for the British war effort.

Also headed for the scrap heap, so to speak, were three other Rockport institutions. In April, 1929, the Rockport Country Club had had a membership of 225; by April 1935 the depression had reduced it to 40. In early May that playground for summer residents was sold for $1,500 to Isaac Hall of Medford. From the remains, his group en-visioned a new corporation, a Rockport Golf Club. Before long such a club was indeed functioning. No such transformation, on the contrary, was possible for the Commercial Cable Company, which had com-menced operations with a fanfare fifty-one years previously. In mid-June, 1935, rumors were heard of its fate; in November the New York headquarters of the Commercial Cable Company took its decision. The office which employed six men under the supervision of William Kirkwood, was closed. Poles bearing telegraph wires were being re-moved from Rockport streets by Thanksgiving week. (Prices for tur-keys that season were 29 cents a pound, and pork had climbed to 25 cents.) By then progress in communications was dramatic. Already Rockporters were looking at newspaper photos transmitted by tele-phone, some from the West Coast in a mere eight minutes.

Glimmerings

Their own telephones with the familiar question, "Number, please?" were things of memory. By September 1930 dialing arrange-ments had been commenced in town, and the new telephone building on Main Street was completed. In anticipation of eliminating the Rockport exchange, the company made arrangements for telephone bills to be paid at Poole's Drug Store beginning on February 2, 1931. The automated dials went into effect on March 5, and, commented the *Times*, local residents took to dialing "like a duck to water." Radio, too, had become so accepted a medium of communication that by 1936 Rockport High School found it appropriate to institute a course for microphone buffs in what it labeled "Announcer's English."

The practical application of learning to cope with radio communications was soon to be had right in town. Back in May 1932 the police department had acquired a motorcycle for speedier service. To keep up with its still more mobile force in 1938, the department branched out into two-way radio communication. A system was installed at police headquarters in Dock Square. As soon as Officer James T. Quinn completed his course in January, he was licensed to operate the device and so keep in close contact with the police prowl car.

At that winter period, when Rockport had already been blanketed with thirty-four inches of snow to date, what appeared to be a setback for better communications threatened Pigeon Cove. The government reportedly planned to reduce the post office there to "a contract station." Despite the weather, a mass protest was immediately raised by what the *Times* claimed were fifteen hundred residents of the cove. The crisis was averted, as such matters generally are wherever local postal facilities are menaced. By August, Pigeon Cove was rejoicing in the luxury of having an outgoing Sunday mail service of its own.

Curiously enough, during the depression years the Boston and Maine in conjunction with other corporations made a number of moves to improve rail communications. To take the heat off the train riders in the summer, in 1932 it began experimenting with ice as a means for cooling overheated cars with their plush seats. Then in June 1936, to attract more passengers, it created a new fare structure—a flat fee of 2 cents a mile. The most daring initiative, however, and a profitable one, commenced with the depression itself. On Saturday, June 21, 1930, a through sleeper from New York City arrived in Rockport at 8:30 A.M. So appreciated was the convenience that the July 4 holiday break rolled five Pullman sleepers plus a baggage car out of Rockport "as a second section to the last train out." The locomotive pulled that string of cars to Worcester, where it was joined to a through train southbound. The project was extended in 1931 to the capital. On April 3 the *Times* informed its readers that from the last week in June through Labor Day there would be a through train between Washington and Rockport—chiefly for weekend traffic. On the way it

would also serve Baltimore, Wilmington, Philadelphia, and New York.
A board of trade folder of the period printed the timetable of "The Surfside," the name given to the weekend attraction, which eventually ran from June 24 through September 16. Departure from Washington was at 4:10 P.M., with arrival at Rockport at 7:29 A.M. Return sleepers left Rockport on Sundays at 8:36 P.M. and arrived in Washington at noon on Mondays.

Up on the hill above the Rockport depot stood another institution which called for reexamination—and got it—during the depression years, the Leander M. Haskins Hospital. From the outset it had been rather a mixed blessing for several reasons. By the time of the March town meeting in 1931, came the proposal for a committee to review the situation and make suggestions for the future. No action was taken until November, however. The hospital facility was taken over and run as a private sanitarium by Dr. Clement Heberle. Back in 1930 the town had had to pay an assessment of $858 toward the addition being built at the Essex County tuberculosis hospital at Middleton. By the end of January 1939, however, the trustees filed a lengthy report pointing out that, given the proximity of the Addison Gilbert Hospital and its far more advanced equipment, Cape Ann had no need for a second hospital. Accordingly, they requested permission to dispose of the property, the grounds of which had already been declared a town "forest."

Early in the depression, Rockport health and Rockport palates began to reap the harvest of faith sown at 15 Main Street. The *Times* carried an announcement on St. Patrick's Day, 1930, that George L. Tuck, pharmacist, had opened his store. "He will carry a full line of medicines." To sugarcoat the pills, so to speak, was a second department. "In the same store with Mr. Tuck is his brother, Walter F. Tuck, who conducts a candy store." To the despair of weight watchers and the relief of the ailing, the "conducting" was to continue for half a century.

Another vote for abolition was passed in January 1939 when the trustees of the Rockport library decided to cease publication of their annual book catalogue. The existence of an accessible, up-to-date card catalogue in the library meant that printed bulletins were no longer cost effective. They did, however, concede to print a list of books held at the library which were in the Swedish language. Sensitive to financial stringencies, the trustees and staffs of both town libraries were always cautious when funds were involved. Halfway through the decade the libraries did receive favorable attention, if not a more liberal budget. November 1935 marked the centennial of Andrew Carnegie's birth. By way of recognition, each library in the nation which had been funded by him or by the foundation he established was given a framed portrait of the philanthropist. From his hook on the wall, Carnegie still beams down beneficently on his library patrons in Rockport, to whom his interest was originally directed by Leander Haskins.

More significant for 1935 and for Pigeon Cove ever since was the transfer of that library to its present home at 138 Granite Street. Begun by the Pigeon Cove Library Association, of which Charles H. Andrews was first president, the Cove library was initially a private project and the recipient of generous contributions from summer residents. In its first years the collection was housed at 189 Granite Street, from which it had expanded until by the time of its opening in the Story building on November 9, 1935, it totaled some two thousand volumes.

Concurrent with the move of the Pigeon Cove library during the summer of 1935 was the restoration of the Old Castle, given by members of the Story family in 1929 in anticipation of its future use as a community center and local museum under the watchful care of the Village Improvement Society. The society was fortunate in having two uncommonly dedicated members to supervise the work: architect Thomas Williams and historian Allen Chamberlain. In 1939 they joined forces and prepared a detailed brochure about the Old Castle.

Burning Lower Lights

To offset some of the losses endured by the North Village during the depression, Pigeon Cove had some gains other than those already mentioned. Two involved Pigeon Hill. The third day of the new decade the community was informed by the press that Rockport's town treasurer "has received the $3,500 recently borrowed by the town, in a note of the same amount, on the Merchants' National Bank of Boston for the purchase of Land Mark Field, Pigeon Cove." Thus, the patrimony of all Rockporters was enriched in a time of poverty. To the hill would soon be added a utilitarian landmark, if not a thing of beauty and joy forever—the water reservoir. On ground purchased for a park, it was proposed to erect a $30,000 standpipe for badly needed water storage. And the need was truly pressing. By the spring of 1930 it became necessary to ban sprinklers and limit yard water to hand-held hoses for one hour a day. To help ease the worsening shortage, the governor signed legislation permitting Gloucester to "sell and convey" water to Rockport. Rockport's annual town meeting in March 1931 ducked taking a decision on construction. Less than two weeks later, however, the water commissioners formally "took over" 61 parcels of land amounting to 315 acres within the watershed of the "new" Babson Reservoir. Damages were awarded in the amount of $13,000.

In May a special town meeting was called at which the decision was made to build the standpipe on Pigeon Hill. By August materials were being trucked up the steep road, and the next month supply pipes were already installed. Exclusive of the foundation, the standpipe was to be about 28 feet tall and have a capacity of 312,000 gallons. The first week in October the foundation was poured: 500 bags of cement, 110 tons of stone, and 75 tons of sand. The result was a platform 2 feet thick and 45 feet in diameter.

During the time Rockporters were arguing over the proposed construction of a tower for Pigeon Hill, they were also looking wide-eyed at photos of a tower being erected in New York City which was to be 85 stories high, 1,100 feet tall, and equipped with a 300-foot mooring mast for dirigibles. That giant was to be called the Empire State Building. Although few if any townspeople had bothered to notice, the *Times* ran a photo of another rising giant on page 8 of its September 18, 1930 edition. His name was Adolf Hitler and the caption read: "The Fascist leader now commands 107 votes in the German legislative body and his party ranks second only to the Social-Democratic faction."

There was considerable excitement in town when the sections of the standpipe arrived from Pennsylvania in mid-October. Assembled, piece by piece on site, the structure was tested the last week of November, the few leaks were caulked, and by early December all was ready for a second test. As residents gathered for carols around the town Christmas tree in Dock Square, they looked across Sandy Bay to the tower landmark on their old hill. The New Year inaugurated a new and more powerful water supply for Pigeon Cove as well as the new 1932.

The South Village also achieved some gains in the earlier years of the depression. In May 1930, for example, with his bid of $3,388, John Anderson of King Street won the contract to build steps and a wall at the Front Beach to run from the property of Joseph O'Connor to that of Fred E. Poole. Iron hand railings were to be provided for security. Over the knoll by the Back Beach on July 25, 1930, the American

Legion met for the first time in its new post headquarters, the former Beach Street School. On that property in due course would be added a bandstand from which the sound of music would lift hearts for decades to come.

While the North Village was toiling upward for water on the hill, the South Village in 1931 was trying to increase its supply of water by digging downward—more salt water was needed for Rockport Harbor. At the March town meeting voters agreed to put up $4,250 for a jointly financed dredging project, to which state contributions would amount to $12,750. Work was begun in June, and the inner harbor was finished by August 5. The pleasure boaters of Rockport had organized a yacht club as early as 1885, but the group suffered from periodic doldrums. Revitalized at the turn of the decade, a group of yachtsmen formally incorporated the Sandy Bay Yacht Club in November 1930 and commenced planning for a proper clubhouse, floats, and mooring facilities.

In August taxpayers, many of them acutely squeezed by the depression, winced to read that their tax rate had gone up $2, to $32. Improvements had to be paid for, it seemed. It was not much consolation to be told that the figure was still lower than in 1929. Fortunately, the $90,000 draining operation being undertaken that summer on the marshlands between Rockport and New Hampshire to help mosquito control were paid for from Governor Ely's appropriations. As an emergency relief project, announced town hall, it would give preference to married men with families and those most in need of work.

The South End also picked up some scraps of betterment in the earlier part of 1930. The county commissioners added $10,000 to a previous $10,000 to be used to assure the completion of South Street from Prospect Street out to Turk's Head Inn. This, rejoiced the *Times,* "is pleasant news to everyone who had looked forward to completion of this scenic highway around the Cape." Again Rockport had done well, since its own $20,000 appropriation had brought in $40,000 more from state and county budgets, sufficient in 1930 to construct "at least two miles of road."

Out at the extreme edge of town Rockport undertook to build a permanent seawall or "bulkhead" at Long Beach. The structure was over thirty-three hundred feet long and required several weeks to build, but it was finished by late November 1931. More roads and mightier bulkheads were being planned in the heart of Europe, some of which would forever alter the lives of Rockporters. A German named Hitler was again shown in a *Gloucester Times* photograph; this 363 time he had moved up to page 7. The October 17, 1930 caption ran: "Today Hitler, because of his belligerent attitude towards the Versailles Treaty, is the most watched politician in Europe." Another bulwark-to-be rated space on the last page of the *Times* just when the Long Beach wall was being finished. The picture explained that the major general, whose name was Douglas MacArthur, would soon take over the duties of chief of the army general staff. At fifty he would be the youngest man to hold the job since World War I.

With the passing years town budgets were scrutinized increasingly. Politics grew more acid. In the town election of March 1932, 78 percent of the voters cast ballots, the highest percentage recorded to date. The year would be remembered above everything else for the election of Franklin D. Roosevelt, to which Rockporters, however, contributed nothing. The Hoover-Curtis ticket got 1,167 votes, while the Roosevelt-Garner one drew only 426 supporters. Gloucester, too, went Republican. All that prolonged unpleasantness about the Bonus Army camped in tents near the Capitol, all the reporting in the *Times* with full photo coverage showing rioters and brickbats only buttressed Republican support for law, order, and conservatism.

Some years later, though, Rockporters in large numbers were grateful to receive the bonus bonds finally awarded to veterans of the World War. On June 15, 1936, the local post office remained open until 8:00 P.M. for their delivery. The next evening it stayed open to certify the bonds of veterans anxious to cash them. That November, when Roosevelt was reelected by a landslide, the town again returned a Republican representative to the State House—Frederick H. Tarr, Jr. Yet a week later, townspeople in general reacted warmly to Roosevelt's plan for social security. The staff at the post office cooperated with the Social Security Board in distributing forms to town businesses and even individuals employing at least one person under sixty-five. Somehow, despite occasional jibes made about socialism, the program seemed saner than that Townsend Plan for the aged about which the *Times* and its readers had a good deal to say in the winter and spring of 1936. Ralph Parker had even run for Rockport selectman on the Townsend Plan, though well before reports were circulated that it was being "investigated" by Washington.

But as for 1932, Rockport had three other highlights recalled later. January was remarkably warm, though not so warm as the record-breaking January 8, 1930, when rhubarb appeared in some gardens. It

364   was so mild on January 15 that Kathleen Fears and Marion Hodgkins went for a dip on the Front Beach and got themselves photographed in the *Boston Post.* Warmer still to hearts as well as minds was the observance of the bicentennial of George Washington. Local celebrations were focused on July 13, which proved to be an ideal summer day. In June, Congressman Andrew was "pleased to inform" the town that the navy would send the destroyer U.S.S. *Tillman* to the harbor for the observances. There was a parade to the high school at lower Broadway, where a tree, a new Washington Elm was dedicated. The Finnish band "Waino" played a stirring concert. At the Congregational church a summer resident, Dr. T. Tertius Noble of St. Thomas', the famous New York church on Fifth Avenue, gave an organ recital, and Dr. Raymond Calkins from Cambridge delivered an address. Rockport schools for years after were graced by bicentennial reproductions of Gilbert Stuart's Athenaeum portrait of the founder of his country. Far more engaging was the oil painting by Rockport's popular summer resident Marguerite Pearson, which appeared on the cover of the *Literary Digest* that same anniversary week.

Mayhem

As chilling as the bicentennial was warming was the first of two murders in Rockport. On March 31, 1930, had occurred a violent episode which, as the *Times* put it, "furnished the residents of High Street enough excitement this morning to last them for a long while to come." About 4:30 A.M. John C. Dinn apparently went berserk, grabbed an ax, and began swinging. By the time he finished and was taken to a state hospital, "his house was a wreck, the street littered with splintered wood and furniture, and four police officers were gasping for breath," having finally subdued him. No persons were injured in the melee.

Quite the reverse was the situation of May 21, 1932. Nothing could have been quieter, but a man was murdered—in his own store on Rockport's Main Street. A. F. Oker, a well-liked, churchgoing, highly respected, Finnish-born tailor failed to return home for lunch with his usual punctuality. Surprised, his son went to the Main Street shop, and found the curtain down and the door locked. When he roused no response to his knocking, he hurried home, got a set of keys, went back to the store, and found the place in chaos. Behind the counter lay his father, bloodied and unconscious. A phone call brought the police and an ambulance, but the victim died en route to the hospital. Investiga-

Town on Sandy Bay

tion turned up a loss of about $17, according to sales slips. The tailor's shears, with which the bloody stabbing had been done, never did turn up. Nor did any clue as to the perpetrator.

Less than a year and a half later, the town was shaken by another murder, that one in Pigeon Cove. The victim, a widow named Johnson, was a member of the same Scandinavian church to which Oker had belonged. She, too, had apparently been robbed; her bludgeoned corpse was on her bed, and her small white house had been set on fire in an obvious attempt to destroy evidence. Although the blaze was extinguished, no evidence was located which led to any likely culprit. Following as it did one unsolved murder, the Johnson case became the subject of mass interrogations by police, local and state. To this date these two crimes against God-fearing Rockporters, having no known enemies, remain unsolved.

Assimilation

By the 1930s Rockport's immigrant groups had become fairly thoroughly assimilated. When the quarries shut down, the breadwinners were forced to find employment out in a larger world. The Swedish Glee Club, which had been organized in 1889 and had joined the American Union of Swedish Singers in 1892, continued giving concerts and being well received. By 1935, however, it was its music more than its Swedishness which drew members. Some competition had set in as early as 1931-32 when the Rockport Community Chorus was organized and began giving its attractive winter and summer concerts. Spiran Lodge, at that period largely Swedish oriented, observed its thirtieth anniversary in its spacious hall on April 12, 1936. A history of the Vasa Lodge in Rockport was reviewed and published in the *Times* for the members and interested friends.

The Finnish community, on the other hand, had arrived somewhat later and maintained a strong cohesiveness considerably longer than the Swedish one. In June 1930, for example, at the newly improved Evans Field the Finnish Athletic Association staged a meet, featuring five competitive events. The association then consisted of fifteen clubs from New England, New York, and New Jersey. At the very end of the month over one thousand members of the Eastern Finnish Temperance League spent two days in town observing midsummer, a festival to be celebrated in later years by the Vasa group. The *Times* reporter decided that the league had selected Rockport as the place for its celebration, "because Rockport, a picturesque little town with its wooded hills, nice sandy beaches and the cool breezes from the Atlantic, is an ideal spot in Massachusetts for just such a celebration." In February 1936 the local society observed its forty-sixth anniversary with a program in the Finnish language held at the Temperance Hall on Forest Street. The year before, on June 6, another group of Finns organized a social club to meet weekly. They gave it the name Ilon Tuojat, Bringer of Joy. Proud of their part in the settlement of the Delaware Valley, Rockport Finns assembled a committee to participate in that historic anniversary event in 1938.

The Finns, like the other newer arrivals in town, had quickly set up their own religious groups. A deeper cleavage existed among them than with the Swedes, however. It was complicated by the church-socialist split and the temperance-nontemperance one. There was also the geographical split between Lanesville and Rockport. An Evangelical Lutheran church society had been initiated in 1889 at the former area and a building begun there in 1891. With the help of Episcopalians at St. Mary's Church in Rockport, itself in a new-old building, a Finnish church was legally established on April 5, 1893. In 1905 the Rockport Finns split away, however, and concentrated their operations on Forest Street. When the Swedish Methodist church, never a hardy plant, withered, a group of Finns took over its building at 147 Granite Street in Pigeon Cove. In January 1939 they launched what they called the "Church of the Lutheran Hour" in response to a "demand for sound conservative Bible preaching in the English language." Vespers were to be held on the first and third Sundays. Some thirty-three turned up to hear the inaugural sermon, "Are We Headed Towards Heaven?"

To any Rockporter reading national or local newspapers, let alone following the radio, heaven seemed an unlikely destination the latter half of the 1930s. The fate of Ethiopia under the Italians and the bloody, internecine conflict in Spain were fully reported. On January 27, 1939, after more than two years of war, Robert Francis Allen, a twenty-seven-year-old Rockporter, was evacuated from Barcelona. He had gone to Spain to join the Loyalists but later became a Reuter's correspondent there. His dispatch the day he left told of forty-six air raids by Franco planes in a four-day period. On one of those days, ice cutting began for the winter at Cape Pond. On another, despite an eight-inch blizzard, over two hundred Rockporters went to the town hall to the annual President's Ball, for polio victims. As a feature

Universalist church Norman Knowlton was rehearsing a troupe for the third annual Black and White Minstrel Show. The Sandy Bay Bowling League, with its six teams, was busily occupied with scores. The *Times* ran a photograph of Hitler's fabulous new Chancellery in Berlin, modeled on Versailles, and another picture with Senator Henry Cabot Lodge snowed under by letters protesting the lifting of the arms embargo on Spain. No, heaven did not appear to be the direction the world was headed for.

Rejuvenation

Nevertheless, a close look at Rockport during that era when so many lamps were being extinguished does show that history is indeed a conflict between creation and destruction, rejuvenation and exhaustion. The decade began with a series of observances of the tercentenary of Massachusetts. Despite the economic slump, townspeople voted $1,000 toward expenditures. From other sources came additional support. On January 1, 1930, the year was launched with an address at the Congregational church by Dr. Frank Sanders on "What the Tercentenary Means to Rockport." Among the many programs which subsequently attracted broad support was a lively enactment by the Red Men of the "Escape of Hannah Dustin," as part of a carnival held at Evans Field on July 10. On July Fourth the DAR had solemnly dedicated its bronze tablet to the unknown local soldiers of the Revolution. The *Boston Transcript* on August 9 ran photos of Rockport tercentenary objects and events. August 14, a fine but somewhat cloudy day, was set aside for a parade sponsored by the Sandy Bay Historical Society. The Methodist church won first prize ($5) for its float, "Hay Rack and Choir." In the evening Professor Robert Rogers of MIT lectured on the Puritans, and Dr. T. T. Noble gave one of his popular organ recitals at the Congregational church. On August 17 the Reverend Mr. W. P. Landers gave an address entitled, "The Story of the Beginnings." Yacht races were sponsored on August 24, and other sporting events provided features for August 30, a town holiday. The destroyer *Crowningshield* was in the harbor; the Art Association's "Old Tavern" held an open house and Main Street was blocked off for dancing and the enactment of "scenes of olden days." There were also fireworks at the Front Beach at 11:30 P.M.

As late as November, the anniversary was still being celebrated. The schools under music supervisor Alice York put on a pageant, "America's Child," and an exhibition of tercentenary posters. Seven memorial markers and tablets were erected that year. As a belated echo, though one still in evidence, in 1931, the town obtained through the interest of Henry A. Tarr of Gloucester, one of the display cannon which for many years was on the old ship *Constitution* as it lay at anchor, "a museum for the whole country, at the Charlestown Navy Yard." The relic was placed outside the Community House, since at that time the museum of the Sandy Bay Historical Society was in that building and Mr. Tarr was a leading promoter of the society.

Among the other evidences of liveliness in a period often thought of as heavily gloomy was the acquisition by the town of the waterfront property of the reorganized Sandy Bay Pier Company. Assessed for $10,000, it was purchased at the town meeting of March 6, 1935, and the deed was signed in October. Thus, T Wharf became public property. Townspeople proved unwilling, however, in 1938 to appropriate $6,500 to purchase sixty-five thousand paving blocks to cover its surface. Considerable pressure was brought to bear on the grounds that work would be provided for thirty-five men for about eight weeks, presumably people connected with the Leonard Johnson-Karl Persson quarry. The cutters had reportedly worked only twenty-four weeks the whole of 1937. Another try was made to use paving blocks for seven hundred feet of Broadway in front of the two new structures being planned for it. That move, too, was defeated (64 to 50) on the theory that one such flagrant subsidy would be followed by demand after demand from other unemployed workers of the town.

The monumental hurricane which created such damage in September 1938 treated Rockport kindly—even in comparison with Gloucester. At Straitsmouth the highest wind velocity recorded was fifty miles an hour. The town was without streetlights and a few homes lost current for awhile, but there was comparatively little waterfront damage (in contrast to the beating suffered by Front Beach in 1933), and the fallen branches and trees proved to be so easy to remove that Rockport actually turned down an offer for WPA financial assistance.

Two other projects, however, did call for notable external financing. Both were for Broadway and both still looked remarkably fresh when the nation was observing its bicentennial. The first was to be a new post office to replace the cramped, wooden quarters on the corner of School and Main streets. As usual, word came out in the newspapers far in advance of the fact—in July 1936, actually. Seven bids were received. It was January 1938 before the site began to be cleared.

Town on Sandy Bay

The Post Office in the Granite Shore property at Main and School Streets about 1910. Postmaster William Parsons stands in the doorway and the clerical gentleman at left is the Rev. Dr. Bartlett of St. Mary's Episcopal Church. (Hoyt)

Originally the structure was to have been brick; but public pressure convinced the federal authorities to use Rockport granite for three sides of the $80,000 building. For its dedication on December 3, the town hall squeezed in a banquet at six-thirty and a five-piece orchestra for festivities and dancing.

During the time the new post office was being erected, many Rockporters and newspaper readers far beyond the town were filled with admiration and concern over Russell and Sherman Woodfall, both in their early twenties, who set sail from town on November 6 on a round-the-world tour in a boat they had built themselves. Their progress was regularly monitored by the press and local radio reports. Far easier for Rockporters to follow was the progress of their rising fire and police station.

A town meeting on September 6, 1938, listened impatiently while the existing hook-and-ladder garage was described as a firetrap itself and the police station as "not a fit place to live in." Reluctantly, voters accepted the burden of providing $80,500 for a combined replacement structure to be erected adjacent to the new post office. On February 16, 1939, the cornerstone was laid, and the facility was

"The Lamps Are Going Out"

finished and opened for inspection by August. A dedication, banquet, seven speeches, and a dance were held on August 8. As Labor Day approached, as many as fifty visitors a day, mainly townspeople, were coming to see their latest achievement. A woman from out of town became quite indignant, reported the *Times,* when told she could not buy stamps there.

War Clouds

Much deeper were the confusions besetting the world in 1938 and 1939. Many former concerns paled into trivia—matters such as the local 1930 "strike" over the school committee's decision to replace the superintendent and the high school principal, the disconcerting affair of turning the "Old Mill" at the mill pond into a tea room (also 1930), even those lively and sometime raucous Art Association annual balls which at first occupied the imagination and talents of so many of the Rockport painters who since January 1930 had been established in their own admired quarters. Throughout 1938 a mounting tide of anxiety was troubling the land. There were more dispatches about Hitler and the Rome-Berlin "Axis," photographs of Londoners being fitted to gas masks, of the Sudeten invasion of Czechoslovakia. Then came the hour-by-hour coverage of the Munich crisis, broken by the September 30 headline in the *Times:* "Chamberlain and Hitler sign Anglo-German Peace Pact."

In January 1939 a thoughtful organization was gathered, the Rockport Foreign Policy Discussion Club, of which Bernard C. Graves was leader, Homer G. Orne treasurer, and Asta Easton secretary. Their first subject was "Shadow over Europe," and their goal was a monthly session. At the time the Gloucester newspaper was editorializing regularly against Roosevelt (e.g., "Are You Tired of Being Regulated") some 150 Rockporters turned out to a meeting consisting of a seventy-five minute address and a thirty-minute question-and-answer period. A two-year peace period was forecast, but as spring unfolded the time frame shrank. On August 31 Sumner York Wheeler returned to town from Germany via the *Bremen.* In a local news interview he informed his neighbors that Hitler and the Germans wanted all of Europe except Russia, France, and Italy. In German hearts Hitler had replaced God. As for Hitler, he admired the American people but hated Roosevelt. The next day World War II began.

In Rockport the new tax rate was announced—$35 per thousand, an increase of $5. The Art Association announced its fancy headdress dance. A three-day baseball carnival was announced, along with a plea for large enthusiastic crowds. Browns of Gloucester announced its fifty-fifth-year sale and parking places for all. The Federated Church at Pigeon Cove announced a benefit party at the Ocean View House at which Dr. Harold Baker would show colored films, and readings would be given by Charlotte DeNoyer and accordion solos by Gertrude Korpi. Washington announced that fifty-two-year-old Dr. Ernest Gruening, who had spent twenty-six summers at Rockport, would be appointed governor of Alaska. The Rockport Golf Club announced its annual jamboree. Red arrows all over Cape Ann would show the way to the fifty-player tournament and the big dance. The Legion band announced its final concert for the season. "Finlandia" would be played by request.

Would they dance the Big Apple at the golf club? The President's Ball the year before with five hundred dancers and a ten-piece orchestra made a $50 profit, but "the dancers passed up the allegedly popular Big Apple routine when the musicians sounded the weird strains for this convulsive movement. Refusing to heed the savage call, the dancers continued in modern routines and classed the Big Apple as just another sour one." Too soon there would be convulsions and savage calls which couldn't be avoided.

Yet, at Christmas, 1939, the Rockport Community Chorus, under Arthur Keene, gave its annual concert, accompanied by Linda Liffler and Mrs. George Lowe. The Swedish Congregational church on Granite Street in Pigeon Cove held a traditional Julotta beginning at 12:01 A.M. The board of trade gave out its candy treats in Dock Square to all the children of Rockport. At the Old Castle in the cove, the Knights of Pythias gave their two hundred bags of candy to children of the North Village. On Christmas Day the new post office received forty bags of parcel post packages, and generous workers left their holiday tables to distribute every last one. On December 26 Finland invaded Russia. Before the strife was over and the battle won, millions of lamps would go out, this time all over the world.

ADDITIONAL READING

There are no exceptional items to be suggested for this more bleak period of Rockport's history. The successive issues of the board of trade's pamphlets, *Rockport, Massachusetts*, with their photographs, have some insights. Two exceptions are John L. Cooley's *Rockport Sketch Book, Stories of Early Art and Artists* (Rockport, 1965), and *A. T. Hibbard, N. A.* (Concord, 1968).

"The Lamps Are Going Out"

22

CENTENNIAL TO BICENTENNIAL

ONLY HISTORIANS make divisions; time does not." That is the view of an historian who spent a lifetime trying to make world history more comprehensible. For the local historian, on occasions the time framework of Rockport's history makes convenient divisions. One of these is the period 1940 to 1976. Babies of 1940 arrived as their town celebrated its hundredth anniversary. In 1976 as their town observed the two hundredth anniversary of the nation's independence, they had grown, married, and produced children of their own—some of whom participated in the festivities. The generation of 1940 had also survived three devastating wars and reached the moon.

Rockport's centennial year began with the coldest January in two decades. On the sixth, the Todd Company was cutting eleven-inch ice at Cape Pond and expected to put twenty-five hundred tons in its storehouse. Despite the freeze, several townspeople braved it to Boston to see a spectacular new film called *Gone with the Wind.* On the twenty-fourth, some pedestrians passing Murray Hall on Jewett Street heard sounds which made them think all was not well, or so the paper claimed. On opening the door, they found a show rehearsal in progress. The tune was "Come seven, come eleven, mah baby needs a new pair of shoes."

Up on Railroad Avenue things were well indeed. After having been closed for over a year the isinglass factory reopened on the eighteenth, though its days were numbered. Luckily, neither the mild earthquake of the twenty-ninth nor the explosion in the power plant of the Cape Ann Tool Company that day caused much damage. Dennis Caffrey, Emil Niemi, and Andrew Habe were treated by Dr. Baker, and the plant itself was repaired in a few days. Fresh statistics were released showing that Rockport births had exceeded deaths by fifty-one to thirty-three. More thrilling by far were letters reporting that Russell and Sherman Woodfall had arrived safely in Australia in the thirty-five-foot ketch from which they had sailed from Rockport Harbor. Money raising was in progress that January for two causes. The annual President's Ball for the polio fund attracted four hundred dancers and cleared $65. Finnish war relief was being vigorously encouraged by such events as a band concert at the town hall and numerous coffee parties, among them Emil Ranta's and Fannie Hendrickson's. At the high school auditorium a lecturer from the *Boston Globe* talked on the "Triple Threat of Europe."

February was the actual birthday month. The Sandy Bay Historical Society announced plans to celebrate the centennial by marking homes more than one hundred years old with a sign giving the name of the original owner and the approximate date of construction. Only a handful remained in place by the bicentennial. They did better than the project launched at a special town meeting in 1940 to consider the installation of water meters. That idea was still in the discussion stage in 1976.

Like the centennial observances of Sandy Bay parish, held on January 1-2, 1854, the festivities of February 27, 1940, were imperiled by storms. Valentine's night brought snow from the northeast. When trains failed to get through, stranded people took refuge wherever they could find it. Over one hundred townspeople were marooned, having gone out to parties and the school basketball game. On February 15 there were gale-force winds, no trains, no local buses, no mail, and no school. Two large town plows broke down under the impact of seventeen-inch snow on the level. Drifts were enormous, one reaching twenty feet in front of the art store at Dock Square. Once the sun came out, it took 115 men to clear the streets and make Rockport passable. Word came through of the death of Thomas Knowlton, two years older than his town. For many years he had been an engineer at the quarries. Then on February 20 in blew a second storm, which knocked out the electric and telephone lines. Thacher's Island was cut off from land communications, and flag semaphores had to be used to signal

374   the Coast Guard at Straitsmouth. Fortunately, both places had enough food and fuel for the emergency.

By February 23 mobility was largely restored, the birthday banquet was in hand, and the churches were ready with their respective anniversary services on the twenty-fifth. The dinner itself came at six-thirty on the twenty-seventh and was enjoyed by three hundred diners at the town hall. The speeches made a pleasant blend of the informative and entertaining. Two items which caught the reporter's fancy were that in 1840 the town's entire budget had been $2,655 and rum had cost a penny a gill. With that occasion the centennial observances took a break until spring.

The storms which had hit Rockport were figuratively hitting Europe that unforgettable leap year and causing mounting concern among Americans everywhere. The all-but-unbelievable Finnish resistance to the Russians gave Rockport's Finns a sense of pride and inner strength. The appointment of Myron Taylor as a presidential emissary to the Vatican broadened the growing ecumenical feeling in town, the ethnic composition of which was underscored in the election of its three selectmen that March: Norman Swanson, Vincent Charte, and William Reed. In rapid succession came the Russian peace demands on Finland; the safe arrival in New York of the new liner *Queen Elizabeth;* the capitulation of Denmark, Holland, Belgium, and Luxemburg, followed by Norway. On June 3 the Germans bombed Paris and on June 11 Italy declared war. All this took place and was fully reported by the radio, newspapers, and magazines during the period Rockporters were gearing up for their next wave of centennial celebrations.

These began with an open-air high school graduation at Evans Field on June 19. To be neatly groomed for the occasion the senior boys paid 40 cents for their haircuts at Cooney's shop. On June 22 there was a gathering of the state historical societies at the Congregational church, as a fraternal gesture to Rockport. The town went all-out that anniversary spring and summer. There was an original historical pageant, "The Voice from the Rock," original poems, a centennial song contest, a centennial march, radio broadcasts reporting bits of Rockport history, and three thousand souvenir programs for the events. Old Home Week extended from August 18 to August 25. The U.S. Navy dispatched the *Hopewell* and the Coast Guard the cutter *Algonquin* to be moored inside the (unfinished) Sandy Bay breakwater. The harbor was full of yachts and smaller boats throughout the week, and the post office was decked with bunting. Town churches enjoyed record-

Float in Rockport's Centennial Parade on August 24, 1940 reflects the concern of the independent shopkeeper over growing competition from the chain stores. (Photograph by William D. Hoyt)

breaking attendance, many worshippers wearing old-fashioned clothing. One of the hits of the "Old Folks' Concert" given by the Community Chorus on the nineteenth was the favorite "Billy Boy." Some six hundred listeners squeezed into the Congregational church that night. A full moon shone down on the band concert directed by Harrison Fears, and on the twenty-first there was open-air, general dancing on Beach Street, with special programs on a stage of Swedish, Finnish, Portuguese, and American country dances. For the sailors from the two visiting ships there was a dance at the town hall. The centennial culminated in perfect weather on Saturday, August 24, with a parade, viewed by an estimated twenty thousand spectators, and a mass display of fireworks. Three days later Rockport commenced to register its aliens.

War Again

For the next five years Rockport lived largely in the shadow of war, though inevitably life went on and local problems had to be tackled, such as the renumbering of portions of Main, Granite, and Mt. Pleasant streets, the need to enforce the law forbidding men to wear topless bathing suits, the call for expanded boiler facilities at the Cape Ann Tool Company, and the subsequent need for round-the-clock police protection there. More earth tremors in December seemed to echo the quakes abroad that centennial year. To some, the reelection of Roosevelt for a third term was a major shock. On the lighter side there were the Community Chorus concerts, the performances by the "Forbes Theater" up in the former Finnish Socialist Hall on Squam Hill, the Legion carnival at Beach Street, the enormous American Legion Convention and parade in Boston, the Halloween parade in Rockport, and the last chances to see the second year of the New York World's Fair. It was also the last chance to take the boat to New York via the Cape Cod Canal, so a few Rockporters enjoyed that luxury.

As the air raids intensified over London, Congress passed a draft act. On October 16, 1940, Rockport men twenty-one to thirty-five years old registered for a call-up. The school enrollment dropped to 485. In December, the tool company added a night shift to the forge plant, and by March 1941 as Yugoslavia fell to the German invaders, it began working night and day—to the annoyance of the Hotel Edward, which endeavored to have the company keep the peace at night in July and August. A few townspeople took a final travel fling. Both Sumner Wheeler and the William Kirkwoods visited South America; the town had yet one more Old Folks' Concert in January, a minstrel show in March, a policeman's ball, and a naval visit (one battleship) in August. Then on December 7, 1941, it had Pearl Harbor.

Within a week, soldiers were quartered in the town hall and the selectmen had called a conference to come to grips with the question of the defense of the town. Those who remembered World War I had learned from the radios and newspapers that times had changed as had the engines of war. Once again a public safety committee was called for and so was a Red Cross unit, staffed and equipped for emergencies, both known and scarcely thought of. To provide reinforcements for those operations, the Red Cross started a nursing course at the high school for senior girls and first-aid courses for the public at large. A first-aid station was established in the new police headquarters, and some forty men and women were given special training.

Unlike previous wars, World War II offered threats from the air. Consequently, Rockporters looked nervously skyward and prepared to defend themselves against air raids. A central air-raid station was established; it was staffed initially by teachers and honor roll students who stood night watches at the center in the conference room at the town hall. Reaching out into the community was a network of wardens, assigned to area posts, and their ambulatory patrol wardens. The core group was made up of 20 men and women; they were assisted by another 125 men and women who were given training, limited authority to issue instructions, and in due course helmets to wear while on patrol. Many of these survive as family souvenirs and were brought out in 1976 during bicentennial show-and-tell sessions.

As protection against potential night raids, blackouts, conducted by a special committee, insured that no lights shone from homes or buildings during tests. The high school initiated instruction in air-raid precautions. In the earlier stages of the war, periodic air-raid tests were conducted on warnings from the fire alarm siren—some were announced, others came as surprises. With the receding danger, however, air-raid drills were dropped and only the signal got its daily test of readiness. One other defense measure was initiated just after Christmas, 1941. Anxious to help and aware from overseas reports of the menace from submarines and saboteurs landed on lonely coasts from smallcraft and underwater vessels, some forty Rockport fishermen and lobstermen augmented by pleasure-boating yachtsmen formed a local Coast Guard Auxiliary.

The story of Rockport during World War II is best heard from those who lived through it. Written documentation is available in the microfilmed files of the *Gloucester Daily Times* and, so far as official matters were involved, in the annual town reports. With few exceptions, Rockport resembled countless other small American coastal towns in its actions and reactions throughout the period. The WPA ended its several vestigial programs in 1942. The depression was clearly over. More depressing were the war news; the draft calls; the mounting shortages; and the subsequent rationing of gasoline, meats, eggs, sugar, and fats. As extensions of the Washington Power center, the town had its local officers, to staff such groups as the committee on food production, the war price rationing board, the war emergency relief committee. An appropriate service flag was raised and an honor roll was created for the veterans. Occasional small gold star flags appeared in the windows of families bereft of sons or husbands.

Another flag of a different nature was raised over the Cape Ann Tool Company, one which inspired a sense of pride in the hearts of those who served in the shops of Pigeon Cove. It was the coveted U.S.

Navy "E for Excellence" pennant. Each employee also got an *E* as a pin to wear, and the newspapers gave full coverage to the honor given the plant and its staff.

Early in the struggle against the Axis both the national and local governments grappled with the future—for American optimism that there would somehow always be a Britain was far greater that there would always be an America. In 1943 a postwar public works commission was organized to provide employment for veterans as they returned from overseas and if they needed assistance. Even then, townspeople, too, were thinking of Rockport itself in the postwar era and set up a postwar planning commission. Some actions did not need to wait for an armistice.

Public employees were provided for as of 1943 by joining the Essex County retirement system for municipal workers. Courses were started at the high school to provide technical training, notably in radio, code, electricity, mechanics, preflight instruction, reconditioning for conservation, and touch-typing. The veritable explosion of paperwork assured anyone who could punch a typewriter a job. As townspeople looked into the more distant future still, they decided to make full-time provisions for kindergarten classes in their public schools. The WPA centers and volunteer classes had demonstrated the need and effectiveness of such activities beyond a doubt. In cooperation with the Massachusetts Department of Education and the War Food Administration a milk program was initiated throughout the school system at 2 cents for a half pint, and a hot-lunch program was put into effect at the high school. Lunches cost 10 cents each, and the cafeteria was reimbursed 4 cents by the WFA. Victory gardens were more productive in World War II, thanks to better agricultural techniques and the pressures from the government. Adults and youngsters alike shared a certain commendable vanity in swapping stories about their successes. Little was said about the occasional pigs raised in private to augment meat shortages and ration coupons. Luckily, the influenza epidemic of 1943 was mild in comparison with the infections of 1918.

As the war effort intensified and eventual victory seemed assured, the Armed Forces Educational Organization requested high schools to introduce preinduction courses. Rockport cooperated with classes for seniors and even juniors. Throughout the conflict the town schools had an exemplary record, beginning with intensified instruction in citizenship, responsibility for government, and information "to know

our allies better." The words "serve, save, conserve" became a motto.
Students worked hard at collecting paper, old clothing, shoes, furniture, even fats. The poor showing and heavy rejections appearing at induction examinations stimulated students of both sexes to devote extra attention to physical education. As in World War I, Rockport students of all ages rallied to support war bond drives and war savings stamp sales. In 1944 the state director of war finances complimented the schools on their responses. On the third anniversary of Pearl Harbor Day, December 7, 1944, Rockport High School students and alumni were paid a special tribute for the 276 of their ranks who had already entered the Armed Forces.

Once the momentum of the Allied drive up from the Mediterranean and across from Normandy got rolling, victory came sweetly. The Pacific theater was never as vivid to most townspeople, even those who had loved ones out there in the unknown islands of the Orient. Even before V-E Day, the American Legion dedicated an honor roll at Evans Field. By the end of the war, however, well over 525 Rockporters had left home for the service. Twelve of them gave their lives in the struggle: Harry E. Andrews, Carl E. Bannion, Robert Barrett, Vincent Charte, William Hakala, Arne Hautala, Leon W. Kantala, Donald F. MacEachery, George C. Mills, Glenn M. Rowe, Charles W. Sears, and George A. Sears.

By 7:00 P.M. on August 14, 1945, the town bells rang and all the whistles blew. President Truman announced that peace terms had been signed. A huge victory parade was organized with townwide participation by the elected officials and the American Legion and high school bands combined under the leadership of Harrison Fears and Herman Erwin. There was the local Massachusetts State Guard with Capt. Ralph Wilson, Lt. John Rapp, 2d Lt. Russell Scatterday, and Sgt. Elliot Grimes. Then came the Rockport Flotilla of the Coast Guard, the civil defense committee under Alvin Brown, Boy Scouts, Girl Scouts, Cub Scouts, Brownies, Council of Pocahontas—everyone. Those not in their organizational ranks followed in cars or on foot blowing horns. At last the war was over—except for sugar rationing, which continued until June 11, 1947!

Peace and War

Much was done in Rockport before the next war exacted its price; some of it involved the war just ended: the work of the veterans' rehabilitation committee and plans for a permanent memorial for the veterans, for example. As a headquarters for their activities the Veterans of Foreign Wars were allowed the use of the former fire and police station in Dock Square. An office of veterans' service was opened in 1946, but the Sixteenth Company of the 24th Massachusetts State Infantry was disbanded after the officers and enlisted men had been given certificates of merit. The town report of 1947 listed the veterans of both world wars. In 1953 Rockport dedicated twenty squares and intersections to its sons who had lost their lives during the two world wars. Signs were erected, each carrying a gold star and the name of the victim.

More of the town's toil was directed to civic matters. There were fresh efforts to improve zoning bylaws, building codes, and a long-range program to replace trees lost by storms and the blight attacking Rockport's stately elms. The Den-Mar Nursing Home expanded its facilities to aged residents generally. In 1947 a sewer extension relieved the contamination of the Front and Back beaches. Work was begun on a housing project. In the national election of 1944, the town had given Dewey 1,212 votes to 701 for President Roosevelt, and 1,437 to Saltonstall as against 383 to Corcoran for senator—totals which the *Times* called a "magnificent endorsement." As for liquor licensing, the ballots were 3 to 1 dry. Four years later, the town stuck by its guns on November 2, 1948, and went Republican more than 2 to 1 (1,401 to 649) against Truman. That spring the novelty of television when shown in the windows of the Mills' radio store attracted crowds even in the rain and tied up traffic on Railroad Avenue. Another traffic problem began on June 27 when St. Joachim's began services in its lovely, enlarged church on Broadway. It was formally dedicated on August 10 by Archbishop Cushing.

The schools of Rockport had made considerable progress during the depression years. Standardized tests revealed the need for improvement in teaching methods and textbooks. Guidance activities were instituted; prizes at graduation gave recognition to the industrious and imaginative students; physical examinations were made more meaningful at a time when social needs among the poor of Rockport were brought to the fore. One particular advance was the cooperative effort of the town, the PTA and the Legion band to provide for a proper high school band. By 1938 it had fifty students enrolled on Saturday mornings. Not much could be done during the war years, when other demands were levied on schools. The town was fortunate in not losing many of its teachers to better jobs.

Town on Sandy Bay

To provide rooms needed in Pigeon Cove, in 1945 the seventh and
eighth grades there were transferred to the high school building on
Broadway. With the end of the war a new and more realistic salary
scale was submitted which finally brought Rockport into line with
other Massachusetts school systems. In 1946 the school committee had
to face the largest enrollment in a decade and to begin planning for
extended facilities. The split between "progressive" and "conservative" theories of education widened. Efforts were made to have the
best of both approaches, but compromise was not easy. Two veterans
of school affairs retired at that period, Lindley I. Dean from the
committee and Superintendent Cottle. Between them they had thirty-
seven years' experience in town schools. As the decade drew to a close,
the town proved willing to spend funds on a summer recreational
program for its youth: swimming, baseball, softball, basketball, even
square dancing and movies. Less engaging was the inauguration of a
peacetime draft, registration for which commenced on August 30,
1948, in the chilly atmosphere of the intensifying cold war.

With 1949 came a campaign for new school buildings. For a time
proponents for regional development clamored for sending all
Rockport students to an expanded Cape Ann High School in Gloucester. The tax rate had climbed to $46 per thousand, and Route 128 was
foreseen as opening Rockport to a heavy immigration from "up the
line." One small indication of increased wheel traffic was the inauguration of driver instruction in 1950, when the Cape Ann Motor Company gave the town a Ford sedan with dual controls for use at the high
school. After a two-year struggle Rockporters finally capitulated to the
baby boom and in 1952 bought land for a new school at Jerden's Lane
and additional property for future expansion there. For the first time
graduation exercises were held for the eighth grade. On January 4,
1954, the new Community School was opened, after expenditures of
well over $100,000. That June the high school graduation drew over
five hundred people to the building.

With town school enrollments having topped the eight hundred
mark, there was need for a two-room addition to the Pigeon Cove
School by 1955, and a planning committee was created to study the
longer-range needs of the town. Some needs were met without much
expansion, such as a voice teacher, facilities for physical education for
the girls, occupational aptitude tests, and in 1955 Salk polio vaccine for
first-and-second-graders.

Even on the war front the Korean struggle made but a moderate impact on Rockporters as a whole. The year 1950 found residents occupied with domestic concerns and rewards. Water consumption had been rising so steadily that the annual meeting voted $40,000 for additional acreage for the watershed and another $9,000 to extend the park area between Pebble and Long beaches. By August the quarry pits off Granite Street were approved for use in water emergencies. On the social service front, the welfare department was reorganized, and the $127,000 housing development for veterans and their families was completed and christened Oak Circle. The Leander Haskins Hospital, not used by the town itself after 1920, was put up for sale with the money to be used for Rockport's needy going to the Addison Gilbert Hospital. The Boy Scout Hall on Mt. Pleasant Street was given a major overhauling. Accessibility to the whole town was heightened when the A. Piatt Andrew Bridge on Route 128 was completed in the autumn.

The board of trade took a mounting interest in town affairs, especially the activities of people with rooms to rent. "If people don't get their money's worth, they move on," was the warning. At T Wharf they undertook improvements to please sport fishing; one was a scale to weigh tunafish which would permit the fisherman to be photographed with his prize. Restrooms were provided for Dock Square. A plaque was unveiled on Motif No. 1, that "symbol of Rockport" of eighty years standing which had even won first prize at the Legion Convention during the Chicago World's Fair in 1933, thanks to the communal cooperation of so many Rockport artists back in the depression days. The board cooperated with the ten-window display featuring Rockport and arranged by Gilchrist's Department Store in Boston with a gung-ho motto: "Let's Go to Rockport."

The fourth annual Fourth of July parade lured "thousands" to town despite the rain, and civic-minded neighbors cleaned up half a ton of "lethal debris" from the Back Beach. A gift made possible the lighting of the Congregational church tower on a nightly basis. One proposal was launched in 1950 which never succeeded, despite repeated attempts from many lovers of the town: the purchase of the four to five acre property at Knowlton's Corner to become a town park. The post office lost its postmaster of fifteen years, William D. Powers, and townspeople that May lost their second daily home delivery of mail. Christmas mail cancellations reached 92,702 items.

Motif No. 1 float, product of local artistic talent, was driven to the 1933 American Legion convention in Chicago to capture first prize. (R. Scatterday)

One by one, Rockporters were called back into the military branches where they had served some years previously. Others were called up for the first time. Out on a battleship in the South Pacific, Richard Salo and Anthony Torrisi, both of Forest Street, met each other by chance. In March 1951 the *Times* started a weekly column, "Interesting Notes from Service Folks," and in April there was excitement when J. Alfred Paradis telephoned his mother from Formosa while on liberty from his ship. May brought "Buddy Poppy Day" and a flock of young schoolchildren to sell them. Recalling their own sacrifices, Legion members played host to ninety hospitalized veterans in June, and Tuck's Drug Store became the deposit center of the "Clothes for Korea Drive." Another veteran, Police Chief Jacob Perkio, returned to duty, but not from Korea—he had had a year of service with the FBI. Thanksgiving brought news that Pfc. Constance Green of the WAF had been chosen queen of her squadron, as well as bringing a photo to the *Times* of Pfc. Richard Wonson on duty in Germany. The Korean relief drive produced half a ton of clothing by the end of November. Unlike World War II, the Korean troubles produced minimal enthusiasm for civil defense activities. Occasional practice alerts were held, and blood-typing teams and blood drives did make

Centennial to Bicentennial

their needs felt. A July 1952 clambake at Knowlton's Field for 125 disabled Korean War veterans gave many townspeople their first direct experience with the war. Up above them on Pigeon Hill, that landmark—sea mark since 1713, was a US radar warning installation. Still higher up, in October, passed an airplane on a training mission. Thanks to carelessness in the aircraft some falling bullets hit five Rockport buildings. Thus, the town was under fire during the Korean War.

It was fire of other types, however, which fortunately kept local residents preoccupied in the second and third years of the far-off conflict. The board of trade continued its efforts to push the town. There were new "Welcome to Rockport" signs for the highways; the continued successful Motif No. 1 days; the institution of an up-to-date publication entitled *Rockport Anchor;* the opening of an information booth at Dock Square to dispense useful trade pamphlets, timetables, and the *Cape Ann Summer Sun.* The town received some welcome publicity for its increasingly popular tourist attraction in Pigeon Cove, the "Paper House" on upper Pigeon Hill Street, when it was featured on John Cameron Swasey's eye-catching TV program, "Caravan." Locally, Rockport made a breakthrough when in October 1952 Margaret E. Condon became the first woman from the town to be drawn for jury duty, at the superior court's civil session at Lawrence.

The Garden Club undertook to beautify the railroad station and succeeded in winning high editorial praise for its efforts. Also exceptionally beautiful were the five greenhouses of the Silva Brothers, which in April 1952 attracted over two thousand visitors. Less successful was Pigeon Cove's Village Improvement Society when it launched a drive for funds to renovate the Old Castle, the only truly historic building in Rockport open to the public and one destined to be placed on the National Register of Historic Buildings a quarter of a century later. For a time the VIS discussed publicly the need to sell the area it owned on Pigeon Hill as a picnic ground in order to secure the cash required at the Castle.

To improve traffic conditions in town the selectmen authorized one-way traffic on Main Street, and the park commission installed a boardwalk leading from Main Street, down beside the Granite Savings Bank (today's Toad Hall), and on to the Front Beach. Stickers were introduced to enable residents and their guests to have parking facilities for picnicking, bathing, and hiking on beaches and near the quarries. Perhaps it was such steps as these and others that earned for

the town its highway safety award for lack of fatal accidents, year after
year.

Further afield, in the 1950s and later Rockport received attention from its growing number of writers in residence. Pigeon Cove had had the William R. Benets and Mrs. George Demetrios ("Miss Burton"), while the South Village had Ruth Holberg, who published some thirty-five children's books between 1930 and 1975 as well as three popular cookbooks. As "Information Please" John Kieran moved into town, his fame and interests in local flora and fauna reached many nature lovers. The newspaper columns of John Cooley, written from his hilltop study on Pigeon Hill, reached as far as the West Coast and the Deep South—wherever North Shore readers took their papers.

It was during the Korean War period that Rockport began entertaining visitors from abroad, especially foreign students from the colleges of Greater Boston and the high school students sponsored by the Rotary Club, the American Field Service, and other internationally oriented exchange programs. Some eighty Italians in August 1952 were part of a pioneer project. American college students, of course, had spent their Easter holidays in Pigeon Cove and at the South End even before World War I. Wellesley, Smith, Dana Hall, and other girls schools sent many of their students to the rocky shores during a period of at least two decades—before the Florida beaches became so accessible by air.

Three Rockport structures in addition to the Old Castle called for attention during the 1950s. Two were rescued—one, thanks to the Rockport Community League, was the old high school on Broadway. It was taken over by the league in 1954 in cooperation with the planning board. "It will not be elaborate, but cheerful and convenient." The second structure saved was that of the first Congregational church, which was given a monumental rehabilitation during 1953-54, the first one in nearly eighty years. The one which was finally doomed was the massive old town hall, by then in sad need of a major restoration to insure its continued usability.

There were other strains put on the town during the 1950s and after. The chief one from the outside was the opening of Route 128, which occurred on July 4, 1953. Enthusiasts cried: "Every home on Cape Ann worth more tomorrow!" Their plan was to extend the highway from today's Blackburn Circle in Gloucester across the old Rockport road down to Nugent's Stretch. Opposition rose and the struggle became intense: "Keep Route 128 out of Rockport. Leave it where it is." There it has lain till today, but traffic began pouring into town, taxing roads, sidewalks, and above all the patience of countless residents. In one month (August 1953), the traffic monitor at the entrance to the town checked in 1,224 more cars than the year previously.

To the merchants, especially the crafts shops on Bearskin Neck and the restaurateurs in downtown Rockport, the new highway was a bonanza. Artists, galleries, silversmiths, the Folly Cove Designers all acquired new clients or at least admirers. Even the putative cooperage shop of James Babson on the way into (or out from Rockport) got a renovation and became a modest tourist attraction once the highway was opened. The possibility of linking Rockport and Gloucester on a single telephone connection at no extra cost in the form of a toll call but a small monthly increase on the bill was not sufficiently attractive to carry the voters of 1952 or 1953. Connections of another kind, and to the past not the present, were warmly appreciated by a small group of historically minded citizens. Work began in the autumn of 1953 in microfilming earlier Cape Ann newspapers. Another peaceful bit of continuity was the initiation in 1946 of a Christmas Nativity Pageant sponsored by the Rockport Art Association. Thirty years later, however, it too had become a major tourist attraction to draw late December shoppers toward the boutiques of Bearskin Neck.

On to 1976

In a somewhat curious way, the end of the war in Korea and the opening up of Route 128 marked the beginning of yet another epoch in Rockport's story. From the middle of the 1950s on, people returning there would quickly discover changes, many purely physical, others intangible but perhaps more significant. There was a new breeze blowing through the old town. Happily, it was not an ill wind, though at times it gusted sharply.

Among the physical improvements which would have been spotted by those coming to town for the annual Motif No. 1 days or the annual Christmas pageant were these. Parking meters on Main Street and other thoroughfares blossomed out in the summer of 1954, to the amusement of cartoonist Dahl of the *Boston Herald*. By 1972, the wiser visitors would have taken advantage of the "Peripheral Parking Lot" at the edge of town and ridden in on the shuttle bus provided. Too few

drivers were, nor are they yet, wise. Drivers venturing into the conges-
tion of Broadway could not fail to observe the attractive renovations
made to the Community House at the cost of two annual budget
appropriations of $9,000 each in 1953 and 1954. By 1960 people
reaching the top of Great Hill would have spotted the new town garage,
erected to hold equipment from the highway, park, water, and tree
departments. People coming in through Pigeon Cove after early 1967
would have found the attractive and helpful Tarr memorial clock,
placed at the heart of the North Village (on a granite shaft from the
Johnson-Persson quarry) by Ella B. Tarr in memory of her public-
spirited husband, Daniel.

To those irrepressible thirteen who graduated from Rockport High
School in 1913 and continued to hold reunions and keep an eye out for
"our town," the opening of a new high school on lower Broadway in
1926 was indeed a "happening." When they began to hear that the
"new" high school was old and a new "new" one must be built, they did
indeed sense "Time's winged chariot." Plans were approved on April
11, 1960, for a new junior-senior high school off Jerden's Lane. Construction commenced on March 13, 1961, and in 1962 the sprawling
building was opened, serving not only students but many community
needs, including adult education classes, and town meetings, and the
great bicentennial observance in 1976.

A decade after the high school opened, Rockport joined fifteen
neighboring communities in providing what it could not hope to offer
alone, a well-equipped, properly staffed vocational school, for grades
nine through twelve. Classes commenced in 1974. Although no public
school activities were involved in the project, a fair number of Rockport residents began profiting from the opportunity of participating in
the Montserrat School of Visual Art, which opened in Beverly in 1971.

In 1973 the school department launched a publication called
Rockport Schools in Action. Coupled with a voluntary program in sex
education for ninth-graders and a mounting demand for a youth
center, youth counseling, jobs for the young, for means to counter the
influence of drugs invading the town, and the mood of indifference if
not rebellion characterizing the "Age of Aquarius" the town had concerns for the future as it reached the bicentennial.

Then, too, the post-Korea decades had projects which failed to
materialize despite well-intentioned efforts. The breakwater, long
since divorced from the once alluring Harbor of Refuge, suffered the
buffetings of storms and hurricanes. In April 1954 an attempt was

made to repair what had survived the lashings of the decades, but Washington remained adamantly negative. Eleven years later the issue was raised again; again Army Engineers—this time in person— refused to recommend funding. Unwilling to be refused, a group of hopefuls surfaced the matter, though not the breakwater, in the spring of 1972. In May the Army Engineers sent three representatives to town to try to explain once and for all why the breakwater would not be maintained by them.

Air pollution was the source of complaints by 1960, and the buses were singled out for spreading noxious gas fumes in "the narrow and house-lined parts of Main Street." It was not until April 1970 that burning was forbidden at the town dump (alias sanitary landfill). Years of planning resulted in the construction of a sewage treatment plant during the 1970s. It, too, began emitting noxious odors. It would take far more than the designation of the lantana as the "official" town flower (a decision of the boards of selectmen and trade taken in May 1961) to offset foul air in parts of Rockport.

Two final irritations rubbed many Rockporters the wrong way during the 1970s. Attempts to halt the town's water fluoridation program stirred up considerable response in 1970. Prolonged agitation against scuba divers and their activities, above and below the surface, brought many complaints, arrests, and a partial ban. The issue was still unresolved by the bicentennial year.

Periodically, transportation has been a source of countless headaches to Rockporters, even more of them once Route 128 was opened to traffic. The advent of a car in every garage, plus heaven alone knows how many second and third cars, meant a fall-off in passengers for buses and trains. The bankrupt state of the Boston and Maine, successive infusions of public monies, takeovers and reorganizations in the metropolitan Boston system, and strikes over hiring policies and wages produced decades of remarks from older Rockporters like this: "My grandfather rode on the first train that came to town back in 1861. I guess my grandchildren and I will ride on the last one." For a period in early 1965 it seemed as if that prediction might come true. For a period in 1974 the Arab oil embargo and all the restrictions it imposed made many townspeople wonder how much longer they might even drive their cars.

Housing, ever a problem for many townspeople, went through an explosive period in Rockport after World War II ended. Construction was still flourishing when the bicentennial arrived. The veterans' housing project built at Oak Circle in 1950 was closed out as a quasi-public entity in July 1965 when its twelve units were sold to the veteran family occupants and the original grants were paid back to the town and the state. In 1963 Rockport residents watched with satisfaction the construction of a housing project for the elderly, located on Poole's Lane adjacent to today's Whistlestop shopping center area. An additional forty dwelling units were agreed upon in 1966. Rockport had built an eighty-bed nursing home, the Den-Mar, on South Street where the town farm had once been. Even the Granite Savings Bank had a housing problem, which it solved satisfactorily by moving to new quarters on Broadway in October 1970.

Housing was not the problem which led three of Rockport's churches, the Congregational, Episcopal, and Methodist, to form a union Sunday school in October 1970. Later the Baptists and Universalist youngsters participated in the challenge to meet the secularization and changes of the age. By the bicentennial, older townspeople recalled their own childhood days when a single church had one hundred or more "scholars" in the Sabbath schools learning their "Tiny Texts" week by week and striving for perfect attendance even at that tender an age. Times had changed.

Rockport had a fair share of shocks in the post-Korean years, including its first fatal airplane crash. A navy Sky Raider out of Quonset, Rhode Island, fell in flames on Marmion Way in July 1954, killing the twenty-four-year-old pilot before the eyes of his horrified twenty-one-year-old fiancée at the Seaward Inn. There was probably more curiosity than shock when on April 3, 1960, the fire department burned down the surviving remains of the Haskins Hospital on Poole's Hill—that place which had symbolized so much for Rockporters concerned about health services back in the our-town age. There was much nostalgia evoked by the burning of another landmark, the Turk's Head Inn, in the summer of 1970. But nostalgia, shock, curiosity, and even anger combined when in 1970 the town had a chance to purchase

Knowlton's Point for $440,000. The price had been $14,000 in 1950. On both occasions and subsequently, too, the failure to act and save the property from exploitation can be regarded only as near tragedy.

Even sporting life shifted its emphasis, partly at least because of the easy accessibility to Boston Garden, Fenway Park, and the great world beyond, once television became popular. The town's passion for baseball gradually cooled, but it probably kept warm longer than it might have because of the unquenchable spirit of artist Aldro T. Hibbard who, when not painting, was laboring on the park commission or for the town team. Its destinies he guided for over thirty years. At Evans Field on June 16, 1957, Rockport staged a memorable Hibbard Day, attended by many old-time local greats and a bevy of out-of-towners. John Kieran gave his view that academician "Hib" would have preferred immortality at Cooperstown, New York, to a niche in the Louvre. The team never quite recovered from the loss of Hibbard's magic once he retired in 1958, though attempts were made by George Walima and Dick Travers in 1964 and with modest success. Hibbard's death in December 1971 was mourned by Rockporters of many interests, as had been the death of Harrison Cady the year before. The "Master of Bugdom" had been beloved by Rockporters of all ages from before World War I.

The institution of the Little League provided an outlet for older enthusiasts and a challenge for Rockport schoolboys. Skating became increasingly attractive. Hockey games could not be played successfully on the mill pond, so 1971 brought the start of a move to build a proper rink at the Evans Field playground. By 1973 some fifteen students and teachers were taking scuba-diving lessons, a hobby far from popular with many townspeople.

International awareness increased among residents as the world shrank and people went traveling in ever increasing numbers. Korea still hung in the background. As late as 1960 schoolchildren were asked to bring in outgrown clothes to be sent to the Pusan area. The Cuban Missile Crisis of 1962 briefly stirred up the town's civil defense office. The Peace Corps held some workshops at the Hotel Emerson in 1970, and the Pigeon Cove chapel continued its international student hospitality program on into the bicentennial period. The creeping malady of Vietnam produced, like the Civil War in the United States, men and families who did what they felt was their duty—some to participate in the conflict militarily, others to protest. The town had several members of the Cape Ann Concerned Citizens, who registered their objec-

The Sewall-Scripture House was built in 1832 by Levi Sewall, president of the Pigeon Hill Granite Company, with stone from his own quarry. It was sold by his descendants to the Sandy Bay Historical Society in 1957. (SBHS)

tions through a newsletter called *Soundings.* In April 1971 about fifty Rockporters went to Washington to protest the war in Vietnam and American involvement in the conflict.

As of May 1, 1960, technology provided direct long-distance dialing to telephone users in Rockport; another number was put upon the minds of unenthusiastic postal users when Rockport became Rockport 01966 in the last month of 1965. In 1962 the once reliable town clock was electrified and became subject to the whims of power failures and distant repair services. It was also a new technology which led to the formation of the Rockport Twine and Rope Company. It moved into the defunct isinglass factory on Railroad Avenue in 1957 and began producing nylon warp for lobster pots, twine nets, and other products.

An atmosphere of festivity was often apparent, especially to those people who stayed in town for more than a few days. The concerts of the Community Chorus drew more singers and still larger audiences. Of later years much of the popularity surrounded the group's engaging conductor, Sonja Dahlgren Pryor. A comparable enthusiasm lured players and listeners to the ambitious programs of the Cape Ann Symphony Orchestra. Square dancing on Saturday evenings at the Art

Centennial to Bicentennial

Association enlivened an already lively place, especially when caller Joe Perkins was giving the orders. Sporadic Old Home Weeks brought many former residents back to Rockport for the nostalgia evoked by those imaginative events with their house tours, garden visits, concerts, demonstrations, and parties. To art lovers there was the joy of the retrospective exhibition arranged on the fiftieth anniversary of the Art Association by William and Telka Beal. The Maddocks Gallery opened a new horizon in July 1970, and in August special tributes were presented to the three surviving charter members, Cirino, Hibbard, and Kitty Parsons Recchia.

Local government, too, was in for changes. Although there was no move to "turn the rascals out," the board of selectmen was increased from three to five members in 1960, and voters felt it necessary to engage a director of public works. Predictably, Rockporters had gone overwhelmingly for Eisenhower when he ran in presidential elections. Not so predictable was the vote on November 8, 1960; yet like Manchester and Essex, townspeople voted better than 2 to 1 for Richard Nixon over native son John F. Kennedy.

Mother Goose sculpture by Richard Recchia is now in Rockport's Carnegie Library.

Town on Sandy Bay

Rockport affection for its past was manifested on many occasions in the 1950s and afterward. Some of the projects undertaken were minor, such as the Boy Scouts' painting the two town cannon outside the Community House and on the Congregational church green. Far more loving was the energy expended to rescue the town's horsedrawn hearse, purchased in 1836, and saved by a heartwarming campaign sparked by Reinhard Speck and Barbara Marshall in 1962.

The Historical Society itself moved. In 1957 it took over the imposing granite Sewall-Scripture House built in 1832; there it enjoyed more appropriate quarters for its remarkably fine collections. Yet by the bicentennial period it, too, was fairly bursting with materials and all but desperate for exhibition and storage space. In 1967 the original six volumes of memorabilia assembled between 1820 and 1870 by Ebenezer Pool were "rescued" from a trunk in an antique shop and given to the Historical Society. They contain much local history and are among the town's most precious possessions. Members of the society warmly supported the republication of Babson's *History of Gloucester* and participated in the landmark picture history of Rockport produced in 1975.

Attempts to raise the intellectual horizons of Rockporters were numerous in the post-Korean War years. In 1956, for example, an organization was created to augment the services of the town's two libraries. Since its inception the Friends of the Library has done yeoman service through purchasing special collections, a film projector, and—most popular—a Xerox reproduction machine. They also cooperated in the acquisition and subsequent display in the children's department, itself a product of the post-Korean era, of sculptor Richard Recchia's delightful *Mother Goose*. A handsome bequest from Nathan Greene made possible the 1963 addition to the Carnegie Library, so badly overcrowded. By the bicentennial, however, more space was urgently being sought.

An attempt to convert the former Straitsmouth Coast Guard Station into a "Land's End Cultural Center" and offer on a nonprofit basis seminars, lectures, round-table discussions, and the like, failed after the season of 1965 because of "apathy." On the other hand, that year the Sandy Bay Historical Museum checked in 752 visitors. Apathy was not the reason the once lively Rug and Quilt Club disbanded—at least its members were still full of energy. To their regrets, however, younger women failed to be attracted to quilt-making on a regular, group session basis.

Bearskin Neck, B.T. (before tourists) about 1922. Sail loft is at extreme left, the old Washington Tarr Tavern left center, and fish houses at the right. (Hillier)

Other horizons were laid open to anyone interested when in the autumn of 1965, the conservation commission achieved its fund-raising goal of $12,000 and acquired still another acre of precious property at the top of Pigeon Hill. The ski trail built on the north side of the Leander Haskins property in January 1967 added another dimension to life on the Rockport slopes. In 1967, too, the town purchased for $4,000 from the Boston and Maine the twenty acres known as the Loop Pond, where trains once turned around to be headed correctly. Down in the valley, so to speak, thanks to alert moves at the outset and to years upon years of "sweat, toil, and tears"— perhaps even some blood, too—Rockport and its visitors can enjoy the Millbrook Meadow with all its waterfalls, brooks, greensward, trees, bushes, flowers, playing area, and granite reminders of the town's history. In 1938 the Allen Chamberlains, the Garden Club, and a deeply motivated committee raised some $1,500 to purchase the area for park purposes. There was staged the bicentennial project, "The Rock in Rockport," inspired and organized by Lura H. Phillips and her dedicated crew of talented exhibitors. There, too, continue to be held many of the town's more attractive programs.

Town on Sandy Bay

Bearskin Neck, W.T. (with tourists) in 1975. Extensive renovations and additions to the Washington Tarr Tavern and fish houses are readily apparent. (GDT)

Two intellectual challenges were offered to Rockporters in the early 1970s. One survives and has become a center for so many townspeople interested in reading, ecology, history, and—in the summer—storytelling for children. The Toad Hall Book Store, a non-profit operation, commenced business in May 1972 in the skillfully adapted Granite Savings Bank building across from the Old Sloop church. The other was a newspaper, the *Rockport Eagle,* first published on January 15 by Mr. and Mrs. Frank Hurnowicz. It drew on several local writing talents, including Mae Heslin, Elizabeth O'Toole, and Ruth Holberg, and it published superb photographs by Merton Webb and J. P. Johansson, one of which, "The Leaning Lamp Post at Rockport," appeared in the international edition of *Life.* In March 1972 the *Eagle* was sold to Walter and Lydia Priest, but in 1974 it followed other, previous Rockport newspapers into oblivion.

Preservation and all its allied activities came to the fore at this period in Rockport's corporate life. Having secured the former Rockport Granite Company's pier in 1956, the town demolished its Victorian town hall of 1869, replacing it by a functional but characterless brick one in November 1957. By 1960 the community had formed an historic district study committee. For more than a decade Dr. William D. Hoyt and Mr. Homer G. Orne, both of the Historical Society, and Town Clerk Esther Johnson persisted in their efforts to lead the town into a more active role in preservation. The acquisition of Lumber Wharf in 1973 by a town meeting decision was followed by the purchase of Middle Wharf in 1975. Wise pressure was applied by the conservation commission to make an inventory of all available land before it was snatched up by developers for building.

A flurry of well-directed activity succeeded in getting the north lighthouse on Thacher's Island declared an "Historic Landmark." Financing the preservation was to be another matter. As the bicentennial drew near, the historical commission in 1973 undertook the mandatory survey of the town's old houses and historic sites. This massive effort, requiring countless hours from truly dedicated volunteer workers, was to lead to the creation of the Rockport Historic District Commission and its commissioners, Mallory Lash, chairman. The project encountered rough waves and headwinds for several months and from varying groups. Preservation of another variety was inaugurated in the 1970s by Selectman Ann Fisk, who by the bicentennial year had transformed a wasteful community into one remarkably aware of the need to salvage paper, bottles, and even cans for recycling purposes.

A group called Citizens for Rockport began work in 1973 studying the broader question of whither Rockport. From those efforts came occasionally bitter encounters between the elements of the town who were still, like the editors of the *Review*, "Boom Rockport" believers and those who, to judge from a survey taken in February 1974, were against increased tourism, motel construction, condominium building, and expansion of shops. By 1976 there emerged a consciousness that fundamental decisions affecting the town would soon have to be taken. For a few days, people drew back that bicentennial weekend in 1976. Rockporters of many backgrounds pondered over their "pleasant town by the sea," as the compilers of their earlier history had described it in 1888.

The town had observances of many types. Among them was the series arranged by Spiran Lodge, reflecting the area's Scandinavian heritage. There was the concert of music written in America during the lifetime of George Washington, programmed by Lois Steele Clapp and members of the town's musical societies. There was the unforgettable eighteenth-century Sunday-go-to-Meeting service at the first church, presided over by the Reverend Mr. Cameron Borton, at which a descendant of both Richard Tarr and Ebenezer Cleaveland read excerpts from the latter's sermons. There was a Sandy Bay Yacht Club boat procession, a week-long exhibition of the "Port in Rockport," a military reenactment by the Sandy Bay Sea Fencibles under Scott Lesch, and the rousing Glorious Fourth Parade by the Firemen's Association.

On the anniversary itself, the Sandy Bay Historical Society mounted a vast special "town meeting" in the high school gymnasium. During that long-to-be-remembered program, Rockporters were told how independence had come to their community two centuries before, and they heard the Declaration of Independence read, line by line, by members from every school class and every society in town. At the conclusion they filed past the original record book and saw that Declaration so painstakingly copied out in a bold, still clear hand. They were reminded that in 1776 their predecessors had stood up in the meeting-house and cast their votes for freedom by walking so that everyone could see how they believed. And as Rockporters in 1976 turned to face their nation's third century and their town's fourth, they heard the advice given to the first settlers in 1628: "Be of good courage, go on, and do worthily."

ADDITIONAL READING

Beginning with the centennial souvenir program of 1940, which regrettably had a number of errors, Rockport has received considerable attention in recent years. Parts of the following books deal with the town, the first with distinction: Melvin T. Copeland and Elliott C. Rogers, *The Saga of Cape Ann* (Freeport, 1960); Herbert A. Kenny, *Cape Ann: Cape America* (Philadelphia, 1971); and the Junior League of Boston's *Along the Coast of Essex County* (Boston, 1970).

There have been successive issues of the board of trade's annual *Rockport Anchor* and their attractive *This Is Rockport*. The Bearskin Neck Association produces "Historic Bearskin Neck," while for art lovers are the detailed catalogues of the Rockport Art Association. The board of trade published in 1968 an outstanding photographic booklet by J. P. Johansson, *Rockport Thru the Seasons*.

The town's best-known landmark, Motif No. 1, was well covered by Eleanor C. Parsons, "Just a Humble Fish House," *Yankee Magazine* (July 1969): 76-77, 150-51. Another beloved landmark, Miss Susie Mae Pettingill, was the subject of Ray Kierman's warm portrait, "Big Enough to Love the Flag," *Yankee Magazine* (June 1969): 141-44. In addition to his newspaper columns and his brochures on the granite industry, the Village Improvement Society, and the Cape Ann Tool Company, John Cooley wrote about a town horse, Kate, and her owner who carried sightseers around the shore for years in a delightful booklet, *Rockport Hobby Horse* (1970).

The 1970s saw two praiseworthy efforts to produce a Rockport newspaper, the *Rockport Eagle* and the *Rockport Horizon.* Regrettably, neither was able to survive long.

Of much worth is *Planning for the Future of Rockport* (Cambridge, 1974).

AFTERWORDS

Of Appreciation

T HE GRAVE is indeed a private
place, as Andrew Marvell long
ago observed; but digging up
the past for local history is an undeniably public pursuit. Since ferret-
ing out facts for this volume was notably expedited by a veritable
platoon of perspicacious co-operators, the author welcomes an opportunity to express in type (and so for posterity as well as for his contemporaries) his debt to each of them. At the head of this list are his patient
fellow members of the Rockport Town History Committee: Margaret
D. Brenner, Myrtle L. Cameron, Robert L. Dixon, Alice Mae Heslin,
William D. Hoyt, Esther E. Johnson, Homer G. Orne, Lura H. Phillips,
and Margery M. Story. With that company should be included three
others who for personal considerations regrettably withdrew but only
after making their contributions to the corporate project: Ann L. Fisk
(the Committee's ebullient first chairman), Elizabeth O'Toole, and
Eleanor C. Parsons.

His gratitude is extended next to three professors: Bernard Bailyn
of Harvard, Robert L. Dixon of the University of Michigan (emeritus),
and William Parker of Yale. Their initial endorsements of this projected account provided the nails, so to speak, without which the critical
shoe might well have been lost. That all-important shoe was the generous grant made to the author by the National Endowment for the
Humanities. Without those funds which helped underwrite typing
(and retyping), research assistance, xeroxing of rare documents, du-
plication of drafts for Committee study, supplies, and travel outlays for
innumerable trips to Salem, Boston, Cambridge, and one to

Washington, this rider-author would surely have been lost and with him at least this particular history of Rockport. Even more certain would have been the loss of its publication without the prudent, sympathetic recommendations of two successive Rockport Finance Committees and the tangible acts of faith recorded by town meeting voters in 1977 and 1979.

Liberal access to documents of numerous types was granted to the author and/or his research associates at the Massachusetts State Archives, the New England Historic Genealogical Society, the Athenaeum, and the Public Library—all in Boston, at the Harvard University Library in Cambridge, and at the National Archives and Library of Congress in Washington. Mining the lodes of historical ore in the deposits of the Essex Institute at Salem became a joy, thanks to Associate Librarian Robinson Murray III and Mrs. Arthur R. Norton, the Institute's encyclopedic Reference Librarian.

In Gloucester, hospitable aid was magnanimously extended at the Sawyer Free Library by Stillman Hilton, Director, and Elizabeth Roland, Reference Librarian, as well as at the City Clerk's Office. In the former rest shelves upon shelves of nearly unique newspapers stretching back to 1828. In the vaults of the latter are those pearls without price, the original records of Cape Ann. Without access to both resources no significant investigations into the area's past could have been effected. Also at Gloucester, Rockport's *alma mater* in the literal sense, were the unfailing services so genially preferred, by Carrie Benham and Dorothy Norton at the Cape Ann Historical Association.

At Rockport itself are the town's own official records, freely provided by Town Clerk Frederick Frithsen and Nancy Carlson, numerous microfilms and printed documents made available by Librarian Stephen Rask, and the treasure-hoard of the Sandy Bay Historical Society, presided over by veteran Curator William Hoyt. Many town organizations furnished helpful background data, and several individuals cheerfully shared family papers, especially diaries and letters. The Committee is confident, however, that far more personal material remains to be uncovered and reported on by future probers, a compelling task, for in the last analysis history, as a sage Briton remarked, is "chaps."

To a few other chaps and to many other women the author and his Committee owe enduring obligations. On the lengthy roster of researchers deserving thanks, Nelda Wright takes precedence for her persistence in scrutinizing reels of microfilm, shelves of brittle newspapers, and rows of town reports and directories. Other stalwarts to whom the author is happy to express public gratitude are: Christine Bonne, Kenneth Brown, Catherine Calabria, Myrtle Cameron, Sandy Crawford, Warren Downie III, Julia Fitzpatrick, Deborah Goodwin, Clark and Lucy Heath, John Lane, Eric Mears, Homer and Sara Orne, Roland Peterson, Ingrid Snelson, and Jo-Ann White. Five people who made contributions to clarifying the manuscript at various stages were Diane Harrington, Garcia Kimball, Thelma Steen, Frances Woodland, and Peggy Wong.

From the beginning to the end and all through the agonizing in-betweens there was Anne Louise Medico. Her adroitness in organizing myriads of manuscript notes, her sagacity in deciphering hundreds of sheets of handwritten texts, crammed with arrows, asterisks, inserts, overstrikes, rewrites, deletions, and afterthoughts; her dexterity and dispatch in churning out nearly flawless copy; and above all her un-wavering patience, gentle humor, and inspiriting encouragement in a very real sense made this book also hers.

On Sources

No attempt was undertaken to include a bibliography with this volume. Generally, the narrative indicates the sources from which materials were drawn. Because of the care taken to check original documents wherever possible, a number of errors which previously appeared in print have been corrected here. Most chapters are fol-lowed by a few suggestions for additional reading for anyone in-terested in pursuing selected topics further. Many more can be had from Gibson's revised and enlarged (1978) *Bibliography of Cape Ann Literature,* originally prepared by Robert F. Brown.

Primary sources for a history of Rockport, of course, include the manuscript records of Gloucester from its inception in 1642 down to 1840. From then to the Bicentennial period, when this story termi-nates, there are the official records of the Town of Rockport, both manuscript and as printed in town reports. The records of the Sandy Bay Parish, and of the area's only church until well into the nineteenth century, are fundamental. Regrettably, few local personal papers of any kind prior to the last century still survive. Furthermore, Cape Ann published no newspapers before late 1827, and Rockport itself had none prior to March 1872.

Fortunately, the six volumes of memorabilia jotted down by Ebenezer Pool—though occasionally contradictory—have been preserved at the Sandy Bay Historical Society. Lemuel Gott's "Centennial Address," John J. Babson's three volumes of local history, and the efforts of John W. Marshall and his colleagues have all been salvaged for posterity through publication. Happily, too, numerous Cape Ann records and newspapers have been microfilmed during the last two decades. Say to say, however, none of the Rockport papers has been so rescued and by now no complete file remains of any of the first ones. As a public service an attempt should be made at the earliest possible opportunity to film those which do exist.

Nearly three centuries now make up the long, rich history of Rockport. Documentary evidence of that fascinating heritage is unfortunately scattered in the Town Hall, the Library, the Historical Society, the churches, lodges, clubs, and in countless family attics. Too much of it has already been lost, most of it is being poorly protected. To safeguard its legacy for those who shall come hereafter, Rockport would do well to establish a central, fireproof, climatically controlled town archive, for "the past is prologue."

The town is indeed fortunate in already having a very extensive, private photographic archive. Down the decades Dr. William D. Hoyt has assembled an extraordinary array of original photographs, prints, and pictures of Rockport as well as adjacent areas. To it he has added copies of items lent by many other collectors. Thus, by now few communities possess so comprehensive a visual record. Dr. Hoyt and his colleagues produced the popular Bicentennial *Rockport as it Was . . . A Book of Pictures* in 1975. For 1980 the Rockport National Bank issued his Rockport Historical Calendar. It is from the Hoyt Collection that the Committee gratefully drew nearly all of the illustrations for this volume, thereby reaffirming the adage that one picture is worth a thousand words.

Those who kindly contributed pictures and other items to illustrate this volume are: John F. Borge, George Caffrey, Cape Ann Tool Company, Gloucester Daily Times, Mrs. John Heslin, Pingree Hillier, William D. Hoyt, Mrs. Elizabeth Knowlton, Massachusetts Archives, William Niemi, Mr. and Mrs. Story Parsons, Miss Cynthia Peckham, Mrs. Stanley N. Phillips, David E. Poole, Rockport Art Association, Rockport National Bank, Sandy Bay Historical Society, Russell Scatterday, Mrs. William P.C. Smith, Carl L. Swan, Village Improvement Society, Miss Dorothy H. Wires.

Afterwords

The Town History Committee is particularly grateful to four corporate donors: the Cape Ann Bank and Trust Company, the Cape Ann Tool Company, the Granite Savings Bank, and the Rockport National Bank. Their generosity made possible the addition of four color reproductions of works by four artists so intimately associated with Rockport: Aldro T. Hibbard, G. Tucker Margeson, W. Lester Stevens, and Anthony Thieme.

Appendices

SOME ROCKPORT ROSTERS

IN THE COURSE OF PREPARING this history, the author repeatedly came upon lists of Rockporters and, before 1840, of residents of Sandy Bay Parish and today's Pigeon Cove. Believing that such documents would be helpful to genealogists and family historians, he commenced transcribing them. Copies have been added to the collections of the Sandy Bay Historical Society and the Carnegie Library. A selection of these rosters follows herewith.

Those who are searching for earlier Cape Ann "roots" should consult the three published volumes of *Vital Records of Gloucester, Massachusetts, to the End of the Year 1849* and the one volume supplementary *Vital Records of Rockport*. Microfilm copies of the decennial Federal Census returns from 1790-1900 are locally available at the Sandy Bay Historical Society, with the exception of the census for 1890. (Data for that year for nearly the entire nation were destroyed by fire before they could be transcribed.) For post-independent Rockport, the vaults of the Town Clerk's Office at the Town Hall include birth, marriage, death, voting, assessment, cemetery, and various other, more specialized lists. The published town reports provide much useful information as to who was doing what and when from 1840 onwards. Comparably helpful are the annual School Committee reports. Rockport church records are often informative sources, as are such fraternal and club registers as have survived. Political party registrations are occasionally accessible. Far fewer are commercial books and payrolls. Published records of all corporations in the Commonwealth of Massachusetts provide considerable insights into the numerous business undertakings of Cape Ann and Rockport from the early 1800s on. Military records are extensive and available but for the most part were not maintained on a geographical basis.

For future probers of the past it would be of great help, if anyone coming across other lists of Rockporters who were members of organizations or participants in events would deposit the original documents or copies of them at the Historical Society or the Library.

In reading and transcribing lists of names, it is important to keep in mind that up until comparatively recent times people often spelled freely. Even proper names were written in a variety of ways, sometimes by the people themselves and often by others. From their first appearance in the area, for instance, Pools were spelled with and without an "e." Tarr was spelled with one "r" and with two and at times with an "o" instead of an "a." Frequently abbreviations and nicknames appear. Mark Twain once quipped that he had no use for anyone who could spell a word in only one way.

An alphabetical list of the 32 Petitioners from "the easterly part of the First Parish in Gloucester called the Cape" who in May, 1738, requested "winter preaching" in their own district. This is the earliest known list of Sandy Bay residents. All but the three names marked with an asterisk repeated the request on December 20, 1738.

Jabez Baker	James Hardy	Jonathan Pool
Jabez Baker, Jr.	Samuel Harris	Joshua Pool
Samuel Clark	Thomas Harris	Jonathan Swift*
Elias Cook*	Thomas Harris, Jr.	Benjamin Tarr
John Davis	Joshua Kendal	Caleb Tarr
Samuel Davis	Eleazer Lurvey	Richard Tarr
Thomas Dresser	James MacCoy	Samuel Tarr
Ebenezer Grover	Moses Platts	William Tarr
Edmund Grover*	Caleb Pool	William Tarr, Jr.
Eleazer Grover	Ebenezer Pool	Henry Witham
Nehemiah Grover	John Pool	

Names on the First Provincial and Town Tax Assessment Lists for the Sandy Bay Parish / October, 1754

Name	Total Tax		
Baker, Anna		Pool, Caleb	2. 0.10
(exec. for J. Baker, Jr.)	£ 1.19.11	Pool, Ebenezer	2. 8. 0
Baker, Jabez	. 5.	Pool, Francis	. 5. 9
Butler, Stephen	. 5. 9	Pool, John	2. 1. 7
Davis, Samuel, Capt.	. 9. 2	Pool, Jonathan	1. 1. 0
Davis, Samuel, 4th	.11. 8	Pool, Stephen	.13. 6
Dresser, Thomas	.17. 3	Row, John	.14. 2
Foster, Nathan	. 0.	Shelton, Ephraim	. 5. 9
Goss, Thomas	. 5.11	Shelton, Israel	. 5. 9
Grover, Ebenezer	.15. 3	Tarr, Benjamin	1. 8. 4
Grover, Edmund, Elder	.17. 4	Tarr, Benjamin, Jr.	. 7. 4
Grover, Nehemiah	.13.10	Tarr, Caleb	
Grover, Nehemiah, Jr.	. 5. 9	(exec. of Estate of)	.16.10
Harris, Samuel	. 6. 8	Tarr, Jacob	. 5. 9
Harris, Thomas	. 2. 2	Tarr, James	. 5.11
Harris, Thomas, Jr.	. 5. 9	Tarr, Joshua	. 5. 9
Hobson, John	. 5. 9	Tarr, William	. 7. 4
Lane, Job	. 5. 9	Thurston, Joseph, Jr.	. 6. 5
Lurvey, Eleazer	. 7. 1	Vincent, Thomas (Finson)	. 5.11
Norwood, Joshua	. 0.	Williams, Daniel	. 5. 9
Norwood, Joshua, Jr.	. 5. 9	Witham, Henry	1.14. 1
Parsons, James, Jr.	. 6. 8	Wonson, Samuel	. 5. 9

During the Revolutionary War men from today's Rockport served in many companies. The majority of the Sandy Bay soldiers enlisted under Captain John Rowe. From the several surviving rolls it appears that at various times between May 29, when enlistment began, and the end of the year, when the company as such was dissolved, some 69 men were accredited to the contingent, some for a very brief period only. Note that of the 66 who allegedly fought at Bunker Hill, six did not even enlist until a month or more after that battle. The name of "Ensign" Isaac Pool does not appear on any list of the Rowe Company whatsoever.

The alphabetical list which follows is based on the officially accepted muster and pay roll from August 1, 1775. To that data has been added the age of the soldier at the time of enlistment, his complexion and height if given on an incomplete muster roll at the Cape Ann Historical Association. Since each soldier was allowed travel pay of one penny per mile, the figure following his date of enlistment places his home as at either Sandy Bay (40 miles), the "Farms" area (38 miles), or Gloucester town (35 miles). Sergeant William Davis(s)on (not Daylon) was given an allowance for only 8 miles, so was apparently not living on Cape Ann then. Two men, a William "Urqhart" and John "Kendol," signed for advance pay on June 28, 1775, but do not appear on any other Rowe Company list. Hence, they are not among the 66 given below. Searchers should be particularly thorough about checking variant name spellings; for example, the family name "Kendall" turns up in 22 variations in the military records of the Massachusetts Archives.

> Allen, Jacob June 3 35 (24) dark 5'6"
> Atkins, Obadiah June 13 35 (17) dark 5'2"
> Averill, David May 29 35 (23) dark 5'4"
> Brooks, Josiah (killed in battle) May 29 40
> Butler, Daniel May 29 40 (16) light 5'6"
> Butman, Eleazer May 29 40 (29) light 5'5"
> Clark, Henry June 12 40 (21) dark 5'8½"
> Clark, John May 29 40
> Clark, Samuel May 29 35 (40) brown 5'10"
> Cleaveland, Eben'r, 2nd lieutenant May 19 40 (21)
> Crage, David June 1 35 (19) light 5'6½"
> Davis, Benjamin, drummer May 29 40
> Davis, Dominicus May 29 40 (21) dark 5'5½"
> Davison, William, sergeant June 15 8
> Doyl, Daniel June 1 35 (35) dark 5'6½"
> Dresser, Joseph June 7 40 (25) dark 5'9"
> Dresser, Richard May 29 40 (20) light 5'7"
> Dresser, Thomas May 29 40 (37) dark 5'10½"
> Edes, Thomas* July 19 35
> Elwell, Caleb May 29 40 (21) dark 5'7½"
> Emmons, Peter* July 19 35
> Finson, Thomas, corporal May 29 40
> Foster, William, sergeant May 29 40
> Gore (Gower), Joshua May 29 38 (26) light 5'4"
> Gott, Ebenezer June 6 40 (17) light 5'4"
> Gott, John, corporal May 29 40
> Haskell, Isaac, fifer June 13 40
> Haskins, Bennett May 29 40 (17) light 5'5½"
> Haskins, William, sergeant May 29 40

Jumper, William June 1 38 (34) light 5'8½"
Lane, Francis May 29 40 (19) light 5'5"
Lane, Joseph May 29 40 (29) light 5'7"
Low, Joseph* July 14 35
Low, Samuel June 6 35 (18) light 5'4"
Lowe, William, corporal May 29 35 (23) light 5'8"
Lurvey, Jacob, private May 29 (19) light 5'4"
Lurvey, James May 29 35
Morgan, Henry May 29 40 (26) light 5'5"
Parkhurst, Hugh May 29 40 (27) dark 5'3½"
Parrott, John* July 14 40
Parsons, Henry June 6 38 (19) 5'11½"
Parsons, Jeffrey June 2 38 (29) dark red 5'11"
Parsons, Jonathan June 10 40
Parsons, Joseph May 29 38 (26) dark 5'7"
Parsons, Wm. (killed in battle) May 29 38
Phipps, James May 29 40 (18) dark 5'5½"
Pool, Francis (killed in battle) corporal May 29 40
Pool, Mark, 1st lieutenant May 19 40
Richardson, Peter May 29 40 age not given brown 5'
Riggs, Aaron* July 14 35
Rowe, John, captain May 19 40 (37)
Rowe, John Jr. May 29 40 (16) light 5'4"
Rowe, Jonathan, corporal May 29 38
Rowe, Joshua May 29 38 (17) brown 5'4½"
Rowe, William May 29 40 (14) light 5'1½"
Sheldon, Ephraim May 29 40 (21) dark 6'0½"
Smith, John June 1 35 (21) brown 5'5½"
Somes, Daniel May 29 35 (26) brown 5'8½"
Tarr, Daniel Barber, sergeant May 29 40
Tarr, Jabez May 29 40 (16) light 5'10"
Tarr, James May 29 40 (16) light 5'4½"
Tarr, John June 12 40 (40) red 5'7"
Tarr, John Jr. May 29 40 (19) light 5'3½"
Thomas, Spencer June 1 35 (29) light 5'5½"
Witham, Ebenezer May 29 38 (22) light 5'2"
Woodbury, William June 1 38 (25) light 5'10"
Youlin, John* July 14 35

Post-Bunker Hill enrollees.

Eleazer Boynton
David Brooks
Reuben Brooks
John Burns
Henry Clark
Moses P. Clark
Samuel Davis
James Goss
William Goss
Ebenezer Gott
Ebenezer Grover, Jr.
Benjamin Hale
John Haskins
Josiah Haskins
Samuel Huston
Thomas Knights
Nehemiah Knowlton
Benjamin Marshall
Caleb Norwood

Francis Norwood
William Norwood
Thomas Oakes
James Parsons
Ebenezer Pool
Ebenezer Pool, Jr.
John Pool, III
Mark Pool
Moses Pool
Stephen Pool, Jr.
Solomon Pool
Thomas Robards, Jr.
John Rollins (Rawlings)
Isaac Rowe
Jabez Rowe
Jabez Rowe, Jr.
Thomas Rowe, Jr.
William Rowe
Aaron Sargent

William Saville
William Smith
Robert Stevens
Abraham Tarr
Andrew Tarr
Benjamin Tarr, Jr.
Benjamin Tarr, III
Benjamin Tarr, IV
Daniel B. Tarr
Francis Tarr
Jabez Tarr
Nathaniel Tarr
Oliver Tarr
Benjamin Thurston
Josiah Thurston
William Thurston
Joshua Webster
Henry Witham

Surviving Proprietors of the Original Sandy Bay Meeting House Who Sold the Building on August 23, 1804

John Gott
Caleb Norwood
Caleb Pool
Ebenezer Pool, Jr.*
Jonathan Pool
Mark Pool

Thomas Roberts
Jabez Rowe
William Rowe
Aaron Sargent
Joseph Smith
Benjamin Tarr

Daniel Thurston
Samuel D. Thurston
Sarah Todd
Henry Witham

On behalf of his father

Scholars at David Jewett's School as of April 1804*

William Adams, Jr.
John Blatchford, Jr.
Ezekiel Bradstreet, Jr.
Reuben Brooks, Jr., son of Deacon Reuben Brooks
Beulah Burns, daughter of Capt. John Burns
John L. Burns, son of Capt. John Burns
William Card, Jr., son of Capt. William Card
Anthony Chipman
Henry Clark, 2nd, son of Ebenezer Clark
Samuel L. Clark, Jr.
William Clark, son of Joshua Clark
William Cook, Jr.
John Davis, son of Daniel Davis
Timothy Riggs Davis, son of Daniel Davis
William Davis, son of Samuel Davis

Felix Doyle, Jr.
Mary Brooks Giddings, daughter of Deacon Reuben Brooks
William Goday
Allen Goss, son of William Goss
William Goss, Jr.
Lucy Grover, daughter of Ebenezer Grover, Jr.
Eleanor Hale, daughter of Benjamin Hale
Thomas P. Knights, Jr.
William Knights, son of Francis Knights
Tobias Leighton, Jr.
Caleb Norwood, 3rd, son of Caleb Norwood, Jr.
Charles Norwood, son of Caleb Norwood, Jr.
Rev. Francis Norwood, Jr., son of Maj. Francis Norwood
John Oakes, son of Thomas Oakes
Thomas Oakes, Jr.
John Phipps, Jr.
George Parsons, son of Capt. James Parsons
Ebenezer Pool, 4th, son of Ebenezer Pool, Jr.
James Pool, son of Stephen Pool, Jr.
Moses Pool, Jr., drowned
Zebulon Pool, son of Stephen Pool, Jr.
Thomas Robards, Jr., son of Capt. Thomas Robards
Allen Rowe, son of Major J. Rowe
Amos Rowe, son of Maj. John Rowe, Sr.
Isaac Rowe, Jr.
John Rowe, son of Isaac Rowe
John L. Smith, son of William Smith, Sr.
Benjamin Tarr, 3rd, son of Benjamin Tarr
Daniel B. Tarr, Jr.
David Tarr, Jr.
Francis Tarr, Jr.
Henry Tarr, Jr.
a son of James Tarr
Nathaniel Tarr, Jr.
Oliver Tarr, Jr.
Richard Tufts

As recollected and identified by Ebenezer Pool in 1866.

Members of Sandy Bay's First Fire Company Organized January, 1807

David Brooks
Reuben Brooks
John Burns
Solomon Choate
William Choate
Josiah Haskell, Jr.
John Haskins

David Kimball
Nehemiah Knowlton
Ebenezer Lowe
Caleb Norwood, Jr.
Francis Norwood
Aaron Pool
Ebenezer Pool, Jr.

Solomon Pool
Simeon Richardson
Andrew Tarr
Benjamin Tarr, 3rd
Jabez Tarr
Nathaniel Tarr

Twelve rosters of men credited with "Service at Gloucester" have been published. In every instance the service period given was in the year 1814. Two of the companies appear to have been raised largely from the Sandy Bay community—those of Captain Charles Tarr and Captain David Elwell, though a handful of taxpaying Sandy Bay parishioners served at the time in the companies of Captains Benjamin Haskell, Joseph Sayward, John Harris, John Smith, and Caleb Williams. The respective rosters are as follows:

Captain Charles Tarr's Company

Charles Tarr, Captain
George Lane, Lieutenant
Timothy R. Davis, Ensign
Henry Tarr, Sergeant

Eben. Pool, Sergeant
Moses Tarr, Sergeant
John Davis, Musician
Edmund Haskins, Musician

Privates

Bickford, Andrew	Hooper, Robert	Pool, William
Brown, Charles	Hoyt, John M.	Robards, Thomas
Butman, John	Lane, Andrew	Stockman, John
Cass, Robert	Merrill, Daniel	Tarr, Jabez, Jr.
Davis, Daniel	Norwood, Daniel	Tarr, James
Gamage, Ebenezer	Oakes, John	Tarr, Nathaniel
Gamage, Samuel G.	Parsons, Eben	Tarr, Robert
Giddings, Aaron	Pool, Aaron	Todd, Asa
Gott, George	Pool, Francis	Todd, Nathan
Gott, James	Pool, James, Jr.	Turner, John, Jr.
Grover, John	Pool, Joshua	Webster, George
Grover, Nehemiah	Pool, Solomon, Jr.	Witham, Henry, Jr.

Capt. David Elwell's Company

David Elwell, Captain
Joshua Clark, Lieutenant
William Low, Jr., Ensign
Moses T. Clark, Sergeant
John Foster, Sergeant

John Haskell, Sergeant
Asa Knowlton, Sergeant
William T. Abbott, Corporal
Henry White, Jr., Corporal

William Thurston, Corporal
Thomas York, Corporal
Eben Pool, Musician
Zebulon R. Davis, Musician

Privates

Adams, William	Clark, Thomas L.	Haskins, William B.
Bagley, John	Clark, William C.	Hodgkins, Henry
Blatchford, John	Cunningham, John, Jr.	Jacob, Abraham
Bradstreet, Ezekiel	Dennin, Job	Knight, Charles
Bradstreet, Nathaniel	Doyl, Felix	Knowlton, Azor
Chipman, Anthony	Dunnaway, Daniel	Lane, George, Jr.
Clark, Abraham S.	Elwell, Caleb	Lee, Nathaniel B.
Clark, Henry	Giles, William	Leighton, Tobias
Clark, Henry, Jr.	Goss, William, Jr.	Low, David
Clark, Samuel L.	Grover, Ebenezer, Jr.	Low, James

Some Rockport Rosters

Low, Nathaniel
Lurvey, William
Morse, Essom
Parsons, John, 4th
Pool, Abram H.
Pool, Francis
Pool, John
Pool, John, 4th
Pool, Moses
Pool, Zebulon
Robards, George

Rowe, Benjamin, Jr.
Rowe, Daniel
Rowe, Eben
Rowe, George
Rowe, Isaac
Rowe, Job
Smith, John L.
Stockman, John
Tarr, David, Jr.
Tarr, Francis, Jr.
Tarr, Francis P.

Tarr, Jonathan, Jr.
Tarr, Joseph, Jr.
Tarr, Joshua
Tarr, Solomon
Thompson, Thomas
Thurston, Joseph
Wainright, Thomas
Webster, Joshua
Weeden, Daniel
Witham, Joseph

Waiters

Brown, David

Clark, John

Members of the Society for the Suppression
Of Intemperance and other Prevalent Vices / 1815

Reuben Brooks*
Reuben Brooks, Jr.*
John Burns, Jr.*
Solomon Choate*
William Choate
George Dennison*
Isaac Dennison, Jr.*
Matthew S. Giles*
Thomas Giles*

James Goss
Jabez R. Gott*
David Jewett*
David Kimball*
Caleb Norwood
Francis Norwood
Gorham Norwood
Ebenezer Oakes
Thomas Oakes

Josiah Page
Aaron Pool
Abraham Pool*
Solomon Pool
Stephen Pool
William Pool*
Joseph Smith, Jr.
William Whipple*
Henry Witham, Jr.

Those 14 names marked with an asterisk signed the dissolution document of March 9, 1829. A note dated January 6, 1818, reads "Mr. Caleb Norwood at his request has withdrawn from the Society, and wishes his name to be erased from the Catalogue of its members. January 6th, 1818."

Taxes Paid to Collector William Smith
by Sandy Bay Residents / 1828-1829

Abbott, Eben Grover	1.13	Boynton, Eliezer, Jr.	5.28
Abbott, William T.	6.66	Boynton, Russel J.	1.92
Allen, Daniel	6.09	Boynton, William	4.52
Allen, Daniel, Jr.	3.09	Bradley, William H.	4.83
Andrews, Benjamin W.	7.32	Bradstreet, Josiah	7.53
Andrews, Samuel L.	2.28	Bray, Gideon	2.72
Babcock, Joseph	1.53	Bray, Jacob	2.72
Bickford, Andrew	9.40	Brooks, David	25.02
Blatchford, Charles	4.15	Brooks, Reuben	15.68
Blatchford, Ebenezer	4.90	Brooks, Reuben, Jr.	12.43
Blatchford, John	4.00	Brooks, Samuel H.	2.78
Blatchford, Kenny	11.42	Brown, Charles	8.68
Blatchford, William	8.89	Brown, James	3.11
Boynton, Eliezer	2.70	Butler, David	5.08

Town on Sandy Bay

Burns, John	25.72	Gamage, Ebenezer	5.10
Burns, William T.	12.39	Gamage, John	2.32
Burrill, Henry	2.70	Gamage, Samuel G.	3.83
Butman, Jeremiah	12.73	Gamage, Stephen	6.83
Butman, Estate of Jeremiah	6.13	Giddings, Aaron	12.61
Butman, John	8.49	Giles, Mathew S.	16.33
Caldwell, William	1.55	Giles, Samuel	5.56
Chipman, Anthony	7.81	Giles, Thomas	20.27
Choate, Solomon	12.43	Goss, James	8.18
Choate, Solomon, Jr.	6.09	Goss, William	8.33
Choate, William	9.02	Gott, Abigail (widow)	5.23
Clark, Henry	10.95	Gott, Eben	5.07
Clark, Henry, Jr.	2.54	Gott, George	20.65
Clark, Moses T., Jr.	12.76	Gott, Jabez R.	15.80
Clark, Peter L.	3.30	Gott, James	16.71
Coffin, Thomas	1.13	Gott, John Captain	36.34
Colby, Benjamin	2.73	Griffin, Josiah	2.70
Colby, Enoch	2.32	Grimes, James	2.72
Colby, Moses E.	2.73	Grimes, Mark, Jr.	2.61
Colby, Moses (in part)	3.75	Grimes, Thomas	1.13
Coose, William III	3.83	Grover, William	4.52
Cunningham, Elias	4.33	Hale, Benjamin	2.70
Cunningham, John	2.32	Hale, George D.	7.49
Cunningham, John, Jr.	4.08	Harriden, Winthrop	3.49
Cunningham, Nehemiah	3.11	Hartley, John	3.49
Cunningham, William	2.78	Hartley, Samuel (in part)	2.00
Dade, Daniel	1.13	Hartley, Samuel L.	3.11
Dade, Reuben	4.39	Haskell, Charles	3.11
Daily, Mathew	1.92	Haskell, Edward, Jr.	1.13
Davis, Ebenezer	4.26	Haskell, John	2.70
Davis, John & Son	6.98	Haskell, Josiah	3.85
Davis, Samuel (in part)	2.00	Haskell, Josiah, Jr.	7.87
Davis, Timothy Riggs	2.70	Haskins, John	5.74
Dearborn, Thomas	2.72	Haskins, John D.	2.72
Dennis, Henry	4.29	Haskins, Moses	2.73
Dennison, George	15.59	Haskins, William B.	5.90
Dennison, Isaac, Jr.	22.88	Herring, Samuel	2.32
Donivan, Job	3.70	Hodgkins, Moses	2.72
Dowcett, David	2.32	Holmes, Robert	4.50
Dowst, Richard	4.29	Hooper, Robert	3.34
Doyle, Abraham T.	6.70	Hoyt, John M.	2.70
Doyle, William	1.13	Huston, Samuel	3.13
Doyle, Estate of William	3.35	Jewett, Eben	1.13
Drown, John O.	3.89	Knights, David	1.13
Elwell, Caleb	6.05	Knights, Jacob	2.32
Elwell, David (in part)	6.00	Knights, James M. K.	1.53
Elwell, David III (in part)	2.52	Knights, Thomas	3.10
Elwell, George	2.06	Knights, Thomas P.	4.08
Foster, George	3.10	Knowlton, Asa & Son	6.19
Foster, John	7.13	Knowlton, Azer	11.87
Foster, Nathaniel	2.31	Knowlton, Charles	3.50
Fretch, William S.	4.58	Knowlton, Charles	3.48
Gamage, Eben	1.92	Knowlton, Harry	3.57

Some Rockport Rosters

Knowlton, Michael	2.70
Knowlton, Nehemiah, Jr.	1.92
Knowlton, Walter	2.70
Lane, Andrew	26.13
Lane, George	18.15
Lane, George, Jr.	2.64
Lane, William	15.43
Low, Daniel	14.93
Low, Ebenezer	4.66
Low, Ebenezer, Jr.	1.53
Low, James	2.56
Low, Kenny	1.13
Low, Nathaniel	2.56
Lurvy, William	5.53
Lurvy, William, Jr.	1.13
Manning, Charles B.	3.10
Manning, James	1.52
Manning, John	39.93
Manning, Joseph B.	3.10
Marshall, Benjamin	1.13
Marshall, Daniel O.	3.21
Marshall, Thomas	6.40
McJannet, Samuel	5.45
Merchant, Daniel	3.49
Merrill, Benjamin	1.13
Noble, Francis	1.92
Norwood, Caleb	1.13
Norwood, Charles	21.43
Norwood, Charles, Jr.	4.91
Norwood, Epes	3.10
Norwood, Esther (widow)	16.43
Norwood, Frederick	3.88
Norwood, George	2.70
Norwood, Joseph E.	7.97
Norwood, Lisey (widow)	15.05
Norwood, William	22.64
Norwood, William, Jr.	3.88
Oakes, Ebenezer	17.51
Oakes, Ebenezer, Jr.	3.10
Oakes, Thomas	19.26
Otis, Samuel	2.32
Parsons, Benjamin, Jr.	3.88
Parsons, Charles	1.13
Parsons, Daniel	2.70
Parsons, James	3.65
Parsons, James, Jr.	2.32
Parsons, Jeffrey	3.88
Parsons, Jeffrey, Jr.	2.08
Parsons, John	2.70
Parsons, John, Jr.	5.92
Parsons, Jonathan 2nd	2.70
Parsons, Jonathan 3rd	1.13
Parsons, Nehemiah	2.56

Parsons, William W.	1.53
Parsons, William, Jr. (in part)	1.00
Parsons, William 4th	1.53
Parsons, Zebulon	2.32
Patch, Frank	4.22
Perry, Allen	1.53
Pool, Aaron	10.55
Pool, Aaron, Jr.	3.54
Pool, Abigail (widow)	3.28
Pool, Abraham	12.47
Pool, Abraham H.	2.32
Pool, Addison	1.13
Pool, Charles	3.35
Pool, Charles III	4.15
Pool, David	3.65
Pool, Ebenezer	40.83
Pool, Eben	5.49
Pool, Eben, Jr.	23.20
Pool, George	1.92
Pool, Gorham	3.34
Pool, James	11.06
Pool, James, Jr.	14.82
Pool, James III	2.72
Pool, John	2.35
Pool, John, Jr.	11.98
Pool, John III	5.07
Pool, Jonathan	4.83
Pool, Josiah	5.63
Pool, Lucy (widow)	3.49
Pool, Mark	2.72
Pool, Nathan	9.31
Pool, Nathaniel	18.50
Pool, Solomon	29.71
Pool, Solomon, Jr.	10.24
Pool, William	2.70
Pool, William III	1.53
Pool, Zebulon	2.26
Richardson, Nathaniel	3.85
Robbins, Nathaniel	3.67
Roberts, George	4.38
Roberts, Polly (widow)	6.98
Roberts, Stephen	2.32
Roberts, Thomas	5.71
Rowe, Eben	7.16
Rowe, Ebenezer (estate of)	2.90
Rowe, Francis	4.58
Rowe, George	4.13
Rowe, Jabez	6.36
Rowe, Jabez (guardian)	8.37
Rowe, Estate of Jabez	8.79
Rowe, James	2.32
Rowe, John, Jr.	9.80
Rowe, John, Jr.	1.13

Rowell, Enoch	3.74	Tarr, Joseph, Jr.	3.11	415
Sanborn, Joshua	2.72	Tarr, Joshua	3.57	
Sanborn, Levi	12.31	Tarr, Moses	2.32	
Sanborn, Levi, Jr.	2.63	Tarr, Nathaniel	15.21	
Sandy Bay Pier	93.87	Tarr, Reuben	3.51	
Saville, William III	2.52	Tarr, Robert	4.37	
Short, James	3.27	Tarr, Thomas	4.61	
Smith, Allen	3.81	Tarr, Washington	4.26	
Smith, Benjamin H.	3.37	Tarr, William	4.14	
Smith, David	1.13	Tarr, William, Jr.	7.66	
Smith, Joseph	24.01	Tarr, Zebulon	5.15	
Smith, Solomon	1.92	Thompson, Thomas	3.94	
Smith, William, Jr.	2.87	Thurston, Daniel	6.55	
Stevens, Oliver II	3.99	Thurston, Joseph	3.83	
Stillman, Amos	2.32	Thurston, William	9.76	
Stillman, Daniel M.	2.68	Todd, Asa	7.77	
Stillman, Peter	2.32	Todd, Sarah (widow)	8.38	
Stillman, Peter, Jr.	2.32	Tucker, Eben	1.92	
Stockman, John	13.72	Tucker, John	2.22	
Stockman, John, Jr.	1.77	Tucker, William H.	2.32	
Tarr, Abner	3.11	Tufts, Richard	8.42	
Tarr, Andrew	6.25	Turner, John, Jr.	2.32	
Tarr, Benjamin	6.95	Turner, Lenard	1.13	
Tarr, Caleb	2.32	Wainright, George	3.11	
Tarr, Charles	21.75	Wallis, David	4.53	
Tarr, Charles, Jr.	3.02	Wallis, George	15.18	
Tarr, Charles III	3.45	Wheeler, Moses	2.72	
Tarr, David	6.04	Webster, George	4.27	
Tarr, Ebenezer	2.76	Whipple, William	9.74	
Tarr, Epes	5.45	White, Harry	2.35	
Tarr, Fitz	3.11	Wilson, James	1.92	
Tarr, Francis	8.71	Wingood, William	1.13	
Tarr, Francis P.	5.05	Witham, Charles	4.10	
Tarr, George	4.12	Witham, Elizabeth (widow)	6.38	
Tarr, George, Jr.	2.32	Witham, George	4.67	
Tarr, Estate of Henry	1.97	Witham, Joshua	5.09	
Tarr, Jabez	11.14	Witham, William	4.72	
Tarr, Jabez, Jr.	16.26	Witham, Zebulon	16.53	
Tarr, John	4.30	Wood, Mark	2.70	
Tarr, Jonathan	5.34	York, Thomas	3.89	
Tarr, Joseph	9.34	Young, John	3.75	

Some Rockport Rosters

Firemen Appointed by the Selectmen to Man Sandy Bay's First Fire Apparatus, Engine No. 5 / October, 1829

Daniel Allen, Jr.
William H. Bradley
John O. Brown
Addison Choate
Benjamin Choate
Dudley Choate
Jeremiah Choate
John Choate
Solomon Choate, Jr.
Henry Clark, Jr.
Benjamin Courtney

Henry Dennis
Richard Dowch
Samuel J. Giles
Ebenezer Gott
George Gott, Jr.
George Knowlton
John Manning
Thomas O. Marshall
George Norwood, Jr.
William Perkins

William Pool, 4th
Nathaniel Richardson
George Robinson
Jabez Rowe
Levi Sewall
Lyman Sewall
Peter Stillman, Jr.
Silas Wentworth
George Witham
Joshua Witham, Jr.

Firemen Appointed by the Selectmen to Man Sandy Bay's Second Fire Apparatus, Engine No. 6 / February 25, 1831

Richard Choate
   Foreman
Nehemiah Knowlton, Jr.
   Assistant Foreman
Abraham Goldsmith
   Clerk
Caleb S. Choate
Prentice Choate

Joseph Davis
Ebenezer Gott, Jr.
James Hooper
Horatio N. Huston
Lot Keen
David B. Knights
Louis Lane
Frederick Oakes

Charles Pool, 4th
Samuel Pool
John Preston
Ebenezer Rowe
Levi Sanborn, Jr.
Benjamin Tarr, Jr.

First 147 Subscribers for the First Hearse at Sandy Bay / 1836

25c

Davis, L.
Elwell, Caleb
Fretch, William S.
Foster, L.
Gott, Widow Abigail
Gott, E.
Gott, H.
Haskins, John
Hodgkins, Moses
Knowlton, Michael
Lurvy, William, Jr.
Pool, Eben
Pool, Ebenezer, Jr.
Pool, F.
Pool, William
Smith, Benjamin H.

Story, J.*
Tarr, Benjamin
Tarr, F.

50c

Abbott, William T.
Andrews, William
Brooks, Reuben
Brooks, Reuben, Jr.
Brooks, Samuel H.
Brown, E.*
Brown, James
Choate, Solomon
Dade, Reuben
Drown, John O.
Elwell, C., Jr.
Foster, George

Gamage, S.
Gamage, William
Giles, William
Gott, Ch.*
Gott, Eben
Grover, J.
Haskins, Moses
Holmes, Robert
Hoyt, John M.
Knights, Thomas
Lane, G.
Lowe, Ebenezer
Lowe, James
Lowe, Kenny
Oakes, Thomas
Parsons, Benjamin, Jr.
Parsons, J.
Parsons, William
Parsons, William W.

Town on Sandy Bay

Pool, C. or G.
Pool, E.
Pool, H.
Roberts, Thomas
Roberts, W.
Rowe, C.
Rowe, Eben
Rowe, J.
Rowe, John, Jr.
Rowell, Enoch
Sewell, L.
Short, James
Smith, Allen
Smith, R.
Stockman, John
Tarr, J.
Tarr, J.
Tarr, J.
Tarr, Washington
Tarr, Zebulon
Tarr, Z.
Thurston, Joshua
Thurston, William
Witham, George
Witham, J.
Witham, Joshua
Witham, William
Witham, Zebulon

75c

Boynton, Eliazer
Boynton, Eliazer, Jr.
Bradley, William H.*
Burns, William T.
Butman, Jeremiah
Butman, John
Davis, John
Dennison, George
Giles, Thomas
Gott, J.
Haskell, J.
Knowlton, Nehemiah, Jr.
Lane, George
Lurvy, William
Lowe, G.

Lowe, H. T.
Oakes, Ebenezer
Pool, Aaron, Jr.
Pool, Ebenezer
Pool, Solomon, Jr.
Roberts, William
Rowe, C.
Rowe, E.
Rowe, Francis
Rowe, George
Tarr, C.
Tarr, George
Tarr, Jabez
Tarr, J.
Tarr, Nathaniel
Tarr, William B.
Tarvis, J.*
Thurston, C.

85c

Norwood, Seth*
Gorman, J.*

$1.00

Andrews, Benjamin
Blatchford, Ebenezer
Blatchford, John
Brooks, David
Choate, William
Clark, Henry
Gennet, William*
Hale, J. C.*
Giddings, Aaron
Giles, Mathew S.
Gott, George
Gott, George W.
Gott, John
Knowlton, Azer
Lane, Andrew
Lane, William
Lowe, Ebenezer
Manning, John
Marshall, Thomas O.

Norwood, Caleb
Norwood, Charles
Norwood, William
Norwood, William, Jr.
Pool, A.
Pool, J.
Pool, Nat.
Pool, Solomon
Sanborn, Joshua
Smith, Joseph
Tarr, Francis P.
Tarr, George, Jr.
Todd, Asa
Tufts, Richard
Turner, John, Jr.

* NOTE: *The names of many donors were entered by first initial only. By cross-checking census and tax lists, it has been possible to identify the subscriber quite specifically. In some cases, however, more than one donor had the same initial, so closer identification is not possible. A few names are all but illegible and must be conjectured. They are marked with an asterisk.*

Abbott, Ebenezer G.
Abbott, William J., Jr.
Allen, Daniel
Allen, David
Allen, David, Jr.
Anderson, Enoch*
Andrews, Benjamin W.
Andrews, Stephen
Beals, Joseph
Bickford, Andrew
Blatchford, Ebenezer*
Blatchford, Henry
Blatchford, John
Blatchford, William
Boynton, David
Boynton, Eliazer
Boynton, William
Bradley, William H.
Bradstreet, Ezekiel
Bray, Benjamin R.
Bray, Jacob
Brooks, David*
Brooks, David, Jr.*
Brooks, Reuben
Brooks, Reuben, Jr.
Brooks, Samuel H.
Brown, James
Butman, Jeremiah*
Butman, John*
Butman, William
Butler, David*
Caldwell, William
Choate, Alfred B.
Choate, Andrew
Choate, Benjamin
Choate, Caleb S.
Choate, Prentis
Choate, R. Paul
Clark, Albert
Clark, Ebenezer
Clark, Henry
Clark, Henry, Jr.
Clark, James, Jr.
Clark, Lemuel J.
Clark, Peter L.
Clark, William P.
Clark, William P., Jr.
Cleaves, Ebenezer
Cleaves, Levi

Cleaves, Moses
Cleaves, Willard*
Colby, Andrew J.
Colby, Benjamin
Colby, Moses E.
Colby, William
Colbey, James
Coose, William
Critchet, Moses
Cross, John
Cunningham, Nehemiah
Cunningham, William
Dade, Reuben
Davis, Daniel
Davis, Ebenezer
Davis, James
Davis, James P.
Davis, John
Davis, Solomon
Davis, Timothy
Davis, Timothy R.
Davis, William G.
Davis, William, III
Day, Samuel
Denen, Job*
Denis, Henry
Doyle, Abraham T.*
Doyle, William
Driver, Stephen*
Dunell, Francis
Elwell, David
Emerson, Fredric
Farnell, George
Fears, Isaac*
Fears, Samuel P.
Fernal, James
Foster, John
Foster, Nathaniel
Fretch, John
Gamage, Daniel B.
Gamage, Ebenezer
Gamage, Epes
Gamage, John
Gamage, Samuel G.
Gamage, William
Gee, Nathaniel
Giles, Darius*
Giles, John L.*
Giles, Samuel

Giles, William
Goady, Thomas
Goday, William
Goldsmith, Abraham
Gott, Addison
Gott, Ebenezer
Gott, Jabez R.*
Gott, James
Gott, John
Gott, Lemuel
Gott, Levi S.
Goss, William
Griffin, Andrew
Griffin, James
Griffin, Josiah, Jr.
Griffin, Timothy
Grimes, James P.
Grimes, Thomas
Grover, John
Grover, William, Jr.
Hadlock, John*
Hale, Albert
Hale, William
Hardy, C. A. S.
Hartley, John
Hartley, Samuel
Hartley, Samuel T.
Haskell, Alexander
Haskell, Charles, III
Haskell, Edward
Haskell, Holden P.
Haskell, John
Haskell, Josiah*
Haskell, William
Haskell, William E. P.
Haskins, John D.
Haskins, Moses
Haskins, Samuel F.
Haskins, William B.
Hill, Joshua P.*
Hodgekins, Aaron, Jr.
Hodgekins, Henry
Hodgekins, Henry, Jr.
Hodgekins, John B.
Hodgekins, Moses
Hooper, Robert, Jr.
Hoyt, John
Huston, Horatio N.
Jewitt, Ebenezer

Town on Sandy Bay

Keen, Lott (from Maine)
Kidder, Luther*
Kinsman, Andrew
Knights, Benjamin
Knights, Charles
Knights, George
Knights, Jacob
Knights, James M. H.
Knights, Thomas P.*
Knights, William
Knowlton, Addison
Knowlton, Asa*
Knowlton, Asa, Jr.*
Knowlton, Azor
Knowlton, Charles
Knowlton, George
Knowlton, Harvy
Knowlton, Jackson
Knowlton, Michael
Knowlton, Nehemiah
Knowlton, Walter
Knowlton, William H.
Lane, Albert
Lane, Andrew
Lane, Andrew, Jr.
Lane, Charles
Lane, James S.
Lane, Lewis
Lane, William
Lane, William, Jr.
Leighton, William
Low, Daniel*
Low, Henry T.
Low, John, Jr.*
Lowe, David, Jr.
Lowe, Ebenezer*
Lurvy, William
Lurvy, William, Jr.
Manning, John*
Marchant, Daniel, Jr.
Marshall, Benjamin
Marshall, Benjamin, Jr.
Marshall, Daniel O.
Marshall, John W.
Marshall, Lafayet
Marshall, Thomas O.
McJannett, Samuel*
McLane, Murdoc*
Millet, Alexander
Millet, Edward
Morgan, Paul
Morse, Essom
Noble, Frank

Norwood, Caleb, III
Norwood, Caleb, Jr.*
Norwood, Charles, Jr.*
Norwood, Epes
Norwood, George
Norwood, Seth
Norwood, Stephen*
Norwood, William*
Norwood, William, III
Oakes, Ebenezer
Oakes, Thomas
Parsons, Benjamin
Parsons, David S.
Parsons, James C.
Parsons, Jeffrey
Parsons, Jeffrey, Jr.
Parsons, John
Parsons, John B.
Parsons, Jonathan
Parsons, Jonathan, III
Parsons, Thomas F.
Parsons, Timothy
Parsons, William W.
Paul, James
Peach, Thomas
Pearson, Nehemiah
Phillips, George
Pickering, Winthrop
Pool, Aaron*
Pool, Abraham H.*
Pool, Abraham H.
Pool, Charles
Pool, Charles, Jr.
Pool, David
Pool, Ebenezer, Jr.
Pool, Ebenezer, III
Pool, Ebenezer, IV
Pool, Eliphalet
Pool, George*
Pool, James*
Pool, James*
Pool, James J.
Pool, John
Pool, John, Jr.
Pool, Joshua
Pool, Lyman
Pool, Mark
Pool, Moses
Pool, Moses, Jr.
Pool, Nathaniel*
Pool, Nathaniel, Jr.
Pool, Solomon, Jr.*
Pool, Theadore

Pool, William
Pool, William, Jr.
Pool, Zebulon
Preston, John
Procter, Addison
Richards, L. E. P.
Richardson, Addison
Richardson, Jabez*
Richardson, Lyman
Richardson, Nathaniel*
Robarts, Charles
Robarts, Stephen*
Robins, Nathaniel*
Rowe, Charles
Rowe, Eben
Rowe, Ebenezer
Rowe, Francis
Rowe, George
Rowe, George, Jr.
Rowe, Jabez
Rowe, John
Rowe, Stephen
Safford, James D.
Sanborn, Isaac
Sanborn, Joshua
Sandborn, Levi*
Sanders, Joel
Saunders, Samuel
Saville, William, Jr.
Sewall, Levi
Smith, Allen
Smith, Benjamin H.
Smith, Cephas*
Smith, Joseph*
Smith, Samuel
Smith, William
Smith, William, Jr.
Standley, Jas. D.
Stanwood, Isaac
Stevens, George
Stevens, Oliver
Stilman, Amos
Stilman, Daniel M.
Stilman, Eleazer
Stilman, James
Stilman, Peter
Stilman, Samuel
Stilman, William
Stockman, John
Sturdivant, Joseph
Tarr, Abner
Tarr, Amos
Tarr, Andrew

Some Rockport Rosters

420

Tarr, Asa
Tarr, Caleb
Tarr, Caleb, Jr.
Tarr, Daniel, Jr.
Tarr, David
Tarr, Epes*
Tarr, Fitz
Tarr, Francis
Tarr, Francis P.
Tarr, James
Tarr, James, Jr.
Tarr, James P.
Tarr, Joshua
Tarr, Joshua, Jr.
Tarr, Nathaniel
Tarr, Stephen N.
Tarr, Thomas
Tarr, Washington
Tarr, William, III

Thompson, Thomas
Thurston, John R.
Thurston, Joseph
Thurston, Joseph, Jr.
Thurston, William
Thurston, William, Jr.
Thurston, William, Jr.
Todd, Asa*
Torrey, William J.
Tucker, John
Tucker, Ebenezer
Tucker, William H.
Tufts, Richard*
Turner, John*
Turner, John, Jr.
Turner, Leonard M.
Turner, William
Walen, Samuel S.

Wainright, George
Wainright, Thomas
Wallis, David*
Wallis, John
Whipple, William*
White, Henry
Witham, Charles
Witham, Charles
Witham, George*
Witham, Joshua
Witham, Joshua
Witham, William
Witham, William
Wormwood, Oliver
York, John
York, Thomas
Young, William

*Names of the 53 people opposed. This is Ebenezer Pool's list (alphabetized) of persons visited in March, 1839.
Note by Ebenezer Pool: "There were quite a number of legal voters who would not mark either for or against a
separation whose names were not returned on the list, therefore they do not appear in the foregoing list. Also some
were absent. No names of Residents living in the North Village were called upon to mark either way, which
village includes those persons living near Pigeon Hill and so on to Folly Cove. If the voters of North Village had
marked, there would have been more than 100 other names besides those who would not mark."

Members of Rockport's Volunteer Fire Department / 1845

Boynton, Eleazar
Brooks, Reuben
Burnham, Newell
Burns, William P.
Choate, Addison
Choate, Dudley
Dennis, Henry
Drown, John O.

Giles, Thomas
Gott, Addison
Gott, Jabez R.
Hale, George D.
Haskell, Josiah
Haskins, William B.
Knowlton, Nehemiah, Jr.
Lane, George

Lane, William
Norwood, Caleb
Pool, Abraham H.
Rowe, Jabez
Tarr, Charles, Jr.
Whipple, William

Founders of Granite Lodge No. 127 I.O.O.F.
Organized May 23, 1848

Babson, David, Jr.
Bryant, William
Burns, Joseph J.
Burns, William D.
Clark, Albert
Colby, William
Dann, William H.
Dennis, Henry

Elwell, Andrew
Flood, Thomas N.
Grover, Charles E.
Hale, Thomas
Lang, David D.
Leach, George
Norwood, Caleb
Parsons, Benjamin

Richardson, Levi P.
Rowe, Charles, Jr.
Sanford, George
Shaw, Edward H.
Tufts, Eli G.
Wallace, John G.
Wallace, William H.

Andrews, Ezekiel
Andrews, S. P.
Blatchford, Eben
Burns, W. P.
Caldwell, William
Choate, Addison
Choate, Dudley
Emver, E. (?)
Giles, Alfred
Giles, John J.
Hale, William

Haskell, Benjamin
Haskell, James
Haskell, Josiah
Haskins, William
Knights, Thomas P.
Lowe, Eben
Lowe, Henry T.
Manning, James
Marshall, Lafayette
Patch, William H.
Pool, John, Jr.

Pool, Theodore
Rowe, Samuel
Shaw, Levi
Simpson, J. H.
Smith, Joseph
Stanford, Daniel
Tarr, Benjamin
Tarr, Charles, Jr.
Tufts, Eli G.
Webster, Joshua
York, Samuel

Founders of Ashler Lodge of A.F. and A.M.
Chartered March 12, 1852

Blatchford, Eben
Caldwell, William
Clark, Henry
Giles, William
Kidder, Luther H.
 (of Vermont)

Manning, William H.
Marshall, Thomas O.
Parker, Samuel
Rowe, Charles

Rowe, Francis
Smith, William
Tarr, Charles, III

School Masters at Sandy Bay as Recalled by Ebenezer Pool / 1866

Jonathan Pool
Moses Parsons
William Clark
William Rogers
Nathaniel Harken
Hugh Parkhurst
Master Berk

Master Cummings
James Goss
William Saville
Oliver Saville
James Saville
Capt. Ebenezer Cleaveland

David Jewett
Joseph Butman
John Dodge
Beniah Morse
John Prentiss
William Whipple

"Of mistresses, there were Mrs. Goodrich, Mrs. [Dorcas] Dresser and many others before 1800. Mrs. William Clark, Thomas Runtsford [Knutsford] and others kept schools at Pigeon Cove."

High School — Sarah Philbrook, Ada S. Tarr, Carrie Wheeler

Broadway Grammar School — James Cogswell, Sarah E. Gray, Ellen Greenwood, Ella Haskins, Hattie McJannet, Ida Manning, Eddie Mills, Jennie Parsons, Nellie Pool

North Village Grammar School — Martha Kendall, Almira Lurvey, Mary J. Lurvey, Susie Lurvey, Nellie Story

Mt. Pleasant Grammar School — Mattie Bradley, Annie Giles, Etta Oakes

North Village Primary School — Ralph Clifford, Mary Parsons, Annie Story, Florence Story, Josie Story

Mt. Pleasant Primary School — Fred Bradley, Sophia Campbell, George Haskell, Sherman Smith, Alice Tarr

Broadway Primary School — Willie Blatchford, Hattie Boynton, Lorenzo Griffin, Lucy Marshall, Eva McJannet, Minnie O'Brien, Jennie Smith

Main St. School — Belle Hodgkins, Josie Paul, Emma Tarr

Beach St. School — Willie Breen, George Cleaves, Sarah Cowen, Martha Parsons, Maggie Sullivan

Young Men's School — John Hooper, Jr., J. E. Pettingill

*Charter Members of the O. W. Wallace Post No. 106 G.A.R. / 1869**

Currier, Sidney	Wingood, William, Jr.	Mitchell, Freeman
Davis, William H.	Witham, John S.	Parsons, Thomas F., Jr.
Parsons, Thomas F., Jr.	Blaisdell, O. H.	Pool, Calvin W.
Pool, Story D.	Bray, Isaac B.	Prior, Eugene R.
Prior, Eugene	Breen, James	Richardson, Nathaniel, Jr.
Sanborn, John E.	Dunlap, C. L.	Rowe, Ozias N.
Shaw, Levi	Fears, Samuel	Stickney, John E.
Stickney, John E.	French, Charles	Stillman, James H.
Townsend, E.	Lane, Andrew, Jr.	Tuttle, Daniel W.

*Post organized August 19, 1869, and reorganized December 31, 1881.

Rockport Taxpayers Paying over $100 / 1886

Allen, Mrs. Ester G.	$ 100.60	Knowlton, W. H.	157.67
Babson, David C.	438.82	Lane, Andrew	221.64
Babson, David W.	102.60	Low, John (estate of)	127.56
Bishop, C. H.	130.05	Manning, J. (guardian)	140.84
Brown, Zenas	127.08	Marshall & Stimson	107.87
Cape Ann Isinglass Company	276.93	McLain, George M.	172.60
Canney, Edwin	147.58	Norwood, Caleb J.	132.14
Colby, W. H.	109.10	Parker, Chas. W. (estate of)	166.39
Day, Charles (estate of)	106.34	Patch, W. H.	129.61
Goodwin, A. C.	145.38	Phillips, Heirs Eben B.	145.35
Gott, Addison	130.37	Phillips, Maria D. (estate of)	796.21
Grimes, Loring	245.92	Pigeon Cove Harbor Co.	137.70
Haskins, L. M.	249.10	Pigeon Hill Granite Co.	278.46
Haskins, M. W.	160.65	Pool, Eben (estate of)	109.60
Hooper, John	105.35	Pool, Nath'l	125.48

Pool, Wm. H.	103.67	Stimson, John	142.29
Richardson, N., Jr.	103.87	Tarr, Chas.	107.42
Robinson, E. S.	215.73	Tarr, George J.	126.10
Rockport Granite Co.	1,353.29	Tarr, Mrs. Lydia G.	147.95
Rockport National Bank	229.50	Tarr, Zebulon	111.40
Sanborn, John D.	343.17	Todd, Asa	151.47
Sandy Bay Pier Co.	294.62	Walker, Theophilus	725.72
Smith, Leverett E.	120.62	Webster, Nath'l	140.76
Stimson, Anson	190.00	Wood, H. N.	198.38

Gloucester Selectmen from the Sandy Bay Parish

1735-1737	Edmund Grover	1796	Ebenezer Pool
1740	Jabez Baker	1797	Benjamin Tarr, Jr.
1756	Ebenezer Pool	1798	James Goss
1760	Ebenezer Pool	1805	John Manning
1768	Francis Pool	1806	Ebenezer Oakes
1775	Francis Pool	1807	Caleb Norwood
1776	Francis Pool	1809	Caleb Norwood, Jr.
1777	Stephen Pool	1810-1812	Francis Norwood
1778	John Rowe	1813-1815	Ebenezer Oakes
1780-1781	Mark Pool	1825	Winthrop Pool
1782	Ebenezer Cleaveland, Jr.	1826-1827	Aaron Giddings
1784	Mark Pool	1830-1835	George D. Hale
1785-1787	Caleb Pool	1836-1838	John W. Marshall
1788	Mark Pool	1839	James Haskell
1789-1795	Caleb Pool		

Rockport Selectmen / 1840-1976

1840

David Babson, Jr.
James Haskell
Thomas O. Marshall

1841

David Babson, Jr.
James Haskell
William H. Bradley

1842-1844

David Babson, Jr.
William H. Bradley
William P. Burns

1845 and 1846

David Babson, Jr.
William P. Burns
George D. Hale

1847 and 1848

David Babson, Jr.
Benjamin Tarr
John Pool

1849

David Babson, Jr.
William Boynton
William P. Burns

1850

David Babson, Jr.
William Boynton
George Gott, Jr.

1851

David Babson, Jr.
William Boynton
James Manning

1852

James Manning
William H. Bradley
Thomas Hale

1853

Thomas Hale
John W. Marshall
Dudley Choate

1854

John W. Marshall
Dudley Choate
Amos Story

1855

James Manning
William H. Bradley
Benjamin Atwood

Some Rockport Rosters

424

1856

John W. Marshall
Washington Tarr
Daniel Wheeler

1857

John W. Marshall
Washington Tarr
Austin W. Story

1858

Austin W. Story
John Manning
Alfred Parsons

1859

John Manning
Moses Haskins
William Marchant

1860 and 1861

John W. Marshall
William Marchant
Addison Gott

1862

Joshua Tarr
Austin W. Story
William H. Bradley

1863

Austin W. Story
William H. Bradley, Jr.
Henry Dennis, Jr.

1864

Henry Dennis, Jr.
William Marchant
David Brooks

1865-1867

Henry Dennis, Jr.
William Marchant
William Caldwell

1868

Henry Dennis, Jr.
Austin W. Story
Ezekiel Bradstreet

1869

Austin W. Story
Francis Tarr, Jr.
William Caldwell

1870

Austin W. Story
Francis Tarr, Jr.
James Fernald, Jr.

1871

James W. Bradley
Henri N. Woods
Abraham Lurvey

1872

James W. Bradley
John W. Marshall
Abraham Lurvey

1873-1877

John W. Marshall
Abraham Lurvey
Henry Dennis, Jr.

1878

John W. Marshall
Abraham Lurvey
Andrew F. Clark

1879

John W. Marshall
Andrew F. Clark
Stillman L. Mason

1880

John W. Marshall
Andrew F. Clark
Abraham Lurvey

1881 and 1882

Jason L. Curtis
George A. Lowe
N. F. S. York

1883 and 1884

N. F. S. York
Nathaniel Richardson, Jr.
Austin W. Story

1885

N. F. S. York
Henry H. Thurston
Joseph B. Dunahue

1886

N. F. S. York
Joseph B. Dunahue
William Lowe

1887

Charles H. Cleaves
Joseph B. Dunahue
Otis E. Smith

1888-1891

Charles H. Cleaves
Otis E. Smith
Isaac P. Fears

1892

Joseph B. Dunahue
Otis E. Smith
John H. Dennis

1893

John H. Dennis
Walter G. Peckham
Bryant Lurvey

1894

Walter G. Peckham
Bryant Lurvey
Charles F. York

1895-1897

Charles F. York
Samuel B. Harris
Andrew F. Clark

1898

Samuel B. Harris[1]
Lorenzo A. Martin[2]
James W. Bradley
John B. Hodgkins

[1] Died April 13
[2] Elected May 16

Town on Sandy Bay

1899 and 1900

Lorenzo A. Martin
John B. Hodgkins
Andrew F. Clark

1901 and 1902

Lorenzo A. Martin
Andrew F. Clark
Otis E. Smith

1903

George W. Tutts
Eli L. Morgan
Otis E. Smith

1904

James A. Cogswell
Otis E. Smith
Eli L. Morgan

1905 and 1906

John H. Dennis
Otis E. Smith
Eli L. Morgan

1907 and 1908

John H. Dennis
Eli L. Morgan
Frank C. Todd

1909 and 1910

John H. Dennis
Eli L. Morgan
John W. Marshall

1911

John H. Dennis
Eli L. Morgan
Walter S. Hale

1912-1919

John H. Dennis
Eli L. Morgan
John W. Marshall

1920

John H. Dennis
Eli L. Morgan
John W. Marshall[3]
Frank C. Todd

[3] Died January 27, 1920

1921 and 1922

John H. Dennis
Eli L. Morgan
Frank C. Todd

1923

John H. Dennis
Eli L. Morgan
Robert L. Murray

1924-1927

John H. Dennis
Eli L. Morgan
Frank C. Todd

1928

John H. Dennis
Eli L. Morgan
Ralph T. Parker

1929

John H. Dennis
Eli L. Morgan
Roy H. Lane

1930

Roy H. Lane
John H. Dennis
Elliot W. Grimes

1931-1933

Roy H. Lane
John H. Dennis
Ralph T. Parker

1934 and 1935

John H. Dennis
William G. Reed
Mrs. Jennie M. Savage

1936

John H. Dennis
William G. Reed
Elliot W. Grimes

1937

John H. Dennis
William G. Reed
Vincent J. Charte

1938

Vincent J. Charte
William G. Reed
Jennie M. Savage

1939

William G. Reed
Jennie M. Savage
John H. Dennis

1940 and 1941

William G. Reed
Vincent J. Charte
Norman T. Swanson

1942-1946

William G. Reed
Norman T. Swanson
Jennie M. Savage

1947

William G. Reed
Norman T. Swanson
Arthur G. Leman

1948-1951

Ernest R. Poole, Jr.
Norman T. Swanson
William G. Reed

1952

Ernest R. Poole, Jr.
William G. Reed
Maurice F. Foley

1953 and 1954

Ernest R. Poole, Jr.
William G. Reed
Norman T. Swanson

1955 and 1956

Ernest R. Poole, Jr.
Frederick R. Grover
William G. Reed

1957

William G. Reed
Ernest R. Poole, Jr.
Karl A. Johnson

1958

Karl A. Johnson
Ernest R. Poole, Jr.
William G. Reed

1959

William G. Reed
Karl A. Johnson
Ernest R. Poole, Jr.

1960

Karl A. Johnson
Ernest R. Poole, Jr.
William G. Reed

1961

Richard K. Manson
Karl A. Johnson
Ernest R. Poole, Jr.
Norman T. Swanson
Frederick R. Grover

1962 and 1963

Ernest R. Poole, Jr.
Karl A. Johnson
Frederick R. Grover
Richard K. Manson
John E. Huttunen

1964 and 1965

Ernest R. Poole, Jr.
Francis P. Brewer
Karl A. Johnson
Richard K. Manson
John E. Huttunen

1966

John E. Huttunen
Francis P. Brewer
Ernest R. Poole, Jr.
Richard K. Manson
Nicola A. Barletta

1967 and 1968

Richard K. Manson
Ernest R. Poole, Jr.
John E. Huttunen
Nicola A. Barletta
Ann L. Fisk

1969 and 1970

Richard K. Manson
G. Herbert Carlson
Ann L. Fisk
Nicola A. Barletta
Ernest R. Poole, Jr.

1971

G. Herbert Carlson
Nicola A. Barletta
Harold F. Beaton
Ann L. Fisk
Ernest R. Poole, Jr.[4]

[4] Deceased

1972-1975

Richard K. Manson
Nicola A. Barletta
Harold F. Beaton
Ann L. Fisk
Frederick H. Tarr, III

1976

Frederick H. Tarr, III
Nicola A. Barletta
Harold F. Beaton
H. Chester Holgerson
Richard J. McGlauflin

Rockport Town Clerks

1840-1868 William Pool
1869-1908 Calvin W. Pool
1909-   Foster H. Saville
1910-1926 Byron G. Russell
1927-1936 Marion C. Dodge

1937-1940 Alvin S. Brown, Jr.
1941-1967 Esther E. Johnson
1968-1973 Nancy A. Waddell
1974-   Frederick C. Frithsen

Rockport Town Treasurers

1840-1842 John Gott
1843-1851 Addison Gott
1852-1854 James Manning
1855-1856 George Gott, Jr.
1857-1864 Henry Clark
1865-1891 Joseph Manning
1892-1899 George W. Tufts
1900-1919 Fred E. Pool

1920   Charles E. Breene
1921-1922 Lois F. Sherburne
1923-October 17, 1933
          Benjamin F. Batchelder
October 18, 1933-1940 (resigned)
          J. Harry Mills
1941-1974 Alvin S. Brown, Jr.
1974-1976 Paul F. Kluge

Town on Sandy Bay

1840	John Davis
1841	Dr. Lemuel Gott
1842-43	William Caldwell
1844	Dr. Lemuel Gott
1845-47	William Caldwell
1848-51	Samuel York
1852	John W. Marshall
1853	William Caldwell
1854	John W. Marshall
1855-56	Samuel York
1857	William Caldwell
1859-60	Samuel York
1861	William Caldwell
1862	Samuel York
1863-65	William Caldwell
1866	Nathaniel F. S. York
1867	William Caldwell
1868-70	Samuel York

1871	William Caldwell
1872	John W. Marshall
1873	Henry Dennis, Jr.
1874	John W. Marshall
1875-77	Henry Dennis, Jr.
1878-80	John W. Marshall
1881	Henry Dennis, Jr.
1882-85	Amos Rowe
1886-88	John W. Marshall
1889-92	Amos Rowe
1893-98	Charles F. York
1899	J. Loring Woodfall
1900-04	Nathaniel S. York
1905-43	John H. Dennis
1944-63	J. Harry Mills
1963-72	H. Lawrence Jodrey
1972-76	Alvin S. Brown, Jr.

Sandy Bay and Pigeon Cove Representatives to the General Court

1806-1807

Caleb Norwood, Jr.

1809-1815

John Manning, M.D.

1830

John Gott
Aaron Giddings

1831

John Gott
Solomon Pool

1832

James Goss
Nehemiah Knowlton
Gorham Babson

1833

George Lane
Josiah Griffin
Gorham Babson

1834

Josiah Griffin
John Blatchford
Gorham Babson

1835

John Blatchford
James Harris
Timothy R. Davis

1836

Timothy R. Davis
John Davis
James Harris

1837

John Davis
Eleazar Boynton
David Dunahue

1838

Eleazar Boynton
William B. Haskins

1839

Samuel L. Andrews

1840

William B. Haskins

Some Rockport Rosters

1841
James P. Tarr

1843
Thomas O. Marshall

1844-1845
William Grover

1851
Addison Gott

1852
Newell Burnham

1855
Benjamin Parsons, Jr.

1856
Samuel York

1857
Thomas Hale

1858
Wm. W. Marshall

1859
Henry T. Lowe

1860
John D. Sanborn

1861
Austin W. Story

1862
Moses Pool

1863
Rev. David Bremner

1864
Austin W. Story

1865
Amos Rowe, Jr.

1866
Wm. Caldwell

1867
Benjamin Hale

1868
Moses Pool

1869
Ambrose Hodgkins

1870
William Marchant

1871
Rev. George Vibbert

1872-1873
James W. Bradley

1874
John J. Giles

1875-1876
Henry Dennis, Jr.

1877
Wm. Marchant

1878
Jason L. Curtis

1879
Amos Rowe

1881
Nath'l Richardson, Jr.

1882
Jason L. Curtis

1883
Edward H. Shaw

1884
George Elwell

1885
John G. Dennis

1887
Theodore L. Pool

Note: From time to time Rockport sent no representative. From 1880 on it shared representatives with Gloucester and, later, other towns.

LIST OF ILLUSTRATIONS

431

Map of Cape Ann as surveyed by John Mason, 1831.

Town on Sandy Bay

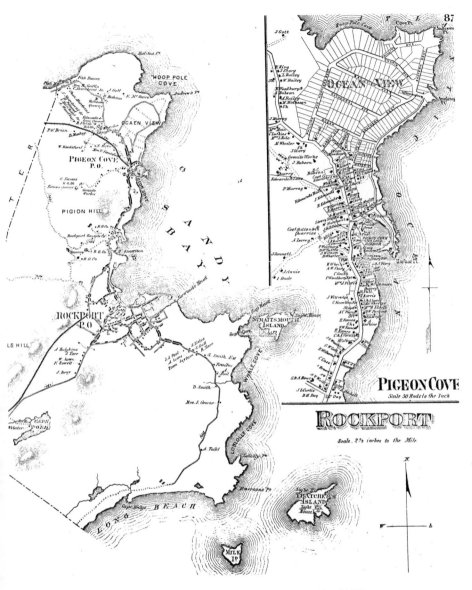

Map of Rockport and Pigeon Cove from "Beers Atlas," 1872.

Maps of Rockport

INDEX

(This is a selective index which combines names and topics. To keep it from becoming too unwieldy, a decision was made to restrict entries for the most part to Rockporters, their predecessors in Sandy Bay Parish, or elsewhere on Cape Ann. Similarly, only those events which directly had an impact on the town appear below. Names in the "Afterwords" and the lengthy rosters of Rockporters beginning on page 403 were also omitted. Thus, numerous people, places, and activities referred to in the text do not appear in this selective index. It should also be noted that people having the same name—and in a venerable area like Cape Ann there are scores—are cited under a single entry. Sorting out juniors, thirds, etc. should be relatively straightforward, since the narrative itself is mainly chronological.)